…se names are under…

…soueraigne Lord King Iames

…aine, franc, & Ireland king.

…& of god, and, aduancement

…r king & countrie, a voyage to

…erne parts of virginia. doe

…ualy in y presence of god, and

…ne our selues togeather intoa

…rdering, & preseruation & fur=

…By vertue heerof to Enacte;

…& equall Lawes, ordinances,

…ime to time, as shall be thought

…erall good of y colonie: unto

…on and obedience gfn witnes

…cribed our names at cap=

…r of y raigne of our soueraigno

…franc, & Ireland y eighteenth

An: Dom. 1620.

IN THE NAME OF GOD, AMEN.

In the name of God, Amen.

Rediscovering Biblical and Historic Covenants

by Daniel J. Ford

Foreword by Douglas W. Phillips

Lex Rex Publishing

Design, layout, and typography by Daniel Ford
Front jacket illustration: *Signing the Mayflower Covenant* by Daniel Ford, 2003
Back jacket illustration: *Upon the Rock* by Daniel Ford, 1996
Flyleaves: redrawn copy of William Bradford's
manuscript of the *Mayflower Covenant*
by Daniel Ford, 2002

Printed in the UNITED STATES of AMERICA
First Edition

This volume is gratefully dedicated:

To the manifold thousands of covenantal faithful whose names may never
grace the pages of a printed volume, yet written into the
Lamb's Book of Life, they were pledged to Him
and have enriched each of
our earthly lives.

Acknowledgments:

The author extends his deepest appreciation to the Zes family: James, Kathleen, Sarah, Rebekah, and Hannah, who have made this volume possible. In February 2001, James initiated the idea of publishing a volume which would extol due honor upon our beloved Christian forebearers. From the beginning of our endeavor together, Jim's dedication to biblical and historic truth has lent overall vision and added specific insight to the content, tone, and integrity of this work. As the project drew into months, and the months drew into years, Kathy's generous hospitality and editorial expertise added grace and professionalism to the countless meetings that we required. Sarah was superb in adding many insightful historic and scriptural contributions; and along with her exhaustive hands-on editing, she lent much to the contextual soundness of the work. Rebekah, through editing, numerous grammatical contributions, and meticulous indexing (not to mention her abundant wit and amazing ability to point out each "redundant redundancy") lent much to the detail and overall content of this project. Hannah lent us her amazing skills in detailed reference checking as well as her remarkable artistic talents to greatly improve the overall integrity and beautify the visual format of each of the books. Frankly stated, mere words are not adequate to convey the abundant generosity, the gracious hospitality, and the exhaustive care that the Zeses have each and together as a family put into the production, editing, and publication of this volume.

My warmest thanks go to my beloved wife, Theresa, whose encouragement, diligent patience, and faithful prayer have provided the greatest contribution and blessed support for this endeavor.

TABLE OF CONTENTS

TABLE OF CONTENTS

FOREWORD

There is no subject more directly connected with the prosperity of the Christian home, the integrity of the local church, or the success of national governments than that of the covenantal nature of life, law, and relationships. The Bible begins and ends with the doctrine of covenant. The history of the world, of nations, and of individuals can only be understood in terms of those who kept covenant with God, and those who did not. The family was birthed from God's directive that man and woman become one through an indissoluble covenantal union. The Church is a testimony to the triumph of God's holy covenant. Even the civil authority is a covenantal creation. And thankfully, from the perspective of the history of our own people, we can gratefully report that no nation in the annals of Western civilization was ever birthed from such a self-consciously covenantal model than the United States.

Centuries ago a bank account was established for our nation. In this account was deposited a spiritual and intellectual treasure trove of the purest gold and silver. This treasure was not easily obtained. It was birthed in the furnace of reformation, baptized in the flames of persecution and martyrdom, and molded by holy hands intent on leaving a covenantal legacy of freedom for generations. Believing our treasure to be inexhaustible, we have drawn from this account for more than two centuries, with little thought toward replenishing our principle. The account is almost dry.

Today, and perhaps only for today, our own nation continues to enjoy the manifold blessings of prosperity, not because of any innate wisdom or righteousness of this present generation, but because of the cumulative efforts of our covenant-keeping ancestors who established a nation with the specific goal of securing the blessings of liberty for their posterity. This historic truth, the memory and honor of which is central to the perpetuation of our present freedoms, is all but forgotten today. Never before in our history have American lawmakers, pastors, and students been more ignorant of who they are and how they got here. I believe we have but a brief window of time to remedy this problem of ignorance and indifference. It must begin with the people of God. It is up to them to embrace these truths, and argue the case on behalf of generations yet to be born.

I know of few better equipped to make this case than Dan Ford. For the better part of a decade he has immersed himself in the original works of the Reformation and the Founding era of America. Dan is not only a walking encyclopedia capable of cataloguing at a moment's notice the many examples of the providential hand of God in our nation's history, but he is the personal owner of one of the most distinguished collections of Reformation and covenantal documents in the world. Consequently, unlike many commentators and historians, Dan not only reads the primary sources, he actually studies the past from the original documents. In fact, many of the rare images you see in this volume come directly from his private collection, making *In the Name of God, Amen* a truly unique and wonderful literary work.

For the last three years Dan has been bringing hundreds of one-of-a-kind, premiere documents to our Witherspoon School of Law and Public Policy. His goal has been to inspire the next generation of fathers, lawyers, pastors, and lawmakers to love the law of God and keep covenant with their Creator. The impact is electric. For many, it is as if "the lost book of the law" was opened for the first time. Students recognize the holy call of God to "remove not the ancient landmarks" and once again proclaim the charters and covenantal documents of our nation's founding. *In the Name of God, Amen* takes the heart and the soul of these messages and makes them understandable and meaningful to a wider audience. Here you will learn of the great covenantal inheritance of Christianity, from the legacy of the martyrs, to the preservation of the "Book of books," to the emergence of God's people of promise, to the gracious fulfillment of His covenant with the triumph of grace and the inheritance of Christ's Church. Here you will discover the noble heritage of our nation's Forefathers, the rise of American covenantal thought, the great Puritan doctrine of covenantal living in every sphere of life, the covenantal principles behind the War for Independence, and the nature of Christian self-government under God. But here also, you will learn rich insights into the practical application of covenantal thinking in terms of our holy responsibilities toward the family, the Church, and the State.

But the book in your hands is more than great history and sound theology artfully presented. It is a passionate labor of love, a gift and a record to our children and their posterity. It is a clarion cry to go back to the ancient paths wherein we will find peace. I am deeply indebted to the author for this thorough, but highly readable contribution. This book is simply landmark. The first and best book of its kind to appear in over a generation, *In the Name of God, Amen* is sure to become a staple for home educators, seminary students, church leaders, lawyers, fathers, and hopefully even civil magistrates. It is my intention to use this tremendous volume to teach my law students, interns, and my own children for years to come.

Douglas W. Phillips, Esq.
Founder, Witherspoon School of Law and Public Policy
President, Vision Forum

In the name of God, Amen.

Book I
Christianity's Covenantal Inheritance

Book I Christianity's Covenantal Inheritance

Introduction: The Cause of the Martyr

The Cause and Cost of Early Covenantal Reformation

ON a midwinter's morning in early 1555, a crowd gathered in Glochester, England as a tall, thin man made his way amid a lingering procession. An estimated seven thousand souls had come out in hope of seeing or hearing the man who, on prior occasions, had often admonished them with his sermons and brotherly encouragements. The mood on this occasion, however, was in sharp contrast to those earlier, more charitable days.

By early February of 1555, the English political and religious winds had radically changed, for although the public was still eager to hear John Hooper's words as before, the new regime of Queen Mary I was intent on silencing him. The Royal reaction to the Reformation seemed to sweep in on Hooper and his fellow reformers[1] as if it had come in the frigid winds of the winter's season. Those reformers had freely preached and propagated God's Holy Writ among the English with unabashed liberty for the past seven years, as Hooper and other like-minded men had begun to speak out against the opposition to God that dominated England during the early reign of Henry VIII. They had seen the rampant medieval ignorance in England as a great evil, and decried the old established order that had deprived the common Englishman free access to God's Word.

Hooper, among many others, had labored tirelessly to undo such evils by providing the realm access to an English-language Bible and an understanding of its high and holy truths. Following Henry's death, his son, Edward VI, had embraced and propagated the Reformation during his brief reign, encouraging and supporting the reformers in their noble work until his untimely death in 1553. But, with the wedding of England's new queen (Edward's older sister Mary) to Prince Philip of Spain in 1555, came the severe chill of the Counter-Reformation. The old order had come back with a new vigor. No longer was there a place for an English Bible anymore than there was for the reformers who had openly preached its covenantal doctrines of grace. The "vulgar"[2] English-language Bible was again banned and the reformers sought out for prosecution. The church establishment was thrown back into Romish hands and reestablished under the banner of an inquisition arriving on shore with the landing of England's new Spanish monarch. Ironically, the queen's matrimonial vows that pledged her in the holy covenant of wedlock plunged the nation into an unholy league of terror.

---

1. See Appendix A: "On the Reformed Christians and the Reformed Movement" on page 279 for a brief sketch of the Christian Reformation and the Reformed movement in Europe and America.

2. "Vulgar": common, vernacular, or national; see Noah Webster, *An American Dictionary of the English Language*, vol. 2 (New York: S. Converse, 1828), for "vulgar."

A.

B.

Dan Ford, 2002

C.

D.

Early Bible editions and the reforming martyrs:

A. William Tyndale published at least two editions of the English New Testament in his lifetime. But, before his translation of the Old Testament was completed, he was martyred in 1536 (title page of Tyndale's 1534 edition).

B. Another martyr, John Rogers, published a complete Bible in 1537 and was martyred in 1555 (text block from Rogers' 1549 title page).

C. Portrait sketch of John Hooper, the powerful voice of covenantal reform, who, like John Rogers, was burned early in 1555.

D. A sixteenth-century woodcut of the typical scene of a public burning. The officials compelled the crowd to gather, hear the pronouncement of the sentence, and witness the proceedings, all as a warning to the town.

The darkening clouds of oppression had loomed heavily for months as the ecclesiastical climate in England cooled. The famous Bible translator John Rogers was the first to suffer the torturing arm of the new order. His crime was that he had disseminated the High and Holy Scriptures in the tongue of the vulgar people. He had not only dared to publish the entire Bible in 1537, but his work carried with it a strong Reformed tone in its marginal notes that was sure to bring a severe official reaction. Rogers' work had proven widely popular among the ordinary people, and the authority of the Sacred Text itself tended to undermine the arbitrary powers claimed by the Church and the Crown. The Bible, as preached by reformers such as Rogers and Hooper, spoke to their nation's lack of integrity when mirrored against the model of the ancient Hebrew Commonwealth. But, England's recent behavior did reflect the corruption of old Israel when it also parlayed with foreign principalities and landed in God's disfavor.

The new English Bible had thus provided a beacon of heavenly light which had not shone into the darkening soul of England since the days of Alfred the Great. It proclaimed God's Laws as the moral integrity of the nation, and its godly standard condemned every rank of Englishmen from the peasant to the king. Commoners, nobility, and royalty were all in need of a thorough scriptural revamping, and the reformers were quick to make the point. Further, their preaching gave England a conscious sense of a mutual moral responsibility before God that had never before penetrated the lowest ranks of its societal order. Common souls could see both liberty and responsibility clearly described in the Holy Writ, giving peasants knowledge of their own direct access to the throne of God. Worst of all, such liberty and responsibility gave the 'common rabble' a sense of cultural dignity and a taste for meaningful self-governance that outshone the claims of their earthly monarchs. So, according to the high ideal of holy royal supremacy, the sweeping covenantal nature of the Reformed faith was seen as an imposing adversary that must be stopped, and following the silencing of John Rogers, John Hooper was next to be put to flames.

Thus, that February 1555 Glochester crowd had come to witness the martyrdom procession of the "Master Hooper," as he had become widely known. They had gathered to pay their final respects for the man who had often predicted beforehand that he was sure to pay a severe price for his open and unabashed public preaching of the Scriptures. In observing their generous friend as he was tied to a stake and decked in the shame of a single loin cloth, the crowd soon became adorned with their own tears while hearing his familiar voice sound aloud for one last time. With his thin figure withering in the flames, his torso holding fast within the chains wrapped to a post, and his lips beginning to fuse in the heat, Hooper opened his mouth in a final breath to address his Lord while still held within his frail, earthbound frame: *"Lord Jesus have mercy upon me: Lord Jesus receive my spirit."*[3]

Thereby was ended the life of another great martyr in the earthly cause of Jesus Christ. Hooper's voice was one of hundreds silenced for the threat they posed to the civil and ecclesiastical establishment of Philip and Mary. The scene of Hooper's fate was reenacted in fiery executions of many such individuals among the friends and the families of the Reformed faith. Death was exacted upon both men and women, masters and servants, adults and children, and in the cruelest of cases, upon one yet unborn. The wicked flames were dutifully endured by Christ's faithful, and the scope of the atrocities were, in part, providentially recorded by the sixteenth-century historian John Foxe. Amid a voluminous number of pages in which he extolled the life and death of Master Hooper, Foxe spoke these most peaceable words of his dutiful Christian sacrifice:

> *Even as a Lamb, patiently he abode the extremity thereof, neither moving forwards, backward, or to any side: but having his neather parts burned, and his bowels fallen out, he died as quietly as a child in his bed.*[4]

A.

A. Shown here is a woodcut depiction of the death of John Hooper in 1555. John Foxe recorded that three fires were required to complete the task. He wrote of the first attempt: *"At length it burned about him, but the wind having full strength it blew the flames from him, so that he was in a maner no more but touched by the fire."* Hooper requested that the people say the Lord's Prayer with him, who *"performed it with tears during the time of his paines."* His death provided a grueling and a powerful testimony for the faith. (Illustration from John Foxe's *Actes and Monumentes of the Martyrs*, 1576 edition.)

B.

B. Foxe's *Actes and Monumentes*, later known as *Foxe's Book of Martyrs*, also depicted the *"lamentable scene"* of the martyrdom of a pregnant woman whose unborn infant fell into the flames and was left there to perish (1576 edition).

Hooper's resignation to martyrdom had an indelible effect on the witnesses of his death, which served to strengthen their faith in his cause rather than intimidate them. For a man to be so compliant in death after being so vigorous in life, lent testimony to the fortitude of the Holy Text for all those who saw, told, and retold the legacy of such a faithful, Reformed Christian. In Hooper's enduring epitaph we still read the impressions upon the historian after nearly four hundred fifty years:

3. John Foxe, *The Actes and Monumentes of the Martyrs*, vol. 3 (London, 1641), p. 156 (also see pp. 145-156).
4. Ibid.

A. This is the title page of Hooper's *Declaration of Christe*, in which he wrote that God binds Himself in Christ directly to the believer.

B. Hooper believed in a covenantal Christian life without the heavy-handed formalities of ecclesiastical or royal innovations.

And he now reigneth, as a blessed Martyr, in the joyes of heaven prepared for the faithfull in Christ, before the foundations of the world: for whose constancy all Christians are bound to praise God.[5]

Hooper, like those who followed, was executed for what he believed, for what he taught, and for Whom he professed. Most vocally, he professed the sovereign authority of Jesus Christ in the Church. He spoke against a formalized regime of human-oriented religion that had usurped the majesty of God's glory and deprived English subjects of their direct access to their true, ultimate Sovereign. Hooper taught that God's Commandments were indeed given to every man and woman by which to see their own depravity and to enable God's elect to taste of the glorious covenant of God's grace. It was also that Law, those same Commandments, by which the people were intended to govern their families and their earthly affairs in covenantal relations. Only through such a thorough reformation could the nation be truly freed from the oppression of sin as well as the bondage of religious and civil tyranny. In time and God's due season, it was thought by the reformers that His Word would relieve the vestiges of many archaic and medieval formulas that had shrouded the liberties which God intended for the souls of men. They could then, in accord with His Word, conduct their lives and affairs in terms of sound relations and engagements; for to truly know the Almighty and to covenant with Him as Lord meant to embrace His heavenly promises through faith, and then to conduct themselves in subject obedience to Him. God's promises of abundant Lordship were fulfilled in Christ and lived out by the faithful in obedience to His Commands. Of such a relation directly with God, Hooper wrote with assurance:

... god hath bound hymselfe by his promes [promise] *to be our god and helper for Christ, so hathe he bound man by his commaundement to be his servant and in his worde to folow Christ and in Christ god for the commaundementes sake ... .*[6]

During the brief reign of Edward VI (1547-1553), Hooper had been at liberty to travel and preach among the regions he served. His preaching was so effective that there would seldom be an unoccupied place to sit or stand in which to hear him casting God's oracles freely among the spiritually-impoverished multitudes. Though it was also commonly observed that he was tirelessly devoted to his mission, he was foremost a man of his family, in which there *"lacked no provision in him, to bring up his own children in learning and good manners."*[7] The Hooper home was also the scene of remarkable hospitality. John Hooper provided a model example of a Christian husband and father, always planting and tilling those covenant responsibilities among others. His mode was to invite various *"beggers*

---

5. Ibid.
6. John Hooper, *A Declaration of Christe and of his Offyce Compylyd* (Zurich, 1547), leaf Liiii.
7. Foxe, *Actes and Monumentes of the Martyrs*, vol. 3, p. 148 (also see pp. 145-156).

and poore folke"[8] to freely dine in his family's common hall, using his generosity as a further opportunity to educate them in the Bible's covenantal doctrines and commandments, as Foxe himself witnessed:

A.

> *Twice I was, as I remember, in his house in Worcester, where in his common hall I saw a table spread with good store of meat, and beset full of beggers and poore folke: and I asking his servants what this meant, they told me that every day their Lord and Masters manner was, to have customably to dinner a certain number of poore folke of the said City, by course, who were served by foure at a messe, with whole and wholesome meats: and when they were served (being afore examined by him or his deputies of the Lords prayer, the Articles of their faith, and ten Commandements) then he himself sate down to dinner, and not before.*[9]

A. The Reformed historian John Foxe (1516-1587) gained wide influence during the Elizabethan era. This engraved portrait was made for the later, 1641 edition of *Foxe's Book of Martyrs*.

Prior to the rise of the reformers of the sixteenth century, the English Church had been a massive ecclesiastical institution with layers of magisterial offices appointed by powerful churchmen. With the rise of Henry VIII in the 1530's came his takeover of the church establishment and its complex scheme of church preferments. Henry reigned as the supreme figure of authority in both church and state. But, to the biblical reformers such as Rogers and Hooper, the true seat of sovereignty remained in the priestly and kingly hands of Jesus Christ. He alone had interceded in His office of High Priest to pay the price for man's sins. He alone had triumphed over all earthly authority, even over death itself, and reigns eternally as the world's only transcendent Sovereign. God did not impart priestly intercession to men beyond the work of Jesus Christ, the only High Priest, nor did He impart a divine right of dominion above that of Christ, the only King of Kings. Hooper recognized that all authority in either church or state resided under Christ, and that, by way of covenantal delegation.

Hooper and the reformers saw the model of Christ's delegation expounded among the pages of a text that had been officially banned from the English tongue. Restricting access to the Bible kept the people ignorant of His true lines of authority, and the reformers saw biblical ignorance as a scheme by the powerful to deprive the commoners of their own just rights and societal responsibilities. Yet, in confronting man's Leviathan (or scheme of supposed authority), those early reformers paid a dear personal price. They had devoted themselves to opening God's Holy Text to every rank of Englishmen and allowing godly lines of authority to break the bondage of ignorance, sin, and the chains of abject human servitude. They gave themselves in the cause of God's Word, sacrificing their own lives so others might enjoy true freedom under Him.[10]

B.

*Regiæ Maiest. Angliæ &c. Mā*datorum Epitome , ex præscripto , Ad subditos suos, tam sacris addictos, quàm Laicos.

Ex Anglico sermone in Latinum conversa.

C.

B. Edward VI's *Injunctions* of 1547 sanctioned public preaching and admonished English subjects to read the Holy Scriptures.

C. Edward VI (r. 1547-1553) was shown here receiving the English Bible from his Reformed advisors.

8. Ibid.
9. Ibid. (A true example of servant leadership.)
10. See *Oxford Encyclopedia of the Reformation*, vol. 2 (1996), s.v. "Hooper," p. 254; also see *Dictionary of National Biography*, vol. 1 (1975), s.v. "Hooper," p. 1001.

Book I Christianity's Covenantal Inheritance

Chapter 1: The Book of Books

The Authoritative Words for Man's Relations with God

Dan Ford, 2002

A.

B.

Fall the texts that have graced the shelves of English and American homes, there is one that stands above all others. The English reformers, as early as John Wycliffe in the late 1300's and William Tyndale in the early 1500's, dedicated their lives to see to its translation and propagation. Thanks to such men and scores who followed, it was the first book to find its place at the common English hearth and has proven the most enduring ever since. Its words have provided solace in times of need, comfort in times of pain, and relief in times of distress.

Replete with passages of both temporary help and eternal solace, the Bible was the most cherished article transported to North America by the first English settlers in the 1600's, and has, until recently, represented a centerpiece of American parlors. Within single volumes were often written scores of records of individual births or deaths, baptisms or weddings, church affiliations or societal associations, along with prayers and supplications for a nation's health and continued blessing. In lists, poems, and prayers, many private aspirations were annexed to the blanks and margins of countless volumes as enduring testimonials of its centrality among the generations.

In a deeper sense, the Bible provided the central precepts of a great cultural reformation throughout Scotland and England, which also found legs in America. Its societal doctrines were foremost in settling colonial America, and its rippling influence guided the founding of an independent nation. It was widely anticipated at the time that its great truths would change the world, beginning with individuals and families, and then on to wider societies and nations. Typical of the aspirations for its timely, ultimate, worldwide success are these words of the eighteenth-century hymnist Isaac Watts:

> *O ALL ye nations, praise the Lord,*
> *Each with a diff'rent tongue;*
> *In ev'ry language learn his word,*
> *And let his name be sung.*[1]

A. This is a sketch of John Wycliffe (1324-1382), who first translated the entire Bible into English.

B. Shown here is a manuscript leaf of a Wycliffe Bible (Romans). English Bibles were outlawed and possessing one was a capital crime.

1. Excerpted from Isaac Watts' rendering of Psalm 117 in Isaac Watts, D.D., *The Psalms of David, ...together with Hymns and Spiritual Songs, ...* (Boston: I. Thomas and E.T. Andrews, 1791), p. 92.

In keeping with the earlier chorus of expectations, by the mid-1900's the Bible had been introduced into well over a thousand languages. By then its historic influence had become as deep as its geographic scope was broad and worldwide. Some consider it merely a compilation of ancient wisdom with its all-familiar quips, as nearly everyone has heard of the popular proverb of Jesus: *"Blessed are the meek: for they shall inherit the earth"* (Matthew 5:5).[2] And even the most committed devotee of humanism, who otherwise would despise the most basic tenets of Scripture, might selectively ascribe wisdom to the fact that *"Blessed are the peacemakers"* (Matthew 5:9). On their face, the Scriptures' two towering Testaments have historically been the starting point for the highest philosophy since the time of Augustine in the late fourth century. They have been noble monuments to the learned, high literature to the scholar, and eternal oracles to all those who have genuinely hungered for truth.[3] Yet, well beyond the fact of their historical impact, the reality is that the Testaments, united together, present the means of man's true solace and the only genuine fount of virtue.

God's Relations With Man

Besides all of these impressive attributes, each one alone marking the Bible as a volume beyond equal, it remains the text above all others that describes the essential relations between the Almighty and His creatures. It divulges God's revealed expressions according to the Majesty of His divine Glory; it expresses His standards for earthly living; and it reveals His heavenly salvation unto its earthly fruition. The compilation of the entire Scripture is therefore the words of greatest importance to man, binding upon the very essence of human life. Simply put, the Bible in its own words, in God's Words, is a book of covenants that incorporates the terms, the ties, and the bonds between God and His property. In the context of the whole Scripture, there is, after all, a much more comprehensive meaning to that often casually thrown-about phrase, *"the meek shall inherit the earth"*:

> *The meek will he guide in judgement: and the meek will he teach his way. All the paths of the LORD are mercy and truth, unto such as keep his covenant, and his testimonies. For thy names sake, O LORD, pardon mine iniquity: for it is great. What man is he that feareth the LORD? him shall he teach in the way that he shall choose. His soul shall dwell at ease: and his seed shall inherit the earth* (Psalm 25:9-13).

A.

Ford, 2002

B.

A. This is a sketch of William Tyndale (1494-1536), who published the first printed English New Testament in 1525.

B. Shown is a page from a Tyndale New Testament published in 1536.

C.

Ford, 2002

D.

C. This is a sketch of the great English hymnist Isaac Watts (1674-1748).

D. Shown here is Isaac Watts' rendering of Psalm 117, entitled: *"Praise to GOD from all Nations."*

2. For an explanation of the Bible version quoted in this volume, see Appendix B on p. 283.
3. See Matthew 5.

The sort of meekness mentioned in such a passage is not at all the kind offered by humanity apart from a direct involvement with the Lord of heaven and earth. The kind of meekness that will inherit the earth, according to both the Old and New Testaments, is not vague or sentimental. The Bible's sense of meekness involves an active league with the sovereign and saving God. The summation of one's personal fate and the fate of one's whole cultural legacy rests upon nothing less than the terms of such an intimate relation with God. From the text of the Old Testament's fiftieth Psalm, for example, the venerable theologian Augustine of Hippo wrote in the early fifth century that the ultimate issue upon every man and woman was who would be eternally gathered to God in heaven or who would be destined for eternal hell. What would decide that issue was how each one stood in relation with God in this life on earth. Augustine thus described those who were to be gathered unto God at the following command to His angels:

> *Then speaketh he to his Angels, Gather my Saints together unto mee: this is done by the Angels ministery. And whome gather they? Those that made a covenant with mee with sacrifice.*[4]

Dan Ford, 2002

This is a sketch of Augustine of Hippo (A.D. 354-430), who was one of the preeminent theologians of early Christian history. Though he lived during the Latin period at the end of the Roman Empire, Augustine's thought had considerable influence on the later reformers.

Augustine saw the covenantal unity of faith and obedience under the terms of God's gift of grace. Later Reformed Christians embraced and developed covenant theology into a comprehensive view of living that invigorated much of northern Europe, and forever changed the face of Western Christendom.

Augustine saw the essence of Christian life in terms of a comprehensive covenantal relation in which God engaged directly with His saints. That life involved both the covenantal grace that the Christian received from God as well as the mirror of that covenant in relations among others. Thus, by the expression *"covenant with mee with sacrifice,"* Augustine meant both the sacrificial acts of mercy received from God in Christ as well as the consistent actions that should be modeled in Christian behavior. Though the sacrifice unto salvation had been completed in the perfect work of Jesus Christ, as Augustine said: *"seeing that his bloud was shed for the remission of sinnes,"*[5] nevertheless, the Christian once in league with God should emulate the covenantal character that Christ demonstrated. And, though the Christian could not be saved by merit of his own covenantal obedience, the Christian in league with God would be blessed (and would be a blessing among others) in covenantal obedience once saved. Thereby, God would still bless the life of the Christian who demonstrated his faithfulness to God by living in reflective obligations among others:

> *In such workes doe the just* [the justified] *make covenants with God, in that they performe them for the promises made them in the New Testament.*[6]

4. Augustine, *The Citie of God*, book 20: *God's judgements continually effected: His last judgement the proper subject of third booke following* (London, 1610), chapter 24: "David's Prophecies of the worlds end, and the last judgement," p. 825.
5. Ibid., p. 646.
6. Ibid., p. 825.

It followed, then, according to Augustine, that the saints who had entered into a bond with the Father through Christ and then lived in covenantal accord with the grace received, would find an eternal reward while escaping God's eternal wrath. Only covenantal obedience on earth would yield its heavenly reward:

> *So then Christ having gotten his righteous on his right hand, will give them this well-come. Come yee blessed of my Father, inherite yee the kingdome prepared for you from the foundations of the world: for I was an hungred and you gave me to eate: and so forth of the good workes, and their eternall rewards which shall be returned for them in the last judgment.*[7]

A.

> Then speaketh he to his Angels, *Gather my Saints together vnto mee*: this is done by the Angels ministery. And whome gather they? *Those that make a couenant with mee with sacrifice*: and this is the duty of all iust men to doe. For either they must offer their workes of mercy (which is aboue sacrifice, as the *Lord* saith, *I will haue mercy and not sacrifice*) or else their workes of mercy is the sacrifice it selfe that appeaseth *Gods* wrath, as I prooued in the ninth booke of this present volume. In such workes doe the iust make couenants with *God*, in that they performe them for the promises made them in the *New Testament*. So then *Christ* hauing gotten his righteous on his right hand, will giue them this well-come. *Come yee blessed of my Father, inherite yee the kingdome prepared for you from the foundations of the world: for I was an hungred and you gaue me to eate*: and so forth of the good workes, and their eternall rewards which shall be returned for them in the last iudgment.

A. Shown here is an excerpt from Augustine's book, *The Citie of God*,* in which he described the covenantal relation between God and His beloved. Early Christians understood the comprehensive nature of the faith in its covenantal sense: God freely justified the sinner, and the saint was then obliged to Him in every way. *(1610)

The heavenly-minded Christian must therefore be bound to Christ and then be involved in the lives of others. He must recognize the spiritual as well as the family, church, and civil implications of such a bond with God. This book, Book I, will attempt to present the basic covenantal concepts demonstrated in the two Testaments of Scripture. Hopefully this will benefit the reader in understanding the basic nature of a biblical relation with God and the wider implications of that life in earthly service.

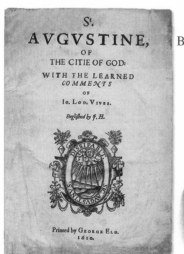

B.

C.

D.

Dan Ford, 2002

B. Shown here is the title page of the first English edition of *The Citie of God*, published in 1610. Begun by Augustine in 413, it was originally written as a vindication of Christianity amid the crumbling ruins of Rome.

7. Ibid., referencing Matthew 25.

C. The scholarly contemporary of Augustine, Jerome (circa 340-403), translated the complete Bible into the "vulgar," or common, Latin language. His charitable work provided the Vulgate Text, which was more easily readable to citizens of his day.

D. Shown here is a manuscript leaf from Jerome's Vulgate translation of Scripture. His work became the predominant version of the Bible read throughout the Middle Ages. This leaf (circa 1250) provides an excerpt from the Book of Romans.

Chapter 2: The Covenants of the Testaments

The Sweeping Legacy of Man's Covenants with God

S illustrated by Augustine's astute theological observations, the Bible presents readers with the idea of covenantal engagements between God and man. Such binding engagements are represented in many ways, and understanding the nature and terms of the Bible's covenants is the key to understanding that which God considers essential for man.

To begin with, the Bible presents itself in its two great "Testaments" as the very source of man's understanding of higher truth. The Scriptures rely upon self-authenticating statements by which their integrity rests upon the exclusive nature of their Words of truth. For example, the Apostle Paul wrote to the young Church at Galatia: *"If any man preach any other gospel unto you, then* [than] *that ye have received, let him be accursed"* (Galatians 1:9). There is simply no way to miss the point of that self-authoritative verse. Such an exclusive statement, which is representative of the many dogmatic passages throughout the Testaments, leaves readers with no room other than to take God's Word as written truth or reject it as wholly untrue. And, because the Bible presents itself as the very standard of *"gospel"* truth, its readers are forced to either take it as such or discard it outright.

Thus, when the Bible presents readers with various interrelations between God and man, its Words must also be held as exclusively authoritative. The Bible embodies the exclusive, written source of understanding healthy relations with God – they are Words by which man either yields and benefits from God's abundant Self-revelation, or he is left to his cold and lonely solitude. For man to have any significant understanding of God or an adequate knowledge of himself in relation to God, he must therefore begin with a compliant and clear reading of the Testaments of God's revealed Word. Simply put, the Bible's twin Testaments provide man with the only mirror by which to see himself from God's point of view.

In order to understand how God regards His relations with man, it is first necessary to understand the terms of man's existence. The Bible therefore begins with an account of how **God** created man and how **He** defined him. As the Creator, God determined how He would relate and interact with His Creation. Man is incapable of dictating the terms of his own existence or overriding the expressed Will of his Superior. To do so would represent a futile attempt to usurp the order of Creation, as if placing man above God. Man's finite will is therefore always inferior, and he must submit to God's infinite supremacy in every engagement.

God chose to deal with men from the beginning – even before the inception of man – by way of binding, interpersonal engagements. From before the advent of man, He graciously initiated cordial interrelations: *"According as he hath chosen us in him, before the foundation of the world, that we should be holy, and without blame before him in love"* (Ephesians 1:4). So, in advance of mankind's existence, God had sovereignly set in place the manner of human engagements with Him.

God's Work of Redemption for Man

Because of God's supremacy, He provided the way by which men entered into covenantal relations with Him. The effort that brought men into a good standing with Him was therefore initiated by God Himself and accomplished by Him in actual deed. God, and God alone, was the "Redeemer," or the One who brought man into a peaceful union with Him. *"I will redeem them from death,"* God had graciously promised through the Prophet Hosea (Hosea 13:14). Man therefore could not "tap into" God or redeem himself at his own beckoned call. Man's separation from God was not a circumstance that could be fixed by willing it away. Oh, how men have wished that it were so! No, man's redemption required real work apart from him – actual work and a real transaction that was undertaken to accomplish man's solace with God. That gracious work required real sweat and real blood, and a definite price had to be paid on the part of man, for sin separated man from God and remained before Him as a very real, legal offense that required His judgment, His justice, and a real prosecution.

Man's redemption was accomplished by a legal transaction undertaken by the triune God. Arranged by a gracious covenant between the three Persons of the Godhead, it was set in motion prior to Creation and before man existed or could have had any say in the matter. It was therefore a gracious, sovereign pact undertaken among His own Persons, with each having agreed to fulfill His part.

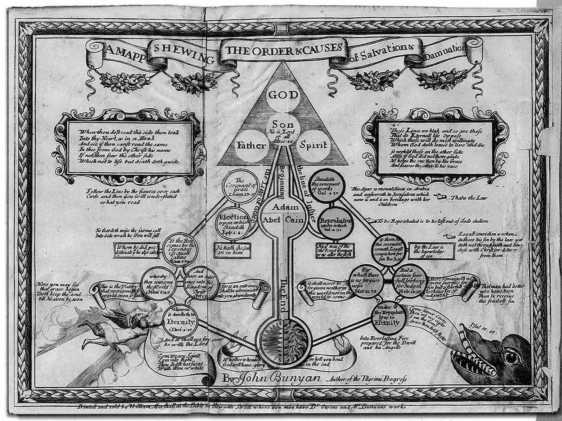

The great Puritan writer John Bunyan understood the essential work of God as the *"Father,"* the *"Son,"* and the *"Spirit"* in the redemption of His elect. This excerpt from Bunyan's detailed *"Mapp Shewing the Order & Causes of Salvation & Damnation"* depicts the *"Covenant"* paths of either salvation by God's grace or damnation by His justice.

The Father's function in the work of redemption would be to declare His Son as the Redeemer unto the world, and then uphold Him by His Spirit: *"Behold my servant whom I uphold, mine elect in whom my soul delighteth: I have put my spirit upon him"* (Isaiah 42:1). The reformers saw within that Isaiah passage an exact unity of the covenantal purpose in the triune God. God, as the divine Father, was the Person speaking in the passage (*"Behold ..."*); He was speaking of the second Person, the divine Son (*"my servant whom I uphold"*); and the first two Persons were in league with the third Person, the divine Spirit (*"my spirit upon him"*). The reformers thus saw man's reconciliation with God as accomplished by a covenantal union of the Three: the office of the Father, the work of the Son, and the strength of the Spirit. The plan was set in motion before the beginning of the world and would be accomplished in fact – in real space and time in the world. A single, perfect man would be offered up to pay the price of man's infinite debt of sin, and the debt would be paid to the Father by the Person of the Son, who would be upheld by the Spirit on behalf of man. God's Covenant of Redemption would therefore provide the sole means for man to satisfy the moral exactness required by the perfect God – and the sole means by which an imperfect man could engage in a personal covenant with Him. The Father, Son, and Spirit together would accomplish the transaction. The reformers' Geneva Bible therefore noted that the above Old Testament, Isaiah passage provided the Father's promise of a pending, redemptive, and *"acceptable"* work which would be performed by His Son:

> *I will establish him, to wit, in his office, by giving him the fulnesse of my spirit. He onely is acceptable unto me, and they that come unto me by him: for there is no other means of reconciliation.*[1]

Several New Testament passages also confirmed the redemptive covenant between the three Persons of God. After Jesus spoke of *"making himself equall with God"* (John 5:18), He acknowledged the Father's directives in His work: *"The Son can do nothing of himself, but what he seeth the Father do: for what things soever he doeth, these also doth the Son likewise"* (John 5:19). Such passages demonstrated the complete agreement among the Godhead's united power and purpose. The reformers therefore observed of that passage in John:

> *In like sort, joyntly and together. Not for that the Father doth some things, and then the Son worketh after him, and doth the like, but because the might and power of the Father and the Son do work equally and jointly together.*[2]

Man, then, had no way to obtain redemption other than through the finished work of God. Only by way of God's sovereign, imputed righteousness could man enter into a cordial relation with Him. Man had no voice in the matter – neither in the fact of his earthly existence, nor in the manner of his being reconciled to God. All relations with God were thereby defined by His covenantal terms. Understanding the sovereign nature of all His engagements provides the roadmap for understanding the nature of man's every relation with God as described in both covenantal Testaments.

1. *The Holy Bible* (London: The Company of Stationers, 1649), Geneva marginal note on Isaiah 42:1, leaf Hh4.
2. Geneva note on John 5:19, leaf Eee5.

Though covenants in the Bible primarily concerned commitments between God and man, there were many that also involved various associations among men. These included binding commitments – whether private, public, or national – between members of families, churches, or the overall commonwealth. These engagements could be as narrowly defined as the marriage covenant between a husband and a wife or as broadly based as an international treaty. But, all binding biblical covenants held one thing in common: they were all pledged under God. They were all sworn before Him and thereby called upon His infinite surety and judgment to ensure their enduring security and righteousness. In their broadest categorical sense, the godly covenants that appeared in the two Testaments therefore represented binding engagements as: within God's Trinity, those engaged between Himself and man, or those among men that were secured and superintended by God.

A.

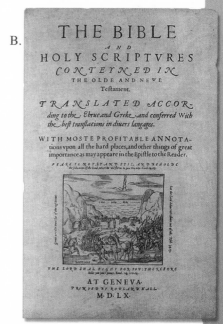

A. Shown here is an example of the extensive marginal notes included in the reformers' Geneva version of the Bible. This small excerpt comprises the Old Testament rendering of Isaiah 42:1-2 and the marginal notes that commented on man's reconciliation with the triune God. Regarding the verse about Christ who *"shall bring foorth judgement to the Gentiles,"* the notes astutely remarked: *"He shall declare himselfe governour over the Gentiles, and call them by his word, and rule them by his Spirit. His comming shall not bee with pompe and noyse, as earthly princes"* (1594 edition).

We can define covenants accordingly. All covenantal agreements are more than mere contracts secured by the fallible words of men, because they call upon divine oversight and the highest self-scrutiny. And, without the acknowledgment of God, human engagements cannot have a secure foundation or an enduring legacy. That sort of commitment is a mere human contract, as fallible as the intentions of the men who engaged in it, and as temporary as the arbitrary language of the finite mortals who secured it. Mere human covenants can indeed be broken and therefore dissolved, and the penalty for covenant breakers would then be great. Yet, without calling on God's divine superintendence to hold committed parties accountable, there can be no surety or security to any human engagement.

B.

B. This is the general title page of the first edition of the Geneva Bible, which was published in 1560. Its centerpiece woodcut depicted God's redemption of the people of Israel, who had been in bondage to Egypt.

Understanding the covenantal nature of the Bible's dual Testaments provides the roadmap for a divine grasp of its sacred history. The Testaments work together as a single, overarching, gracious covenant by which God historically imparted His redemptive grace to man. And, together they present an appropriate understanding of the covenantal nature of His involvement with us, and of our covenantal obligations among our fellow man.

The Hebrew Ideas of Covenant

The idea of covenants was pervasive throughout both Testaments and presented in several ways. The Old Testament Hebrew term that translated into English as "covenant" was "berith," which could be used in describing many types of committed agreements between parties. An early example of a berith was the commercial truce of Abraham with Abimelech, king of the Philistines, which involved the respect of each other's tribal interests.[3] On the other hand, one of the most significant covenants involving God and man was the unconditional berith promise that God Himself made to Abraham. God thereby sealed His pledge by way of a berith engagement of "cutting" a covenant. He utilized a ritualistic rite of dividing a beast in two and passing between the two divided halves. All parties who pledged were to pass through the parts to dramatize that their covenant was irrevocable. The graphic parts symbolized that if one of the parties violated the terms of the covenant, he was as much as dead – as if he were the carcass split in twain. The Genesis narrative described how God, being infinite, represented Himself in passing through the parts:

> *And it came to passe, that when the sun went down and it was dark, behold a smoking furnace, and a burning lamp that passed between those pieces. In that same day the LORD made a covenant with Abram, saying, Unto thy seed have I given this land, from the river of Egypt unto the great river the river Euphrates* (Genesis 15:17-18).

Because God unilaterally engaged Himself in an unconditional promise to Abraham, the Genesis narrative illustrated His covenant promise in such a manner that God's representative presence alone passed through the divided beasts. God alone made the pledge signifying to Abraham that He would be as much as dead if He failed to perform on His promise, having sworn upon His own sovereign integrity. By singularly passing between sacrificial animals as a sign of His solemn promise, God made a pledge that was to the complete benefit of Abraham with no performance required by him in return. God, as sovereign, granted an infinite surety in His promise which demonstrated His sovereign grace to Abraham as well as unto his most distant descendants. That berith was a defining moment in the Bible's covenantal narrative. Because God was divine and could not lie any more than He could die, His promise demonstrated an infinitely secure, unbreakable oath and an irrevocable, covenantal engagement with man.

The idea of berith was continued in the development of Israel as a nation. Following the release of the descendants of Abraham from their extended captivity in Egypt, God formed their twelve tribes into an independent nation. He then entered a contractual bond of obedience between Himself, as their Redeemer, and Israel, as the redeemed. Upon embarking on their wilderness journey at Sinai, God presented the sons of Abraham with a most significant engagement.

A.

B.

Das Ander teil des alten Testaments,

Wittemberg.

D. D. XXXIIII.

A. Shown here is an excerpted portrait of the original Hebrew patriarch, Abraham, as he was depicted on the Old Testament title page of the first edition of Martin Luther's German Bible in 1534.

B. This is the text block of Luther's Old Testament title page of 1534.

3. See Genesis 21:22-27.

There the berith motif came in the form of written statutes as a national constitution. It was not the kind of berith in which God had engaged their forefather, for this time it came by way of a mutually binding agreement with terms binding upon both parties. The consensual nature of the pledge by vassal (bonded servant) Israel put them under the obliging ownership of their Redeemer. The people unitedly consented to the terms of His Law in becoming a nation, as demonstrated by the exchange between God's mediator (or representative), Moses, and the people:

> *And he took the book of the covenant, and read in the audience of the people: and they said, All that the LORD hath said, will we do, and be obedient* (Exodus 24:7).

God was theirs and they were God's by right of His redemption and their consensual vow. God provided the Israelites with guidance, protection, and prosperity in exchange for their obedience. As a chosen people, an earthly priesthood, and the physical repository for God's Promise to Abraham, they were completely obliged to the Law of their Lord. Such an engagement was the most common use of Old Testament berith: as a written contract with obligations on the part of God as well as upon His people: *"... if ye will obey my voice indeed, and keep my covenant, then ye shall be a peculiar treasure unto me above all people: for all the earth is mine"* (Exodus 19:5). God thereby entered into a berith promise in which His part would be secured by His infallible Word, and theirs by their solemn vow.

The conditional covenant Law did not contradict God's prior, unconditional covenant promise to Abraham. The one did not lessen the other nor undermine or nullify its sovereign terms.[4] The two worked hand in hand, with faith in the promise of grace working through Abraham's covenant and with earthly blessing working through their obedience to His Law. But, both looked forward together toward their fulfillment in the coming of the Messiah, as solemnized and symbolized by another berith sign used by Moses in the sprinkling of blood upon the covenant people of Israel:

> *And Moses took the blood and sprinkled it on the people: and said, Behold the blood of the covenant which the LORD hath made with you concerning all these words* (Exodus 24:8).

Moses' sprinkling of the blood upon the people signified the sacrificial price that was necessary to pay for transgressions against God's Law. The blood thereby foretold the forgiveness that would be accomplished in the sacrificial death of the Messiah as a kinship redemption which would be performed by Jesus Christ. The Geneva Bible's marginal notes on the Book of Hebrews therefore associated all of the "Old Testament" sacrificial ceremonies as foreshadows of the real sacrificial death and kinship redemption to be accomplished by the Messiah in the "New Testament": *"Christ shed his blood also for the fathers, for he was shadowed by these old ceremonies."*[5]

Moses and the two tables of the Covenant Law were depicted on the general title page of the first edition of the 'King James' version of the Bible in 1611.

4. See Galatians 3:17.
5. Geneva note on Hebrews 9:15, leaf Nnn.

Dan Ford, 2002

A.

B.

C.

A. This sketch, based upon a nineteenth-century Bible illustration, shows Jeremiah pronouncing God's judgment before the king of Judah.

B. This is the opening of the Book of Jeremiah as it appeared in the Geneva Bible (1594 edition), with its introductory notes explaining God's charge to the prophet: *"The Lorde sheweth him the destruction of Jerusalem. Hee commaundeth him to preach his word without feare."*

C. This is the Geneva Bible's rendering of Jeremiah 22:8-9, the text in which the Lord announced that *"many nations"* will wonder what had happened to Jerusalem. After its judgment by God, the prophet said, *"they shall say every man to his neighbour, Wherefore hath the Lord done thus unto this great citie?"* The Lord told the prophet that the people would then reply: *"Because they have forsaken the covenant of the Lord their God, and worshipped other gods and served them."*

Another dramatic application of the Hebrew idea of "berith," used again in reference to "cutting" a covenant, was employed when God later judged His people in the land of Judah because of their disobedience. God had promised the land to Abraham's descendants[6] and later delivered on His pledge through Moses. When their descendants failed to be obedient to their covenantal obligations, God announced that they were destined for ruin and captivity. Though the promise of the land had been made unconditionally to Abraham, the total depravity of his later descendants made continued prosperity in the land impossible. God therefore compared Judah itself to the pieces of the sacrifice He used in the original Abrahamic berith "cutting." Using His prophet Jeremiah, God announced His judgment that the people of Judah would temporarily be removed from the Promised Land, as the marginal note in the Geneva Bible explained: *"to signifie that the transgressour of the same covenant should be so divided in pieces."*[7] Jeremiah spoke in such a manner as to illustrate the certain death that was due them – that is, apart from God's sovereign promise to preserve Abraham's offspring.[8] They would thereby graphically understand the justice of the punishment to be inflicted upon them because of their breaking the berith Law.

Judah indeed suffered God's judgment in Babylon, though its captivity did not nullify God's promise to Abraham. The Hebrews were restored to their homeland and God's sovereign promise continued in effect until its fulfillment in the coming of Messiah. Pointedly, God then used the same Prophet, Jeremiah, to announce that He would reaffirm the original promise of grace made to Abraham in the fruition of a "New Covenant": *"I will make a new covenant with the house of Israel, and with the house of Judah ... "* (Jeremiah 31:31). That promise signified the Messiah's grace which would

6. See Genesis 15:18.
7. Geneva note on Jeremiah 34:18, leaf Ll.
8. See Jeremiah 34:18-20.

remove the penalty of the sins of many: *"For this is my blood of the new testament which is shed for many for the remission of sins"* (Matthew 26:28). The reformers therefore referenced in the Geneva Bible's footnotes: *"Whereby the new league and covenant is made: for in making of leagues, they used pouring of wine and shedding of blood."*[9]

As representative of the whole of sinful humanity, the nations of Israel and Judah had repeatedly failed in their obligation to obey God, yet God still demonstrated a continuing performance on His sovereign promise. It would be in the gracious substitution demonstrated in the perfect, obedient life and sacrificial death of Messiah Jesus that sinful man would see the true manifestation of God's original berith promise to Abraham.

The Apostle Paul, who was the inspired author of much of the Apostolic text of the Bible, used the Greek term "diatheke" in the Old Testament berith sense as contractual covenant in his Epistle to the Galatians.[10] Throughout the third chapter of that book, Paul referred to the promissory aspect of Christ as a fixed covenanted pledge in the various ancient Hebrew applications of the term.

In the New Testament, though, we find another important aspect of the overall understanding of Jeremiah's pronouncement of the "New Covenant."[11] God's original proclamation of the "New Berith" (through Jeremiah) also foretold that which would be described in the New Covenant's Book of Hebrews as a "testament."[12] There, the author of the epistle described the perfect life and sacrificial death of Jesus as associated with a sonship inheritance by way of His "last will and testament" following His death. The Reformed theologians therefore considered both the Old and New Testaments as manifestly united in the person of Jesus Christ. "Jesus," as man, uniquely fulfilled the requirements of the Law and left an inherited will and testament to His brethren. And "Christ," as God, satisfied the original promise of covenantal grace and now lives to intercede on behalf of His elect. In His gracious death, Jesus left a testament bestowing His inheritance upon His fellow heirs, and by still living, Christ continues to maintain His sovereign Lordship over them in an everlasting dominion. Jesus Christ therefore remains gloriously sovereign over man's entire covenantal inheritance.[13] The reformers also saw both the "Old" and "New" texts pointing to the same covenantal mediation for sin, as Christ died equally for both the "Old" and the "New" Covenant believers. The Book of Hebrews' reference to Christ as *"the Mediatour of the new testament"* (Hebrews 9:15) was thus explained in the Geneva Bible's comments:

> ... *this testament is called the latter, not as concerning the vertue of it, (that is to say, remission of sin) but in respect of that time, wherein the thing itself was finished, that is to say, wherein Christ was indeed exhibited to the world, and fulfilled all things which were necessary to our salvation.*[14]

The Apostle Paul, an inspired New Covenant author, was shown in this illustration armed with God's Word by which the faithful could rightly divide and weigh all issues of justice and truth on earth. (Also see Hebrews 4:12-13.) This allegorical woodcut of Paul was included in William Tyndale's 1536 edition of the English New Testament.

9. Geneva note on Matthew 26:28, leaf Bbb4.
10. See Galations 3:15, 17 for "covenant."
11. See Jeremiah 31:31.
12. Compare Galations 3:15 "covenant" and Hebrews 9:15 "testament."
13. See Paul's Epistle to the Ephesians 2:13-14 and Epistle to the Colossians 1:14-17.
14. Geneva note on Hebrews 9:15, leaves Nnn1 and Nnn2.

Many would indeed be saved by way of the mediation of Jesus Christ. All of God's elect, both Jews and Gentiles, would then be redeemed as Abraham's covenant descendants in the extension of the same promise called the "New Covenant," or "New Testament." Old Israel was replaced by Messiah's worldwide dominion as He now rules over all of the world as its King of Kings and Lord of Lords.

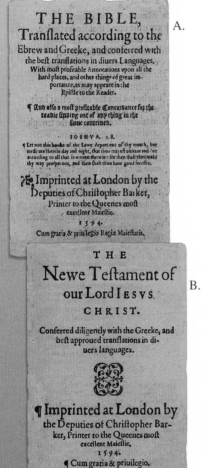

A. Shown here is the text block from the general title page of an Elizabethan era Geneva Bible. It quotes Joshua 1:8: *"Let not this booke of the Lawe depart out of thy mouth, but meditate therein day and night, that thou mayest observe and do: according to all that is written therein..."* (1594 edition).

B. The text block from the New Testament title page of the same Bible shows the Scriptures divided as two "Testaments."

The Titles of the Testaments

To the English reformers of the sixteenth and seventeenth centuries, the textual sense of the Bible was that it was composed of two "covenants" rather than "testaments." Covenants certainly best explained to them the relations by which God conducted His engagements with man. As reflected in the promissory agreements made to Adam, Noah, Abraham, Moses, David, and Jeremiah, and the promises' subsequent fulfillment in Messiah Jesus, God's gracious engagements with all were covenantal. The twin volumes were best described in their theological sense as two volumes of covenantal engagements between the Creator and His Creation, between the Sovereign and His vassal subjects, between the Redeemer and His redeemed. The English reformers' Geneva Bible footnotes clearly indicated that the textual content of both was considered covenantal: *"They are called two covenants, the one of the old Testament, and another of the new."*[15]

Nevertheless, the same Geneva version that referred to the Bible's main theological themes as "covenants" still continued the long tradition of titling the Bible's two major divisions as "Testaments." This was due to the well-established practice of titling the two major sets of biblical texts as "Testaments" – a tradition which dated back over a thousand years to the time of the old, original Uncial Greek texts (large, square characters) of A.D. 250-400.

Historically speaking, those two major divisions of the Bible's books came to be known as "Testaments" due to the manner of their early transmission and subsequent translation into various languages. Early in the Church Age, the Apostolic Scriptures were transmitted in their original Greek or Hebrew languages. They were initially disseminated as individual scrolls of Gospels, Epistles, or volumes of a few of the various Apostolic books. At that time the various compilations of new writings had no official general title. Yet, like the older, authoritative Hebrew texts that preexisted the Apostles, their writings were also circulated by the faithful as Scripture.

15. Geneva note on Galatians 4:24, leaf Lll.

The entire Hebrew Old Covenantal text had already been translated into the Greek language by the beginning of the second century before Christ. That Greek Scripture, known as the *Septuagint*, was widely read by the early Christians and accompanied their Apostolic (New Covenant) texts. After the fall of Jerusalem in A.D. 70, the Hebrew language ceased to be commonly used in Judea and the entire text of Scripture was widely disseminated only in the Greek format. By the end of the second century, both the Old and the New Covenant sets of (Greek) texts were generally accepted by Christians as two individual volumes. But, it was the gradual process of accumulating both sets of texts into a double volume format (the Old with the New) by the Greek-speaking Christians that distinguished them with the two titles of "Old Testament" and "New Testament." Then, borrowing from that Greek custom, Jerome, in the early fifth century, translated both sets of texts together into the "vulgar" (common) Latin language, also titling each of the two divisions of the Vulgate as a "testamentum." Elsewhere in the Vulgate text, Jerome also rendered the idea of "berith" in Latin terms such as "foedus" (covenant) or "pactum" (contract). Thus, the overall use of the Bible's covenantal motif was variously expressed in the text of the Latin-language Bible as federations, pacts, treaties, or binding agreements, as well as testaments, though both the older and newer Scriptural divisions were titled as simply "testamentum."[16] When the 'official' (Roman) Church put its stamp on Jerome's Vulgate version, it officially established the major title divisions as the Old and New "Testaments."

Beginning with John Wycliffe's reforms in the late fourteenth century came the first complete translation of the Vulgate into English. He simply followed the form and linguistic traditions established by Jerome's version. English-language Bibles also began rendering the divisions as "Testaments," borrowing from Jerome. With the English Reformation in the early 1500's came the first English translations of the Bible from the best obtainable early Hebrew and Greek texts. Beginning with William Tyndale's "New Testament" in 1525, the title pages were titled "Testaments." Later English translations, including the historic Genevan and the "Authorized" (King James) texts, likewise adopted the divisions as "Old and New Testaments." Interestingly, even when the Bible was translated by the Puritan John Eliot into an American Indian dialect, he, too, used the traditional term "Testament" following the English tradition.

It is somewhat ironic that in the first English translation directly from the *Septuagint* (published by the former secretary of the American Continental Congress, Charles Thomson, in 1808), the general title page was rendered without further explanation: *The Old and New Covenant, commonly called the Old and New Testament. Translated*

A. This is the text block from the general title page of the first complete Bible printed in English, showing its divisions as the *"Olde and New Testament"* (1535).

B. This title page from the first Bible printed in an American Indian language showed its divisions as "Testaments" (1660).

16. *Encyclopedia Britannica*, Eleventh Edition, vol. 3 (1910), s.v. "Bible: The Process of Dissemination and Collection. Influences at work," pp. 876-877.

from the Greek. His specific title page to the first volume (including the Books of Moses) similarly read: *The Old Covenant, Commonly Called The Old Testament: Translated from the Septuagint.*

Many researchers of the last century also came to agree with the sixteenth-century reformers that the better term to refer to the theological theme of the Scriptures was the term "covenant." For example, a century after Thomson, the *Encyclopedia Britannica*'s comprehensive article on the historic development of the Biblical text considered the term "covenant" to preempt the term "testament" in describing the Apostolic writings as well as the understanding of the older Hebrew texts:

> *By the last quarter of the 2nd century the conception of a Christian Bible in two parts, Old Testament and New Testament, may be said to be definitely established. Already at the beginning of this period Melito had drawn up a list of the twenty-two Books of the Old Covenant, i.e. of the documents to which the Old Covenant made its appeal. It was a very short step to the compiling of a list for the New-Covenant, which by another short step becomes the New Testament, by the side of the Old Testament.*[17]

More current historians likewise agree in respect to the term *"covenant"* that Jeremiah used in the *"new covenant"* prophecy of the coming Messiah (Jeremiah 31:31). That reference leads them to conclude as does contemporary author Paul Wegner: *"Probably the better term to refer to the parts of Scripture would be the word covenant."*[18]

"Covenants" indeed best describe the overall scope of the relations of God with His people as they are described in the text of Scripture. It would therefore be just as legitimate to use the term "covenant" in referring to the Bible's two major division titles. Indeed, both the narrative of Scripture and the broad sweep of history show that God's chosen way of relating to man has been through covenantal relations. Men are certainly both individually and corporately obliged to their Creator by such means whether they realize it or not. Therefore, the following chapters are intended to provide a brief overview of the scope of man's historic obligations to God and of His abundant covenantal grace toward man.

Dan Ford, 2002

A.

B.

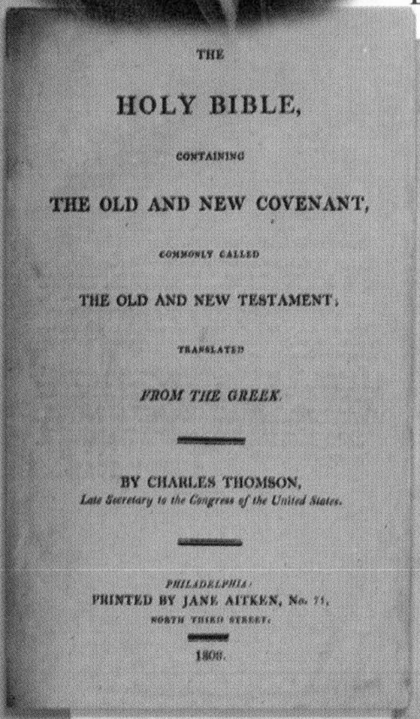

C.

THE
HOLY BIBLE,
CONTAINING
THE OLD AND NEW COVENANT,
COMMONLY CALLED
THE OLD AND NEW TESTAMENT;
TRANSLATED
FROM THE GREEK.
BY CHARLES THOMSON,
Late Secretary to the Congress of the United States.
PHILADELPHIA:
PRINTED BY JANE AITKEN, No. 71,
NORTH THIRD STREET.
1808.

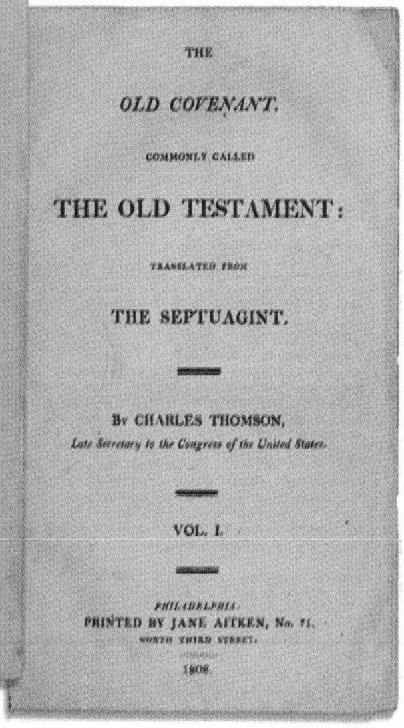

THE
OLD COVENANT,
COMMONLY CALLED
THE OLD TESTAMENT:
TRANSLATED FROM
THE SEPTUAGINT.
By CHARLES THOMSON,
Late Secretary to the Congress of the United States.
VOL. I.
PHILADELPHIA:
PRINTED BY JANE AITKEN, No. 71,
NORTH THIRD STREET.
1808.

A. This is a portrait sketch of American Charles Thomson, who first published an English-language translation of the *Septuagint* Greek Bible in 1808.

B. Shown here is Thomson's general title page called: *"The Holy Bible, containing The Old and New Covenant."*

C. Thomson's *Septuagint "Old Covenant"* title page noted that it was also *"Commonly Called The Old Testament."*

17. Ibid.
18. Paul Wegner, *The Journey from Texts to Translations* (Grand Rapids, MI: Baker Academic Books, 2000), chapter 2, subheading: "What are Testaments," p. 31.

Chapter 3: The Creation of Man

The Covenant of Works and Mankind's Fallible Limitations

THE first glimpse of a covenantal mandate between God and man appeared on the sixth day of Creation. On that day, the first day of man's existence in Eden, God established the first obligations of His choicest creature. That Creation Covenant was presented in terms of man's obedience to God as well as God's obligations to man. On God's part, He promised to provide every sufficiency for man: *"And out of the ground made the LORD God to grow every tree that is pleasant to the sight, and good for food ..."* (Genesis 2:9).

God took the initiative as the superior party in the covenant. He therefore *"took the man and put him into the garden of Eden,"* and created a subordinate obligation on man's part *"to dresse it, and to keep it"* (Genesis 2:15). The man found his perfect fit in his natural setting. And, with perfect subjection to God, man's obligations were not burdensome and he enjoyed the full extent of genuine liberty through his stewardship. Man was perfectly designed for his position and exactly suited to the pleasurable terms of his work. His Lord, though, had given him personal responsibility through expressed limits upon his governance:

> And the LORD God commanded the man, saying, Of every tree of the garden thou mayest freely eat: But of the tree of the knowledge of good and evil, thou shalt not eat of it; for in the day that thou eatest thereof thou shalt surely die (Genesis 2:16-17).

In the Creation Covenant, man was given dominion over *"every beast of the field, and every fowl of the air"* (Genesis 2:19), as God brought each of them to man for naming. And, as God's immediate subordinate, the man was then given his own name by God: Adam.

Man's Responsible Dominion

Thus were drawn the lines of superiority and subordination in Paradise, with God over man and man subject to God, and with man over Creation and Creation subject to both man and God. Man's authority and dominion was then, as always, to be subordinate, and his stewardship subject to his Lord. Adam was charged neither to take orders from the beasts, which he himself had named, nor to eat *"of the tree of the knowledge of good and evil."*

In spite of all the good that surrounded him, there was one thing lacking in Adam's Paradise. By creating another union for Adam, God initiated the second covenantal motif, known as the Societal Covenant. As long as man lived alone under God there was but one, vertical covenant responsibility. But, at the moment when the one became two, man's covenantal horizons took on a new dimension. God created another human being and man took on additional responsibilities as a co-member of the new community of mankind. In the creation of mankind, societal bonds were required to bind man with woman, and they were not left to themselves, for the fact that man would enter mutual commitments with others did not mean that he was freed from his first, or preemptive, bond with God. The horizontal societal covenant did not lessen man's prior, vertical responsibilities to his Creator.

A.

B.

A. God formed Eve from Adam's rib on the sixth day of Creation, as illustrated in this woodcut from an incunable Italian-language Bible printed in 1494.

B. By eating of the forbidden tree, Eve and Adam willingly rebelled against their Creator. They broke His direct command by obeying the voice of a creature, over whom they had been charged by God to demonstrate their dominion. This illustration of mankind's original sin was included in John Speed's *Genealogies*, which accompanied the first edition of the 'King James' version of the English Bible, printed in 1611.

With the creation of Eve, man was given the most adequate sustenance through the helpmeet of a covenant wife. Man and woman together now comprised the first societal covenant in which God required them to *"cleave"* (Genesis 2:24), becoming one with the other. Now, together in an additional covenant bond, they acquired multiple responsibilities under God. Their first duty was each maintaining their responsibilities directly to God, and their second duty was maintaining their responsibilities with each other. Individually, the husband and the wife held an account with God for the good of each, and jointly they had an account with God for the good of the whole. For the sake of the other they were to be uniquely subservient to God; for the sake of the family, or the first human society, they were to be unitedly subservient to God and to their union. Then again, in the broadest sense, together they represented the whole body of mankind, and as such, they represented the whole cooperative responsibility of mankind to the Creator. Simply put, Adam and Eve were each: one under God as an individual; together: one united under Him as a family; and corporately: one under Him as the entire commonwealth of mankind. God thereby placed the Creation Covenant's responsibilities upon them in each and every sphere of their existence, with God Himself as the Initiator of each human society and reigning as the continuing Lord over all. Eve then, being included in God's perfectly divine sustenance for herself, her husband, her family, and mankind, acknowledged herself to be responsibly and responsively included in all the stipulations that had been given to Adam by God.[1]

1. See Eve's acknowledgment to the serpent of her covenantal responsibility to God in Genesis 3:2-3.

The Covenant of Works

Such a covenantal engagement, with all obligations dependent on man's perfect performance, was described by the reformers as "The Covenant of Works."[2] Adam and Eve were given specific terms of obedience with no margin for error, since the terms of their Paradise provision were dependent on their "Works" of obedience. The Covenant of Works was to be perfectly kept, or else it would be completely broken by a single infraction. Because God is perfect and infinitely righteous, obedience to Him must be maintained accordingly. He could not legitimize imperfection without lowering Himself, and according to His engagement, His terms were perfectly precise. Adam's and Eve's lives, ever maintained under the watchful care of their perfect Creator in the perfect Paradise covenant, necessitated perfect "works" of submission.

The term "Covenant of Works" was employed by Reformed theologians as early as the mid-sixteenth century[3] to describe man's pre-fall life in Paradise. The covenanted parties were: God as the moral Ruler and mankind as the moral agent representing His dominion over the earth. On God's part, His work was in giving mankind life and perfect sufficiency. Man's work was to submit to God's supreme authority and live in perfect Paradise obedience. The terms of man's life were therefore perfectly conditional. The *"tree of life"* (Genesis 2:9) was the visible sign of life. The forbidden *"tree of knowledge of good and evil"* (Genesis 2:9) was the visible sign of death. Both were visible seals of the covenant. The Tree of Life represented *"a signe of the life received of God"*; the Tree of the Knowledge of Good and Evil represented *"miserable experience, which came by disobeying God."*[4]

Perhaps the most succinct definition of the Covenant of Works was that of the Reformed scholar John Preston in the early 1600's. His explanation of *"reasons why God is willing to make a Covenant with men,"* provided the following straightforward statement:

> *The Covenant of Workes runs in these termes, Doe this, and thou shall live, and I will be thy God. This is the Covenant that was made with Adam ... .*[5]

Adam and Eve thus received their directives from on high, from God Himself. They failed the terms of their covenant when they complied with the directives from a subordinate creature – a serpent over whom they were required to demonstrate their dominion. Then, in their submission to the serpent they subsequently partook of the forbidden tree, disobeying God's direct commandment and violating the visible sign of their eternal life: *"Adam deprived of life, lost also the signe thereof."*[6] Thus, mankind was shown to be incapable of adequate performance under the Covenant of Works, and God had them removed from the garden of perfect Paradise provision.

2. *Oxford Encyclopedia of the Reformation*, vol. 1 (New York & Oxford, 1996), pp. 128, 241, 442.
3. Ibid.
4. Geneva note on Genesis 2:9, leaf A6.
5. John Preston, *The New Covenant, or the Saints Portion. A Treatise Unfolding the All-sufficiencie of God, Mans Uprightnes, and the Covenant of Grace*, 8th ed., corrected (London, 1634), p. 317.
6. Geneva note on Genesis 3:22, leaf A7.

Chapter 4: The Fathers of the Promise

The Early Legacy of God's Covenant People of Promise

ACCORDING to the terms of Adam's fall, God would only continue to deal with man according to either His judgment or His grace. Lest He execute man's deserved judgment and he utterly perish, God has, since the Paradise fall, sovereignly chosen to deal graciously with man by continuing covenantal relations. For instance, an explicit gracious promise was made by God just prior to the great deluge of the earth. Though mankind had utterly and repeatedly demonstrated its disobedience, God, even in judging the sins of the world, spared mankind through His mercy displayed upon the single family of Noah:

> *But with thee will I establish my covenant: and thou shalt come into the ark; thou, and thy sons, and thy wife, and thy sons wives with thee* (Genesis 6:18).

The Gracious Noahic Covenant

God delivered on His gracious pledge immediately after delivering Noah's family. In a covenant grounded purely in grace, God affirmed: *"And I will establish my covenant with you, neither shall all flesh be cut off any more by the waters of a flood, neither shall there any more be a flood to destroy the earth"* (Genesis 9:11).

Noah's Ark was shown in this 1611 depiction resting safely on the *"Mountaines of Ararat."* Noah's family had carried with them God's gracious promise of man's continued life on earth. (From John Speed's *Genealogies* in the first 'King James' edition.)

To the Reformed, God's covenant with Noah represented a restatement of the Creation Covenant. It was conferred upon *"all flesh,"* meaning that the whole order of the earth had been mercifully restored and recreated. Matthew Henry, the "non-conformist"[1] author of a voluminous set of Reformed Bible Commentaries, proclaimed it: *"the Magna Charta – the Great Charter of this new kingdom of nature."*[2] He saw that mankind was given a new earth gifted by God's grace, renewed in its original terms of submissive dominion.

As a Covenant of Grace, the ark narrative stood as God's redemptive deliverance, with Noah standing in the gap of mankind's total annihilation. Henry remarked: *"God here makes Noah a monument of sparing mercy."*[3] The act of

---

1. *The Compact Edition of the Dictionary of National Biography*, vol. 1 (Oxford, U.K.: Oxford University Press, 1975), s.v. "Henry, Matthew," pp. 574-575.
2. Matthew Henry, *An Exposition of the Old & New Testaments*, book 1 (London, [circa 1841]), commentary on Genesis 9:1-7, p. 29.
3. Ibid., commentary on Genesis 6:18, p. 24.

saving mankind by such an unmerited, miraculous deliverance caused Henry to see the narrative as God's special providence in the manifestation of His Covenant of Grace: *"... a great honour was thereby put upon him and his* [Noah and his family]. *The covenant of grace, that God would be to him a God and that out of his seed God would take to himself a people."*[4]

Thus, a new sign would be manifested as the physical seal of the covenant. The rainbow was affixed by God as an often-repeated reminder of His grace toward mankind. That great seal would remain affixed in the heavens as a continual display that God's promise would not fail as long as there remained generations upon the earth. As long as one sees the bow, the seal remains affixed and the "New" Creation Covenant, that great *"Magna Charta of the new kingdom of nature,"*[5] still endures:

> *And God said, This is the token of the covenant which I make between me, and you, and every living creature that is with you, for perpetuall generations: I do set my bowe in the cloud, and it shall be for a token of a covenant between me and the earth* (Genesis 9:12-13).

Though God's promise of continued grace was secured, His covenant was marked by continuing terms of obedience. All subsequent human posterity, as Noah's descendants, were obliged by God's terms to maintain their earthly sufficiency by obedience to His commands. For example, God covenantally commanded all men to forever respect human life: *"Whoso sheddeth mans blood, by man shall his blood be shed; for in the image of God made he man. And you, be ye fruitfull, and multiply, bring forth abundantly in the earth, and multiply therein"* (Genesis 9:6-7).

A.

Dan Ford, 2002

A. Noah is here depicted with his three sons, who together represented the entire male posterity of the human race at the time of God's gracious covenant with the new world.

The Earliest Covenantal Documents

God had thus contracted terms of divine Law, and the idea of contracted covenantal laws was implanted in the generations descending from Noah. Among the earliest physical records of post-Noahic civilization were the seals and tablets of the Near East, which recorded various contracts and agreements regarding business, religious, or civil activities. These transactions, recorded with an array of terms that vary from common exchanges to royal decrees, were inscribed on clay tablets or stone. Among the most fascinating artifacts for archaeologists are the seals that were rolled or stamped over a document before it was fired.[6] Once fired, the seal's impression represented a binding commitment, or pledge, stating the terms of the contract. The seals were often illustrated

B.

B. This is a typical cuneiform contract written upon a clay tablet from Ur in Babylonia. It dates from approximately 2000 B.C., when God called Abram from that city.

4. Ibid., commentary on Genesis 6:21, p. 24.
5. Ibid., commentary on Genesis 9:1-7, p. 29.
6. See Harriet Crawford, *Sumer and the Sumerians* (Cambridge University Press, 1992), pp. 155-156.

A. This is a Sumerian cylinder seal shown in its two sides with the entire impression rolled upon clay. It depicts a Babylonian priest or ruler worshipping a deity of half-man, half-beast (Babylon, circa 2700 B.C.).

with the image of a particular deity which supposedly would have oversight to see that the obligations were met and then intervene through natural forces as necessary. It could be well-argued that such practices (though all too-soon corrupted by man) stemmed from the prior understanding of binding laws and superintended covenants that God had deposited with Noah. Large numbers of the earliest written contracts, deeds, and decrees dating from the third millennium B.C. are, in fact, from Babylonian Ur, predating Abraham and the Hebrew Patriarchs by centuries.

The Usurping Pride of Tyrants

Babylon's great ruler, Nimrod, *"Meaning, a cruell oppressour and tyrant,"*[7] was the first to establish a dominion-styled rule in which a mortal lorded absolute dominion over people as if they were mere possessions. Nimrod ruled as though he was nearly divine,[8] and arbitrarily controlled man's first great multinational empire. This included Babel, as well as the vassal provinces of Erech, Accad, Calneh, and that of Ashur, in which he founded the historic city of Nineveh.[9] Simply put, Nimrod was seen by the Reformers as the world's original tyrant: *"His tyranny came into a proverb, as hated both of God and man: for he passed not to commit cruelty even in Gods presence."*[10]

By the second millennium B.C., the Hittite people (to the immediate north of Canaan) had begun to establish written covenants in the spirit of Nimrod. They defined reciprocal obligations of their imperial lordship over vassal provinces.[11] By then, the idea of a dominion empire based on the servitude of provincial vassal states had become established in the Near East. Such covenants often took the form of military treaties and were used to specify terms of peace between a conqueror and his defeated foe, or to record the obligations of tribes that sold themselves into the protection of a more powerful nobility. Both to Canaan's Hittite north, as well as to its south in Egypt,[12] lay two empires that had become great by the practice of the contracted vassalage of subject peoples. They both declared their supremacy according to the powers granted them by their local deities, who were seen as reigning over their

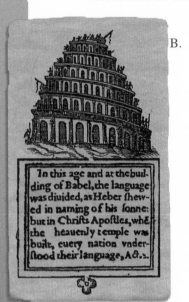

B.

In this age and at the building of Babel, the language was divided, as Heber shewed in naming of his sonne: but in Chrifts Apoftles, whē the heavenly temple was built, every nation vnderftood their language, A&.2.

B. The Tower of Babel was the first symbol of human dominion built upon the idea of pride and autonomy from God. It was here depicted in Speed's *Genealogies* (1611).

7. Geneva note on Genesis 10:8-9, leaf B1.

8. See *The Encyclopedia Britannica*, Eleventh Edition, vol. 19 (Cambridge & New York, 1910-1911), s.v. "Nimrod," p. 703.

9. See Genesis 10:8-12.

10. Geneva note on Genesis 10:8-9, leaf B1.

11. *Encyclopedia Britannica*, 11th ed., vol. 9, s.v. "Egypt," pp. 84-85; vol. 13, s.v. "Hittites," pp. 534-535.

12. Ibid.

vanquished fellow gods. Thus, the idea of gods preying upon other gods, defeating them, and reigning over their vanquished foes, served to multiply the numbers of admired deities. Such imaginative pretenses simply gave the empires their own sense of divine justification for magnificent human dominions. The emperor alone seemed to have the reign over all the most favored gods, and being declared a god himself, his will also was easily confirmed as divine.

Man had once again become abjectly corrupt. A trend by monarchs to subjugate people and provinces as if they were livestock was inconsistent with the covenant that God made with Noah. God did not divest Himself of His own overarching supremacy by legitimizing any localized alternatives, nor did He sanction mankind to permanently divest itself of the subordination it owed to Him. And further, God had never invested man with a level of dominion in which he could himself *"subdue"* the earth (Genesis 1:28) to the extent of dominating people in hopeless and endless servitude. God had limited such dominion over the lesser creatures, as He had told Noah:

> *And the fear of you, and the dread of you shall be upon every beast of the earth, and upon every foul* [fowl] *of the air, upon all that moveth upon the earth, and upon all the fishes of the sea; into your hand are they delivered* (Genesis 9:2).

The usurping pride of tyrants did not suit a people created in God's image. He did not mandate an arbitrary right to subdue men as if they were beasts to be ground down through brutally oppressive toil. All absolute dominion was reserved by God, and no absolute subordination of men would be countenanced as righteous by Him. God could and would use servitude as a form of His judgment upon individuals, tribes, or nations, or He could even destroy them according to His overarching purposes. But that divine right was exclusive to God and not man's for the taking. Thus, the Puritan author John Bunyan wrote in his *Exposition on the First Ten Chapters of Genesis* of the beginnings of a cancerous rise of prideful and godless human dominion:

> *Nimrod having began to exalt himself; others, that were big with Desires of Ostentation, did soon follow his Example, making themselves Captains and Heads of the People, and built them strong Holds for the Supportation of their Glory.*[13]

A. *Now, Faithfull, play the Man, Speak for thy God, Fear not the wicked's Malice, nor their Rod: Speak boldly, Man, the truth is on thy Side; Die for it, and to Life in Triumph rids.*

A. This engraved portrait of John Bunyan (1628-1688) was used as the frontis for the first complete edition of his collected *Works*, published between 1736 and 1737.

B. In this allegorical scene, Bunyan urged *"Faithful"* (the Christian) to *"play the Man"* in contending for God's truth before a world of petty human tyrants (engraving from *Works*, 1736).

13. John Bunyan, *The Works of that Eminent Servant of Christ, Mr. John Bunyan, ... Being Several Discourses upon Various Divine Subjects*, vol. 1, (London, 1736), *An Exposition on the First Ten Chapters of Genesis*, pp. 80-81.

God's Continuing Judgment

God's destruction of Sodom was an example of His continuing judgment of sin and rebellion, as illustrated in John Speed's biblical *Genealogies* (1611).

Other forms of moral depravity accompanied the great rebellion of human tyrants. Though God had promised Noah never again to judge the world by way of a general deluge: *"the waters shall no more become a flood to destroy all flesh"* (Genesis 9:15), His judgment would come again in a powerful local display of *"brimstone and fire"* (Genesis 19:24). Nevertheless, God locally poured out His wrath against Sodom and Gomorrah to demonstrate His general condemnation of all human depravity. The Apostle Peter looked back to God's judgment of Sodom as *"making them an ensample unto those that after should live ungodly"* (2 Peter 2:6). Thus, God would always retain the right to judge people or nations, even under His grace.

God's Gracious Intervention

In spite of man casting God's covenant aside, He again would patiently demonstrate His grace. With His judgment of Sodom, His sovereign grace would also be demonstrated in a localized exchange as a promise presented to a mere tribal patriarch. Significantly, God did not choose to contract with the likes of the prideful image of Nimrod. No, in what would have appeared at the time to be a vow of prosperity to the childless head of a relatively small clan of nomads, God engaged Himself in a great covenant that would impact the farthest points on earth. His simple but sovereign vow would bring the likes of Nimrod to their knees. Just as Sodom's hour of wrath foretold God's eternal sentence upon all wickedness, His moment of promise wrought the eternal hope of gracious forgiveness.

Adam's fall had proven that mankind could not live before God in perfect obedience, and the general rebellion of Noah's offspring served to confirm the point. God's grace would then be mediated by way of divine intervention in a sovereign, transcendent promise. In contrast to the more familiar contracts of the time, this covenant would neither originate with men nor be mediated through the incantations of the deities formed at their hands.

A Babylonian from Ur named Abram was approached by the Almighty. Someone with his cultural background would have been aware of the solemnities of a pledge to a deity. But, such a pledge actually coming from God Himself would have been manifestly different. That would have drawn Abram's attention back to the Author of the original covenant with Adam, and then on to His gracious redemption through Noah. By culturally knowing of contracted promises, and knowing of God's great covenant bow in the sky, Abram would have been given a profound sense of a great new engagement. God's words would bypass all the prayers, rituals, and gestures toward mere local deities when the great Almighty spoke to him:

... And I will make of thee a great nation, and I will blesse thee, and make thy name great; and thou shalt be a blessing. And I will blesse them that blesse thee, and curse him that curseth thee: and in thee shall all families of the earth be blessed (Genesis 12:2-3).

In spite of the apparent impossibility of the aged Abram and his wife Sarai to naturally produce such an abundance, Abram had faith in the Lord: *"And he beleeved in the LORD; and he counted it to him for righteousnesse"* (Genesis 15:6). Righteousness was appropriated to Abram when he demonstrated his trust in God, as the Geneva Bible noted in its margin: *"Abram is justified by faith."*[14] Abram's righteousness *"justified,"* or blotted out, all of his sins before the holy sight of God and removed his transgressions from God's righteous court of justice. Faith in God's promise, or rather, faith in the God of the promise, was the sole condition for Abram being apportioned such grace. But, God was the One who had taken the initiative in making His promise: He had graciously intervened to evoke Abram's faith, and Abram was then graciously credited with righteousness in spite of his own sinfulness. Abram's righteousness was therefore an explicit gift, and God's promise to him brought with it the implicit grace by which Abram could be viewed by God as righteous and could then personally interact with His perfectly holy, heavenly Being.

Just as Abram believed the promise and God accounted it to him as *"righteousnesse,"* the reformers also saw faith as the sole condition necessary for others to become *"justified"* before God and receive a pardon for their sins. Personal faith in the biblical promises of God therefore became the centerpiece of the reformers' understanding of personal salvation. Abram's trust in God's promise had saved him, and that which brought Abram's righteousness and his pardon would likewise do so for all those who God chose for salvation. To the reformers, genuine trust had its specific object, but faith directed either toward man's merit or toward mankind's hope for future achievements were both futile. So, like Abram, there was only one way for the reformers to engage with God on gracious, cordial terms. To them, Abram's saving Covenant of Grace (by faith alone) was the same, saving Covenant of Grace (by faith alone) that brought the righteousness needed for them to personally engage with a holy God.

Abraham (Abram) had faith in the God of the promise even though he died not having seen the real, physical fulfillment of the atoning work by the actual Lamb of God (see Hebrews 11:8-13). Abraham's faith in the future Lamb of God was depicted in this endearing woodcut that was included on the general title page of the first complete English-language Bible, printed in 1535.

The association of God's covenant with unmerited grace was based upon the fact that all of His pledges to man were absolute. God's promise to Abram was just as sovereign as the one He had made previously to Noah. God's promises to Noah and Abram would be kept on His part despite man's continuing, foul, and foreboding disobedience. Simply put, the unconditional promises made by an infallible God would always trump man's fallible failures. God had thereby pledged Himself by Himself and bound Himself by His own oath, so the terms of all His covenants had more surety than the physical world itself (that He created), and His sovereign promises would define the covenantal destiny of all the world's future events.

14. Geneva Bible headline banner above Genesis 15, leaf B2.

Abram and his seed would surely become a great nation in the Promised Land and would miraculously carry the physical promise of man's redemption in their multigenerational seed. That "Seed," by a timely coming to fruition in the person of the Messiah, would then bring His sovereign kingdom upon the earth and establish His dominion forever.

This sixteenth-century Bible woodcut depicts Abraham's wife, Sarah, giving thanks to God for the miraculous gift of her son, Isaac. God had delivered on His gracious promises to Abraham and Sarah, and would then graciously bless the whole world through the covenant "Seed" of their offspring.

Abram would indeed become the earthly father of a great nation, but as the *"father of many nations,"*[15] he was to be the patriarch of the world by extension through the Messiah. The Geneva Bible noted that the covenant modeled the promise of a nation from Abram, not only to Jews in their inheritance as Abram's fleshly nation, but to those everywhere by faith in Christ: *"Not onely according to the flesh, but of a far greater multitude by faith."*[16] On this point, John Preston, one of the most renowned Puritans of the early 1600's, wrote that God's *"promise of the Messiah"*[17] signified the same Christ to Abram and Sarai as to all the faithful that would follow them, whether they were Hebrews (B.C.) or Christians (A.D.). Abram and Sarai were then covenanted as Abraham and Sarah, as their change in names would be an eternal testimony of the enduring Covenant of Grace. Just as the Covenant of Grace had been sealed to Noah in the continuing legacy of the rainbow, the same Grace Covenant was sealed to Abraham in the continuing legacy of his potent name. Thus, the change from Abram to Abraham was noted in the Geneva Bible's margin: *"The changing of his name is a seal to confirm Gods promise unto him."*[18]

The Obedience of Covenant Faith

Even so, the Covenant promise did not mean that Abraham would escape severe consequences by continuing to sin before God. God's earthly sufficiency was still tied to terms of obedience, as disobedience would retain its most deadly earthly consequences. A promise of grace did not loose the fetters of the earthly consequences of sin; included along with God's unconditional promise of grace was His strong admonition: *"I am the Almighty God; walk before me, and be thou perfect"* (Genesis 17:1).

When righteousness had been previously imputed to Abram by faith, God predicted that he and his offspring would suffer for their disobedience. The fact was foretold in the symbolism of the rite by which God cut His covenant with

---

15. See Genesis 17:3-5.
16. Geneva note on Genesis 17:4, leaf B3.
17. Preston, *The New Covenant, or the Saints Portion*, p. 366.
18. Geneva note on Genesis 17:5, leaf B3.

Abram. God commanded him to divide the ceremonial animal parts: *"And he took unto him all these, and divided them in the midst"* (Genesis 15:10). Again, later reformers interpreted this rite as God demonstrating His pledge of grace as He alone passed through the parts, yet they saw the graphic visual of the grotesque animal parts signifying human consequences for sin. The Geneva Bible's notes explained that although they would suffer greatly in God's temporal wrath, the sons of Abram would prevail: *"This was the old custom in making covenant, Jer. 34:18. to the which God added these conditions, that Abrams posterity should be as torn in pieces, but after they should be coupled together: also that it should be assaulted, but yet delivered."*[19]

Grace and obedience accompanied the same promise: grace for justification and imputed righteousness, and obedience for the enjoyment of God in His abundance. The original "obedience" stipulations of Noah's covenant were still obliging on men as demonstrated by God's judgment of Sodom for its disobedience: *"... the men of Sodom were wicked, and sinners before the Lord, exceedingly"* (Genesis 13:13). Interestingly, at the same time that God was confirming His righteous wrath against man in the judgment of Sodom and Gomorrah, He was reimplementing the Covenant of Grace to Abraham. On the very day that Abraham negotiated with God, trying to keep Him from destroying Sodom,[20] God reconfirmed that Abraham's posterity would become a mighty nation[21] and through his Seed all the nations would be blessed.[22] At the same time, God showed Abraham that both faith and obedience were required of man, just as both grace and wrath were still powerful forces at work by His hand.

The Promise of God's Covenant Lamb

It followed that Abraham's covenant was to be carried through his physical lineage, and God had miraculously given him a son as a confirmation of His promise. God told Abraham regarding his son: *"and thou shalt call his name Isaac: and I will establish my covenant with him for an everlasting covenant, and with his seed after him"* (Genesis 17:19). The legacy of grace was confirmed in God's incomprehensible command that Abraham sacrifice the life of his son. Abraham believed that God would deliver Isaac from the hands of death, since losing his son would be inconsistent with his faith in God's promise. He had faithfully told Isaac prior to his intended act: *"God will provide himself a lamb"* (Genesis 22:8). Abraham's assurance was completely consistent with his faith, and believing that God could raise his son from the dead, Abraham was willing to carry out God's command.[23] His faith was in the God of the promise who would

In this early nineteenth-century engraving used in an American Bible, Abraham was shown bowing before messengers of the Lord with Sarah attentively listening.

19. Geneva note on Genesis 15:10, leaf B2.
20. See Genesis 18:23-32.
21. See Genesis 18:17-18.
22. See Genesis 18:18.
23. See Hebrews 11:19.

33

A.

B.

A. God had providentially spared Isaac's life (from Abraham's sword) in a demonstration of His promise to provide the sacrifice of His own Son, as shown in a woodcut from William Caxton's publication of *The Golden Legend* (1483), the first history book printed in English.

B. God would provide His Son to be sacrificed (by way of His cross) as the substitutional Lamb. That Lamb rose to reign triumphantly, as He was portrayed on the title page of the first 'King James' Bible in 1611.

provide, just as He had before in the miraculous birth of Isaac. Thus, he saw by faith that the promise of a lamb would not be fulfilled by anyone but God Himself. To Abraham then, the Lamb toward whom he looked was indeed the Lamb of God.

As God had originally provided Isaac from the barren womb of Sarah, Abraham knew that God *"could have raised him from the dead; when I had killed him, as.. with .. Sarahs wombe, when that was dead."*[24] Abraham demonstrated his faith in God before Isaac was born as well as after, and upon God sparing the life of Abraham's son, God reaffirmed the promise to him. Abraham in turn reconfirmed his faith: *"And, Abraham called the name of that place Jehovah-jireh"* (Genesis 22:14), which the Geneva margin explained: *"to shew that God doth both see and provide."*[25] God would provide the sacrifice and that sacrifice would indeed be the Lamb He provided.

Abraham's faith and obedience thereby built upon one another. References to God's promise of abundant offspring were expansive in passages conveying vast visual imagery such as *"the stars of the heaven, and as the sand which is upon the sea-shore"* (Genesis 22:17). Unlike the Babylonian potentates who relied on frail deities that vanished along with their petty imaginations, God's promise was invested with an enduring inheritance over all heaven and earth, in visions of both heaven's *"stars"* and the earth's *"sand."*

24. Preston, *The New Covenant*, p. 366.
25. Geneva note on Genesis 22:14, leaf B3.

C.

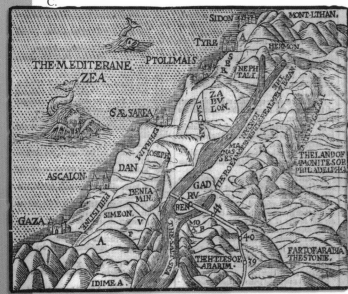

D.

C. God had promised Abraham a homeland for his (Hebrew) descendants. This unusual English map of 'The Promised Land'* shows the territory that God had covenanted to Abraham. Later, that 'Land' would yield the promised 'Lamb' who would bring Abraham's Seed to the world. *(From a 1599 Geneva Bible.)

D. God also covenanted that the entire world would be blessed through Abraham's Seed, the Lamb of God. Shown here is the first printed map of the (known) world by Gunther Zainer in 1472. Oriented with East to the top, it depicted the lands of Noah's sons: *"Sem"* (Asia), *"Cham"* (Africa), and *"Jafeth"* (Europe).

The Patriarchs

The mantle of God's promise would expand Abraham's offspring to millions of souls. Abraham's lineage was indeed blessed with the very inheritance of God's own Seed, as there was to be another gracious covenant seal. This time a sign was to be physically cut upon all of Abraham's male kindred as God's seal upon those who carried the promise: *"This is my covenant, which ye shall keep between me, and you, and thy seed after thee; Every man-childe among you shall be circumcised. ... and my covenant shall be in your flesh for an everlasting covenant"* (Genesis 17:10,13).

To Abraham's offspring, circumcision was an outward sign which showed that all those of his household partook of the promise. As the covenant was affixed to the fleshly household, all males were therefore sealed: *"He that is born in thy house, and he that is bought with thy money, must needs be circumcised"* (Genesis 17:13). The reformers taught that circumcision also provided a physical reminder intended to keep a male obedient to all his vows, for it was an ever present sign to men that they were born of such a nature that might otherwise go the typical way of human flesh: *"That privie part is circumcised, to shew that all that is begotten of man is corrupt, and must be mortified."*[26]

Abraham left a legacy of a great family, not only in its numbers, but in its continuing godly constitution:

> *... he will command his children and his houshold after him, and they shall keep the way of the LORD, to do justice and judgement ...* (Genesis 18:19).

It was therefore the responsibility of the patriarch to teach and train his children by both word and example. The Hebrews were to know that they were the repositories of God's promise and His Word. God's promise ensured that Abraham would leave a legacy in the godly governance that his offspring, the Hebrew Patriarchs, would continue.

Abraham and his offspring were to be God's harbingers of good government. Genuine government had been awakened again when Abraham was called out of Babylon to be separate from its corrupted dominions, and by the time of his death he had become the Patriarch of a considerable self-governing tribe of people. For generations his kindred would be identified as Abraham's household under the rule of one father (or patriarch), with authority

A. This eighteenth-century illustration from an Anglican prayer book depicted the covenantal rite of ancient Hebrew *"Circumcition"* (1762).

B. Shown here is the text of Genesis 17:9-12 from a 1649 'King James' Bible with its additional, Reformed Genevan marginal notes. The notes explained that the ordinance of circumcision was associated with the promise of God's covenant grace: *"Circumcision is called the covenant, because it signifieth the covenant, & hath the promise of grace joyned to it: which phrase is common to all sacraments."*

26. Geneva note on Genesis 17:11, leaf B3.

passed down through his successive sons. The *"justice and judgement"* that God foretold was thereby established in the patriarchal family. To *"keep the way of the LORD"* was therefore the responsibility for the head of the family; the man as patriarch was to represent the delegated authority that God had deposited in family leadership to legislate, administrate, and conduct the family altar. The Puritan scholar Thomas Goodwin noted that the responsibilities of the Hebrew fathers were thus in two distinct spheres of authority, *"being both Kings and Priests, in their own houses. They had power over their own Families."*[27] Each family was ruled as a self-governing whole, with its devotions led by the father, who also administered the civil power by the same Abrahamic constitution given by the God of their fathers.

The Patriarchal Character

The vulnerable, pilgrim nature of the early Hebrews required their strength and continued confidence in God's promise to Abraham. Their exposure was shown in this 1555 Bible woodcut.

Each patriarchal leader of that nomadic race lived under constant outside threats. According to Matthew Henry: *"he was among jealous and envious Neighbours, for the Canaanite and the Perizite dwelled then in the Land."*[28] Exposed to such ever-present danger, the Hebrew patriarch had a duty to protect his tribe by governing them under God's care and safety. God chose the leader for such a purpose, because an appropriate patriarchal character was one of submission to God and a reflection of His interest in the overall good.[29] Unlike the surrounding heathen tyrants, the role of the Hebrew patriarch was to first be God's servant and then His authoritative steward over those under his charge. Like his fathers, he was to administer leadership for the overall good and not merely for his own good.

Each generation was therefore to be sealed in the knowledge of their covenant, recalling their continuing duty to do all things according to their providential inheritance: *"and so Abraham begat Isaac, and circumcised him on the eighth day: and Isaac begat Jacob, and Jacob begat the twelve patriarchs"* (Acts 7:8).[30]

To the reformers, the Old Covenant provided many exemplary models for the Christian character. For example, when Isaac was anticipating the return of his father's servant with his bride, he *"went out to meditate in the field at the eventide"* (Genesis 24:63), to which the Geneva Bible noted the contemplative character of the Patriarchs: *"This was the exercise of the godly fathers to meditate Gods promises, and to pray for the accomplishment thereof."*[31] Matthew Henry thus appropriated the passage as a charge for the newly-modeled Christian patriarchs: *"Meditation and prayer ought to be both our business and our delight,*

---

27. Thomas Godwyn [Goodwin], *Moses & Aaron. Civil and Ecclesiastical Rites, Used by the Ancient Hebrewes*, 7th ed. (London, 1655), p. 1.
28. Matthew Henry, *A Church in the House. A Sermon Concerning Family-Religion* (London, 1704), p. 22.
29. See Romans 13:3-4.
30. Quoted in the Book of Acts from the testimony of the first Christian martyr, Stephen.
31. Geneva note on Genesis 24:63, leaf B6.

when we are alone; while we have a God, a Christ, and a Heaven, to acquaint ourselves with, and to secure our interest in."[32]

Upon the occasion of Isaac meeting his future bride, Rebekah had pulled a veil over her countenance (Genesis 24:65). The practice was noteworthy to later reformers, as explained in the margins of their Geneva Bible: *"The custom was that the spouse was brought to her husband, her head being covered in token of shamefastnesse* [humility][33] *and chastity."*[34] Rebekah carried herself in a demeanor which showed respect for her own inner beauty by way of the outward honor she demonstrated to both God and her patriarchal groom. Matthew Henry therefore noted that divine consciousness behind her gracious countenance: *"having seen Providence going before her in the affair, she accommodates herself with cheerfulness to her new relation."*[35]

The biblical narrative of Isaac and Rebekah demonstrated the godly lines of orderly submission within a patriarchal home. Isaac, the future husband of Rebekah and future Patriarch of his father's posterity, had directed his submissive attention toward his Lord. That inward demeanor toward God then directed him to the outward strength he owed his bride and future family. His bride likewise presented herself in submission to him as the future Patriarch's wife – the two united under God in covenant purpose. Can there be any wonder why the example of Rebekah's veil has been adopted in later, Christian matrimonial ceremonies?

Patriarchal Continuity

Isaac, whom Abraham had offered to the Lord at Jehovah-jireh, then inherited the covenant mantle from God: *"I am the God of Abraham thy father: fear not, for I am with thee, and will blesse thee, and multiply thy seed for my servant Abrahams sake"* (Genesis 26:24). Isaac consented to the appointment: *"And he builded an altar there, and called upon the name of the LORD"* (Genesis 26:25). It then became Isaac's duty to pass the legacy and the covenantal obligations of the promise on to the family that he begat. Isaac's son Jacob thus inherited God's covenant promise conferred upon him accordingly:

> *... I am the LORD God of Abraham thy father, and the God of Isaac: the land whereon thou liest, to thee will I give it, and to thy seed. And thy seed shall be as the dust of the earth; and thou shalt spread abroad to the west, and to the east, and to the north, and to the south: and in thee and in thy seed shall all the families of the earth be blessed* (Genesis 28:13-14).

A. The patriarch was to demonstrate his inward submission to God by asserting his outward honor and respect for all others. His strength was then carried in proper, manly restraint. This late fifteenth-century illustration showed the manner of a young man's chivalrous demeanor toward a lady.

B. The patriarch inherited an historic obligation to see to the education of his future generations, as was shown in this sixteenth-century woodcut.

---

32. Matthew Henry, *Exposition of the Old & New Testaments*, book 1, commentary on Genesis 24:63, p. 67.
33. *"Shamefastnesse"* is a (now) extinct Saxon word, which once meant "humility."
34. Geneva note on Genesis 24:65, leaf B6.
35. Henry, *Exposition of the ...Testaments*, bk. 1, commentary on Genesis 24:65, p. 67.

Jacob then became the father of twelve sons, who were the continuing Patriarchs of twelve united tribes of Israel. They often exhibited abhorrent behavior, particularly in selling their younger sibling Joseph into Egyptian slavery. God, though, intervened by His steadfast Providence to bring famine on the sons of Jacob who had wreaked such havoc and judgment upon Abraham's lineage. God honored His covenant pledge to Abraham, Isaac, and Jacob, and used their lineage to carry on His promise to future generations.

A. According to God's providential plan to redeem His people, Jacob's family had to travel into Egypt to join Joseph. The scene was depicted on a 1590 Dutch map's cartouche which featured God's promise in Genesis 46 (verse 3): *"I am God, the God of thy father, feare not to goe downe unto Egypt: for I will there make you a great nation."*

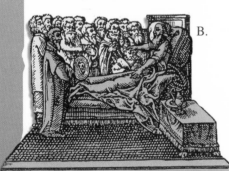

B. On his death bed, Jacob blessed the sons of Israel as twelve patriarchal tribes. That blessing providentially sealed the Hebrew identity as a great people who would eventually become a nation of God, even though at the time they were on the eve of a prolonged period of servitude. Jacob's prophecy thereby affirmed God's promise of gracious redemption, as was illustrated in this engraving included in the *Genealogies* by John Speed in 1611.

It was due to Joseph's stalwart obedience and God's intervening graciousness that his eleven brothers were drawn back to unified submission. God providentially used the course of Joseph's life, first by way of his sonship as one of the Patriarchs, then by his Egyptian slavery, and finally by his rise to a seat of great civil authority in a corrupt foreign nation. God honored Joseph's consistent obedience by bringing his kindred back from oppressive famine into covenantal continuity. *"Notwithstanding the corruptions of Egypt, yet Joseph taught his family to fear God."*[36] Despite his brothers' prior evil and his own subsequent rise to ascendancy, Joseph's faithful devotion to his family drove him to have boundless compassion for them. His prior obedience to God had simply prepared him for the moment and allowed him to stand in the gap for Israel's future generations. Out of godly compassion, Joseph poured out his devotion for his father's continuing legacy in reassuring his brothers: *"I will nourish you, and your little ones"* (Genesis 50:21).

God had a purpose in His providence, and it was His own covenantal faithfulness which bore Joseph's kindly fruits. The true and sovereign God among a world of petty lords once again delivered on His pledge of grace to the sons of Israel.

The twelve sons of Jacob as Israel's tribal Patriarchs were thereafter honored as the forefathers through whom the faithful God demonstrated His promise, placing within them the theme of covenantal fidelity as a multigenerational charge. Following the Bible's great Genesis narrative, the remaining books of the Pentateuch (five Books of Moses) presented the reconfirmation of God's continued grace in the ongoing bonds between God and His chosen people. He would establish them in a further covenant relation in which their faithfulness and obedience would yield His ongoing blessing and protection.

36. Geneva note on Genesis 43:23, leaf C6.

Book I Christianity's Covenantal Inheritance
Chapter 5: The Covenant Law of God
The Covenant Laws of Israel as Moral Mandates for Mankind

THE great Exodus saga of Israel is another great monument to the theme of Christianity's covenantal inheritance. God would redeem His people and establish them as a covenant nation. Later, Christians would see the events and terms of Israel's Exodus saga providing both the model of sovereign redemption and the covenantal standard by which to govern their lives. Reformers were particularly drawn to references of Israel's covenantal character, as noted by Richard Baxter: *"No man was to live a member of the commonwealth of Israel that entered not into the covenant of God."*[1]

God commenced Israel's Exodus from Egypt through an amazing series of events, the likes of which had never been recorded before or since. God was demonstrating a powerful testimony to the nature of His redemptive work and the covenantal life that necessarily followed. God would initiate and drive the events by raising a Hebrew man for that purpose. Jonas Clark, a patriot minister from Lexington, Massachusetts, cited the *"high station"* of Moses as *"the head of the commonwealth of Israel."*[2] In comparing America's own revolutionary circumstance with the moral obligation that God imparted to the people of Israel, Clark cited the Law of God as *"the constitution GOD had given them."*[3] He saw Moses' character as that suited for America's own rulers, and saw that the former Israelite *"constitution"* had been the moral example for the new Commonwealth of Massachusetts. Clark could then quote Moses with assurance to those in his own audience who were newly elected to rule over a similar commonwealth:

> *Set your hearts unto all the words which I testify among you this day: For it is not a vain thing for you; because it is your life: And through this thing ye shall prolong your days in the land.*[4]

Moses' life had indeed set the example for many noble rulers who followed in his stead – those who later ruled in accord with God's great Laws, which were providentially extended to them as His great governing statutes for men. Moses' life was consequently central to many later world-changing events. And, even from his youth, Moses' life would be one of God's great historic providences. Clark and many other Puritans before him saw that God had designed history for that very purpose. All men were to look back on the powerful events of Moses' life to better appreciate God's providence in their own. Moses was thus the central figure amid a very extraordinary set of circumstances surrounding Israel's departure from Egypt and its birth as a covenanted nation.

1. Richard Baxter, *A Holy Commonwealth, or Political Aphorisms, Opening The True Principles of Government* (London, 1659), p. 249.
2. Jonas Clark, *Sermon Preached before John Hancock, ...* (Boston, 1781), pp. 36-37, citing Deuteronomy 32:45-47.
3. Ibid.
4. Ibid.

Egyptian Bondage

The sons of Abraham had settled in Egypt by way of Jacob (whom God had renamed Israel) and his twelve sons when they had sought relief from famine. Following Israel's death, his sons (then identified as the tribes of Israel) were afraid that they would lose the civil favor of their brother Joseph. Up until that time, Joseph had cared for them due to their common lineage and his own love and devotion toward his father. Upon Israel's death, his sons found themselves prostrated before their brother in repentance for what they had done to Joseph in his youth. Willing to be his slaves themselves rather than to become destitute, they knew that their continuing maintenance would depend upon his graces: *"And his brethren also went and fell down before his face; and they said, Behold, we be thy servants"* (Genesis 50:18).

Joseph, though, did not see himself as their master nor as their father figure. Therefore, as a faithful brother, he directed them to the One who had provided for him during his troubles at their hands. Joseph, as a mere civil officer, pointed to the fact that he was not their ultimate judge and that the God who had mercifully saved him, would in turn also save them:

> *And Joseph said unto them, Fear not: for am I in the place of God? But as for you, ye thought evil against me, but God meant it unto good, to bring to passe, as it is this day, to save much people alive. Now therefore fear ye not: I will nourish you, and your little ones. And he comforted them, and spake kindely unto them* (Genesis 50:19-21).

After first pointing his brothers toward God, Joseph then offered his hand of assistance. While Joseph expressed God's genuine concern toward the *"little ones"* of Israel, their road would still not be an easy one. With the passing of Joseph, the Israelite tribes gradually lost their prestige and internal independence in Egypt. But, even in bondage, they were able to maintain their tribal allegiances. They would subsist as slaves, but due to God's undergirding provision they would not be vanquished as individual wards of Egypt. The sons of Israel would remain the sons of Abraham's promise, and God would preserve their tribal identities. Just prior to his passing and centuries of pending servitude for Israel, Joseph prophetically renewed his brethren in their forefathers' promise of covenantal continuity: *"I die: and God will surely visit you, and bring you out of this land, unto the land which he sware to Abraham, to Isaac, and to Jacob"* (Genesis 50:24). Due to the tribes' continuing Patriarchal identity they maintained their cultural integrity, despite the loss of their original liberty. Their unity and common purpose were preserved in spite of their slavish and exhaustive toil.

The twelve tribes of Israel were named and providentially sealed by Joseph at the time that they were about to enter a prolonged period of servitude in Egypt. They were thereby preserved by God as twelve familial units within one overall body of Hebrew people throughout their ordeal. The twelve tribes were depicted with allegorical family crests on many of the early 'King James' Bible title pages, as with this engraving from 1621.

As a twist of irony, it turned out that the brothers who had originally sold Joseph into slavery also ended up slaves through their descendants. Each tribe became identified by its servitude to Egypt under the increasingly brutal regimes of the Pharaohs, and the Israelites found themselves in an ever-tightening grip of successive tyrants.[5] But, God sovereignly had them in preparation; for despite losing the former lordship of their earthly fathers, they grew in their understanding of God's Lordship. Under Him they increased in power and numbers as the Israelites *"waxed exceeding mighty, and the land was filled with them"* (Exodus 1:7). God was preparing a people and a nation for Himself, growing a population that would again demonstrate His gracious redemption, and cultivating the seeds of a promised nation. In the bowels of Egyptian toil they grew strong until the tyrannical taskmasters were eventually threatened by their numbers and implemented a social policy to eliminate their lineage.[6] By ordering the Hebrew midwives to destroy their own innocent kindred, Pharaoh simply pitted his will against the promise, proving himself to be just another obstinate and petty prince. All the forces of Egypt could not stand for long against the arm of the Almighty, and the Hebrew midwives thus disobeyed the order to destroy the Hebrew male infants in order to preserve their posterity: *"But the midwives feared God, and did not as the king of Egypt commanded them, but saved the men-children alive"* (Exodus 1:17). Pharaoh called them to answer for their disobedience, to which the Geneva Bible noted: *"Their disobedience herein was lawfull; but their dissembling* [deceptive concealment] *evil."*[7] They could rightly answer Pharaoh that God's promise to their people was higher than his arbitrary commands, although the Hebrews still remained obliged to honor God in their subservient demeanor to Pharaoh.

Nevertheless, by continuing in high rebellion toward God, Pharaoh (as if he had a divine right to command life and death) compounded his cruel offense by further targeting the Hebrew families. In contrast, due to the midwives' respect for God's promise and His Laws in their homes, God blessed the institution of their families: *"And it came to passe, because the midwives feared God, that he made them houses"* (Exodus 1:21). In spite of Pharaoh's attack on the Hebrew sons, God increased His blessing on their families. God incubated the covenant in the Hebrew homes, and the reformers interpreted that as God's providential means to grow a great people: *"That is, God increased the families of the Israelites by their means."*[8]

A. The Hebrew women prospered their people by honoring God and watching over the sons of Israel.

B. Though they disobeyed Pharaoh's tyrannical command to kill their offspring, God increased their numbers, as was told in the Geneva marginal notes to Exodus 1:19-22 (1649 edition).

A.

B.

Hannah Zes, 2002

g Their disobedience herein was lawfull, but their dissembling evil.

h That is God increased the families of the Israelites by their means.
i When tyrants cannot prevail by craft, they brast forth into open rage.

. 19 And the midwives said unto Pharaoh, Because the g Hebrew women *are* not as the Egyptian women : for they *are* lively, and are delivered ere the midwives come in unto them.

20 Therefore God dealt well with the midwives : and the people multiplied, and waxed very mighty.

21 And it came to passe, because the midwives feared God, that he h made them houses.

22 And Pharaoh charged all his people, saying, Every son that is born ye shall i cast into the river, and every daughter ye shall save alive.

5. See Exodus 1:8-14.
6. See Exodus 1:16.
7. Geneva note on Exodus 1:19, leaf D1.
8. Geneva note on Exodus 1:21, leaf D1.

41

Seeing that the outraged Pharaoh simply continued to increase the Hebrews' strife by further demanding that every male Hebrew infant be cast into the Nile,[9] the reformers noted another timeless principle: *"When tyrants cannot prevail by craft, they brast forth into open rage."*[10] God then set in motion His sovereign work of redemption. Despite Pharaoh's continued family limitation policy, God prospered His plans over the scheme of Pharaoh.

Hannah Zes, 2002

A.

B.

2 And the woman conceived, and bare a son: and when she saw him that he was a goodly childe, she hid him three moneths.

3 And when she could not longer hide him, she took for him an ark of bulrushes, and daubed it with slime and with pitch, and put the childe therein; and she laid it in the flags by the rivers brink.

4 And his sister stood afar off, to wit what would be done to him.

5 ¶ And the daughter of Pharaoh came down to wash her self at the river, and her maidens walked along by the rivers side: and when she saw the ark among the flags, she sent her maid to fetch it.

A. The infant Moses was depicted in this drawing as he was providentially saved from the tyrannical death edict of Pharaoh.

B. The scene was recorded here in Exodus 2:2-5 of a 1649 'King James' edition with a Genevan comment that also noted: *"the rage of the tyrant."*

The Call to an Exodus

God chose an infant born of two Levite parents (tribal descendants of Jacob) to execute His designs for Israel. The infant Moses was, by way of an incredible providence, placed in prominence[11] and called by God to facilitate Israel's deliverance.[12] Moses, though, would not stand as a father figure as had Abraham, Isaac, and Jacob. The sons of Israel would no longer be identified as much under a human father as they would be under God Himself. They would be pledged as twelve tribes directly under their Lord with their rulers representing His administrative assistants, and His Laws being the laws of their land. God chose Moses to model the role, and he would be a figurehead and a mediator, although God Himself would be the true Father of the nation. The Israelites would be covenanted as a civil and an ecclesiastical nation, and as a confederation[13] of tribes they would become a commonwealth.[14]

Moses would simply be Israel's first representative administrator as well as the first public servant to the people of God. Just as God had used Joseph's obedience and compassionate heart to administer good will to his brethren,[15] Moses would not be lord over the Israelites, but would remain one among them, by them, and for them. The people of Israel would thereafter be identified as a family of tribes – the sons of a common forefather named Israel – constituted as a nation of twelve in one commonwealth under God.

9. See Exodus 1:22.
10. Geneva note on Exodus 1:22, leaf D1.
11. See Exodus 2:1-10.
12. See Exodus 3:9-10.
13. "Confederation": from the Latin *confoederatus*, meaning a league as in a covenanted association. See Noah Webster, *American Dictionary of the English Language*, vol. 1 (1828), for "confederation."
14. "Commonwealth": from the Latin *communis*, meaning common as in common together, and from the Saxon *weal*, meaning strength; together meaning *common strength*. See Webster, *Dictionary of the English Language*, vol. 1 for "commonwealth," "commonweal," and "common"; vol. 2 for "wealth" and "weal."
15. See Genesis 47:11-12.

The entire Exodus saga thus represented much more than the struggle by Israel to escape the tyranny of Egypt. It represented a uniquely miraculous deliverance by the Lord, and the establishment of a union directly under a total Sovereign. Though constituted as independent of any other nation, the Hebrews would remain directly dependent upon the God of their covenant. The Genevan introduction to Exodus therefore pointed to the ongoing saga of their departure:

> ... he still governed them, and gave them his word and law, both concerning the manner of serving him, and also the form of judgements and civil policy: to the intent that they should not serve God after their own inventions, but according to that order, which his heavenly wisdom had appointed.[16]

Though the actual events of Israel's departure from Egypt were initiated and orchestrated directly by God, He chose Moses to carry the representative mantle of His power and majesty, of His mediation, and of His deliverance. Early in the Book of Exodus, God called Moses at Mount Horeb to such a purpose: *"and I will send thee unto Pharaoh, that thou mayest bring forth my people the children of Israel out of Egypt"* (Exodus 3:10). God thus identified the Hebrews as *"my people,"* but Moses, knowing of his low status before Pharaoh, questioned such a high calling upon himself: *"Who am I, that I should go unto Pharaoh ..."* (Exodus 3:11). In reply, God graciously told Moses of the purpose for which He had delegated authority to him: *"Certainly I will be with thee; and this shall be a token unto thee, that I have sent thee: When thou hast brought forth the people out of Egypt, ye shall serve God upon this mountain"* (Exodus 3:12).

But, also knowing his lack of sufficient status to speak for the God of their fathers, Moses needed nothing less than a divine proof of his sanction. To the Hebrew elders, he would certainly appear to be challenging the time-honored order of their tribes. Moses needed more than his own words. He needed to prove an immediate sanction from the Almighty, so Moses questioned the Lord a second time:

> And Moses said unto God, Behold, when I come unto the children of Israel, and shall say unto them, The God of your fathers hath sent me unto you; and they shall say to me, What is his name? (Exodus 3:13).

At that point, God declared His magnificent transcendence which Moses was to declare to the elders and the people. Moses was to reveal the ever-present nature of God's Being as not only above the elders of Israel, but also above Pharaoh, Abraham, Noah, Adam, and Creation itself. God revealed Himself in a way that was more timelessly eternal, yet more profoundly immediate, than ever before: *"And God said unto*

In a dramatic gesture of gracious intervention, God initiated the redemption of the tribes of Israel. God specifically revealed Himself to Moses in a flaming bush, calling and sanctioning him to become His spokesman to the sons of Israel as well as to the power structure of Egypt. As God's servant, Moses was himself led to lead others out from bondage. The initial moment of God's powerful intervention was depicted in this mid-sixteenth-century Bible woodcut.

16. See Geneva commentary: *"The Argument"* for *The Second book of Moses, called Exodus*, leaf C8.

Moses, I AM THAT I AM: And he said, Thus shalt thou say unto the children of Israel, I AM hath sent me ..." (Exodus 3:14). God manifested Himself as ever present and ever eternal, the God of the present as well as of every generation. Thus, the eternal God, henceforth to be known as *"I AM THAT I AM,"* reconfirmed the promise to Moses with renewed freshness and fervor:

And I appeared unto Abraham, unto Isaac, and unto Jacob, by the name of God Almighty, but by my name JEHOVAH was I not known to them. And I have also established my covenant with them, to give them the land of Canaan, the land of their pilgrimage, wherein they were strangers (Exodus 6:3-4).

God then further clarified the former promise to include a pledge to act in the generation of Moses:

Wherefore say unto the children of Israel, I am the LORD, and I will bring you out from under the burdens of the Egyptians, and I will rid you out of their bondage: and I will redeem you with a stretched out arm, and with great judgements (Exodus 6:6).

Moses declared the transcendent God, *"I AM,"* to the families of Israel. Before that time, God's existence had been identified with His relation to their circumstance. For example, He had been known as the great Leader of their fathers: *"the mighty God of Jacob"* (Genesis 49:24). He had also revealed Himself as the source of their promises: *"the God of thy father who shall help thee, and by the Almighty who shall blesse thee with blessings of heaven alone"* (Genesis 49:25). But, God revealed Himself to Moses in His immediate, self-existent Being, and Moses was shown in this sixteenth-century biblical woodcut pointing upward to God's immediate transcendence over the people of Israel.

The Passover

God powerfully demonstrated His Name as well as His sovereignty over the household of Pharaoh. In a devastating series of public plagues administered through the hands of two Hebrew men, Moses and Aaron, God let His true transcendence be manifested to His obstinate foes: *"And the Egyptians shall know, that I am the LORD, when I stretch forth mine hand upon Egypt"* (Exodus 7:5). God used Moses to mediate, or come between, Himself and Pharaoh on behalf of the Israelites. Moses delivered God's message, and then Moses and Aaron raised His standard to signify the beginning or ending of the various plagues. In the first nine plagues God demonstrated His dominion over Egypt's natural circumstances, but in His final plague against the callous Pharaoh, He demonstrated His power over Egypt's own inheritance: *"And all the first-born in the land of Egypt shall die"* (Exodus 11:5). Due to Pharaoh's obstinate demeanor, he had sacrificed the blessing of his firstborn, which, incidentally, had been the very blessing secured to Abraham by faith. In submitting to God, Abraham had retained his son and fruitful inheritance; in not submitting to God, Pharaoh had lost his firstborn as well as his dominion over the sons of Abraham.[17]

17. Comparing Exodus 11:5 with Genesis 22:12.

The Lord thereby prosecuted the final plague as a sign of His sovereign protection over His covenant families. To the Israelite families, the final plague both symbolized and enacted their very deliverance from bondage. God had given them specific instructions so that none of the Hebrew firstborn were taken in His judgment upon Egypt. Due to their obedience to His instructions, their Passover ceremony also effected their families' redemption in actuality. Accordingly, God's angel of death had bypassed the homes that had the seal of the sacrificial lamb upon their door posts.[18] God had once again demonstrated the faithfulness of His covenant promise to Abraham, Isaac, and Jacob:

LO, the destroying angel flies
To Pharaoh's stubborn land!
The pride and flow'r of Egypt dies
By his vindictive hand.

He pass'd the tents of Jacob o'er,
Nor pour'd the wrath divine;
He saw the blood on ev'ry door,
And bless'd the peaceful sign.[19]

A.

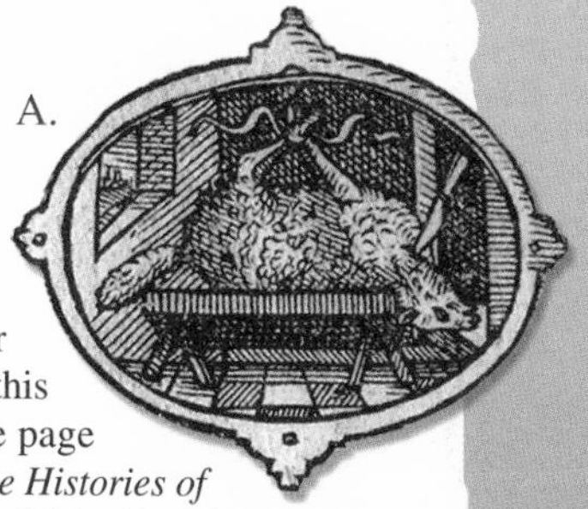

A. God provided His own Son to be slain for the elect, as shown in this woodcut from the title page of *A Continuation of the Histories of the Forreine Martyrs*, published in 1641.

That momentous Passover represented Israel's new beginning. It was therefore to be remembered in each Hebrew home in an annual celebration, as God commanded Israel: *"thorowout your generations"* (Exodus 12:14). They were commanded to repeat the sacrifice of a lamb, *"without blemish"* (Exodus 12:5). As an everlasting *"memoriall"* (Exodus 12:14), the Passover was thus the second Hebrew covenantal sacrament given by God after the first rite of circumcision that He had given through Abraham. Circumcision remained as their symbolic seal of covenantal distinction and the Passover became the memorial to their covenantal redemption.

The new Passover ordinance was to be followed by seven days of eating *"unleavened bread"* (Exodus 12:17).[20] Thomas Goodwin, a Reformed antiquarian of the mid-seventeenth century, explained the Passover ordinance as it was practiced by the Hebrews in association with unleavened bread:

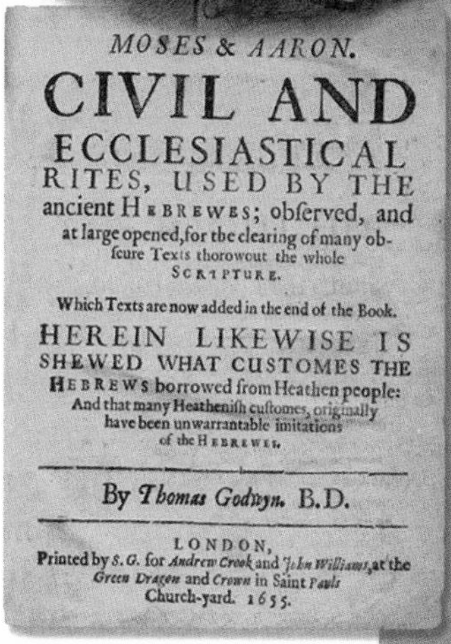

The Rites and Ceremonies observed by the Jewes in the eating of this Sacrament their Paschall Lambe, agreed with those generall ceremonies used in their solemne Feasts. They blessed the cup, and blessed the bread, and divided amongst their guests, and washed the feet of those that sat at the table, ...[21]

B.

C.

MOSES & AARON.
CIVIL AND
ECCLESIASTICAL
RITES, USED BY THE
ancient HEBREWES; obſerved, and
at large opened, for the clearing of many ob-
ſcure Texts thorowout the whole
SCRIPTURE.

Which Texts are now added in the end of the Book.

HEREIN LIKEWISE IS
SHEWED WHAT CUSTOMES THE
HEBREWS borrowed from Heathen people:
And that many Heatheniſh cuſtomes, originally
have been unwarrantable imitations
of the HEBREWES.

By Thomas Godwyn. B.D.

LONDON,
Printed by S. G. for Andrew Crook and John Williams, at the
Green Dragon and Crown in Saint Pauls
Church-yard. 1655.

B. This is a sketch of the Puritan historian Thomas Goodwin (1600-1680).

C. Shown here is the title page of his scholarly work on Hebrew customs: *Moses & Aaron* (1655).

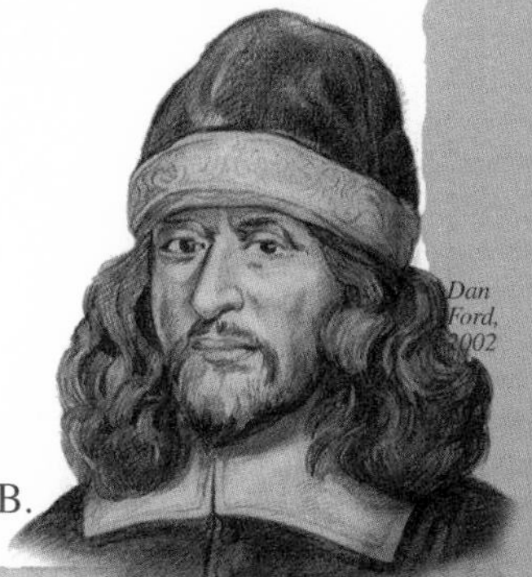

18. See Exodus 12:3-11.

19. Isaac Watts, *The Psalms of David*, Hymn 155, stanzas 1-2, p. 202.

20. See also Exodus 12:39.

21. Goodwin, *Moses & Aaron*, book 3, p. 105, also citing Maimon, *de sermento & Azymo*, c.6. Sec. 1.

The Passover was thereby used in "catechizing" (instructing) the Israelites of the means of their redemption. Every family was to be informed: *"... the whole body of the Israelites was divided into twelve tribes, the tribes into families, the families into houses; if the house were too few for the eating of the Lambe, then the next neighbour joyned with them in the eating thereof."*[22]

According to Goodwin, intimate groups of about a dozen men as communicant students of a rabbi (instructor) would also gather to celebrate together as a *"company of guests, so many as can sit at the same table."*[23] Thus, like the Hebrew families, these groups of celebrants also represented a small "society" as *"The number of communicants in this Paschall society was never less then ten, nor more then twenty."*[24]

A.

B.

Of their Paſſeover.

This kind of *Catechiſing* they ſay is commanded, *Exod.* 12. 26. They called it הגדה *Haggada*, (i, *Annunciatio*, the *declaration* or *ſhewing forth* of the *Paſſeover.* Hence the *Apoſtle* borroweth his phraſe; As often as ye ſhal eat this bread, and drink this cup, ye ſhall *declare* or *ſhew forth* the *Lords* death, 1 *Corinth.* 11.26.

A. Depicted in this sixteenth-century woodcut by Holbein is a teacher instructing his communicant disciple (1534).

B. This is an excerpt of Thomas Goodwin's description of the Passover celebration in which he noted the wording of the ancient Hebrew practice as adopted by the Apostles: *"They called it Haggada, Annunciatio, the declaration or shewing forth of the Passover. Hence the Apostle borroweth his phrase; As often as ye shal eat this bread, and drink this cup, ye shall declare or shew forth the Lords death, I Corinth. 11.26"* (*Moses & Aaron*, 1655).

Goodwin described this aspect of the Passover celebration as looking forward to a man of *"peerless vertue of our Saviour, whom it did typically shadow forth."*[25] The Hebrew Passover therefore recalled the Israelite (household) covenantal redemption in their past as well as looked forward to the covenantal redemption of the future household of faith with the coming of the Messiah.

Both the covenant rites of Circumcision and Passover were commanded to those of the wider household of Israel. When, for instance, a stranger came in to live among them, he would be required to undergo the first sacramental rite of circumcision before partaking in the second sacrament of the Passover: *"And when a stranger shall sojourn with thee, and will keep the Passover to the LORD, let all his males be circumcised, and then let him come neer and keep it: and he shall be as one that is born in the land"* (Exodus 12:48).

The two sacraments worked together to permanently seal and then repeatedly remember the Israelite covenant. Both looked back to the covenantal origins of Israel as well as pointed forward to the covenantal nature of the Kingdom of God yet to come. In every new generation, circumcision and Passover were to serve as testaments and memorials of their forefathers' deliverance and toward the deliverance of their future offspring. Each father passed the sacraments on to the next generation with an explanation of its meaning: *"... thou shalt shew thy son in that day, saying, This is done because of that which the LORD did unto me, when I came forth out of Egypt"* (Exodus 13:8). All sons of Israel were to know the terms of their fathers' covenant – to know the rites and the meanings behind them in looking ahead to their future.

22. Goodwin, *Moses & Aaron*, book 3, p. 106.
23. Ibid.
24. Ibid.
25. Ibid.

The Flight From Egypt

Following the last awful plague, the Israelites were ordered by Pharaoh to depart from Egypt. Led by Moses, they fled eastward into the desert. God not only delivered them by way of their Passover escape, but by the deluge of their pursuant enemies. Due to Pharaoh's prompt change of heart, the *"host of Pharaoh"* were fast upon the Israelite's heels (Exodus 14:28). The destruction of his great army was swift and final, as once the Israelites had safely set foot across the Red Sea, Pharaoh's chariots were overwhelmed by the collapse of the separated walls of water.

Once confirmed by such a miraculous deliverance in newly-founded liberty and independence, the sons of Israel sang of God's gracious redemption. In a magnificent confirmation of Israel's covenantal self-identity, Moses led the people in praise to their God as Savior and Lord:

A.

> *I will sing unto the LORD, for he hath triumphed gloriously; the horse and his rider hath he thrown into the sea. The LORD is my strength and song, and he is become my salvation; he is my God, and I will prepare him an habitation; my fathers God, and I will exalt him* (Exodus 15:1-2).

A. The Hebrews' approach to the Red Sea was depicted in this cut on the title page of the Geneva Bible's first edition (1560).

During Israel's approach to the Red Sea, God had placed a cloud of smoke and a pillar of fire in front of them as visible signs of His provision. Then, as the armies of their former captors approached, God moved to their rear as a visible sign of His protection.[26] They could have, and seemingly should have, rested assured that such a magnificent providence would be an unquestionable confirmation of God's continued care. The smoke and fire were certainly signs that, to God, the Israelites were unique among the peoples of the world. Yet, despite all that God had done for the sons of Israel, they began to complain of their plight to Moses. They looked to the figurehead Moses with lament instead of looking to God in faith. Their humanistic tendencies caused them to focus on themselves and their wilderness condition instead of their triumphant position, and on their problems instead of God's promise.

One of the first manifestations of their humanistic complaints was displayed at Marah where the people *"murmured against Moses"* (Exodus 15:24) because of the detestable drinking water. Moses demonstrated his role of intercessor again, pleading to the Lord on their behalf. They had turned to a man, but he had turned to their Lord. God delivered on Moses' petition by providing Israel's refreshment,[27] but in so doing,

B.

B. In His gracious providence, God used faithful Moses to intercede on behalf of His people. God provided fresh water for the sons of Israel at Marah, as illustrated in this Bible woodcut (1555).

26. Comparing Exodus 13:21 and 14:20.
27. See Exodus 15:25.

He began to reveal His intention to bind them directly to Himself and make them a covenant nation unlike any other. God had no intention of allowing them to drift into unchecked humanism, and through the interceding words of Moses, the Lord spoke of redirecting their focus back upon Himself:

> *... If thou wilt diligently hearken to the voice of the LORD thy God, and wilt do that which is right in his sight, and wilt give eare to his commandments, and keep all his statutes, I will put none of these diseases upon thee, which I have brought upon the Egyptians...* (Exodus 15:26).

But still, regardless of God, the people again blamed Moses for their plight: *"... for ye have brought us forth into this wildernesse, to kill this whole assembly with hunger"* (Exodus 16:3). The fight for their hearts was on. Moses petitioned yet again, and God provided a miraculous sign by furnishing them with a harvest of quail in the further demonstration of Moses' mediation.[28] God next provided them with manna, which settled daily around their camp to be gathered directly, family by family and day by day – an ongoing demonstration of His immediate presence and providence.[29] Moses' repeated intercession and God's repeated provision were intended to reinforce the knowledge of the people's direct position under God. Because their hearts were not given to God, they continued on in their complaints.[30] The Israelites also piled the growing complaints and disputes among each other upon Moses,[31] seeing him as their intercessor among one another. He complained of that burden to his father-in-law, Jethro: *"... the people come unto me to enquire of God"* (Exodus 18:15).

This map depicts God's redemption of the *"Children of Israel"* in their Exodus from Egypt. Oriented with East to the top, it portrays their journey from the city of Ramses (*"Exod. XII.v.34"* at the bottom) up to and through the Red Sea. It shows the destruction of Pharaoh's pursuing chariots in the tumult of the sea and the people's praise of God on the other side (*"Exod. XV."*). It then shows Israel's procession upward through the wilderness to the thundering manifestation of their covenant God at Mount Sinai (*"Exod. XIX."*). This folding map was included in an early federal period American Bible (1816).

Moses could not bear the crown that the people had placed upon him, and through Jethro, Moses saw that if the people were to live in liberty, they would be required to become knowledgeable and responsible themselves before God: *"teach them ordinances and laws, and shalt shew them the way wherein they must walk, and the work that they must do"* (Exodus 18:20). Moses was thus directed to delegate authority to qualified judges by selecting *"able men, such as fear God, men of truth, hating covetonsnesse"* (Exodus 18:21). The Reformed theologian Richard Baxter saw those qualities as the key to all good governance in any commonwealth of free people: *"Officers should be such as God will own; that is, men fearing God and working righteousness; men sober, righteous and godly, that by Faith and Love are subjected themselves to God their Creator and Redeemer."*[32]

28. See Exodus 16:8, 12-13.
29. See Exodus 16:14-16.
30. See Exodus 17:3.
31. See Exodus 18:13.
32. Baxter, *A Holy Commonwealth*, p. 213.

Baxter also warned that such a fear of God was central to any representative officer, for to judge rightly he must understand where he stood in relation to both God and the people. On the contrary, those who might attempt to rule without such a check on themselves were woefully insufficient to carry their charge from God: *"If the inferior Magistrates be Infidels, or ungodly men, they are false to their highest King: and how can they be fit to Govern for him, and promote his interest?"*[33]

Israel was to be ruled by many levels of men in authority: *"rulers of thousands, and rulers of hundreds, rulers of fifties, and rulers of tens"* (Exodus 18:21). With authority delegated as close to the people as possible, the people were apt to retain their own sense of immediate responsibility in their governance. On the other hand, to place all authority in one man would lack the heart of representative responsibility, and the people would soon lose sight of their own duties in the commonwealth. With authority delegated in a well-constituted order at various levels, Israel was aptly constituted as a self-governing nation:

> *And Moses chose able men out of all Israel, and made them heads over the people, rulers of thousands, rulers of hundreds, rulers of fifties, and rulers of tens. And they judged the people at all seasons: the hard causes they brought unto Moses, but every small matter they judged themselves* (Exodus 18:25-26).

A HOLY
Commonwealth,
OR
Political Aphorisms,
Opening
The true Principles of Government

This is the title page of Richard Baxter's *A Holy Commonwealth*, in which he deciphered the biblical precepts of Hebrew civil governance and applied them as the standards of all godly nations (1659).

Being God's people, Israel was required to register its consent and enter vassalage according to an oath dictated by its Sovereign:

> *And Moses came and called for the elders of the people, and laid before their faces all these words which the LORD commanded him. And all the people answered together, and said, All that the LORD hath spoken, we will do. And Moses returned the words of the people unto the LORD* (Exodus 19:7-8).

Upon taking their oath, Israel became a covenanted nation. With their multitiered judges, Israel embarked upon nationhood without a man as an absolute potentate. As a distinguished nation, Israel would be ruled according to specific terms that defined them as God's nation, united as families and vassal tribes, to their Redeemer. *"Now therefore, if ye will obey my voice indeed, and keep my covenant, then ye shall be a peculiar treasure unto me above all people: for all the earth is mine"* (Exodus 19:5).

Israel's status as a new nation required both the people and the rulers alike to bow before His throne and together worship their Sovereign. And in Israel's case, its Sovereign was also the exalted Lord of heaven, giving them a distinctive charge on earth. Israel became a nation established upon a covenant that involved God's direct Lordship over them, and they became an example of His extended Lordship over the world.

---

33. Ibid.

The Commandments

As God's vassal nation, Israel was to be devoted to Him and obedient to all His subsequent commands. But, unlike the other nations, its obligations emanated from His eternal Will, giving them an enduring temper and a timeless standard of blessings or cursings far beyond all others. And, unlike the codes of the other nations surrounding them, God's Commandments were the codification of the One who looked out for their welfare rather than the rules of a taskmaster who lived lavishly upon the sweat and toil of his subjects. God was the source of all their resources, and His covenant nation could partake of His prosperity. He was to them a Provider rather than a potentate that put a drain on their resources and labor to gain the unjust fruits of spoil. He was already in possession of all the material goods as well as all moral good: *"... for all the earth is mine"* (Exodus 19:5). It was upon this principle that God established His model for Moses' administration.

That unique relation made Israel radically distinct among all the nations of the world. God had called the sons of Israel out from Egypt for a purpose unlike any other, and such a purpose required the institution of God's transcendent Laws. Other potentates of the time relied upon the forceful administration of their own wills. As their codes and their modes were built upon the "grand" tradition of Nimrod,[34] the monarch's voice had the force of law, and his will embodied the constitution of the nation under him. He might codify laws and delegate authority, but the laws and their administration were simply a reflection of his human will. However, in Israel, Moses would not rule according to any humanistic precedent, nor would the people make their own ordinances.[35] In the beginning, Israel was neither a monarchy nor a democracy. Neither its rulers nor its people were to become arbitrary in their judgments, nor were they to be licentious in their understanding of Israelite society. God had vested self-governance with His people; Israel's elders were united under one supreme Lord who dictated His sovereign Will both to the people and rulers alike. Richard Baxter described the principle behind such a noble constitution as a simple matter of covenantal fidelity:

> *Laws are the subjects' Rule of Duty,*
> *and the Judges' Rule of Judgement:*
> *therefore most certainly if God have Laws,*
> *he will have judgement according to his Laws.*[36]

Redeemed by God, the sons of Abraham were given new life under Him. As the fruitful tribes of Israel which came out from human bondage, together they forged the pillar of a united commonwealth which rested squarely upon the foundation of God's continued, gracious, covenantal relation with man. Graphically portrayed with Adam and Eve at the bottom and with Moses and the tables of the Law at the top, that 'fruitful' column was depicted in this woodcut on the title page of a folio English Bible printed in 1632.

34. See Genesis 10:8-12.
35. See Acts 7:37-38.
36. Baxter, *A Holy Commonwealth*, p. 15.

It was God Himself who had redeemed His people from bondage, and they were to become His bonded servants in accordance with such Laws as He commanded. Therefore, as the sons of Israel approached Mount Sinai and *"camped before the mount"* (Exodus 19:2), the Lord reconfirmed their status: *"Ye have seen what I did unto the Egyptians, and how I bare you on eagles wings, and brought you unto my self"* (Exodus 19:4).

They were to engage with God as their Lord and keep themselves set apart from the world through devoted obedience to Him. God graciously presented them with a national Law by which to govern themselves, as the Puritan John Ward later observed:

> *They had engaged themselves by solemn Covenant to Reformation, to depart from the customs of Egypt, and to keep themselves unspotted from the manners of the Nations, to receive a forme of worship from God, a Law of Ordinances, and to keepe his Commandements and be obedient.*[37]

Moses received Israel's Covenant Law directly from its true Sovereign, as shown in this woodcut from the title page of the first complete English Bible, printed in 1535.

Neither Moses nor the magistrates were such potentates as to demand the property of their subjects. They stood in the shadow of Israel's true Provider and were called by Him to govern for the common good. Israel's governors were not constituted to be a drain upon the people; they were to facilitate God's Laws so they could enjoy the fruition of their Sovereign's sufficiency for them. God could and would supply; the civil government was not to look to the people nor would the people look to the government. Israel's governors were designated to serve their Lord and His people, to facilitate the common good, and to simply direct them in His statutes toward a "common-weal," or commonwealth.[38]

The Preamble of the Law

Israel was hereby prepared for its Lord's Commands. God's covenant Law, the Ten Commandments, which He then gave them at Sinai, began with a preamble as a brief, memorial statement of their stature under Him:

> *And God spake all these words, saying, I am the LORD thy God, which have brought thee out of the land of Egypt, out of the house of bondage* (Exodus 20:1-2).

Moses and the judges were subject to the terms of that preamble, as were the rest of the people, who, together as an entire nation, were subject to the whole Law which followed. This represented another distinction between Israel and other nations. All Israelites stood obliged to uphold the Law of their Sovereign, each within his or her appropriate sphere.

37. John Ward, *The Good-Will of Him that Dwelt in the Bush: Or, the Extraordinary Happinesse of Living under an Extraordinary Providence* (London, 1645), p. 29.
38. Referencing Baxter's aforementioned title: *A Holy Commonwealth.*

51

By way of covenantal application, the *Westminster Larger Catechisme* concluded that the preamble of the Commandments further stipulated: *"He is a God in covenant, as Israel of old, so with all his people... ."*[39] The preface which set the stage for the Commandments of Israel thereby set the stage for all covenantal people to follow.

A.

B.

The First Table of the Covenant Law

God gave Israel *"ten Commandments, which were delivered by the voyce of God on mount Sinai."*[40] The books of Exodus and Deuteronomy both noted that they were presented *"in two tables of stone"* (Deuteronomy 5:22).[41] The first table of the Covenant Law, or the first four Commandments, were specific statutes regarding the obligations of every Israelite and the nation as a whole toward their Lord. They directed all private as well as public concerns in Israel, and, on a larger scale, they represented the overall duty of mankind. And, they were the four Commands which, according to Richard Baxter, directed all of us to love and serve God without reservation or qualification:

> The summe of the dutie commanded towards God, is to love him with all our hearts: more particularly it is, that we love most highly esteem, honour, reverence, believe and trust him, and adhere to him in love, and seek him, and depend upon and serve him with all our powers and faculties.[42]

The *Westminster Larger Catechisme* added that: *"The summe of the four Commandements containing our duty to God, is, to love the Lord our God with all our heart, and with all our soule, and with all our strength, and with all our mind,"*[43] concluding that man's love and inner devotion to God must precede all outward devotion and active obedience.

A. This is a manuscript section of a Hebrew-language Torah scroll (scroll of the five books of Moses). From the first column (on the right) into the second column (on the left), it shows the text of Exodus 20, including the complete 'Ten Commandments' as given by God to ancient Israel. This particular fragment was written on red heifer hide and dates from the late seventeenth century.

B. Shown here is the title page of the Westminster Assembly's *A Larger Catechisme*, published in London by Reformed biblical scholars in 1648.

39. Westminster Assembly of Divines, *The Humble Advice of the Assembly of Divines... Concerning A Larger Catechisme...* (London, 1648), pp. 26-27.

40. Ibid., p. 25.

41. Ibid. (Also see Exodus 24:12.)

42. Richard Baxter, *A Holy Commonwealth*, pp. 50-51.

43. *Westminster Larger Catechisme*, p. 27.

I. The First Commandment

The First Commandment demanded exclusive vassalage to God as Lord:

Thou shalt have no other gods before me (Exodus 20:3).

God was the Lord of Israel's forefathers and had newly expressed Himself to them in the most profound way as *"I AM THAT I AM"* (Exodus 3:14). God was immediate though timeless to them, and He was personal to each but universal to all. He therefore commanded and deserved their every and exclusive allegiance.

A. As a Commandment to Israelite individuals: they each owed their first devotion to the *"I AM"* alone. God was the only One worthy of their ultimate individual loyalty and He reigned over their personal, household, and public affairs. The Israelite was to own God alone as the only object of his or her most immediate trust, and Moses gave that foremost trust further clarity again at Horeb:

And thou shalt love the LORD thy God with all thine heart, and with all thy soul, and with all thy might. And these words which I command thee this day, shall be in thine heart. And thou shalt teach them diligently unto thy children, and shalt talk of them when thou sittest in thine house, and when thou walkest by the way, and when thou liest down, and when thou risest up (Deuteronomy 6:5-7).

The Israelite parents were therein charged to teach their children to love God, training and instructing them in the precepts of His Law on a regular basis.

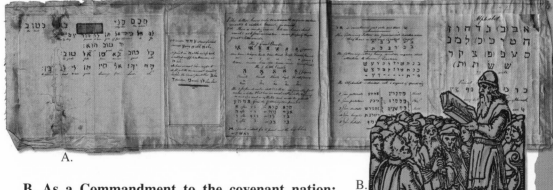

A.

B. As a Commandment to the covenant nation: Israel's exclusive allegiance to God represented the starting point of all governance and law. It embodied a straightforward demand that the vassal nation acknowledge its status before the one and only true God as its Lord. He was their God because He was the God of all men, but He had specifically called them as a people out of Babylon through their forefather Abraham. He was their Lord because He had called them out from their bondage under Pharaoh, and Israel was now pledged to Him as a nation by its consensual vow. God gave Israel its legitimacy and He alone gave the nation its sanction.

B.

A. Shown here is a manuscript Hebrew primer scroll used in teaching children to read and write the ancient script (circa 1800).

B. The public reading of God's Law was depicted in this woodcut used on the title page of the first complete Bible printed in the English language in 1535.

C. As a moral Mandate to mankind: the First Commandment represents the universal acknowledgment of man's only true God. All the blessings that mankind will ever possess are due to His gracious providence. All that men possess in their lives or property, families or homes, neighbors or communities, and societies or nations, belong to His gracious providence in creating and providing for them. And, trust in Him alone is the only way to salvation through His grace, as is further stated in Scripture: *"... without faith it is impossible to please him: for he that cometh to God must beleeve that he is, and that he is a rewarder of them that diligently seek him"* (Hebrews 11:6).

The only genuine object of mankind's worship is God as He has revealed Himself in Scripture. He is One Being in three Persons: as the Heavenly Father, the Savior Son, and Holy Spirit. The idea of the Triune God was depicted in this engraving on the title page of an English 'King James' Bible in 1632.

In the covenantal application of God's Law, the *Westminster Larger Catechisme* stipulated that the First Commandment centered around *"yeelding all obedience and submission to him, with the whole man."*[44] We are obliged to acknowledge God's sovereignty and to make Him the sole object of our inward trust and outward obedience. On the other hand, the denial or mistrust of God facilitates continued disobedience.[45] Richard Baxter went further in writing that without our acknowledgment of His explicit sovereignty in all our affairs, there can be no legitimate sanction of any human engagements: *"The denial of the Sovereignty of God, and his Moral Government is the denial of Deity, Humanity, Religion, Morality, and Policy."*[46]

II. The Second Commandment

The Second Commandment prohibited worshipping God by inventive human methods. Other man-made deities have been worshipped by flattering homages, images, and appeasements. Human potentates were themselves often worshipped as idols, and the gods devised by them were the objects of human imaginations. But, the God of Creation, the God of Israel, the God of the Apostles, exists beyond human comprehension. He dictated the modes of man's worship, and with His Second Commandment, inventive human forms of worship would not be tolerated:

> *Thou shalt not make unto thee any graven image, or any likenesse of any thing, that is in heaven above, or that is in the earth beneath, or that is in the water under the earth. Thou shalt not bow down thy self to them, nor serve them: for I the LORD thy God am a jealous God, visiting the iniquity of the fathers upon the children unto the third and fourth generation of them that hate me: And shewing mercy unto thousands of them that love me, and keep my commandments* (Exodus 20:4-6).

44. Ibid.
45. See Psalm 14:1-4.
46. Baxter, *A Holy Commonwealth*, p. 39.

A. As a Commandment to Israelite individuals: they could not approach God by any other means than by His specific directives. His manner of receiving worship and His modes of appeasing their sin were not matters entrusted to inventive individuals. God gave them the proper forms of approaching Him. They were matters of grave consequence and called for strict obedience and deep humility. A clearer explanation behind God's prohibition of inventive forms of worship was given when the covenant was repeated at Horeb:

> *Take ye therefore good heed unto your selves (for ye saw no manner of similitude on the day that the LORD spake unto you in Horeb, out of the midst of the fire) Lest ye corrupt your selves, and make you a graven image, ...* (Deuteronomy 4:15-16).[47]

A.

The individual Israelite was then to guard himself against corrupting himself through innovative schemes or creative imagery. True mediation for sin was promised through God Himself, so each Israelite was to fix God's promise within his heart and mind. Each was to own God as the only "object" of faith, lest he fall short of His perfect standard of devotion. Individuals were to worship God by His chosen means, or not approach Him at all.

A. When Christ found money changers defiling God's Temple, He drove them off (John 2:15). The scene was shown in this engraving by Rembrandt van Rijn in 1635.

B. As a Commandment to the covenant nation: God dictated Israel's means of approaching Him as its Lord. Israel had not been delivered by way of earthly images. God alone was above them and manifested Himself at His own discretion. Moses did not initiate God's intercession in Egypt nor did Aaron conjure up His image. Israel could therefore neither dictate to God nor appease Him on its own terms, and any effort to do so represented a display of humanistic pride and arrogance and was not befitting the vassal nation.

In Israel, no earthly image could represent God as an object of devotion. Moses did not represent Israel's object of devotion, for he was simply presented in the reflective light of its true Lord.[48] He and the Israelite priesthood simply acted in an intercessory role according to God's own design.[49] Moses was not the source of Israel's deliverance, nor were the people capable of creating their own. Thereby, for Israel to suppose that it could create a figure of worship would represent the height of self-devotion. The people of Israel would see their own hands as providing their deliverance, and, when they created a golden calf, that is just what they had done: *"... they have made them a molten calf, and have worshipped it, and have sacrificed thereunto, and said, These be thy Gods, O Israel, which have brought thee up out of the land of Egypt"* (Exodus 32:8).

B.

B. When Moses found the Israelites defiling their covenant by creating and worshipping a false god, he smashed the original tables of the Law in outrage (Exodus 32:19). He then burnt the idol, ground it into powder, and made the people drink it (Exodus 32:20). The scene of Moses' righteous fury was depicted in this sixteenth-century woodcut.

47. Also see Deuteronomy 4:17-19.
48. See Exodus 34:34-35.
49. See Exodus 32:11-13, 29, 31-32; 33:9, 13-17; 34:8.

C. As a moral Mandate to mankind: the Second Commandment is a demand to approach or worship God only by the means which He provides. Man is incapable of making his own way to God, for he is finite and will inevitably attempt to do so by means dependent upon self-limitations. Ever since Creation, man has been required to worship God in the manner prescribed by Him. Adam's first son, Cain, erred in offering God an unacceptable sacrifice.[50] Adam directed his sons to offer devotion according to God's discretion, as the Geneva Bible's note explained the background of Cain's error: *"This declareth that the father instructed his children in the knowledge of God, and also how God gave them sacrifices to signifie their salvation, ..."*[51]

A.

From the time of Adam and his sons, fathers were required to explain the means of devotion to God to their families. Early on, that was done by means of a family altar or place of familial worship. Noah reconfirmed that obligation by building an altar with his entire family following the flood.[52] Yet, in spite of men continually inventing their own ways of worshipping various deities, God provides us with the only rightful way to approach Him. Humanity cannot find access to God simply by multiplying its modes of religious activity. The Puritan Thomas Goodwin therefore noted the futility in a man's attempts to intimately approach God by way of human creativity or inventiveness:

A. God has always required appropriate worship, as was seen in the comparison between the means of worship by Adam's sons, Cain and Abel, in Genesis 4. Their two, distinct sacrificial objects were shown in this late fifteenth-century illustration.

> *... when he hath multiplied the number of his gods, according to the number of the Starres in Heaven, and creeping things on earth, yet still his heart will be doubtful, whether he hath worshipped the true God, nay, whether the true God be not utterly unknown.*[53]

God is indeed known and worshipped by man. People will continue to worship Him in His true glory, but they will come to Him only by the way prescribed by Him:[54] *"For there is one God, and one mediatour between God and men, the man Christ Jesus"* (1 Timothy 2:5). Men and women must therefore have the Lord Himself as a Mediator by which to approach the only true and transcendent God. The means of worshipping Him was therefore graciously provided by Him. And, considering man's fallen and fallible state, we ought not complain that there are not many ways to legitimately approach God, but we ought to be grateful that He has provided the one.

B.

B. God's written Word does not condone pluralistic religions or modes of worship, as was described by Thomas Goodwin's first chapter on man's manifold forms of idolatry in his book, *Moses & Aaron*.

50. See Genesis 4:5.
51. Geneva note on Genesis 4:3, which set up verse 5, leaf A8.
52. See Genesis 8:18-20.
53. Goodwin, *Moses & Aaron*, p. 140.
54. See John's Gospel 14:6.

III. The Third Commandment

The Third Commandment strictly prohibited the use of the Lord's Name in any derogatory way:

> *Thou shalt not take the name of the LORD thy God in vain: for the LORD will not hold him guiltlesse that taketh his name in vain* (Exodus 20:7).

According to the Geneva Bible's annotation, that meant *"either by swearing falsly or rashly by his name, or by contemning it."*[55]

A. As a Commandment to individual Israelites: it demanded the awesome reverence that was due to God's Name as Lord. No Israelite was to use His Name in a way that would reduce His honor or defame His glory. God's Name was to them the *"I AM,"* or the *"I AM THAT I AM,"* which connoted His self-supremacy and self-sufficiency. To the Israelites, that Name represented God's own heavenly supremacy and their own covenant's sufficiency. Whether privately at home or publicly among a larger community, God's Name was never to be profaned in either their casual or formal speech.

God superintended every sphere of covenantal duty in ancient Israel. His Name alone was Holy and to be revered at all times, in all public discourse, and with all private conversation. That Hebrew reverence was depicted in this seventeenth-century woodcut.

The Lord's integrity was the basis of the Israelite either at home or in public. For his personal associations to be corrupted with falsehood would weaken the fabric of Israel's larger societies. The Israelite was therefore strictly forbidden to enter into covenants or engagements under false pretense, which would render his Lord's Name in league with hypocrisy: *"And ye shall not swear by my name falsly"* (Leviticus 19:12). To incriminate the Lord in a sworn lie was both hypocritical toward Him and a practice that weakened the fabric of their mutual obligations.

B. As a Commandment to the covenant nation: Israel had been redeemed by its Lord and was identified with His Name. His title was Israel's banner among the nations. Israel was established under His holy standard and had pledged its unfeigned allegiance to God in its covenant oath. His Name marked them; it was revealed to Moses at the beginning of their exodus journey at the commencement of the plagues; they were to reverence it throughout their wilderness travels and establish it in the Promised Land. The gift of God's Name represented Israel's distinction as the nation which carried His promise and His Laws. It was to remain solemn and revered. It was not to be profaned in speech or action, for it was holy, or *"hallowed,"* as in "set above," and that which set Israel apart: *"Neither shall ye profane my holy name, but I will be hallowed among the children of Israel: I am the LORD which hallow you"* (Leviticus 22:32).[56]

---

55. Geneva note on Exodus 20:7, leaf D7.
56. Also see Numbers 6:24-27.

C. As a moral Mandate to mankind: God's Name is to be held above all others. God was the Creator of all mankind. Both Adam and Noah, mankind's most distant common ancestors, were covenanted with Him at the beginning of our lineage, and His Name is uniquely worthy of our submissive reverence: *"Give unto the LORD the glory due unto his name,"* proclaimed David to all *"ye mighty"* (Psalm 29:1-2).

To speak profanely in God's Name is a great offense to Him. Using His Name irreverently in boasting or blasphemy, coarseness or cursing, or lies or lusts are all universally offensive to God. It does not matter whether or not the offenders are ignorant of God or His Name, or whether they even recognize any accountability to Him. Richard Baxter wrote: *"They could violate a Law, and deny obedience to it; but they could not nullifie it, or prevent, or destroy its obligation."*[57] Speaking against His Name therefore puts everyone and anyone at enmity with God, because *"thine enemies take thy name in vain"* (Psalm 139:20).

Bringing a 'bad name' upon God by way of one's misconduct is equally prohibited by the Third Commandment. For example, through the prophet Amos, God complained that His people *"profane my holy Name"* (Amos 2:7) by way of a long list of public injustices and lewd iniquities. The later Hebrew Apostle Paul similarly charged that non-Hebrew peoples were defaming the Lord's Name due to their hypocritical misconduct, writing: *"the name of God is blasphemed among the Gentiles, through you"* (Romans 2:24). All those who claim God's mantle upon their lives, their families, their communities, or their nation can simply not afford to desecrate that integrity in either word or deed.

Further, God's Name alone is sovereign and His Name alone fulfills the promise of grace: *"... there is none other name under heaven given among men whereby we must be saved,"* declared the Apostle Peter (Acts 4:12). His Name alone is worthy of universal devotion: *"Who shall not fear thee, O Lord, and glorifie thy name? for thou onely art holy"* (Revelation 15:4), profess the multitude of angels upon the great *"sea of glasse"* (Revelation 15:2). It is therefore most befitting that mankind be commanded to hold God's Name in highest respect, gracious trust, and universal devotion by not taking it *"in vain."*

IV. The Fourth Commandment

The Fourth Commandment mandated conformity of all human affairs to the order of God's seven days of Creation. God mandated labor for six days of the week and rest for one:

> *Remember the sabbath-day, to keep it holy. Six dayes shalt thou labour, and do all thy work. But the seventh day is the sabbath of the LORD thy God: in it thou shalt not do any work, thou, nor thy son, nor thy daughter, thy man-servant, nor thy maid-servant, nor thy cattell, nor thy stranger that is within thy gates. For in six dayes the LORD made heaven and earth, the sea, and all that in them is, and rested the seventh day: wherefore the LORD blessed the sabbath-day, and hallowed it* (Exodus 20:8-11).

57. Baxter, *A Holy Commonwealth*, p. 45.

A. As a Commandment to individual Israelites: they were each to *"hallow,"* or set aside, the Sabbath as a day to rest, to worship, and to remember the God of their devotions:

> *And remember that thou wast a servant in the land of Egypt, and that the LORD thy God brought thee out thence, through a mighty hand and by a stretched-out arm: therefore the LORD thy God commanded thee to keep the sabbath-day* (Deuteronomy 5:15).

Every seventh day was more than an occasional reminder of Him, it was an obligation to be pledged to Him in a regular weekly practice. They were to be set aside unto Him in an attitude that remained with them throughout the toils of the remainder of their week.

The Sabbath also put an Israelite's affairs in line with the Creation Covenant. At Creation, God set the example of resting on the seventh day of the first week with the first man. There was a completion represented within each cycle of days, each seven days representing a new cycle, and each cycle representing a new beginning among each continuing week. Each Israelite was commanded to follow that tempo in his private affairs. His household would therefore be paced on a sequence of six days for work, then one for rest: *"... and on the seventh day thou shalt rest: that thine ox and thine asse may rest, and the son of thy handmaid, and the stranger may be refreshed"* (Exodus 23:12).[58]

A.

B.

A. God ordained labor for six of the seven days each week. An example of a man's domestic labor was shown in this anonymous sixteenth-century illustration.

B. An example of a woman's domestic labor was shown in this companion illustration.

B. As a Commandment to the covenant nation: Israel was to honor and worship its Lord on a regular basis. The nation was to corporately be set aside on the Sabbath in mindful devotion to its Lord as Sovereign and Creator. He was always to be the object of its cultural identity and His Sabbath was to be strictly enforced in its national statutes.[59] The Fourth Commandment set the cultural tempo for the nation, with six days of labor and one day of rest to be consistently observed throughout its societal order. As Creator, God Himself was the example to His people and He determined the limits of their earthly burden, and as their Redeemer, He brought them out from the oppression of ongoing, slavish labor. It would therefore be tyrannical for Israel to once again put its people under the punitive oppressions of Pharaoh by an endless, seven-day workweek.[60]

The word "Sabbath" also signified Israel's covenantal rest as the term was applied to its solemn festivals. Thomas Goodwin explained this dimension of the Sabbath in an exposé of the various ways that Israel either kept or broke it in its public festivals, with God condemning the people accordingly: *"They polluted my Sabbaths, Ezek. 20. 21: That is, my Feasts."*[61]

58. Also see Leviticus 23:3; Deuteronomy 5:12-14.
59. See Exodus 31:15; 34:21; 35:2; Leviticus 23:3.
60. See Exodus 5:4-5; Deuteronomy 5:15.
61. Goodwin, *Moses & Aaron*, p. 97.

There was also a Sabbath rest mandated for Israel's stewardship of the covenant land itself: *"But in the seventh yeer shall be a sabbath of rest unto the land, a sabbath for the LORD: thou shalt neither sowe thy field, nor prune thy vineyard"* (Leviticus 25:4). Therefore, Israel went into Babylonian captivity under God's judgment for seventy years in order to accomplish the Sabbath's rest for its land. Israel had violated the principle of giving its fields a Sabbath's rest every seventh year, and the seventy years of captivity represented the years required to restore the land: *"... untill the land had enjoyed her sabbaths: for as long as she lay desolate, she kept sabbath, to fulfill threescore and ten yeers"* (2 Chronicles 36:21).

To Israel then, the Sabbath represented both a blessed redemption and a solemn obligation. It was intended to keep Israel on the path between licentious laxity and tiresome toil, and between the lines of societal extravagance and cultural famine.

C. As a moral Mandate to mankind: the Fourth Commandment dictates man's general obligation to serve God in accord with our Creation Covenant. The Command paces human life with the Creator's given cycle, as well as directs us toward His grace, for in God's fulfillment of the promise, the faithful find their ultimate Sabbath's rest in their Redeemer:

> For we which have beleeved do enter into rest, as he said, As I have sworn in my wrath, if they shall enter into my rest: although the works were finished from the foundation of the world. For he spake in a certain place of the seventh day on this wise, And God did rest the seventh day from all his works (Hebrews 4:3-4).

To the believers, the true Sabbath's rest is found in the completed work of Messiah Jesus. Therefore, the cycle of six days of work for one day of rest still follows in the regular practice of the New Covenant faithful, though they were free in Christ to change the particular day of its observance.

The Sabbath was observed by Reformed Christians as a day for families to gather with others to hear God's Word publicly preached and to corporately worship Him as befitting His Holy Name. Those two aspects of the Sabbath assembly were shown in this single sixteenth-century engraving from Foxe's *Actes and Monumentes* (1576 edition).

Nonetheless, in God's general mercy upon mankind, He still sets constraints on all earthly burdens and limitations upon the oppressions of any humanistic tyranny. The general mandate of setting a day apart signifies the Creator's everlasting transcendence above all, as all are to honor Him for their common gift of creation. Our created design calls us to acknowledge Him in the general cycle of a weekly day of rest. And, as there still remain many spirits of Pharaoh amid the fallen world of humanity, God's Fourth Commandment is a merciful statute to rein them in, to strengthen mankind, and to help replenish the earth. According to God's earthly design, all people should regularly be *"resting from worldly travails."*[62]

62. Geneva note on Exodus 20:8, leaf D7.

The Second Table of the Covenant Law

The remaining six Commandments were each specific Laws regarding the covenantal obligations of people in relation to one another. The second table of the Covenant Law thus defined the relations of the Israelites among themselves, and of their nation amid all other nations of the world. Moreover, the last six Commands mandate the moral obligations of all men among our fellow man. Yet, these obligations to love one's neighbor come only in accord with the former Commands to love God, as we can only love a neighbor, as He requires, with His assistance. As each of the Commandments tend to build upon the former, we cannot hope to keep the last six if we do not first have a heart to keep the first four. According to Richard Baxter, the final six Commandments determine the sum of our duty to our fellow man:

Dan Ford, 2002

God gave Israel two tables of the Law, as shown with this sketch of Moses drawn from a painting by Rembrandt van Rijn (circa 1650).

> *Our duty towards our Neighbor as such, is to love him as ourselves, that is, to love him with an Impartial Love, not drawing from him to ourselves, by an inordinate selfishness: which must be expressed about his Life, Chastity, Estate, Honour, and any thing that is his: Godliness, Soberness, and Righteousness, are the general Titles of all these.*[63]

V. The Fifth Commandment

The Fifth Commandment dealt with honoring all forms of parental authority. As it was the first of the Commandments that presented mankind's distinct obligations among one another, it established the proper attitude and demeanor of the duty owed to all who are in authority. Thus, the Geneva Bible's note on the Commandment also read: *"By the parents also is meant all that have authority over us."*[64]

> *Honour thy father and thy mother: that thy dayes may be long upon the land which the Lord thy God giveth thee* (Exodus 20:12).

Though the Fifth Commandment simply demanded that honor be given to parents, its intended application was much broader.

A. As a Commandment to individual Israelites: it first spoke of their duty to respect the order in family government. The Hebrew people themselves began by way of a miraculous birth from two parents:

> *Therefore sprang there even of one, and him as good as dead, so many as the stars of the skie in multitude, and as the sand which is by the sea shore innumerable* (Hebrews 11:12).

63. Baxter, *A Holy Commonwealth*, p. 51.
64. Geneva note on Exodus 20:12, leaf D7.

Ever since Abraham and Sarah, the Hebrew households were to be sanctuaries of parental honor. The parents held the reins of governance within the family as the reigns outside the home were deposited among the rulers of tens, fifties, hundreds, and thousands.[65] Hebrew parents were charged by God with the power to enforce His commands in the home so as not to leave sons and daughters to their own devices: *The rod and reproof give wisdom: but a childe left to himself, bringeth his mother to shame*" (Proverbs 29:15).[66] Israel's King Solomon took great pains to repeatedly drive home the importance of parental honor.[67] He also placed disrespect toward parents among such aggravating sins as moral filth, boundless pride, blinding rebellion, and even violence. Solomon therefore warned the Israelite:

A.

There is a generation that curseth their father, and doth not blesse their mother.

There is a generation that are pure in their own eyes, and yet is not washed from their filthinesse.

There is a generation, O how lofty are their eyes! and their eye-lids are lifted up.

B.

There is a generation, whose teeth are as swords, and their jaw-teeth as knives, to devour the poor from off the earth, and the needy from among men (Proverbs 30:11-14).

The Fifth Commandment's clause: "... *that thy dayes may be long upon the land,*" also implied a multi-generational continuity that Hebrew parents were obliged to bestow to their children. A child's education in the home therefore included learning a hearty respect for their more distant forefathers of the past. And, by ways of both instruction and example, parents would also honor their own children's future authority by training them to have the highest respect for the Laws of God:

A. It was the obligation of each Hebrew father to teach his own children the ways of their forefathers, as was shown in this illustration depicting the Hebrew Habdalah, or service of separation at the end of the Sabbath.*

B. Led by the father, it was the whole family's duty to help search for and remove Leaven, or corruption, from the home.*

*A. & B.: Woodcut illustrations of Hebrew rituals and holiday customs by Solomon Proops (early eighteenth century).

And ye shall teach them your children, speaking of them when thou sittest in thine house, and when thou walkest by the way, when thou liest down, and when thou risest up. And thou shalt write them upon the doorposts of thine house, and upon thy gates: That your dayes may be multiplied, and the dayes of your children, in the land which the LORD sware unto your fathers to give them, as the dayes of heaven upon the earth (Deuteronomy 11:19-21).

65. See Exodus 18:25.
66. Also see Proverbs 19:18.
67. See Proverbs 1:8; 6:20; 10:1; 19:26; 20:20; 23:22; 28:24 (among others).

B. As a Commandment to the covenant nation: the Fifth Commandment mandated Israel's duty to honor its various spheres of authority.

As a nation, Israel was to respect the private government of the family. The household covenant was basic to Israel's whole covenantal fabric, for its beginnings lay in the depths of bondage in Egypt as families under the yoke of the household of Pharaoh. The sons of Israel escaped in the form of Passover families and they were covenanted as a nation to rule as protectors of that most commonplace familial institution. If vassal Israel hoped to prosper, it must maintain a most noble respect for the great nursery beds of all its institutions. And, the nursery beds of Israel were always to remain its Passover homes.

A. Parental honor was central to understanding all Israelite authority. Israel's various tribes were, after all, composed of individual families, as was depicted in this engraving by Leone de Modena in 1629.

Respect for parental rule was paramount in a nation covenanted with God. God had placed parents over children, by whom they would be nurtured in all of His rules of authority and submission. Then, as they were raised into maturity, they would respect the order of authority and submission required of them in their wider societies. Such children would become the fit managers of the vassal nation. The Fifth Commandment thus included due respect for all ruling authority. It indeed acknowledged the supreme honor of the domestic establishment, but it also implied the honor of all human order established under God. As authority and submission extended into every venue of Hebrew life, the Fifth Commandment encompassed the honor and respect of the eldership that would administer God's Law. The covenant nation could then serve its Lord in uniform submission, and honor all subsequent authority with appropriate private carriage and public decorum. The manner of covenant Israel's private occupations, its public congregations, and civic associations therefore all began with the command to *"Honour thy father and thy mother."*

When Israel succeeded and indeed lived *"long upon the land,"* it was due to its reverence for God and His Law. But, God's pledge of prosperity came with expressed conditions, and when Israel failed, as it often did, it was due to a lack of honor for its own heavenly Father. God therefore asked His ministers through the Hebrew prophet Malachi:

> *A son honoureth his father, and a servant his master: if then I be a father, where is mine honour? and if I be a master, where is my fear? saith the LORD of hosts unto you, O priests, that despise my name...* (Malachi 1:6).

B. Israel's overall civility demanded honor and respect for its system of ruling elders, as was depicted in this seventeenth-century engraving of a dispute brought before a Hebrew judge (1695).

C. As a moral Mandate to mankind: the Fifth Commandment is a demand to continue the honor that God deposited with the first human institution on earth. It was therefore fitting that this was the first Commandment in which God stipulated our relations among our fellow man. As a published statute, it requires honor for all legitimate authority, but as a practical matter, it reflects the fount of godly wisdom: *"A wise son maketh a glad father: but a foolish man despiseth his mother"* (Proverb 15:20).

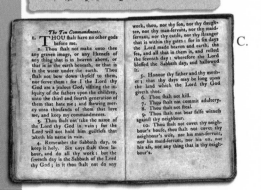

A.

B.

C.

A. God vested His dominion authority with man at Creation, and mankind was to honor God with its own respect for all legitimate authority thereafter. Man's creation dominion was allegorically depicted by this woodcut in Martin Luther's *Small Catechism* in 1529.

B. This text shows the wording of the Fifth Commandment as repeated in Deuteronomy 5 in an early English Bible published in 1537.

C. The text of the Ten Commandments was also provided for generations of new readers in the *New England Primer*, published throughout the eighteenth century.

With the Creation Covenant, God invested His honor in representative human authority. Any position of authority under Him is simply reflective of His first honor. In the first marriage covenant, God initiated a bond between Adam and Eve, associating His honor in the union of husband and wife. It followed that since the arrival of their first offspring, all marital parents have been vested with His representative responsibility and dominion over their children. Their children (as with all subsequent children since Adam and Eve's) have been vested with a primary duty to honor that authority. Thus, to pay honor to parents is to pay honor to the representative image of the original and highest Authority. The continuity of godly parental honor has thus been passed down through all generations. And, as confirmed in the Fifth Commandment, each new generation has been given God's charge to honor its parents, and all new parents have a duty to impart that understanding on to the next.

The honor due anyone's superiors, whether in family, work, or wider society, is also derived from the first honor in respecting God. Thereby, in the Fifth Commandment God provided for adequate societal stability without the need for oppressive tyranny. In so far as parents train their children with a working understanding of the godly principles of authority, they will grow in godly self-discipline and, as adults, be prepared to submit to the legitimate constitutions of the institutions under which God's providence places them. And, only then will they be adequately prepared to hold their civil authorities to their vows and solemn oaths of office. It is therefore incumbent upon every individual to have a working understanding of the various civil constitutions, whether written or unwritten, which they are also morally obliged to honor in accord with the Fifth Commandment.

VI. The Sixth Commandment

The Sixth Commandment was a straightforward demand to respect life:

"*Thou shalt not kill* [murder]" (Exodus 20:13).[68]

As life and death were the sole purview of God, man was not sanctioned on his own to either give life or take it away. God alone was the Creator of life in both body and soul, and He alone was the arbiter of man's natural and spiritual ends.

A. As a Commandment to Israelite individuals: the Hebrew man could not cause the death of another without his Lord's specific sanction. The Sixth Commandment specifically denied that sanction to individuals acting on their own,[69] and the crime of murder, or the unsanctioned taking of a life, was thereby an offense requiring severe restitution:

> *And if he smite him with an instrument of iron (so that he die) he is a murderer: the murderer shall surely be put to death. And if he smite him with throwing a stone (wherewith he may die) and he die, he is a murderer: the murderer shall surely be put to death. Or if he smite him with an hand-weapon of wood (wherewith he may die) and he die, he is a murderer: the murderer shall surely be put to death* (Numbers 35:16-18).

Under God's mandated principle of retribution, the Israelite murderer was to pay back the life taken with that of his own. Because the Commandment also prohibited arbitrarily inflicting harm upon others, the principle of personal retribution was therefore to be enforced by the civil magistrate: "*Eye for eye, tooth for tooth, hand for hand, foot for foot, Burning for burning, wound for wound, stripe for stripe*" (Exodus 21:24-25).[70] The sovereign Lord was the covenant Preserver of the life of each Israelite, and His Sixth Commandment also implied the positive duty of each to protect life and to actively safeguard the lives of the innocent, as the Geneva Bible's margins noted: "*But love and preserve thy brothers life.*"[71]

The Sixth Commandment not only prohibited Israelites from injuring or taking the lives of others, but it required them to have a high personal regard for the preservation of life. One of Christ's parables spoke of a man who had been assaulted by thieves on his way from Jerusalem to Jericho. Two Israelites, a priest and a Levite, who should have known their covenant mandate, *"passed on the other side,"* but a mere Samaritan tended to the wounds of the man. By his intervention, the 'Good Samaritan' revealed the two Israelites' passive cruelty (see Luke 10:30-37). The scene was carefully depicted in this engraving from an early nineteenth-century American Bible.

B. As a Commandment to the covenant nation: the Sixth Commandment demanded an institutional respect for those who carried the covenant promise. Israel carried the promise of its fathers, and its rulers were charged with preserving the lives of its continuing inheritance. The Commandment was

---

68. The Hebrew word used in Exodus 20:13 is *rasah*, which especially indicates killing or slaying that is premeditated, and is thus better translated as "murder." See *Vine's Complete Expository Dictionary of Old and New Testament Words* (Thomas Nelson Publishers, 1985), p. 128.
69. See Deuteronomy 19:10-12; 27:25.
70. Also see Exodus 21:18-20, 26-34.
71. Geneva note on Exodus 20:13, leaf D7.

therefore so expansive that it prohibited arbitrarily oppressing the people or taking away any life without the specific sanction of their Lord. Under the nature of its covenanted constitution, Israel was to conform to the character of its Lord God in the preservation of lives that He alone created and ultimately owned. In His Laws of the land, His character was therefore reconfirmed in further sanctions to protect and defend the lives of all those under Israel's charge:

> *Thou shalt neither vex a stranger, nor oppresse him: for ye were strangers in the land of Egypt. Ye shall not afflict any widow, or fatherlesse childe. If thou afflict them in any wise, and they cry at all unto me, I will surely hear their cry. And my wrath shall wax hot and I will kill you with the sword; and your wives shall be widows, and your children fatherlesse* (Exodus 22:21-24).

As God gave Israel its strict terms of obedience, it was not authorized for arbitrary rule or sanctioned to condone the death of a single innocent life without the nation being chargeable before Him.[72] God's justice, however, did require punishment in the death of the guilty in many instances. For example, Israel's judges were merciful to the nation when requiring the life of a capital offender due to an ardent respect for the Commandment's wider positive protection of life and limb. The adjudicated death of the guilty would then best protect and secure the lives of the innocent.[73] For the nation not to take life for life would be blatant disobedience.[74]

In its international affairs, Israel sat tenuously before its Sovereign. It was to move upon other nations only at its Lord's behest, for unless otherwise commanded, it was to remain at peace with others.[75] But, when so directed, Israel had no option other than to move with unwavering force against others: *"Behold, the LORD thy God hath set the land before thee: go up, and possesse it, as the LORD God of thy fathers hath said unto thee; fear not, neither be discouraged"* (Deuteronomy 1:21).[76] God owned all land and all peoples. When He had allowed others to possess the land ahead of Israel, He had done so by grace. He had previously promised and prepared the Land for the sons of Abraham, and in His timing, He chose how long such temporal graces would continue. When Israel was then commanded to move, it had no option but to move. For Israel not to utterly destroy the inhabitants in such an instance would have represented rebellion.[77] For the sons of Abraham to hesitate would have been to neglect their first covenantal duty and necessitate that their Lord Commander pass His sentence upon their insubordination.[78]

Herein, safeguarding Israel's own existence was seen in terms of its obedience to its Sovereign. The sons of Israel existed by God's promise, and rampant disobedience would rain death upon their heads.[79] On the other hand, Israel's abundant life was set in terms of maintaining His standards of life and goodness:

72. See Jeremiah 26:15; Isaiah 59:1-7.
73. See Exodus 21:12, 29; Leviticus 20:2; 24:17; Numbers 35:16-18, 21, 30.
74. See Exodus 21:23; Numbers 35:31; Deuteronomy 19:21.
75. See Deuteronomy 2.
76. Also see Deuteronomy 6:10-11.
77. See Numbers 14:9; Deuteronomy 7:1-7; Joshua 8:1-2.
78. See Exodus 24:7-8; Numbers 14:23.
79. See Deuteronomy 28.

See, I have set before thee this day life and good, and death and evil; In that I command thee this day to love the LORD thy God, to walk in his wayes, and to keep his commandments and his statutes, and his judgements, that thou mayest live and multiply (Deuteronomy 30:15-16).

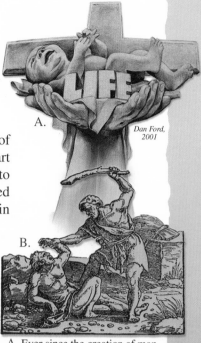

A.

Dan Ford, 2001

B.

In spite of God's irrevocable promise to preserve the sons of Abraham, they did not have a divine right to an abundant life apart from obedience to their Lord's sanction. Though they continued to exist by way of that promise, covenantal disobedience still yielded rampant death and destruction. And, ultimately, Israel's success in preserving life rested upon its overall covenantal faithfulness.

C. As a moral Mandate to mankind: the Sixth Commandment is a statute that prohibits the taking of innocent human life. From man's beginning under the Creation Covenant, the shedding of innocent blood was cursed by God, as recorded in the Genesis record of the original murder of Abel by his brother Cain. God confronted Cain according to his Creation responsibility:

A. Ever since the creation of man, protecting innocent human life has been mandatory. The Upholder of life requires His subordinates to do likewise, as shown in this sketch.

B. The first murder by man, of Abel by Cain, was illustrated in this woodcut in Luther's *Small Catechism*, published in 1529.

And he said, What hast thou done? the voice of thy brothers blood crieth unto me from the ground. And now art thou cursed from the earth, which hath opened her mouth to receive thy brothers blood from thy hand (Genesis 4:10-11).

The God of the earth abhorred all murder, as the covenantal nature of the earth itself cried out against Cain. Again, in God's covenant with Noah, all murder was specifically prohibited, as God yet again sanctioned retribution: *"Whoso sheddeth mans blood, by man shall his blood be shed; for in the image of God made he man"* (Genesis 9:6). The Sixth Commandment is thus another codified moral statute which absolutely prohibits harming or taking any human life without God's specific sanction. This Commandment includes safeguarding the preborn.

The destruction of human life violates the Creation Covenant in that God has deposited His image (at conception) within every man and woman: *"So God created man in his own image, in the image of God created he him; male and female created he them"* (Genesis 1:27). For one to unjustly destroy, harm, or use another man or woman would violate a certain property right imparted within each person by God. Since God still retains the exclusive right to His image in a person's body, heart, and soul, the Commandment is thus morally expansive to prohibit harmful afflictions of the heart as well as of the body, or of the internal as well as of the external lives of others.[80] Such wider moral obligations further prohibit the harming of one's own life – thus, to intentionally harm or deface one's self, or to violate the distinctive nature of one's manhood or womanhood,[81] would also violate the obligation of the Sixth Commandment.[82]

80. See Psalm 143:11-12; Isaiah 5:22-23.
81. See Genesis 1:27.
82. Reference principles behind Israel's own statutes: Leviticus 19:28, 29; 20:13, 15, 16; Deuteronomy 22:5.

VII. The Seventh Commandment

The Seventh Commandment appeared as a straightforward command against marital infidelity:

Thou shalt not commit adultery (Exodus 20:14).

Though simple in its wording, it carried much wider implications; for on one hand it negated a host of destructive vices, and on the other it necessitated all positive virtues. *"But be pure in heart, word, and deed,"* was the Geneva Bible's simple notation aside the text.[83]

Vows of covenantal fidelity were exchanged in the Hebrew marriage ceremony, as illustrated in this late seventeenth-century woodcut by Solomon Proops.

A. As a Commandment to Israelite individuals: the Seventh Commandment was a moral statute against all infidelity. The Lord demanded purity and faithfulness in His people – as His vassals they carried His standard, and at the time, represented Him among the peoples of the earth. The representative image of all fidelity was therefore modeled in their most basic obligations of marriage, because to the Israelite, faithfulness in all things began with covenantal fidelity in the home.

The Pilgrim preacher John Robinson saw that the fidelity of every Israelite man also meant choosing an Israelite wife. Simply put, intermarriage with foreign idolaters would produce disaster:[84] *"When the sons of God take for themselves the daughters of men, giants are borne, and all monstrous confussion followeth, first in the family, and after in the church, and then in the Commonwealth."*[85]

Thus, for either the Israelite or the Christian to be covenantally yoked[86] outside of their community would be incompatible with covenant faithfulness in all other spheres of life. The English reformers adopted God's mandate for fidelity as a principle to be observed by His New Covenant faithful: *"as the Lord hath vouchsafed* [vowed safety for] *the name of his children,* [they] *must keep themselves pure, not onely in minde, but also in body, that they may wholly be holy unto the Lord."*[87] Certainly, the Seventh Commandment's demand for the Israelite's covenant faithfulness carried a multiple charge, because according to its positive implications, it provided the abundance of the people, the success of the domestic family, and the prosperity of the nation.

On the other hand, marital unfaithfulness yielded all sorts of unsavory fruits. When the people of Israel committed adultery, their Lord removed the blessed joy of their wedlock: *"Moreover, I will take from them the voice of mirth, and the voice of gladnesse, the voice of the bridegroom, and the voice of the bride ..."* (Jeremiah 25:10). Nevertheless, once God had purged them through severe judgment, He returned their joy through grace:

---

83. Geneva note on the Seventh Commandment, Exodus 20:14, leaf D7.
84. See Deuteronomy 7:3-4.
85. John Robinson, *Essayes. Or, Observations Divine and Morall...* , 2d ed. (London, 1638), p. 520.
86. See 2 Corinthians 6:14-16.
87. Geneva note on 2 Corinthians 6:14, leaf Kkkk5.

The voice of joy, and the voice of gladnesse, the voice of the bridegroom, and the voice of the bride, the voice of them that shall say, Praise the LORD of hosts, for the LORD is good, for his mercy endureth for ever (Jeremiah 33:11).

Here, the Israelite's espoused faithfulness to God ultimately foretold of the future joys in the pending union of the promised Bridegroom with His Bride.[88]

B. As a Commandment to the covenant nation: adultery represented the breaking of Israel's corporate vow of fidelity. God used the imagery of a marital commitment to illustrate His devotion to His chosen nation. When it strayed in its numerous infatuations with other lords, God harshly condemned its infidelity. Such adultery was the chief cause of Israel's broken covenant and subsequent Babylonian captivity: *"for all the causes whereby back-sliding Israel committed adultery, I had put her away, and given her a bill of divorce"* (Jeremiah 3:8).

Due to Israel's national adultery, it also failed to protect its offspring. The future sons of Israel had been given to the Lord in the national covenant, and they were to be guarded from worldly wickedness. In the course of Israel chasing after false gods, it had handed its sons over to destruction: *"... with their idols have they committed adulterie, and have also caused their sons whom they bare unto me, to passe for them thorow* [through] *the fire, to devour them"* (Ezekiel 23:37).

Yet, God provided hope for the sons of Israel, as portrayed in the imagery of Israel's ancient form of marital engagements. According to its tradition of matrimonial engagements, a man's faithfulness to his future spouse was pledged by way of an espousal price. Upon a future groom pledging his promise to marry a bride, he paid a dowry to the girl's father amid a small company of witnesses. The future groom would confirm his promise in the *"like forme of words; Loe thou art betrothed unto me."*[89] The espoused man and woman were thereafter covenanted to mutual faithfulness not to pursue another, and they were prohibited from consummating a physical union until marriage. In that imagery lay Israel's ultimate hope in God's like engagement.

The Church, or the espoused Bride of Christ, has pledged her fidelity to her Beloved and retains all the obligations of devoted faithfulness. This woodcut of avowed Christian adoration was included in Luther's *Small Catechism*, first published in 1529.

Similarly, Christ Jesus has been revealed as the Espoused of His beloved Church. He has paid the full dowry price to her Father. He has thereby pledged His full fidelity to her amid His company of witnesses. She, as His espoused, now retains the Seventh Commandment's full obligation of fidelity to Him. Having also pledged her covenant fidelity to Him, Christ's Church thereby retains the Commandment's charge to keep herself from adultery with the other gods of the world. Like the espoused nation of Israel before His coming, Christ's holy nation (Christ's Church) now remains pledged as His espoused. And, according to the Apostles' witness, she is faithfully looking forward to the fruition of the marriage to come. Christ's beloved Apostle, John, therefore wrote at his Lord's behest:

88. See Isaiah 61:9-11.
89. Goodwin, *Moses & Aaron*, p. 231.

Let us be glad and rejoyce, and give honour to him: for the marriage of the Lamb is come, and his wife hath made her self ready. And to her was granted, that she should be arayed in fine linen, clean and white: for the fine linen is the righteousnesse of saints (Revelation 19:7-8).

C. As a moral Mandate to mankind: the Seventh Commandment prohibits all illicit behavior. God universally sanctioned marriage for man and woman in the Creation Covenant.[90] God thereby defined the terms of sexual purity between a man and a woman within wedlock, as well as established it as the legitimate means of procreation. Therefore, implicit in the Seventh Commandment is also a prohibition against homosexuality, bestiality, incest, and other abominations.[91] The intimate union of a man and a woman is to always be within the covenant as husband and wife according to God's universal standard: *"Marriage is honourable in all, and the bed undefiled: but whoremongers and adulterers God will judge"* (Hebrews 13:4). God thereby imputed within mankind's nature the marriage covenant of a man and a woman, and it has ever since proven to be a universal practice. The Seventh Commandment therefore stipulates the continuity of His standard of covenantal faithfulness among all peoples in all places.

The Command also implies certain safeguards to the union. For example, maintaining marital faithfulness also stipulates a modesty befitting the marital station. A committed spouse would not have a reason to attract another suitor, therefore he or she would be sure to adopt an attitude and demeanor to secure the perimeters of their commitment. The Puritan William Perkins noted the dignified adornment of the covenantal carriage: *"... the garments we make to cover our bodies, must bee such as may expresse the virtues of our minds; specially the virtues of Modestie, Frugalitie, Shame-fastnesse* [humility]*, They should be as a booke written with text letters, wherein, at the first, they may reade the graces that bee in the heart."*[92]

Besides defensive safeguards, covenantal fidelity also requires the aggressive exercise of faithfulness in the home. To Matthew Henry, it was apparent that the best means to prevent vice was to implement regular behaviors that would tend to the contrary:

> *Where no Fear of God is, no Reading, no Praying, no Devotion, what can one expect but all that's bad? Where there is Impiety there will be Immorality; they that restrain Prayer, cast off fear, Job 15:4. But if Religious Worship have its Place in the House, it may be hoped that Vice will not have a Place there.*[93]

Keeping the Seventh Commandment therefore requires an active family practice. Overcoming the humanistic tendencies that lead toward spiritual or physical adultery involve ongoing commitments within the home. Both horizontal safeguards and vertical devotions combine to protect the purity and fidelity of covenant family members.

Not guarding his heart and home, King David cast his gaze upon Bathsheba and soon fell into overt sin. The moment of his betrayal was depicted in this woodcut from Luther's *Small Catechism* of 1529.

90. See Genesis 2:22.
91. See Leviticus 20:11-21; also Romans 1:26-27; 1 Timothy 1:9-10.
92. William Perkins, *The Whole Treatise of the Cases of Conscience...* (London, 1632), p. 334.
93. Henry, *A Church in the House*, p. 39.

VIII. The Eighth Commandment

The Eighth Commandment was a statute that prohibited acting against the property of others:

> *Thou shalt not steal* (Exodus 20:15).

It was brief and to the point, but like those before it, it also had far-ranging implications. Though the Command was foremost a directive not to take from another, it also implied promoting a neighbor's increase. The Genevan margins noted its positive obligation: *"But study to save his goods."*[94]

By not looking to God for honest provision, the thief seeks satisfaction by underhanded means. Shown here in an early seventeenth-century English woodcut is a "cutpurse," or a man who secretly picks the pockets of others (1612).

A. As a Commandment to individual Israelites: the Eighth Commandment demanded an active respect for the private ownership rights of others. Under terms of their covenant, it also demanded that each Israelite keep a caretaker's trust in the property which the Lord had deposited with him. Each family was merely a steward of what it possessed, and its responsibility involved its entire estate, including all the possessions and resources of its household, all the lands and animals, as well as all the profit and investments associated with its individual station within the tribe and commonwealth.

Everything they had belonged to their Lord, including their tithe: *"Bring ye all the tithes into the store-house, …"* (Malachi 3:10).[95] In neglecting its payment, they were stealing from their Sovereign, as He asked them, *"Will a man rob God? yet ye have robbed me: but ye say, Wherein have we robbed thee? In tithes and offerings"* (Malachi 3:8).

The object of the Commandment was for one to be content with the possessions that the Lord had sovereignly provided, and to respect the property rights of others: *"Better is a little with righteousnesse then* [than] *great revenues without right"* (Proverbs 16:8). There was vigorous restitution applied to violations of property rights, and the Israelites punitively paid for their theft or destruction of others' goods: *"If a man shall steal an ox or a sheep, and kill it, or sell it; he shall restore five oxen for an ox, and four sheep for a sheep"* (Exodus 22:1).

Since God was concerned about all victims of theft, restitution was also required for any unauthorized use of another's property: *"For all manner of trespasse, whether it be for ox for asse, for sheep, for raiment ..."* (Exodus 22:9). Even in such a circumstantial claim such as the mere misuse of someone's property, either the accuser or the accused could bring his case before the judges. Regardless of who brought the complaint, both sides must be fairly heard: *"the cause of both parties shall come before the judges"* (Exodus 22:9). The fact that the Israelites' Laws required the hearing of both parties pointed to the impartial nature of God and His Laws. His Laws rendered equal justice. A uniform respect

---

94. Geneva note on Exodus 20:15, leaf D7.
95. Also see Exodus 13:1-2; Leviticus 27:30.

for them made it necessary for each Israelite to have an adequate understanding of the application of the Law in order to honor the terms of their covenant. Thus, as seen in the broad application of the Eighth Commandment, God established the comprehensive sanctity of private property rights among the people of Israel, and He required the people to both know and honor the rights of others.

B. As a Commandment to the covenant nation: Israel's stewardship rights over the Promised Land were also held tentatively. It possessed the land by God's unconditional promise, but that promise had stewardship responsibilities that would determine the extent of its enjoyment of the possession.

A.

Israel's continued prosperity was therefore conditional. The Lord ultimately owned all of its lands and possessions, and He jealously oversaw and protected His primary property right. All that was entrusted to Israel was sanctioned by Him and must be rightfully maintained and possessed. If Israel desired its own increase, it had to submit to its Lord's terms of blessing, and explicit covenantal obedience to His Laws provided the means: *"Keep therefore the words of this covenant and do them, that ye may prosper in all that ye do"* (Deuteronomy 29:9). Seeking to serve its covenant Lord and being content with that which He provided was therefore the key to Israel's continued abundance and prosperity.

A. Even if ill-gotten gain could be hidden from others, it could not be hidden from the oversight of Israel's Lord. This early sixteenth-century woodcut depicts a man vainly trying to hide the spoils of his thievery from Israel's elders.

When the Lord disciplined the nation for disobedience, He therefore afflicted it in its property holdings. He had given Israel a pointed warning of the One who truly held its account:

> *And if ye shall despise my statutes, or if your soul abhor my judgements, so that ye will not do all my commandments, but that ye break my covenant: I also will do this unto you, I will even appoint over you terrour, consumption, and the burning ague; that shall consume the eyes, and cause sorrow of heart: and ye shall sowe your seed in vain, for your enemies shall eat it* (Leviticus 26:15-16).[96]

B.

All disobedience to God was therefore, in effect, stealing from national prosperity. For example, attempting to increase the nation's public wealth at the expense of the people's private capacity was also theft and ignored the terms of the nation's vassal position under God. God was not a respecter of persons in high positions,[97] and Israel's public officials were not sanctioned to increase their own wealth by way of expansive taxation.[98] Thus, to come full circle, theft, whether public or private, would be a futile endeavor for the nation, for in the long run, stealing would prove counter-productive under the aggressive oversight of Israel's covenant-keeping Lord.

B. As themselves servants of God, Israel's rulers were not to require punitive tribute from the people. However, this late fifteenth-century woodcut depicts a man of public nobility wielding his power to exact bounty from his vassal subject (1493).

96. Also see Luke 16:1-2.
97. See Acts 10:34.
98. See Deuteronomy 17:16; 2 Kings 23:35.

C. As a moral Mandate to mankind: the Eighth Commandment confirms the original ownership rights of property as a universal statute given by God. Private property was originally given a sacred sanction through man's original dominion mandate over the earth. Men were handed God's directive to work for their substance.[99] The principle of increasing private wealth by way of one's labors has been reconfirmed by God ever since: *"Wealth gotten by vanity, shall be diminished: but he that gathereth by labour, shall increase"* (Proverbs 13:11). For one person to take property from another by theft, bribery, blackmail, extortion, fraud, force, or coercion are all ways in which one violates the steward ownership of others.

Just as a violation of the Sixth Commandment: *"thou shalt not kill,"* is a violation of the image of God granted to man in the Creation Covenant, a violation of the Eighth Commandment: *"thou shalt not steal,"* is a violation of a dominion right granted concurrently.[100] Under the Creation Covenant, men still remain accountable to God in their property holdings. They are mere caretakers who maintain an ongoing account with their Sovereign Creator,[101] and, according to William Perkins, all men are but the stewards of His possessions: *"God is not only their sovereign Lord, but the Lord of their riches, and that they themselves are but the stewards of God, to employ and dispense them, according to his will."*[102]

Every family has thus been given a responsibility for the dominion that Providence has placed in its hands. God knows the needs of each household and His purpose for the abundance which He has provided:

> *And the end of a mans calling is not to gather riches for himselfe, for his familie, for the poore; but to serve God in the serving of man, and in seeking the good of all men; and to this end, men must apply their lives and labours.*[103]

Alms and charity were given on a needs basis in the Scripture. Accordingly, when someone or a group of individuals were in specific need, individuals or churches would assist. Assistance was not given as a programmed public show, but provided through discreet donations or privately to individuals, as Christ commanded: *"That thine almes may be in secret: and thy Father which seeth in secret, himself shall reward thee openly"* (Matthew 6:4). And, according to the Apostles, private family assistance was required by one's own faithful family members for all mutual members in need: *"If any man or woman that beleeveth have widows, let them relieve them, and let not the church be charged; that it may relieve them that are widows indeed"* (1 Timothy 5:16).

According to the models presented in Scripture, assistance to others is to be provided as actual needs present themselves. True charity is a matter of a heart's specific response to the immediate distress of others. It stems from one's own gratitude for God's gracious sustenance in the past, and carries the promise of one's continued blessings in the future (see Deuteronomy 24:17-19). Personal welfare and care for the sick was appropriately shown in this late fifteenth-century illustration from a devotional prayer book.

99. See Genesis 3:19.
100. See Genesis 1:26.
101. See Matthew 25:14-30.
102. Perkins, *The Whole Cases of Conscience*, p. 308.
103. Ibid.

Each person has an obligation (according to God's blessing upon him or his family) to care for others in need: *"Then the disciples, every man according to his ability, determined to send relief unto the brethren which dwelt in Judea"* (Acts 11:29). Charity is therefore to be given on a needs basis and not on a social basis, as there are commands to feed the hungry, but none to eliminate world hunger; there are admonitions to assist those in need, but none to eliminate all human needs through social engineering or civil redistribution of wealth.

Nehemiah, the leader of the Hebrews following their seventy years of captivity in Babylon, certainly respected private property rights. He was thus outraged when excessive imposition, or *"usury,"* was forced upon them by their own *"nobles"* and *"rulers,"* and decried: *"You exact usury, every one of his brother"* (Nehemiah 5:7). Nehemiah accordingly charged them *"to make a covenant of restitution"* (Nehemiah 5, introductory note), and demanded: *"Restore, I pray you, to them, even this day, their lands, their vineyards, their oliveyards, and their houses"* (Nehemiah 5:11). The nobility and rulers then conceded by avowing:

> *We will restore them, and will require nothing of them; so will we do as thou sayest. Then I* [Nehemiah] *called the priests and took an oath that they should do according to this promise* (Nehemiah 5:12).

A. This is an early sixteenth-century woodcut showing nobles and public officials extracting usury from their subjects. Such corruption resulted in private iniquity and public injustice.

According to many such biblical precedents, neither the private person nor the public servant can tread upon another's goods without treading upon God's sanction of private property. Both excessive interest rates and excessive public fees, that Nehemiah called *"usury,"* represent infractions of God's Commandment not to steal. And, no individual or nation has a right to arbitrarily dispossess families of their goods or property without violating God's statute against fraud or theft.[104]

B. Immediately following the restoration of Jerusalem at the time of Nehemiah, Judea was the dominion of a potentially thriving commonwealth. God's public Temple was shown here set peaceably amid the Israelites' private dwellings at a time when proper respect was given to both Judea's private and public interests. This depiction of Judea's capital city of Jerusalem was included in a Venetian *Haggadah* (circa 1740).

Private property is recognized as having a legitimate title which can be transferred by the mutual consent of various parties.[105] In that case, the property may be sold or given to assist others to relieve their needs. And, those in public authority should encourage that as a private practice.[106] But, the title to one's private property is not to be obtained by way of public fraud under the pretext of public charity. That is simply 'playing God' with another man's goods. It is not a governor's prerogative to decide who more 'fairly' deserves the moneys or goods held in private possession, nor is he authorized to use coercive civil power to exact one's charity. As God alone reigns over all private and public property interests, His Eighth Commandment sanctions both private charity and public restraint within one universal moral Law.

104. See God's condemnation of public fraud and theft in 1 Kings 21.
105. See Acts 4:34-35; 5:4.
106. See Leviticus 25:35-37.

IX. The Ninth Commandment

The Ninth Commandment was an unqualified statute to preserve truth:

> *Thou shalt not bear false witness against thy neighbour* (Exodus 20:16).

A.

Truth is the basis of all surety, and falsehood is the basis of discord and instability. Bearing slander or a false witness therefore undermines all positive relations. Societies of men can neither be built nor maintained upon lies, libels, perjuries, or slanders. Therefore, the early reformers saw the Command as an obligation to speak in a positive light of others as best one could in truth: *"But further his good name, and speak truth."*[107]

A. Falsehoods, lies, slanders, or gossips undermine the integrity of any society. Two talebearers were portrayed in this illustration by Holbein (circa 1530).

A. As a Commandment to individual Israelites: they lived under their Lord, *"long-suffering, and abundant in goodnesse and truth"* (Exodus 34:6). Each individual was avowed to honor Him and model His character. In modeling Him, they were each granted subordinate responsibilities to *"Speak ye every man the truth to his neighbour: execute the judgement of truth and peace"* (Zechariah 8:16). The Israelite was commanded to be a testimonial witness among God's chosen people and to therefore honor His nature in all his dealings with others. Their Lord was Himself the mark of honesty, and He consistently commanded devout honesty among each and every one: *"Thou shalt not go up and down as a talebearer among thy people: neither shalt thou stand against the blood of thy neighbour"* (Leviticus 19:16).

Dishonesty was a vile pollutant to the fabric of Israelite society. So, in the words of King Solomon, public lies and perjury could not be overlooked: *"A false witness shall not be unpunished ..."* (Proverbs 19:5). Throughout Israel's existence there were many (not too gentle) reminders to be honest in one's dealings, for each Israelite had the highest obligation to maintain the Lord's integrity in his associations and transactions. As His covenanted people, they were thoroughly admonished to *"neither deal falsly, neither lie one to another"* (Leviticus 19:11). Also, being true to God's Law was being true to God. Thus, later, the Hebrew Apostle John could also warn the New Covenant "Israelite": *"He that saith, I know him, and keepeth not His commandments, is a liar, and the truth is not in him"* (1 John 2:4).

B.

SALOMON REX

B. King Solomon of Israel was the author of God's timeless Words of wisdom in the *Book of Proverbs*. The youthful king was illustrated here by Holbein (circa 1530).

B. As a Commandment to the covenant nation: Israel knew its Lord as the true God and the sole source of justice.[108] It had a double obligation to uphold His truth as the standard of its own legal legacy, and by reflection, uphold His standard to the world.[109] The fact that Israel was redeemed from Egypt as a nation

107. Geneva note on Exodus 20:16, leaf D7.
108. See Psalm 89:8, 13-14; Proverbs 21:2-3.
109. See Deuteronomy 4:5-8.

A.

A. The object of the Israelite court was to determine the true facts behind a dispute and to render a judgment based on those facts in light of God's Statutes. Perjury, or a *"false witness,"* before the court would undermine its primary object of obtaining truth and thereby corrupt the entire Israelite system of justice. This early sixteenth-century woodcut shows witnesses presenting the facts of a case before a Hebrew court (1529).

B.

B. The Covenant Law and the King:

As illustrated in this woodcut included on a title page of the first printed English Bible in 1535, Josiah, the king of Judah, renewed the Covenant Law. Here, Josiah was shown having the Law read in his presence (2 Kings 22:10-13), and he repented due to its sharp condemnation of his nation. Then, gathering the elders and people of Judah, he *"made a covenant before the LORD, to walk after the LORD, and to keep his commandments and his testimonies and his statutes with all their heart and all their soul, ..."* (2 Kings 23:3).

and was the repository of His covenantal promise toward the world bound them in a double engagement to represent the true and living God.[110] When Israel, which was commanded to practice truthfulness under its double mantle, fell into dishonest and deceptive practices, it failed in both its national covenant as well as in its charge before the world. Thus, the prophet Jeremiah declared that the Hebrews had become estranged from their Lord: *"... they are not valiant for the truth upon the earth; for they proceed from evil to evil, and they know not me, saith the LORD"* (Jeremiah 9:3). As they continued to ignore God's demand for truthfulness, they lost trustworthiness among themselves as a nation. Their Lord therefore warned them again by way of Jeremiah: *"Take ye heed every one of his neighbour, and trust ye not in any brother: for every brother will utterly supplant, and every neighbour will walk with slanders"* (Jeremiah 9:4). At that point the nation had lost its integrity and thus its worth. God's nation had collapsed as a heap of immoral ruin; Jeremiah then proceeded to proclaim God's judgment: *"I will scatter them among the heathen, whom neither they nor their fathers have known"* (Jeremiah 9:16).

Since God's chosen nation failed to uphold His standard of truth among the nations, God used the nations around Israel as His means of humiliating His own. God used those who had not known the intimacy of His truths to purge those who did know His truths of their lies.

By contrast, God's purpose in the Command can be seen in its healthy light. The Law of God as a positive Commandment asserted that Israel serve the Lord *"in sincerity and in truth"* (Joshua 24:14). Thus, the key to Israel's health was for it to be fixed upon its high and holy Sovereign and be devoted to His Law.[111] God would then secure the nation and maintain it in His truth as a matter of its trust: *"Trust in him at all times: ye people pour out your heart before him: God is a refuge for us. Selah. Surely men of low degree are vanity, and men of high degree are a lie, to be laid in the balance..."* (Psalm 62:8-9). King David indeed understood the principle of maintaining a nation's high and healthy trust in God as a matter of its own high and honest integrity.

110. See Jeremiah 10:10.
111. See Proverbs 3:7-8.

C. As a moral Mandate to mankind: the Ninth Commandment demands the honesty and integrity that God first established in the Creation Covenant. Those two virtues were lost amid the lies in man's fall from Paradise. By falling for the serpent's lie, the first man and woman set mankind up to be deceived ever since.[112] By believing the lies of the creature rather than the truth of the Creator, they inverted man's integrity and destroyed the honest openness that they had enjoyed in their innocence. Deception is antithetical to God's nature, and lies about His truth and sovereignty have been successfully propagated upon mankind ever since. For mankind to be deceived into thinking that it can make its way safely and peaceably apart from God's overarching truth is merely the natural extension of that original lie. For human associations to maintain any semblance of integrity, they must rest firmly upon the essential truth that God is the Creator and Preserver of mankind.[113] To deny such a fundamental fact is to deny the source of all truth and bring an end to the integrity of any people.[114] Richard Baxter correctly asked, *"Can the infinite God make a temporary finite imperfect Creature the ultimate end of his intentions ... ?"*[115] In earlier times, such notable societal thinkers understood an essential link between the truth of society's accountability to God and the strength of its social fiber. For instance, the seventeenth-century philosopher John Locke, who was heavily influenced by Puritans such as Baxter, wrote that the bonds of all legitimate associations rest upon this simple truth: *"Promises, Covenants, and Oaths, which are the Bonds of Humane Society, can have no hold upon an Atheist. The taking away of God, though but even in thought, dissolves all."*[116] Thus, for mankind to live in any integrity requires us to live in the basic truths underpinning our existence. Though the Ninth Commandment specifically pertains to lies against one's neighbor, all human untruth stems from the first lie against the Creator.

Whether coming in the form of deceits, slanders, or frauds among individuals, families, congregations, or communities, all falsehood destroys the fabric of any personal or societal commitment. Solomon, a man gifted with great wisdom and the earliest (and likely the greatest) of all mankind's philosophers, wrote that among the things that God hates are: *"A false witnesse that speaketh lies, and him that soweth discord among brethren"* (Proverbs 6:19). All untruth yields discord and instability, and no falsehood escapes God's gaze. Truth is therefore a great prize to be continually sought by all godly men and women. The love of God and one's fellow man causes them to continually fight to preserve God's truth as well as to resist all societal tolerance of untruth. The cause of maintaining truth has indeed been the historic mantle of those who have, in the past, lived in genuine conviction of God's foremost precepts.[117]

The ultimate *"false witnesse"* came in the betrayal of Jesus Christ by His disciple Judas Iscariot. Judas lived the epitome of a deceptive life by pretending on one hand to be a close friend of the Savior, yet acting as His staunchest enemy on the other. The two juxtaposed positions came together in the form of a (apparently) friendly kiss that Judas gave to Jesus just after he had secretly received a generous bounty for the betrayal. The scene was depicted in this fifteenth-century woodcut with another disciple, Peter, naively ready to defend his Savior against approaching soldiers (1497).

112. See Genesis 3:4-5.
113. See Psalm 100:1-5.
114. See Jeremiah 10:10-12.
115. Baxter, *A Holy Commonwealth*, p. 28.
116. John Locke, *A Letter Concerning Toleration* (1690), p. 67.
117. See Proverbs 12:15-22.

X. The Tenth Commandment

The Tenth Commandment, typically summarized as *"Thou shalt not covet"* (Exodus 20:17), forbade the aggressive desire for either the persons or property belonging to others. It also spoke of a solace with things remaining out of our grasp and a security with God's current provision. Like the Seventh Commandment, it involved respect for the person of others, and like the Eighth Commandment, it involved respect for their property. Thus, the whole Commandment read:

> *Thou shalt not covet thy neighbours house, thou shalt not covet thy neighbours wife, nor his man-servant, nor his maid-servant, nor his ox, nor his asse, nor any thing that is thy neighbours* (Exodus 20:17).

Among the several vices engraved on the title page of a 1522 annotated Latin New Testament, were these figures representing warnings against suspicious jealousy, craft, and envy. The Tenth Commandment forbids all such sins of the heart.

To fix one's desires upon a neighbor's wife, servant, or property was to ignore God's provision and sufficiency. Because coveting focused on illicit gratification, it put desire above the source of blessing. Covetousness again inverted the order of Creation. God was to be the focus of one's desires and His provision was to bring earthly satisfaction.

Neither the secularist nor the humanist can have such peace with the world, as they must find ever more creative systems of transferring or redistributing material abundance.[118] But, material gratification cannot satisfy, as the Christian reformer William Perkins wrote centuries ago that the simple key to true satisfaction was in establishing one's heart upon God's providence: *"They whiche seek the Lord, shall want* [lack] *nothing that is good."*[119]

Presenting genuine needs and desires before God was clearly not forbidden in the Command,[120] nor was there a prohibition to *"covet"* greater service to Him.[121] The Tenth Commandment prohibited selfishness and ill desires toward one's neighbor. The Geneva notes therefore contributed: *"Thou mayest not so much as wish his hinderance in any thing."*[122]

A. As a Commandment to Israelite individuals: God demanded that others' ownership rights be aggressively respected. Mutual respect was an essential feature of soundly self-governed people. There was no place for selfish discontent or flames of jealousy that would surely lead to the unraveled discord among a covenanted people. Illicit desires would not captivate their affections as long as their Lord commanded their hearts. His terms stated that those who sought Him[123] would find their true satisfaction in the increase of His blessing, and His blessings

118. Contrast with Psalm 34:10.
119. Perkins, *The Whole Cases of Conscience*, p. 310.
120. See 1 Kings 13:6; Psalm 5:1-3; 55:1-2; Daniel 6:11; Malachi 1:9.
121. See 1 Corinthians 12:31.
122. Geneva note on Exodus 20:17, leaf D7.
123. See Psalm 107:9.

came by way of the abundance of their own labors: *"And sow the fields, and plant vineyards, which may yeeld fruits of increase"* (Psalm 107:37).

Their Lord, in His surety, had pledged Himself to increase all those that honored Him: *"He will blesse them that fear the LORD, both small and great. The LORD shall increase you more and more, you and your children"* (Psalm 115:13-14). In return for their covenantal obedience, He would prosper them in a multigenerational abundance. When illicit gratification captivated the Israelite's attention, vanity became his ravenous master which could not be satisfied. He was left to either be consumed by its temporary and insufficient desires or live with his Lord's formidable promise, because God's terms were binding even upon his innermost affections. The terms of the covenant therefore required each Israelite to depend on the Lord for his enduring satisfaction: *"He hath given meat unto them that fear him: he will ever be mindfull of his covenant"* (Psalm 111:5).

B. As a Commandment to the covenant nation: Israel was to keep its whole vision fixed upon its Lord. Its vision for national prosperity was set before the nation in specific terms of blessing. Its fruitful increase was a matter of consistent obedience to its Lord:

> *If ye walk in my statutes, and keep my commandments, and do them: Then I will give you rain in due season, and the land shall yeeld her increase, and the trees of the field shall yeeld their fruit* (Leviticus 26:3-4).

But, Israel's hopes for increase would be disappointed without true inward devotion to its covenant Lord:

> *And if ye shall despise my statutes, or if your soul abhor my judgements, so that ye will not do all my commandments, but that ye break my covenant: ... ye shall sowe your seed in vain, for your enemies shall eat it* (Leviticus 26:15-16).

Israel kept the two tablets of the Law in the *Ark of the Covenant*, which was itself kept by the priestly tribe of Levites. When the Israelites first entered the Promised Land, Joshua commanded that the Ark precede them as a sign of God's leading (Joshua 3). The procession of the Ark was shown by this woodcut in Martin Luther's publication of the complete German Bible in 1534.

Gratitude, and not covetousness, yielded Israel's prosperity. Its gratitude to its Lord resulted in national obedience. The nation's prosperity therefore did not rely upon its own desire for increase, nor upon its devotion to prosperity; those two tendencies reflect mere humanism and would lead to the nation's ruin. Its most exuberant display of passionate patriotism could not in itself bring Israel's abundance. Because of its covenanted nature, Israel's success rested with its continued humility and hearty dependence upon its faithful Sovereign. Its increase would neither come by faith in its own potentiality nor in its own ability to legislate social equality. The people of Israel were not equipped to legislate national increase or continued prosperity, for they were not equipped to play the role of their own Lord. *"The LORD maketh poor, and maketh rich: he bringeth low, and lifteth up"* (1 Samuel 2:7).

79

Coveting the Lord and His blessings were the true objects of national patriotism: *"... the LORD shall give that which is good: and our land shall yeeld her increase"* (Psalm 85:12). For Israelite rulers to remain patriotic as zealous supporters of their nation meant for them to be even-handed in their judgments – to neither favor one group to the exclusion of the rest, nor beguile one class (either the rich or the poor) at the expense of the other: *"Ye shall do no unrighteousnesse in judgement; thou shalt not respect the person of the poor, nor honour the person of the mighty: but in righteousnesse shalt thou judge thy neighbour"* (Leviticus 19:15). If Israel longed for the national good, it was to work to prevent covetous public or private greed and corruption: *"... O princes of Israel: remove violence and spoil, and execute judgment and justice, take away your exactions from my people, saith the Lord GOD"* (Ezekiel 45:9).

God's Word is necessary for justice: *Foxe's Book of Martyrs* illustrated justice as *"the weight and substance of God's blessed Word, against the doctrines and vanities of mens traditions"* (1641 edition).

Preventing national injustice was essential to the Israelite Commonwealth. As Richard Baxter put it: *"If injustice be predominant in the stated exercise of Government, it is but a combination of Robbers and deceivers."*[124] Thus was the weight of responsibility that the Lord put upon Israel's rulers. They were not placed in positions of authority to enable them to fix their gazes on the property of the people; they were only to administer justice under God's Laws in order to prevent the unbridled manifestation of greed and to protect the people's private property, thereby procuring the people's private increase. Administering God's justice would then secure the nation's own increase. National blessing would be advanced among all if all patriotically honored their Lord, as according to Moses:

Hear therefore, O Israel, and observe to do it, that it may be well with thee, and that ye may increase mightily, as the LORD God of thy fathers hath promised thee, in the land that floweth with milk and honey (Deuteronomy 6:3).

Coveting the property of others was clearly a negative-sum-game for Israel. Fixing its affections upon its true Sovereign and simply administering His holy ordinances meant true gain and wealth across the covenant land.

C. As a moral Mandate for mankind: God forbade all men and women to fix their hearts upon the things that could not satisfy. Obtaining the possessions of others could, at best, bring an illusion of gratification, for obtaining them would inflict a moral violation that would itself destroy the desired satisfaction. Like the delusion that accompanied Adam and Eve's desire when they fixed their eyes upon the forbidden tree, it appeared *"pleasant to the eyes, and a tree to be desired"* (Genesis 3:6), though it brought death into the world. All covetousness is likewise merely a mirage, for it delivers a far different result from that which appears at a distance.[125]

124. Baxter, *A Holy Commonwealth*, p. 130.
125. See Genesis 3:16-19; Proverbs 14:12.

Like the commandments that forbid adultery and stealing, the Tenth Commandment reconfirms the Creation Covenant's mandates to respect the sanctity of the possessions of others. But, unlike the former commands, it speaks specifically to the greedy passions of the heart. It goes to the vanity of the motivation behind the action. God therefore condemned the Gentile Chaldean *"who enlargeth his desire as hell, and is as death, and cannot be satisfied"* (Habakkuk 2:5). Whether Jew or Gentile, all worldly lust is expressed as the insatiable greed of covetousness.[126]

All those who covet have lust as their earthly lord and pride as their taskmaster.[127] Such men are ruled by an unbridled will, and become captive to the constraints of their limited, human imaginations. The all-knowing, clear-sighted God condemns such vanity as an attempt to construct a hedge against evil by means of mere human efforts: *"Wo to him that coveteth an evil covetousnesse to his house, that he may set his nest on high, that he may be delivered from the power of evil"* (Habakkuk 2:9). The best human efforts can therefore provide little security. Covetousness does not shield us from evil; it encourages our further evil as lust simply plants the seeds for a host of additional sins.[128]

A. This early seventeenth-century cartoon showed the vanity of coveting riches. The man who lived his life with a heart fixed on worldly fortune was here compared with the swine who professed: *"Mine is the desire, To roote in earth, and wallow in Mire."*

If, by relying on all the power that we possess is not enough to find satisfaction, where can it be found? The Puritan John Preston asked: *"What can a man desire more than to be satisfied?"*[129] Preston saw that a man's genuine satisfaction would only be found in his contentment within the "sphere" in which God had placed him. Far from contentment in illusions, a man or woman's earthly satisfaction would be found only through the actual means that God has ordained, such as honest work and honest gain, as well as using the unique positions in which God has placed them:

> *Consider thy selfe, that the varieties of the sufficiencies that God gives to men, ... every man in his place, he may have it within his spheare, so that there shall be no want of at all: for the Lord, out of his Almighty power, is able to doe it, that the desire may be satisfied as much, they may be filled in a lower condition as well as in a greater.*[130]

B. The allure of coveting glory:

This early seventeenth-century moral cartoon, *"Behoulde Your Glory,"* spoke to one of the most ravenous sins of the heart in which a man covets the kind of exaltation that God strictly retains for Himself. The all-too-prevalent appetite for glory by mortals actually represents the height of human pride and humanistic vanity. It causes individuals, nations, and even mankind to be blind to critical flaws and fatal insufficiency. Therefore, coveting self-glory was depicted here as the very reflection of death itself.

126. See Exodus 15:9; Numbers 11:4, 34; Psalm 78:18, 30; 81:12; 106:14; Proverbs 6:25.
127. See 1 John 2:16-17.
128. See James 1:14-15.
129. Preston, *The New Covenant*, p. 133. (Also see James 4:2.)
130. Ibid., p. 132.

81

A. The family hearth was the gathering place for household devotions, education, and personal conversation. The simple comfort of such discourse was shown in this late fifteenth-century illustration.

The way to find contentment in all human spheres is by submitting to God as our Provider and conforming to His design for our sufficiency. Abundance is found, for instance, by men and women living as husbands and wives and as fathers and mothers working together within the stations that God ordained. Our focus is therefore to be on both our distinct obligations to God as well as the general needs of our entire household. God's sufficiency is thus maintained in the coordinate work and mutual help of the whole, and not in pursuing unsatisfiable illusions of individual fulfillment. True satisfaction is found only in coordinate or covenantal commitments because we were made for no other. Fixing our desires upon the roles, positions, or stations of others ignores God's overall design as well as His individual calling for each man and woman. And, in the end, pursuing the kind of futile covetousness that is forbidden in the final Commandment will prove just as deadly for us as was the serpent's advice pursued by Adam and Eve.

The Covenant Law and Grace

B. By washing His disciples' feet, Christ demonstrated the gracious character in covenantal obedience, as was shown in this sixteenth-century Bible woodcut by Bernard Solomon (1555).

Faithfulness to God and care for one another was the key to keeping God's Ten great Statutes. Loving God with one's whole heart, with one's whole soul, and with one's whole mind, as well as loving one's neighbor as one's self, formed the crux of the requirements that God placed upon Israelite individuals, the Hebrew nation, and all mankind.[131] The Covenant Law of God therefore did not take away from the unqualified promise of grace that followed the lineage of Israel. The Law was not a new Covenant of Works that replaced the old Covenant of Grace.[132] It defined, refined, and reinforced the terms of obedience that were resonant with the same Grace Covenant that was imparted after the fall to Adam, to Noah, to Abraham, and then to Moses. The moral Law given through Moses confirmed the terms of obedience required in all the manifestations of God's grace from Creation up to the redemption of Israel from Egypt.

The Law thus perfectly defined an individual Israelite's obligation in his free self-governance; it perfectly commanded the obedience of a liberated covenant nation; and it perfectly confirmed God's moral Mandates for the faithful service of mankind. Though not intended by God to effect perfect works of obedience by which we might earn our salvation (for therein they simply prove our perfect cursedness), nevertheless, the Ten Commandments were God's great covenantal expressions of His moral will and a gift to all men as a radiant revelation of the standards of His perfect Being:

> *And he declared unto you his covenant, which he commanded you to perform, even ten commandments, and he wrote them upon two tables of stone* (Deuteronomy 4:13).[133]

131. See Matthew 22:37-40; Deuteronomy 6:5; Leviticus 19:18.
132. See Galatians 3:17-18.
133. Also see Deuteronomy 10:12-13.

Book I Christianity's Covenantal Inheritance

Chapter 6: The Gracious Fulfillment

The Triumph of Grace and the Covenantal Inheritance of the Church of Messiah Jesus

PON issuing the Covenant Law, God proceeded toward the promise of its fulfillment. As stated before, the moral Law required the Israelites' obedience for their earthly fruition, and they in fact suffered greatly for breaking it. But, as a means to heavenly fruition, its perfect fulfillment could only come by the promised One who would live in the perfect obedience required for salvation. His ancient promise was that God Himself would see to its perfect fulfillment in grace. Therefore, as Moses sprinkled the blood of the covenant over the people when he presented them with the Law,[1] he prophetically signified *"that the covenant broken, cannot be satisfied without blood shedding."*[2]

The Prophetic Priesthood

Besides that of Moses, there were many other signs and directives pointing toward a future sacrifice, king, and covenant. For example, a sacrifice was foretold in Abraham's prophetic statement that God would provide a lamb for the fulfillment of the promise. Upon his willingness to give up his own son Isaac, Abraham's faith had assured him that God would provide His own sacrifice to pay the irreconcilable debt of men to God.[3] The Levitical, or priestly, ceremonies were then added as covenantal signs – as prophetic illustrations – of the promise's true, future priestly sacrifice.[4] The Israelite priesthood offered temporal symbols of that which would come in the acceptable, eternal fulfillment of the ceremonial Law, as the priestly sacrifices instituted under Moses and Aaron pointed to God's own provision. Thus, the Levitical rites or rituals themselves also illustrated (in intricate and graphic detail) their own fulfillment through the priestly sacrifice in Messiah's future death and resurrection. The Israelites were therefore to look ahead to that perfect fulfillment of both the moral Law and its priestly rites.

For the Israelites, the covenantal rites of their ceremonial Law also required the same faith as that of Abraham's: *"Of things which are everlasting, which were promised to the fathers, and exhibited in Christ."*[5] The priestly sacrificial

1. See Exodus 24:7-8.
2. Geneva note on Exodus 24:8, leaf E.
3. See Genesis 22:8.
4. Compare Exodus 29:1-12 with Hebrews 9:18-22.
5. Geneva note on Hebrews 10:1, leaf Nnn2.

Moses and Aaron were placed in the roles of covenant judge and priest, both flanking the Law:

In this early seventeenth-century engraving, Moses was pictured on the left pointing heavenward to God, who would come to fulfill the Law as Christ. Under the two tablets was engraved: "... *grace and trueth came by Jesus Christ.*" To the right of Moses stood Aaron, dressed in his more formal priestly garments. Both men were pictured before the Ark of the Covenant, the temple, the altar, and various articles used in the Hebrew sacrificial rites, all which symbolically foretold the perfect sacrifice of Christ. This illustration was used as a vignette on John Speed's famous English map of Canaan (1595).

rites prophetically pointed toward that same blessed satisfaction in the coming Messiah. The covenant of promise given to Abraham was simply visually enhanced with the elaborate demonstrations of the ceremonial rites added through Moses. But, the covenant was one and the same promise, one and the same grace, and one and the same fulfillment in the one true sacrificial offering of the one and the same Lamb. The whole of the priestly ordinances which were demonstrated in the ceremonial Law was thereby finished[6] – satisfied once for all – in the physical sacrifice of the true covenant Lamb: *"By the which will we are sanctified, through the offering of the body of Jesus Christ once for all"* (Hebrews 10:10). Abraham's substitutional Lamb was pictured in the Mosaic ceremonial rites. The images of both the Lamb and the rites pointed toward the same sacrificial life that fulfilled the terms of the moral Law. Thus, all the souls in ancient Israel that were eternally redeemed were saved by one and the same faith, looking forward to the covenantal Lamb, to His substitutional life and death, to His covenantal sacrifice, and to His covenantal fulfillment.

The Prophetic Men of God

It is at this point that we can see the dual role of the historic "Old Covenant" prophets. Both Abraham, in prophesying the Lamb, and Moses, in sprinkling the blood, were used by God in powerful testimonies of heavenly glories to come. Yet, they were also both used by Him to reveal the obedience that always accompanied His eternal promise on earth. Therein we see the similar roles that the Almighty had designated for the prophetic men who followed. As God, He called men out to repeatedly remind His people that the covenant Messiah was on His way, and as Lord, He called them out to repeatedly remind them to love and obey His Laws. Time after time the prophets extolled the promise, and time after time the same prophets extolled the Law. The prophet Zechariah, for example, could lament in reflection:

> *Yea, they made their hearts as an adamant-stone, lest they should hear the law, and the words which the LORD of hosts hath sent in his spirit by the former prophets: therefore came a great wrath from the LORD of hosts* (Zechariah 7:12).

6. See John 19:30.

And, the same prophet could also rehearse in hopeful anticipation: *"And I will pour upon the house of David, and upon the inhabitants of Jerusalem, the spirit of grace and of supplications, and they shall look upon me whom they have pierced"* (Zechariah 12:10).

Both passages were concurrent Words of their covenant Lord and God; the former lamented the wrath due their circumstance, and the latter rehearsed the unconditional hope in the Messiah. It grieved the souls of the prophets that Israel and Judah would not obey their covenant Lord, but it delighted the souls of the prophets that many foresaw the coming of the promise. The failure of Israel did not cause God to create the promise, as the promise preceded the founding of the nation by centuries. The Law, then, did not negate the purpose of the promise, nor did the promise negate the purpose of the Law,[7] though proclaiming both was (lest we forget) the often thankless task of the prophet:

> *Who through faith subdued kingdoms, wrought righteousnesse, obtained promises, stopped the mouths of lions, Quenched the violence of fire, escaped the edge of the sword, out of weaknesse were made strong* (Hebrews 11:33-34).

The promise and Law came together in the testimonials, in the lives, and even in the deaths of the prophets who died *"having obtained a good report through faith received not the promise"* (Hebrews 11:39). Though the prophets did not live to see the fulfillment, they faithfully obeyed God, proclaiming that both the Law and the promise were essential in the coming manifestation of the Messiah to the world:

> *But now is made manifest, and by the scriptures of the prophets according to the commandment of the everlasting God, made known to all nations for the obedience of faith* (Romans 16:26).

A.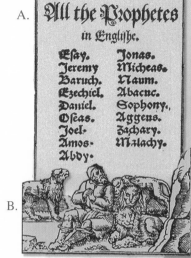

A. This is a list of *"All the Prophetes in Englishe,"* from the title page of the Prophets in the first complete English Bible, printed in 1535.

B. Daniel, one of the many long-suffering prophets, sat precariously amid a den of lions, as illustrated on the same English title page.

C. This is a section of a rare Hebrew sheepskin scroll of the Prophecy of Isaiah. It contains the text of chapters 48 through 54, which foretold the suffering of Messiah Jesus (Isaiah 53). This copy dates from the seventeenth century in eastern Europe.

D. This woodcut depicts the actual events prophesied by Isaiah, in which Messiah Jesus bore the sins of many. Consistent with Isaiah's ancient words and Jesus' own notice of His eminent death (Matthew 23:28), Messiah Jesus sacrificially fulfilled all the requirements of the Law for salvation and delivered on God's gracious promise to Abraham. The scene was illustrated by Jan Chistoffel in 1649.

7. See Matthew 5:17-19.

The Prophetic Covenant of David

Israel's King David also knew the equation; he recognized that the transcendent God was the true Ruler of his realm and that his own title simply pointed toward the One far greater than himself. As a governor, David bowed to the Law of his Lord, and as a king, he merely pointed to the true King of Kings. Just as Israel's government had been under Moses and the judges before David's time, the covenant of Israel also defined his vertical obligation to his Lord. David, as monarch, bowed to his Lord, saying, *"Thou art good, and dost good: teach me thy statutes"* (David's prayer: Psalm 119:68). God therefore demanded that Israel's king be *"a man after his [God's] own heart"* (1 Samuel 13:14), meaning that the Israelite title of "king" was subjective, and the real object of "King" was reserved by God. David was therefore not considered an omnipotent monarch by his fellow brethren. At Hebron, David was merely anointed among his fellow brethren, the elders of Israel.[8] He remained one of them. As chosen by their consent, his horizontal authority was confirmed according to a covenant between them: *"So all the elders of Israel came to the king to Hebron, and king David made a league with them in Hebron before the LORD: and they anointed David king over Israel"* (2 Samuel 5:3). The nature of Israel's covenantal king could then be seen in its twofold covenantal directive. In his vertical duty, David retained all the obligations of Israel's covenant with the Lord: *"And David perceived that the LORD had established him king ..."* (2 Samuel 5:12), and in his horizontal duty, he maintained all the constituted obligations among his fellow elders: *"and king David made a league with them ..."* (2 Samuel 5:3).

All rulers must attend to the supreme Lord over the earth. King David of Israel was depicted worshipping God in this engraving that appeared in an early American, federal period Bible (1792). David was shown admonishing all nations: *"O praise the Lord all ye nations: praise him all ye people"* (Psalm 117:1).

Israel then had its vassal king. The reason God permitted a king to exist in Israel was to use its symbolism just as He had used the symbolism of the Levitical priesthood – to point toward their Messiah. The title of "king" in Israel was simply pointing toward that real and everlasting Monarch. David's title was a mere signpost and an illustration of One to come in his lineage who would be the omnipotent Ruler. God thus made still another extension of His promise of grace, this time involving David, and this time including a most kingly feature: *"I have made a covenant with my chosen, I have sworn unto David my servant, Thy seed will I establish for ever, and build up thy throne to all generations"* (Psalm 89:31). The successive kings that followed David simply carried the prophetic mantle of his covenant. They also carried a governing mantle between the king and the nation, as they were to be vassal kings. For example, at the coronation of King Joash, the priest Jehoiada anointed him with the royal title, but he reigned as a vassal both under God and alongside the people:

> *And Jehoiada made a covenant between the LORD, and the king and the people, that they should be the LORDS people; between the king also and the people* (2 Kings 11:17).

8. See 2 Samuel 5:1.

The priest mediated God's covenant between the king and the people, binding the king with his nation. The priest represented God in the anointing of royalty, showing the covenantal connection of Messiah's heavenly lineage (as God) with Messiah's earthly lineage (as David's seed). The life and death of Messiah would indeed manifest His manly service to God's people,[9] as His resurrection would manifest His godly dominion over the world. He would rule over all men, all families, and all nations, in accord with His divine Kingship:

> To make known to the sons of men, his mighty acts, and the glorious majesty of his kingdom. Thy kingdom is an everlasting kingdom, and thy dominion endureth thorowout all generations (Psalm 145:12-13).

In adopting the governing mode of kingship over Israel, God also reintroduced the patriarchal succession of father to son that existed before. The idea of fatherly succession pointed to God's supremely royal lineage passed on to His divine Son. King David therefore said toward the end of his forty-year reign: *"Howbeit, the LORD God of Israel chose me before all the house of my father, to be king over Israel for ever"* (1 Chronicles 28:4). David saw the covenant as an unfathomable grace. He was in awe that God had sovereignly chosen to enter a covenant with him in order to demonstrate the manner of the promise's fulfillment. God's engagement taught David to *"magnifie the mercy of God."*[10] David was humbled that the great God of heaven and earth would enter a compact to *"tye himselfe, and bind himselfe to be a debtor to me,"*[11] and he saw it as no small event for a mere earthly king to be allowed to engage with the promised King of Kings. David had prophetically addressed the eternal dominion of his own future Sovereign. Speaking under the inspiration of God's Holy Spirit, the Apostle Peter later recalled that kingly covenant, showing that David had fully understood the implications of God's promise to him:

> Therefore [David] *being a prophet, and knowing that God had sworn with an oath to him, that of the fruit of his loyns, according to the flesh, He would raise up Christ to sit on his throne* (Acts 2:30-31).

The Messiah would therefore come with kingly dominion. Like His natural forefather David, He would serve God for the benefit of the sons of Israel, and like David, He would fulfill God's qualification for a true Israelite king, being *"a man after his* [God's] *own heart"* (1 Samuel 13:14). But, unlike David, He would come in perfect obedience to the comprehensive Commandments of

A. This is the beautifully designed opening page of the Psalms as it appeared in the first edition of the 'King James' Bible in 1611. It included God's declaration: *"O yee Kings: be instructed ye Judges of the earth. Serve the LORD with feare, and rejoyce with trembling. Kisse the Sonne lest he be angry ..."* (Psalm 2:10-12).

B. Christ was shown ruling the earth, ascendant above His creation and sitting upon the covenant rainbow, as illustrated on the title page of *Foxe's Book of Martyrs* (1641 edition).

9. See Isaiah 53:7.
10. Preston, *The New Covenant*, p. 331.
11. Ibid.

A. The 'Transfiguration' (Luke 9:31) showed a unity of the Law and the prophets with the New Covenant, as portrayed in Tyndale's New Testament (1636 edition).

A.

God. And, unlike David, He would have a timeless dominion over the whole earth. As Messiah's dominion was universal, He would reign over every human authority *"... visible and invisible, whether they be thrones, or dominions, or principalities, or powers, all things were created by him, and for him"* (Colossians 1:16). His office was not confined to the physical lineage of the sons of Israel, as both the circumcised Hebrew and the uncircumcised "Gentile" (non-Hebrew) would be under His glorious dominion. Gentiles who had not previously known the promise, *"being aliens from the commonwealth of Israel, and strangers from the covenants of promise"* (Ephesians 2:12), would partake in the promise by way of Christ's victory and His eternal reign over the earth.

The New Covenant Dominion

Along with David's covenant came a greater manifestation of the kingly promise, as it pointed to a much wider dominion. In that covenant promise, all majesty was added to the former promises of grace given to Adam, Noah, Abraham, the Patriarchs, and Moses, as well as to the prophets. Each successive manifestation of the promise had been spoken with greater clarity, all pointing toward the same fulfillment. The entire Old Covenant period represented one massive arrow pointing toward Christ. All of the gracious covenants from Adam through Malachi thereby represented one continuous shaft with a single promissory point.

All the prior covenants therefore came together in God's first proclamation of the *"new covenant"* (Jeremiah 31:31). As the reformers' Geneva Bible concurred: *"Though the covenant of redemption made to the Fathers, and this which was given after, seem divers, yet they are all one and grounded on Jesus Christ ... ."*[12]

B.

The New Covenant's historic shaft was therefore forged with each of God's prior covenants, with its tip honed into a single, royal priesthood. The whole of mankind's prior hopes for eternal redemption were thereby targeted in the life, death, and resurrection of a single, distinct Soul.

All the old covenants pointed to the coming of Messiah. All targeted the heart of the "New Covenant" foretold by Jeremiah: *"I will put my law in their inward parts, and write it in their hearts"* (Jeremiah 31:33). The New Covenant was directed at the heart of man's bondage to sin, a servitude that gripped all men due to their hapless and inescapable violations of God's Commandments. Inherent disobedience was in the heart of all men and

B. This is an excerpt of Jeremiah's prophecy (chapter 31) in which God promised the *"new covenant."* The Geneva Bible's side-note *"h"* showed the Reformed view that all of the gracious biblical covenants are one, in so far that they are all *"grounded"* on Jesus Christ. Both Old and New *"are all one and grounded on Jesus Christ, save that this is called new, because of the manifestation of Christ, and the abundant graces of the holy Ghost given to his Church under the Gospel"* (1594 edition of the Geneva version).

12. Geneva note explaining Jeremiah 31:31, leaf Kk8.

their greatest bondage was a matter of their inward makeup. The New Covenant therefore targeted that inward heart, and also marked the fruition of a marvelous covenantal inheritance. All the outward forms, rites, and promises of Israel's kingdom and priesthood came together in the defining moment of man's redemption. All Jews, as well as Gentiles, were otherwise hopelessly bound under the weight of uniform rebellion, as God's entire sweep of covenantal history folded together in the arrival, or "incarnation," of His divine kingly Son. All of human and divine history thereby formed Christianity's rich covenantal inheritance. All pointed to the same *"glad tidings"* of God's eternal promise of His own Son to mankind, as the Apostle John, a beloved friend of Jesus, declared:

> *And we declare unto you glad tidings, how that the promise which was made unto the fathers, God hath fulfilled the same unto us their children, in that he hath raised up Jesus again, as it is also written in the second psalm, Thou art my son, this day have I begotten thee* (Acts 13:32-33).

The *"tidings"* of which John spoke were not merely directed to the prior people of the promise. When the Jews turned Jesus over to Rome for execution, they turned their inheritance over to the world. Jesus was presented as a king,[13] and He presented Himself as King.[14] He was thereby crowned and robed, as well as mocked and condemned, accordingly.[15] The chief legal issue of Christ's Roman trial was over His Kingship. The Jewish officials recognized the kingly Roman jurisdiction above them, so they turned their King over to Rome for death at its hands.[16] The issue was one of royal authority, as Jesus was not stoned to death by the Hebrews, as would have been the case of a heretic.[17] By proclaiming Rome's sovereignty over Judah and giving Christ up for execution in the manner of a royal usurper or rebel, the Hebrews effectively handed their own legitimate King to the world. So, in an historic (and earth-shattering) irony, they turned Messiah over to the world to become its King. It brought a bittersweet (though sublimely ironic) fulfillment of God's great promise to Abraham in which the nations of the earth were to be blessed through his "Seed."[18]

The nations of the world would then become the inherited dominion of Jesus Christ upon His resurrection.[19] He rose not merely triumphant over Israel, but He rose as the King of Kings over the earth. His own brethren handed Him over, and in so doing, they gave up their own exclusive title

A.

B.

Jesus Christ as King of Kings:

A. Jesus was handed over to the Roman authorities and questioned concerning His royal status (see John 18:37). He was mocked as a king and scourged as a supposed usurper of the imperial system, as shown here in a devotional woodcut (1565).

B. Christ was then risen as King of Kings, as shown in this woodcut of the Lord standing holding His royal orb (globe), signifying His royal status as the King of the Earth (1497).

13. See John 19:14, 19.
14. See Matthew 21:2-5; 27:11; John 18:36-37.
15. See Matthew 27:29, 37.
16. See John 19:15.
17. See Deuteronomy 17:2-6.
18. Compare Genesis 18:18 with Galatians 3:16.
19. See Revelation 11:15; Colossians 1:16-20.

as Abraham's seed. Abraham's one "Seed" (Christ) therefore became the dominion ruler of the world as God had promised. Now, Christ as that Seed is the true dominion King of all. It was one nation's kingly loss but the whole earth's gain – it was one people's great sin but others' greater covenantal inheritance. The New Covenant therefore spoke to the kingdoms of mankind, as the Psalm that the Apostle John had addressed spoke to the *"kings of the earth"* and all the rulers who *"take counsell together, against the LORD"* (Psalm 2:2). The New Covenant therefore addresses both the innermost man and all the kingdoms of men – the hapless heart, as well as the rebellious nation.

The New Covenant Administration

Another key difference between the Old and the New Covenants is found in their distinct types of inner ministrations[20] and outward administrations.[21] Both Covenants, or Testaments, are grounded in Christ, and both embrace the same redemption, but the inner forms and the outward practices greatly distinguish the New from the Old.

The chief inner form, or ministration, of the Old Covenant had been servile obligation.[22] It was impressive but heavily imposing,[23] as both Moses and the people all quaked in fear at the Law's presentation.[24] Their inner motivation was thereby commanded by an outward manifestation through the senses – mainly by a sense of great awe in the demonstration of God's sovereign power. Nevertheless, the inward ministration of the Old Covenant was sufficient for the salvation of many through the Holy Spirit working faith in them, even though humanistic vanity still worked its destruction in the others.[25] The Old Covenant thus carried a heavy emphasis on the outward administration of its forms[26] by way of *"Promises, Prophecies, Sacrifices, Circumcision, the Paschal Lamb, and other types of Ordinances ... all signifying Christ to come."*[27] These outward forms and practices of administering the Old Covenant would be effective for a *"full remission of sins, and eternal Salvation,"*[28] but only for those Old Covenant saints operating in the genuine motive of faith by way of God's Spirit. The outward forms of administration were intended to direct their inward faith toward the substitutional obedience of Jesus Christ to come. In the future, He would pay the actual price for their *"remission of sins."*[29] So, just as the Apostle Peter looked back in time to the finished work of Christ in the remission of his sins, David had looked forward. Peter thus noted David's fore-faith in Christ: *"He seeing this before, spake of the resurrection of Christ, ..."* (Acts 2:31).

20. See John Preston, *The New Covenant*, pp. 319-320; and Westminster Assembly of Divines, *The Confession of Faith, Together with the Larger and Smaller Catechismes ...* (London, 1658), pp. 27-28.
21. Ibid.
22. See Preston, *The New Covenant*, p. 319.
23. Ibid.
24. See Hebrews 12:20-21.
25. See 1 Corinthians 10:1-5; and 2nd Geneva note on 1 Corinthians 10:3, leaf Iii7.
26. *Westminster Confession of Faith*, p. 27.
27. Ibid.
28. Ibid., p. 28.
29. See Acts 10:43; Psalm 130:7-8.

Whereas the Old Covenant was expressed in *"Types, and shadowes, and figures,"*[30] the New Covenant came to actual fruition with the *"death of Christ, and the satisfaction that He gave to his Father in his death, and likewise the inward satisfaction of the spirit."*[31] The Spirit works the sovereign will of the Father inwardly without the aid of priestly formalities, as described by John Preston: *"we* [Christians] *serve the Lord in spirit and truth, but there is not that visible light which was a help in their* [the ancient Israelites'] *weakness."*[32] By weighing the New Covenant's inward Spirit against the Hebrews' *"visible light,"* Preston was describing the heavier inner ministration of the New Covenant as opposed to the heavier outer administration of the Old. The inward ministration of faith now looks backward to the realization of a Christian's redemption in Christ. Types, shadows, and figures were put away, and a fuller ministration of God's Spirit now works within the New Covenant believers – with few outward formalities:

> Which, though fewer in number, and administered
> with more simplicity, and lesse outward glory: yet
> in them it is held forth in more fullness, evidence,
> and spiritual efficacy.[33]

There is therefore both a deeper and a wider focus to the New Covenant. It is more powerfully manifested inwardly to Christians and more powerfully manifested as obliging to the whole world. It represents a greater focus on the single convicted heart and the whole constituted world. The Old Covenant became New by the historic fact of Christ's perfect work on earth, though both Old and New Covenants point to the same Covenant of Grace in Him:

> There are not therefore two covenants of Grace,
> differing in substance but one and the same,
> differing in Dispensations.[34]

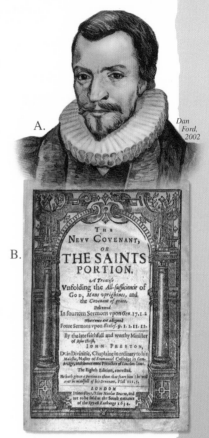

A.

Dan Ford, 2002

B.

A. John Preston (1578-1628) was a staunch advocate of the Reformed cause in England and regularly drew large crowds to hear his powerful preaching on covenantal Christianity.

B. Published following his death, Preston's book, *The New Covenant*, eventually became one of the most influential works of Reformed theology in both Old and New England. Shown here is the title page of the 1634 edition.

The variance of two *"dispensations"* mentioned in this quote from the Reformed *Westminster Confession of Faith*, refers to the two differing administrations, and was not a reference to two distinct works of God's sovereign grace. The same is true with other references to the term dispensation in the Scriptures. They simply refer to differences in terms of the administration of the same grace, as it now pertains to a new administration under Jesus Christ.[35] There is but one overall Covenant of Grace as there is but one way to salvation. Jesus

30. See Preston, *The New Covenant*, p. 326.
31. Ibid.
32. Ibid.
33. *Westminster Confession of Faith*, p. 28.
34. Ibid.
35. See 1 Corinthians 9:17; Ephesians 1:10; Ephesians 3:2; etc.

declared Himself to be the exclusive *"way, the truth and the life"* (John 14:6) of redemptive salvation: *" ... ye shall die in your sins: for if ye beleeve not that I am he, ye shall die in your sins"* (John 8:24). The old priestly forms were done away with in the New Covenant as they were all performed *"once, for all"* (Hebrews 10:9-10) in the sacrificial death of Jesus Christ. Jesus Himself replaced the old forms in the completion of His high priestly service.[36] Therefore, the new administration (or new outward forms) replaced the old. The New Covenant represented a new form of administration and not an alternate form of grace. Both Old and New Covenants involved the same ministration of the eternal, overall Covenant of Grace, though each simply differed in its forms of administration.

Features of Christianity's Covenantal Inheritance

New Covenant saints indeed have a glorious covenantal inheritance. First and foremost, as faith was the prime inner sign of gracious salvation in the Old Covenant, God has likewise graciously infused many hearts with that same essential criteria for salvation in the New Covenant. Yet, despite several obvious distinctions in their outward forms, many ordinances were continued or paralleled under the administration of Christ and His Apostles. And, without each of the following principled ordinances having been first authoritatively ordained and faithfully observed in Christ's Old Covenant, they would not be demonstrative of any significance in the lives of His New Covenant saints. The four central features of Christianity's covenantal inheritance are as follows:

I. The Inherited Covenantal Signs and Seals

Intended as a descriptive graphic, this woodcut illustrated the essentials of a Reformed congregation. Prominently featured was the covenant assembly gathered to hear God's Word, with the communion table and the baptismal (Foxe's *Actes and Monumentes*, 1641).

Ever since the great return to the purer administration of faith and fidelity in the sixteenth century, several essential elements of the Old Covenant have been traditionally recognized and practiced as part of a Reformed Christian ordination. Just as faith was once again more fully appreciated as the inward manifestation of salvation, so, too, was the purer meaning in its outward covenantal ordination.

Prime among the outward, or visible, features was the ordination of two parallel covenantal signs and seals. Whereas the Old Covenant was administered with seals by God through Abraham's ordination of circumcision and through Moses' ordination of the Passover, God has reordained these seals as Christian *"Baptisme and the Lords Supper."*[37] As the physical reality of God's grace was fully manifested in the sacrifice of Christ's body, thus completing the Abrahamic promise and Mosaic redemption, Christ

36. See Hebrews 10:19-22.
37. See Preston, *The New Covenant*, p. 326.

now *"hath new seales put to it."*[38]   Whereas the two visible signs (or sacraments) of circumcision and the Passover pointed toward Christ's actual ministry, their fulfillment in Him is now reconfirmed in two parallel, visible signs (or sacraments) of our remembrance.

Baptism

"*Baptisme,*" as a New Covenant sacrament or outward ceremony, represents the *"giving up unto God through Jesus Christ."*[39] The ordination of baptism thereby signifies the *"death of the old man, or sin,"*[40] according to the Geneva Bible's annotation. It represented admission into the covenant community as the New Covenant's direct representation of the Jewish circumcision, which was formerly *"a sign or seal of God's Covenant."*[41] The former covenantal rite was administered once to each male Israelite, sealing him as a member of the people of the promise. Its object was the seal of righteousness that was actually imputed to Abraham and his sons by faith.

A. Circumcision was an outward seal of an Israelite's covenant within the community of God's chosen, shown in a woodcut by Solomon Proops (1707).

New Covenant baptism is an ordinance that reflects circumcision in that it also signifies righteousness by faith: *"that is, to what end it is used, to wit, not onely to signifie, but also to seal up the righteousnesse of faith."*[42] Its object is the seal of the righteousness of Christ that is imputed to His covenant faithful. Old Covenant circumcision and New Covenant baptism therefore point to the same imputed reality. The actual inward working of God's Word is signified in its administration, which is the outward seal of the inward righteousness obtained through faith.

Baptism is also a sign that points toward the sanctification of all those who are raised to a new life in Christ. Both men and women are therefore outwardly sealed as those who actually partake of the inward *"vertue"* of Christ in a New Covenant: *"we which are his members rise for this end, that being made partakers of the self-same vertue, we should begin to lead a new life."*[43] Once baptized, the saint will thereafter outwardly demonstrate that inward life, as to *"walk in newness of life."*[44] New Covenant believers are thus both signed and sealed, each marked once by the sacrament as those who are expected to demonstrate covenantal lives amid fellow Christlike brethren and before the world.

B. Jesus was baptized by John the Baptist as a demonstration of His union with the Father and Spirit, and of His identity with those later baptized unto Him. Christ's baptism was depicted by this woodcut in Luther's *Catechism* (1529).

C. Like circumcision, the sacrament of baptism is an outward seal of the covenant within the body of God's chosen. The rite of infant baptism as adopted by the Anglican Church was shown by this woodcut in John Foxe's *Actes and Monumentes* (1641).

38. Ibid.
39. *Westminster Confession of Faith* on Baptism, p. 94.
40. Geneva note on Romans 6:3, leaf Hhh5.
41. Goodwin, *Moses & Aaron*, p. 213.
42. Geneva note on Romans 4:11, leaf Hhh5.
43. Geneva note on Romans 6:4, leaf Hhh5.
44. *Westminster Confession of Faith* on Baptism, p. 94.

A.

B.

A. Shown here is the text inset from the title page of a *Seder Haggadah* ("Passover Narration"). The narrative featured the ceremonial rites of the Hebrew Passover feast, as described in the Venetian *Haggadah* of 1740.

B. This is a small woodcut from an earlier *Seder Haggadah*, showing a Hebrew father teaching his son the meaning of the Passover table (from the Venetian *Haggadah* of 1629).

C.

D.

C. Christ instituted the sacrament of the Lord's Supper during His final Passover observance with His disciples, just prior to His death and resurrection. The setting was depicted here in an English *Devotional* engraving (1762).

D. The reformers restored the Lord's Supper and the Communion Table to the simplicity of its two elements of bread and wine, as illustrated in Foxe's *Actes and Monumentes* (1641 edition).

The Lord's Supper

The sacrament of the *"Lords Supper"* represents the Old Covenant's Passover that had previously sealed Israel's redemption. To the reformers, the Lord's Supper, or "Communion," was the New Covenant parallel of the Passover redemption *"when the Lord appeared unto them, and redeemed them out of the hand of the enemy."*[45] The Lord's Supper was instituted by Christ, the true Lamb of God, as *"the Sacrament of his Body and Blood"*[46] to be regularly *"observed in his Church unto the end of the World."*[47]

The object of the Old Covenant Passover had been Israel's seal of redemption, imputed by God in its deliverance from bondage to Egypt. The object of the Lord's Supper is the seal of the believers' redemption, imputed by Christ in their deliverance from bondage to sin. The Old Covenant Passover and the New Covenant Supper therefore both point to the redemption of God's covenant people. Like the Passover, the Lord's Supper is an outward ordinance regularly administered for a *"perpetual Remembrance,"*[48] and like the Passover, it outwardly seals the benefits of the reality in Christ. That seal is a repeated symbol of the continued nourishment from Christ, and the faith and obedience owed to Christ because of His gracious death.

As the Passover's *"Paschal Lamb"* was the element partaken in the Old Covenant ordinance, new *"elements"* of the Lamb of God[49] are partaken in the New Covenant sacrament. The Lord's Supper is administered by taking the elements of bread and wine, which represent the body and blood of Jesus Christ who was sacrificed once for the forgiveness of sins. Christ's single sacrifice paid the full price for remission of the sins of all those chosen by God unto salvation: *"For this is my blood of the new testament which is shed for many for the remission of sins"* (Matthew 26:28). Jeremiah's prophesy of God's New Covenant, stating: *"I will put my law in their inward parts"* (Jeremiah 31:33; also Hebrews 8:10), was completed in the sole sacrifice of Christ. His institution of the two sacraments of the Lord's Supper and Baptism therefore seal the gracious New Covenant.

45. Goodwin, *Moses & Aaron*, p. 106.
46. *Westminster Confession of Faith* on the Lord's Supper, p. 97.
47. Ibid.
48. Ibid.
49. See John 1:29; John 1:36.

II. The Inherited Covenantal Prayer and Worship

The New Covenant retains the Old Covenant's ordination of prayer and worship. Communication with God was represented by many different ways in the Old Covenant, such as confession, supplication, intercession, petition, thanksgiving, song, praise, prayer, and worship.[50] Of all these, prayer was the most basic term for addressing the Lord.[51] And, of all these, worship was the most basic term for expressing reverence to Him.[52] All of these ancient forms of communication were retained in the Christian covenantal inheritance, and all are essential expressions of people who are bound in a covenantal relation with God as their Lord.

Prayer

Prayer in the Old Covenant was a foundational way of addressing the Lord of Israel. Abraham's way of speaking with God was much more significant than the distant, formal, ritualistic rites common in his contemporary Babylon. Abraham's prayer exhibited a humble intimacy and a trusting understanding of God.[53] And, as each of Abraham's descendants prayed, they were also to address God in submissive humility, acknowledging His sovereign Lordship and understanding the terms of their overall covenant engagement. It followed that all Israelites were to pray, and all were to have faith that the merciful God would hear them:

> *What prayer and supplication soever be made by any man, or by all thy people Israel, ... Then hear thou in heaven thy dwelling place, and forgive, and do, and give to every man according to his wayes, whose heart thou knowest* (1 Kings 8:38-39).

On the other hand, when the Israelites failed to obey their covenantal obligations, the Lord would not answer their petitions, rendering their deserved judgment by His disregard.[54] Prayer therefore retained an important place in the relations of the people of God, as it was demonstrative of God's blessings and judgments, as well as His essential graces upon His beloved. When they prayed in abject repentance, calling upon His Name and His grace in *"keeping the covenant"* (Daniel 9:4) with them, God would often enact His mercies and (at times) reconfirm His covenant promise as an act of encouragement.[55]

With Messiah's incarnation on the earth, the Lord Jesus continued the practice of addressing God in prayer. As the prayers of a Son to His Father, He reconfirmed the former modes of prayer, both by His own example and by His direct admonition to His faithful. Prayer for the New Covenant

The importance of covenantal prayer was demonstrated by the ancient prophet Daniel, who faithfully fasted and prayed on behalf of Judah during its Babylonian captivity. Daniel was depicted praying in this early sixteenth-century woodcut; the Lord answered and showed him *"that which is noted in Scripture of trueth"* (Daniel 10:16-21).

50. See Daniel 9:4; 1 Kings 8:25; Jeremiah 27:18; 1 Samuel 1:27; Psalm 69:30.
51. See 2 Chronicles 6:40; 30:27; Psalm 17:1, et al.
52. See Exodus 34:14, et al.
53. See Genesis 18:27.
54. See Jeremiah 11:14.
55. See Daniel 9:21-27.

believer therefore carries the same modes as before: praying in accord with covenantal humility under God, praying in accord with the covenantal mercies of His promise (now fulfilled), and praying in accord with the reverence due all of His covenantal commands.

To the English reformers, to pray to God was to do so *"in the name of Christ."*[56] This was done because Christians must still plead the mercies of the Covenant of Grace before God. That practice addressed the need for fallible man to have a *"Mediator"* (as One who is worthy to come between) by which to approach or plead before the perfect God. As with the prior mode of Old Covenant prayer, whereby the Israelites pleaded the mercies of the promise, the New Covenant saints plead the mercies of its gracious fulfillment. Christ alone has gained the legitimate right to access the Father's throne on His own merit, and He alone can intercede on behalf of those who cannot have that right on their own. But, they must be in league with Christ for Him to be their Advocate. Christ goes before the Father for the faithful, because *"we can have no access into His presence without a Mediator."*[57] Christ thereby remains the continuing Mediator of the New Covenant,[58] just as He was in the fulfillment of the Old.[59]

A.

B.

A ND so it was, that as hee was praying in a certeine place, when hee ceased, one of his Disciples said vnto him, Master, teach vs to pray, as John also taught his disciples.

2 * And hee said vnto them, When ye pray, say, Our Father, which art in heauen, halowed bee thy Name: Thy kingdome come: Let thy will be done euen in earth, as it is in heauen:

3 Our daily bread giue vs for the day:

4 And ‖ forgiue vs our sinnes: for euen wee forgiue euery man that is indebted to vs: And lead vs not into temptation: but deliuer vs from euill.

The reformers' *Larger Catechisme* defined the New Covenant mode of prayer as: *"an offering up of our desires unto God, in the name of Christ, by the help of his Spirit, with confession of our sins, and thankfull acknowlegement of his mercies."*[60] The Lord Jesus gave us the example of such a prayer which exhibits the various sanctions, pleadings, and petitions that are honorable to God: *"... so that it be done with understanding, faith, reverence, and other graces necessary to the right performance of the duty."*[61] His historic model for Christian prayer was commonly called *"The Lord's Prayer"* by the English reformers, for they said it was given by Christ as a: *"pattern according to which we are to make other praiers."*[62]

Each of the Lord's Prayer's individual petitions[63] were those which had been earlier suited to God's covenant people of Israel. Now, with Christ as our covenant Mediator, we access the throne of the Heavenly Father with confidence in the Son:

A. The Lord Jesus taught His disciples the manner of addressing God in New Covenant prayer, as was depicted in this sixteenth-century woodcut from a *Devotional* (circa 1530).

B. This is the Lord's Prayer as it appeared in the context of Scripture (Luke 11:1-4) in a sixteenth-century Geneva version of the Bible.

56. See Westminster Assembly, *Confession of Faith, Together with the Larger and Smaller Catechismes* (1658), on *Larger Catechisme*'s Question, *"What is it to pray in the name of Christ?"*, p. 141.
57. Ibid.
58. See Hebrews 12:24.
59. See Galatians 3:19-20.
60. *Confession of Faith, Together with the Larger and Smaller Catechismes*, on *Larger Catechisme*'s Question, *"What is Prayer?"*, p. 140.
61. Ibid., p. 144.
62. Ibid.
63. Ibid.

Our Father which art in heaven,[64]

We are to honor His transcendence and have highest esteem for Him:

Hallowed be thy name.[65]

We are to acknowledge His sovereign Kingship over both heaven and earth:

Thy kingdome come. Thy will be done in earth as it is in heaven.[66]

We are to see God alone as our earthly and providential Provider:

Give us this day our daily bread.[67]

We are to see our continued need of confession under the Covenant of Grace and the concurrent need to extend it in our relations with others:

And forgive us our debts, as we forgive our debters.[68]

We are to acknowledge our continued fallibility and tendency toward sin and plead His continued Grace:

And lead us not into temptation, but deliver us from evil:[69]

We are to pledge our uniform submission to an exalted, omnipotent, and eternal Lord:

For thine is the kingdome, and the power and the glory, for ever. Amen.[70]

With the various examples and modes of prayer demonstrated by Abraham, Moses, David, and the great *"cloud of witnesses,"*[71] Christians can begin to understand the long, prior tradition of speaking with God as a covenant Lord. With the gift of the Lord's Prayer given by Christ, along with the abundant admonitions by His Apostles to confess, repent, petition, plead, and intercede in prayer, we indeed have a greatly honored place before His holy throne.

64. Matthew 6:9-15; also see *Westminster Larger Catechisme* (1648), pp. 54-56.
65. Ibid.
66. Ibid.
67. Ibid.
68. Ibid.
69. Ibid.
70. Ibid.
71. See Hebrews 12:1.

A. Christ admonished His faithful not to prohibit *"little ones"* from coming unto Him (Matthew 18:6). The reformers therefore considered it a covenant duty for parents to honor Christ in teaching their children to pray. This woodcut depicting Matthew 18 was included in an illustrated edition of a William Tyndale New Testament (1551).

The LORDS PRAYER,
Matth. 6.

Our Father which art in heaven, Hallowed be thy name, Thy kingdom come, Thy will be done on earth, as it is in heaven, Give us this day our daily bread, And forgive us our debts, as we forgive our debters, And lead us not into temptation, but deliver us from evil: For thine is the kingdom, and the power, and the glory, for ever. Amen.

B. Understanding the Lord's Prayer, shown here as it appeared in the Westminster Assembly's *Smaller Catechisme*, was central in catechizing Reformed families on how to address God. A descriptive narrative of the Lord's Prayer explained that it was *"an offering to God up of our desires unto God for all things agreeable to His will, in the nature of Christ, with confession of our sins, and thankful acknowledgment of his mercies."* It also stated that the conclusion of the Lord's Prayer *"teacheth us to take our encouragement in prayer from God onely, and in our prayers to praise him, ascribing kingdom, power and glory to him"* (1648).

The Lord's Prayer.

Our Father, who art in heaven, hallowed be thy name. Thy kingdom come. Thy will be done in earth as it is in heaven. Give us this day our daily bread; and forgive us our debts, as we forgive our debtors. And lead us not into temptation, but deliver us from evil. For thine is the kingdom, and the power, and the glory, forever. Amen.

C. During the colonial and founding eras of America, the Lord's Prayer was taught as an essential part of a child's education. It often appeared in juvenile literature, as shown here in the *New England Primer*, published from the seventeenth to nineteenth centuries.

Worship

The Reformed Westminster Assembly's *Larger Catechisme* also stated that *"Man's Cheifest and Highest end is to glorifie God, and fully enjoy him for ever."*[72]   In the Old Covenant, worship was the most immediate act of glorifying God. His glory is resonant in the basic fabric of Creation, and throughout time and history, Creation itself sings an ongoing declaration of His glory: *"The heavens declare the glory of God: and the firmament sheweth his handy-work"* (Psalm 19:1). But, God's glory was declared above Creation and His glory was manifest above all nations.[73] Before the incarnation of Christ, covenant keepers worshipped God in accord with their Lord's mandates. At that time, corporate worship centered both around their families and the larger Israelite community during their times of feasts.[74] For example, the feast of Purim, celebrating God's deliverance of the Jews from Haman's destructive plot, was an annual worship ceremony celebrated by *"every family, every province, and every city, and that these dayes of Purim should not fail from among the Jews, ..."* (Esther 9:28). Their worship was to remain inwardly motivated, contrary to the time of Malachi when worship had become purely ritualistic, as if it was a great burden of *"wearinesse"* (Malachi 1:13). So, for the covenant people of the promise, the Psalms were to provide them with lively songs for individual, family, and community worship. The Psalms were full of the Spirit-inspired praises of true and hearty worship. Their worship was to have as its intended objects God the Father and His Holy Word: *"I will worship ... and praise thy name, for thy loving kindenesse, and for thy truth: for thou hast magnified thy word above all thy name"* (Psalm 138:2).

A.

B.

A. King David was inspired by God to write the historic, devotional Psalms. He was here depicted in song on the New Testament title page of the first complete Bible printed in English (1535).

B. This is the opening section of an 'Esther Scroll,' as was used since ancient times by Hebrew families in devotional worship during the feast of Purim (circa 1800's).

Christ reconfirmed that the manifestation of God's glory was inherited in the New Covenant. But that divine glory which had always obliged man's worship was now also clearly manifest in the person of Jesus Christ, as demonstrated in His prayer to His heavenly Father: *"Father, I will that they also whom thou hast given me, be with me where I am, that they may behold my glory which thou hast given me"* (John 17:24). God therefore still remains the object of devotion in the New Covenant. God is the object, and worship remains the means of expressing devotion. The Apostles therefore reconfirmed the Old Covenant practice of worshipping God by way of singing personal, familial, and community psalms:

72. *Confession of Faith, Together with the Larger and Smaller Catechismes*, on *Larger Catechisme*'s Question 1, p. 151.
73. See Psalm 113:4.
74. See Deuteronomy 26:10-11.

Let the word of Christ dwell in you richly in all wisdom, teaching and admonishing one another in psalms and hymns, and spirituall songs, singing with grace in your hearts to the Lord (Colossians 3:16).

A.

Without the continuity of the Old Covenantal practices of prayer and worship, the New Covenant would lack its interpersonal modes of communicating with God and of offering Him His due reverence. Through the continuance of the former practices of prayer and worship (which incorporate the continuance of supplications, intercessions, petitions, thanksgivings, and praises), covenantal continuity has been maintained in Christianity's rich inheritance.

A. New Covenant devotion is infused with Spirited worship, as was depicted by this woodcut in Tyndale's New Testament (1636).

III. The Inherited Covenantal Study of Scripture

Thirdly, the New Covenant also retains the Old Covenant's obligation of the regular study of God's Word. The entire written Scripture was given for the comfort and hope of its readers, as the Apostle Paul wrote to the first-century Church at Rome, and through them, to all the New Covenant faithful: *"For whatsoever things were written aforetime, were written for our learning, that we through patience and comfort of the scriptures might have hope"* (Romans 15:4).

In that instance, Paul was revering the Old Covenant text while in the process of composing the New. Thus, by God giving two Testaments of His Word, the Christian inheritance is a comprehensive manifestation of His historic promise and its timely fulfillment. And, in that sense, both Covenants are still one – of grace.

The Old Covenant itself was pertinent not only to historic Jews. The Old Testament represented God's covenant working toward all sorts of men, both those of the "promise" and those of the "flesh." For example, in the Book of Galatians, Paul wrote to the Gentile believers, contrasting the two distinct sons of Abraham: Ishmael and Isaac. Paul argued that Abraham's first son, Ishmael, *"was born after the flesh"* (Galatians 4:23), and his second son, Isaac, represented *"the children of promise"* (Galatians 4:28). The Covenant of Grace had thus extended God's grace to some after the flesh (Gentiles) as well as to some of the promise (Jews). The reformers therefore saw Paul's argument as proclaiming God's single Covenant of Grace within both the Old and New Covenants: *" ... They are called two covenants, the one of the old Testament, and another of the new: which were not two indeed, but in respect of the times, and the diversity of the government."*[75] Both Old and New Covenants are thereby necessary for Christian study in that they are both essential to understanding our own entire Covenant of Grace. And, without a thorough knowledge of the Old Testament, Paul's comprehensive teachings on God's grace would sadly fall upon deaf ears.

B.

B. Moses and two prophets, here representative of all the inspired authors of the Old Testament texts, were depicted discussing the covenant promises of God. This scene was included in Isaiah Thomas's American Bible printed in 1792.

75. Geneva note on Galatians 4:24, leaf Lll.

Thus, even in its antiquity, the Old Covenant contains the essential covenantal background for all New Covenant saints – whether they were Jews or non-Jews. The Hebrew Scriptures were certainly not just for Hebrews, as the Old Testament contains the only complete repository of facts pertaining to mankind's common Creation Covenant, as well as to our common grace by way of Noah's Covenant. Subsequently, either by way of Abraham's promise or Ishmael's flesh, the Old Testament must be seen in light of every Christian's covenantal inheritance. The New Covenant thus inherits all the wealth of the Old. The moral Law, for example, though no longer representing the obligations of the vassal nation of Israel, now represents God's mandates for New Covenant sonship obedience. The Christian covenantal inheritance fully embodies the Old Covenant obligations of faith and obedience summarized in the Ten Commandments.[76] God, in three Persons, as our almighty Father, our fellow Son, and our guiding Spirit, has sovereignly ordained both faith and obedience as enduring features of His eternal grace. His twin Testaments work together for New Covenant saints, showing us the long and continued richness of our inheritance.

The regular reading and study of God's Word has been an important part of covenantal obedience since originally instituted through Moses. That Old Covenant mandate has simply been continued, reordained in the work and ministry of Christ and His Apostolic authors. God has, again, sovereignly confirmed His Word (all of His Words – both Old and New Covenant Words) for the Christians' edification. The moral Law now becomes the ally of the New Covenant saints, as it ever radiates the perfect moral will of our heavenly Father. Because of His Son, His Laws are now inwardly lively and richly given for our brotherly self-governance. Through His Spirit they are abundantly pleasing by the inner ministration of their hearty truths. As coming from the perfect Will of our inheritance through Christ, God the Father has adopted us as fellow sons, and it is our divine privilege to partake of the abundant gift of His complete Word as best befitting our whole covenantal inheritance.

IV. The Inherited Covenantal Community of Saints

Lastly, the New Covenant retains the Old Covenant's ordination of a covenant community. Christian baptism itself signifies one's entry into a new community in which he or she becomes one among a covenanted body of believers: *"For if we have been planted together in the likenesse of his death: we shall be also in the likenesse of his resurrection"* (Romans 6:5). The sacrament of the Lord's Supper is also know as "communion," as in the communion of saints partaking of the body and blood of Christ – not as individuals, but together as a body of believers. The Apostle Paul argued

Called to preach the Gospel of the Kingdom of God to both Jews and Gentiles, Christ's Apostles championed the whole counsel of God's written Word among the dominions of men. Shown here are the twelve Apostles as they were depicted on the title page of a typical early 'King James' Bible (1621).

76. See *Westminster Larger Catechisme*: *"Where is the Moral Law summarily comprehended?"*, p. 56.

accordingly in his letter to the Romans: *"... The bread which we break, is it not the communion of the body of Christ? For we being many are one bread, and one body: for we are all partakers of that one bread"* (1 Corinthians 10:16-17). God's adopted sons are therefore in covenant with one another as the fellow (circumcision) sons of Abraham and the fellow (Passover) families of Israel. They are also fellow heirs of the Kingdom of David with the common Lord as the King of Kings.

The community of saints is, in a bodily sense, assembled together and united under Christ as their Head, with each of them as His various parts. God desired that His people gather under Him, as first demonstrated by the united Patriarchs of Israel. When the great Patriarch Jacob died, he gathered his sons around him and blessed them together as tribes.[77] When the sons of Israel departed Egypt, they were composed of covenant families, although united together as one congregation. God led them together under His direction by the pillar of a cloud by day and of fire by night.[78] Later, Moses gathered all the people of Israel together to read to them the "Book of the Covenant," first uniting them as a covenanted nation pledged under Him.[79] God then gathered the people to Himself before *"the tabernacle of the congregation"*[80] in initiating the worship obligations and ordinances as a single congregation.

When Israel was gathered together under God they remained strong, but when they lingered apart from Him they were weak. The key was always to be under Him – that is, under His sovereign will. God had formed the Israelites together as a *"covenant ... people"*[81] and *"an assembly of saints,"*[82] and later would have had them unite under Christ – but they rejected Him. Jesus Christ therefore equated Jerusalem's refusal to gather under Him with rebellion to God: *"O Jerusalem, Jerusalem, ... how often would I have gathered thy children together even as a hen gathereth her chickens under her wings, and ye would not!"* (Matthew 23:37).

Christ's Church was therefore called to such a purpose. Both His Jewish and Gentile chosen were called to gather under His wings. They were to gather to Him before the *"tabernacle of the congregation,"* called together as His Kingdom and nation, covenanted together before the "Book of the Covenant." And, in departing

A. Ancient Hebrew congregations gathered in synagogues as the customary places for their local assemblies to publicly study, discourse, and hear the plain teaching of God's Word. According to the Bible's narrative, Jesus attended, taught, and ministered in synagogues on the Sabbath (Matthew 12:9; Luke 1:21; Luke 6:6). Such an assembly was depicted in this woodcut included on the title page of the *Prophets* in the first complete English Bible (1535).

B. Reformed congregations gathered in local church buildings as the customary places for families to assemble, fellowship, and hear the plain preaching of God's Word. Such an assembly was depicted in this woodcut showing the Christian Sabbath, or Lord's Day, service (circa 1530).

77. See Genesis 49:1-28.
78. See Exodus 13:21.
79. See Exodus 24:7.
80. See Leviticus 8:3.
81. See Exodus 34:10.
82. See Psalm 89:7.

101

from their bondage in Egypt together as covenant families, they were called to be united, guided by His Pillar both by day and by night. Christianity has thus adopted Israel's rich inheritance as God's covenant people and as His assembly of saints. Thereafter, the New Covenant ministers of His Word were also to administer the Sacraments to a new community of believers. The other features of the Old Covenant grace that have continued under the New Covenant grace, such as prayer, worship, and the reading of God's Word, are all presented as objects of community obligation as well as of familial and individual duty. The community of saints, or the family of believers, is also compared to a physical body that works together toward a common purpose: *"From whom the whole body fitly joyned together, and compacted by that which every joynt supplieth"* (Ephesians 4:16). The common purpose of that body is to work the Father's will on earth, with Christ as its head, His Spirit as its heart, and its members being all the believers joined together.[83]

The reformers of England and Scotland fully embraced the notion of the church as a body of believers. The Assembly of Divines wrote of their understanding of the role of the church in the *Westminster Confession*'s *"Of the Communion of Saints"*:[84]

> And as being united to one another in love, they have communion in each others gifts and graces, and are obliged to the performance of such duties, publicke and private, and do conduce to their mutual good, both in inward and outward man.[85]

Christ Jesus handed the Keys of the Kingdom of Heaven to His Church by way of His Apostles (Matthew 16:19). That charge involved preaching the Gospel to all nations and transferring covenantal responsibilities from a single nation to those of a worldwide Kingdom. The transfer of Christ's 'Keys' of authority was symbolically represented in this woodcut included on the general title page of the first printed English Bible in 1535.

Such a statement marked a comprehensive summary of the inward motives and outward workings of the covenant church. Under Christ, worldliness is to be kept out by keeping true to God's Words within, *"and the gates of hell shall not prevail against it"* (Matthew 16:18). Christians, all the more, have a covenantal obligation to guard their own brethren and extend a hand of charity within the body: *"Watch ye, stand fast in the faith, quit you like men, be strong. Let all your things be done with charity"* (1 Corinthians 16:13-14).

On the other hand, the saints were to have an outgoing demeanor. *"Neighbors!"* New England's Cotton Mather referenced all Christians within a wider community, *"You stand related to each other; and you should contrive how others should have reason to rejoice in your neighborhood."*[86] Typical of the Puritans, Mather saw a very positive societal role for Christians. The church was to gather together as saints and learn from Christ's oracles, but also to be faithful in outwardliness within the world proclaiming God's great standard. Christ admonished His disciples that wherever they taught, He would be with them:

83. See Ephesians 3:14-17.
84. *Westminster Confession of Faith* on the Communion of Saints, p. 90.
85. Ibid.
86. Cotton Mather, *Essays To Do Good, Addressed to all Christians* ([1710], 1824 edition), p. 61.

Teaching them to observe all things whatsoever I have commanded you: and lo, I am with you alway, even unto the end of the world. Amen (Matthew 28:20).

The inherent obligation of wider Christian involvement in the world was foretold by Israel's prophets of old. From before its inception, Christ's kingdom was foreordained with His power and dominion: *"that all people, nations, and languages should serve him ..."* (Daniel 7:14). As a community, the church is to adopt the full mantle of its mission to the world to be both its *"salt"* and its *"light,"*[87] as commanded by Christ.

Like redeemed Israel of old, the Christian community also retains its association as a body composed of covenant families. Moses had pleaded the cause of the Israelites as a community of families in stating the purpose for their Exodus from Egypt: *"We will go with our young, and with our old, with our sons, and with our daughters: with our flocks, and with our herds will we go ..."* (Exodus 10:9). God later honored the family institution in the nation of Israel, and, like ancient Israel, the family covenant is to be honored in the church as its basic covenantal building block. Richard Baxter asked of the role of the Christian family: *"Who shall lead the way in holiness but the father and mother of the family?"*[88] The families of the church, like Israel's families, retain their full covenantal obligation before their Lord. The obligations to pray, to read, to study, to lead, to teach, to disciple, to preach, and to worship apply as much to family devotions as to the community at large.

Understanding the comprehensive nature of the Old Covenant community is therefore essential to understanding the church's basic identity. Only by knowing Christianity's covenantal inheritance can one see how richly it still embodies an abundant variety of ancient biblical titles, such as: *"the kingdome of God,"*[89] *"an holy nation,"*[90] *"a royall priesthood,"*[91] *"the assembly of the saints,"*[92] *"the whole family in heaven and earth,"*[93] as well as *"one body in Christ."*[94]

A.

A. The church, as the Kingdom of Christ, went out from Jerusalem *"to the uttermost parts of the earth"* with the *"inheritance"* of God's promise (Psalm 2:8). This image is a composite of two engravings that appeared on the title page of Samuel Purchase's *Hakluytus Postumas or his Pilgrimes*, allegorically showing the great throngs of New Covenant faithful as if they were the redeemed tribes of Israel providentially going forth to inhabit the entire Promised Land. Purchase's *Pilgrimes* was influential in encouraging England's establishment of colonies in North America (1626 edition).

B.

B. Christianity's rich covenantal inheritance can be seen in much of the symbolic imagery used in the past. For example, the title page of the *Roycroft Polyglot* (multiple language) *Bible* printed in London between 1653 and 1657, shows the Law, the priests, and the prophets standing upon the foundation of Adam and Noah. On the 'pillars' of the entire Old Covenant sit Christ's Apostles and His Church. Such graphic imagery portrays how the Bible's entire narrative is structured in one, unified covenantal theme.

87. See Matthew 5:13-16.
88. Richard Baxter, *The Saints Everlasting Rest* (London, 1656), part 3, p. 363.
89. See Matthew 6:33.
90. See 1 Peter 2:9.
91. Ibid.
92. See Psalm 89:7.
93. See Ephesians 3:15.
94. See Romans 12:5.

Conclusion of Book I

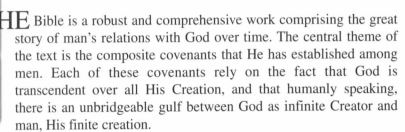

HE Bible is a robust and comprehensive work comprising the great story of man's relations with God over time. The central theme of the text is the composite covenants that He has established among men. Each of these covenants rely on the fact that God is transcendent over all His Creation, and that humanly speaking, there is an unbridgeable gulf between God as infinite Creator and man, His finite creation.

By the nature of His own Being and Essence, God is beyond our comprehension, beyond our grasp, and distinct from anything which we can conceive here on earth. It is thereby impossible for us to establish relations with Him on our terms. He is infinitely sovereign, so God chose to speak to man in condescending Words in order to bridge the gulf of communication between man and God. He thus took the initiative and His sovereign truths were revealed, first to man's earliest fathers and then to the early Hebrew Patriarchs. They were first recorded in writing by Moses and continued through the prophets and apostolic authors. God's Words were composed as human language to reduce them to our understanding, yet they were all composed to maximize our surety in Him. Consequently, King David could gratefully express back to God: *"Thy testimonies are wonderfull: therefore doth my soul keep them. The entrance of thy words giveth light: it giveth understanding unto the simple"* (Psalm 119:129-130).

God's written text, however, cannot of itself bridge the gap between ourselves and the Almighty. Reading a description of God or of His decrees is not sufficient to bring us into meaningful contact with Him or to establish cordial relations with Him. Written words are sufficient to let us know of Him, but are not, in and of themselves, sufficient to become interconnected with Him. Knowing about God is not the same as knowing Him or interacting with Him in any relational way. There remains therefore a relational separation which written words alone cannot gap.

For man to encounter God in a relational sense requires God's initiative by way of His additional supernatural intervention or divine *"revelation"* (Romans 16:25). For a man to truly have a direct revelation from God in a taste of His immediate glory provided a powerful event, and such instances were few. The prophet Jeremiah, for example, became speechless as *"a childe"* (Jeremiah 1:6), in awe before a direct, firsthand revelation of God's Words. Even the Apostle John, who had known Christ when He walked on the earth, and knew Him as his divine Savior after the Resurrection, had a striking encounter when directly confronted by an unbridled revelation of the glorified Son of God: *"And when I saw him, I fell at his feet as dead"* (Revelation 1:17). Dealing directly with the Almighty, then, is no small moment; neither, then, is the significance of His sovereign promises, His tenets, nor His terms upon those entering engagements with Him. Though we may not see their significance in their full glory, they exist in His full majesty. They represent Him in His full majesty. They represent His divine Will and He condescends to us in order to cordially relate them to His creatures. In so doing, He may mask much of His glory, but that in no way means that He has lost any of His sovereign authority.

Covenants were therefore sovereignly instituted by God from the start, conceived in the infinite majesty of His three Persons: The Father, the Son, and the Holy Spirit. From before the foundation of the world, God initiated His Covenant of Redemption, and that Redemption Covenant was His first Covenant of Grace. Yet, from the start of Creation, He conducted His first relations with Adam and Eve under the condition of their perfect obedience to His commands. That Covenant of Works did not work for long, as they soon failed in their obligations and were promptly removed from their perfect Paradise. God would only enter into relations with man from that time forward under terms of His grace, for mankind was no longer capable of perfect obedience. Because the perfect God could not continue to relate to man under imperfect terms of obedience, man's continued existence meant for him to live under the merciful terms of grace. That Covenant of Grace would be at the base of all future engagements between God and man. Man deserved non-existence and his mere existence alone was an act of God's infinite grace. Thus, the Covenant of Grace is the sole means by which God presents cordial relations to men, and grace is the means by which He could henceforth conduct any affairs with mankind.

The central feature of the overall covenant theme was God's timeless promise to man. The promise of grace was repeated throughout the old Hebrew texts in the revelation of God's immediate providence to man, yet with a corresponding future pledge of grace toward His elect. The Scripture's great covenantal theme of grace always combined the issues of faith and obedience within a covenant pact. Grace was always sovereignly fixed, but man's obedience was always annexed, making the various covenants also conditional. The various covenants within the overall Covenant of Grace united both salvation and earthly sufficiency under the purview of God.

For Adam, though he had departed Paradise, the Covenant of Grace represented his temporal maintenance, though it also pointed toward a future deliverance from sin. For Noah, the Covenant of Grace represented the immediate sparing of his family from the deluge, yet it pointed toward the future hope for salvation from the destruction due to disobedience. For Abraham, the Covenant of Grace represented success for his fleshly lineage, yet it pointed toward mankind's future redemption through his spiritual Seed. For Moses, the Covenant of Grace represented the national blessings of God's Law, yet it pointed to the removal of its curse through a High Priestly sacrifice for God's elect. For David, the Covenant of Grace

From the beginning, God created man to be relational and covenantal. Men and women were always to be accountable to their Creator and subject to His decrees. This late fifteenth-century illustration showed the obliging nature of the first covenant of Adam and Eve with the eternal Creator. Though they failed under the perfect Covenant of Works, their marriage covenant and all other covenantal associations continued under God's terms of grace toward man.

represented a multigenerational kingdom from God, yet it pointed toward man's future hope under the true King of Kings. For the prophets, the Covenant of Grace represented Israel's national call to return to God, yet it pointed toward His future victory over the whole world.

But, for the Apostles, God's Covenant of Grace represented the fulfillment of all that had been promised before. It represented the deliverance from original sin and from destruction of disobedience by redemption through Abraham's Seed. It represented victory over the condemnation of the Law through the genuine High Priestly sacrifice. It represented the manifestation of the eternal reign of the King of Kings and pointed to His ultimate victory over the world. For the Apostles, the promises had all come together in the life, death, and resurrection of Jesus Christ. For them, all that remained of the future promise was that the Covenant of Grace was yet to be imparted upon future believers. His sovereign grace would be deposited by means of a union of His Spirit with the covenant church, which would be unleashed upon the earth. That Church would bring temporal earthly fruition, as well as eternal covenant redemption to many. Therefore, the Apostles looked forward to what still remained of the grace, for only at the end of this earth would come the perfect consummation of the Covenant of Grace in a glorious wedding feast between Christ, the perfect Groom, and His espoused Church. That will mark the end of all promises, as observed sixteen hundred years ago by the early church father Augustine, who also looked forward to that final consummation:

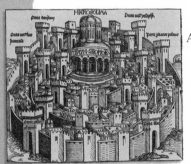

A.

When this Promise is fulfilled. O what shall wee bee then? How glorious shall the soul of man bee, without all staine and sinne, that can either subdue or oppose it, or against which it need to contend; perfect in all vitrue, and enthroned in all perfect peace?[1]

A. Old Jerusalem was creatively but fancifully depicted in this woodcut from the *Nuremberg Chronicle*, a highly illustrated history of the world (1493).

Much later than Augustine, one of America's own early church fathers, Thomas Shepard, also looked forward to that glorious day in *The Parable of the Ten Virgins*, as a series of sermons preached during the first decades of colonial New England:

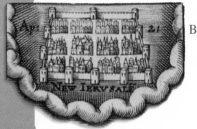

B.

Our faith indeed shall not then by such glasses see Christ, nor adhere unto Christ by such means as Promises and Ordinances as we do now, but without them we shall both see, and forever adhere to him as our King at that day; and tho' indeed though the law be abolished, as a Covenant of life, yet it shall ever remain as a Rule of life; perfect subjection to it, is the happiness of the Saints in Heaven.[2]

B. New Jerusalem (the part of God's gracious promise yet to be fulfilled) was imaginatively depicted in this engraving on the title page of Purchase's *Pilgrime* (1626 edition).

Thomas Shepard retained a vision for that part of God's promise yet unfulfilled. As a visionary, he therefore warned *"all the Churches of Jesus Christ, here planted in these Western parts of the World,"*[3] to be on their guard. American congregations at that time viewed themselves as *"pure, chaste Virgin-churches,*

1. Augustine, *Citie of God*, book 22, chapter 24, p. 909.
2. Thomas Shepard, *The Parable of the Ten Virgins Opened & Applied...* , [preached in Cambridge, N.E., circa 1636-1640] (London, 1660), p. 5.
3. Ibid., p. 37.

not polluted with mixtures of men's inventions, not defiled with the company of evil men, pure Ordinances, pure People, pure Churches,"[4] and were to covenantally endure until the end, to rise victoriously in the arms of their Groom.

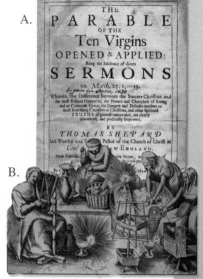

A. This is the title page of Thomas Shepard's *The Parable of the Ten Virgins*, printed in 1660.

B. This woodcut by Pieter Bruegel depicts wise virgin churches, busy with lamps aglow (circa 1560's).

Though the overall Covenant of Grace was confirmed by various signs and seals as ordinances, they each contained God's pledge. The same fulfillment of grace was annexed to all, and for the Reformed Christian such as Thomas Shepard, the covenantal life signified the same trust that it had before to Adam, Noah, Abraham, Moses, David, the Prophets, and the Apostles. Their bond with God signified both faith and obedience, as bringing salvation through the one and His earthly sufficiency through the other. Their covenant tied godly dominion with manly service, and wedded heavenly devotion to an earthly service still to be completed by His Church.

As the covenant sons of God, New Covenant believers became interrelational, and, being bound in service to their King, they had a significant impact on the nations about them. Being covenantally united with Christ allowed them to be charitable to one another, and being bound to Him called them to be servants to yet others.

The crux of the promise allowed Christians to enter a cordial (vertical) relation with Him and still have a significant (horizontal) life through Him. Then, to the august Reformed Christians such as John Hooper, William Perkins, John Preston, Richard Baxter, Thomas Shepard, Cotton Mather, Matthew Henry, and so many others, their callings directed them to reap the widest heavenly abundance amid their greatest earthly good. God's moral Law, His Commandments, were not seen as foes to grace, but as God's blessed directives in their private family governments, as well as in their public church, societal, and civil engagements. The promise reaped both individual souls and societal stewardship; thereby, the Christian life, the covenantal life, had its farthest reaching impact.

The English reformers, beginning with Tyndale, Rogers, Hooper, and the first generation of English martyrs, perhaps best understood Christianity's great covenantal inheritance. They understood the great legacy presented to them in the *"book of the covenant."*[5] They indeed paid a great price for what they knew to be true, yet by putting their knowledge to practice they also constructed a wide cultural framework built upon those biblical mandates. That frame of private, Christian duty and societal responsibility is what we, their cultural descendants, have come to enjoy. But, far too much of our covenantal legacy has also been neglected, rejected, or long forgotten. It has, at least, been taken for granted, which alone puts the enjoyment of our liberties at risk, for historically speaking, liberties were not defined as doing what we want, but as doing what we must under God to keep from bondage. The following book will therefore present a brief historic overview of how such ideas were originally effected, first in shaping England's, and then in providing America's, rich covenantal inheritance.

4. Ibid.
5. See Exodus 24:7.

In the name of God, Amen.

Book II
America's Covenantal Inheritance

Book II America's Covenantal Inheritance
Introduction: The Noble Inheritance
The Forefathers of America's Forefathers

AT the beginning of the tensions with Great Britain that would eventually bring America's independence, a young lawyer from Massachusetts paused to consider the rich history of his colony. A decade before the first volleys were exchanged at Lexington and Concord, he weighed the American cause by reflecting upon the first settlers of New England. John Adams was awed by the sacrifice, strength, and motivation, but mostly by the inherent virtues of the earliest immigrants, as he wrote to admonish his own generation in passionate terms:

> *Recollect the civil and religious principles, and hopes, and expectations, which constantly supported and carried them thro' all hardships, with patience and resignation!*[1]

In 1765, Adams looked back from a distance of over one hundred years, not merely to an historic legacy, but to a character that had been deposited in the soul of New England. In the first New England planters he saw lives that had been tough – soul-wrenching tough – but they were not made of the stuff that we might suppose. They certainly were not the kind of self-determined individualists as many today might imagine early Americans to have been, nor were they ruthless adventurers staking wild-eyed claims upon the soil and toil of others. No, their character would be barely recognizable today as seen through our secularized lenses. They were a devout people, and they were devoted to God and to one another. They were devout families, they were devout churches, and they were devoutly self-governed commonwealths. John Adams saw in them a tireless quest for the purest brand of Christianity, for which they purchased their own freedoms and then planted its liberties upon the New England shores. He saw in them the character of a people who loved their Lord with such an unfathomable devotion that they were willing to sacrifice themselves for the good of those who would follow. Adams saw in them the kind of strength and thirst for Christian liberty that, to him, must once again enliven the souls of New England:

> *Let us recollect it was liberty! the hope of liberty for themselves and us and ours, which conquered all discouragements, dangers and trials! – In such researches as these let us all in our several departments chearfully engage?*[2]

---

1. John Adams, *A Dissertation on the Canon and the Feudal Law*, printed as part of *The True Sentiments of America...* , published by John Almon (London, 1768), p. 139.
2. Ibid.

Long before the shots were fired on the fateful morning of April 19, 1775, which began America's contest in arms, there were indelible principles woven into the fabric of American ideas. These principles could only be maintained by another generation – Adams's generation – if it, too, was willing to sacrifice. Those of his generation would also be called upon to give of themselves for the good of the future, but they must first be willing to patiently study and learn the precepts of Christian liberty, and only then, to act upon them: *"In such researches as these let us all in our several departments chearfully engage? But especially the proper patrons and supporters of law, learning and religion."*[3] John Adams was studiously aware of a most remarkable inheritance that had been passed down to his generation – an inheritance that was now for his generation to embrace and then to pass along to those who would follow.

He admired those first New England planters who, in spite of such a material disadvantage, accomplished so much good. They had put before him an example which required his generation to become patrons of like virtues. It was the original settlers who had framed New England's character and, more than any people in history, had broken the shackles of tyranny. But, those to whom John Adams ascribed so much honor and thanks are seldom recalled with like gratitude in our day. Today they are most often considered with scorn as their name has been branded as the very byword for that which is bigoted, backward, and ignorant. Yet, ironically, their education and central principles were both highly esteemed and endorsed by our founders' generation – that very generation which we now esteem with a most hearty debt of gratitude. How is it that we now despise those from whom our forefathers found their own inspiration? John Adams and the host of his day surely remembered them as the most noble people who had set the example for their age. They had provided them with an inheritance grounded in opposition to royal tyranny in either church or state, for theirs had been built before *"on the foundation of the Bible and common sense."*[4] Those early settlers, who were such a remarkable people, those whom Adams recalled as *"intelligent"* and *"learned,"* were, after all, *"a sensible people, I mean the puritans."*[5]

Adams was writing on the eve of the most critical years of America's history. He admonished his fellow colonial English subjects to learn from their past, then for them to write, to speak, to awaken their own first principles, and then to rise to the cause of liberty. For, at the time, Adams recognized that danger was at hand as there was a *"design on foot, to enslave all America."*[6] An education in history's great lessons was the same critical issue for that Braintree (later Quincy),

Dan Ford, 2002

A.

THE TRVE SENTIMENTS OF AMERICA:
CONTAINED IN A COLLECTION OF
LETTERS SENT FROM THE HOVSE
OF REPRESENTATIVES OF THE
PROVINCE OF MASSACHVSETTS
BAY TO SEVERAL PERSONS OF
HIGH RANK IN THIS
K I N G D O M :

TOGETHER
WITH CERTAIN PAPERS RELATING TO
A SVPPOSED LIBEL ON THE
GOVERNOR OF THAT PROVINCE,
AND A DISSERTATION ON
THE CANON AND
THE FEVDAL
L A W.

LONDON, PRINTED FOR I. ALMON, IN PICCADILLY.
1768.

B.

A. This is a portrait sketch of the young Massachusetts lawyer, John Adams, as he appeared in the mid-1760's.

B. This is the title page of *The True Sentiments of America*, which contained John Adams's *Dissertation on the Canon and the Feudal Law*, published in opposition to Great Britain's tyrannical American policies.

3. Ibid.
4. Ibid., p. 121.
5. Ibid., p. 117.
6. Ibid., p. 141.

Massachusetts lawyer and his fellow provincials as it had been for their forefathers. For someone with a Puritan backbone such as that of Adams, to allow his inheritance to slip away would prove the highest offense:

> *... that consenting to slavery is a sacrilegious breach of trust, as offensive in the sight of God, as it is derogatory from our own honour or interest or happiness; and that God almighty has promulgated from heaven, liberty, peace, and good will to man!*[7]

Adams was speaking of principles better understood in his day than ours, nevertheless, he still admonished his generation to engage them all the more. Privileges and responsibilities were considered more precious at that time, for they were recognized as both gifts and obligations which tied them directly to the Almighty. All that was right (and thus considered as "rights") was derived from eternal truths, giving them a status unrecognizable today. Those essential principles of colonial times which would later be implanted in the infant charters of a new nation that Adams would help form, were those of the Christians known to him as the *"intelligent," "learned,"* and *"sensible"* Puritans.

A.

A. As with many of America's impressive monuments, Mount Rushmore beckons citizens to be mindful of their history (designed by Gutzon Borglum, begun in 1927).

America's history, though, did not cease with either a John or Samuel Adams, or with a George Washington or Thomas Jefferson, or with a subsequent Abraham Lincoln or Theodore Roosevelt. Images of the latter four have been inscribed into a monumental tribute to America's continuing legacy. America has moved on since its founding years, continuing to some extent in the manner of a principled republic, and boldly proceeding with her greatest institutions at the fore. By these we mean her great institutions of the family, the church, the township, the city, the county, and the state republics, as well as the national federation at large. Each of these has had an important place as the United States moved through her early years of development. Each institution has faced many pressures and survived many challenges. The federation added dozens of new states and eventually brought her borders beyond unimaginable Pacific shores. Each additional state republic was itself a monument to the greatness of those far-reaching first principles which John Adams admired. Other great American achievements, such as a massive output of Christian missionaries over the past two centuries, and still other exports in produce,

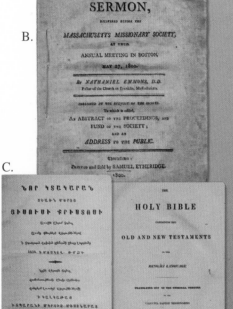

B.

C.

Early American Exports:

B. This is the title page of a sermon preached in support of one of the many American foreign mission societies (1800).

C. These are the title pages of two Bibles published in India by American foreign missions in 1839 and 1845 respectively.

7. Ibid., p. 139.

products, and improvements far too many to mention here, have gone well beyond America's borders to bless foreign and distant peoples as a result of those first principles that the Almighty so graciously planted along her eastern shores. As her continuing history has shown, America has indeed changed much from her earlier days.

As each generation passed into the next, each had reshaped itself to some extent according to various influences and innovations of the day. The problems and fears of one age have given rise to hopeful new ideas for the next. For example, the Progressive movement of the past century and a half was based on a notion that social changes themselves could bring about the remedies for past ills. The values of human nature thus came to the fore as Americans began to assume that humanity was evolving toward its ever more competent potential. Progress itself became the byword to such an extent that mere self-confidence and self-awareness replaced the historic public reverence for (and dependence upon) God.

Unfortunate for America's ideologues of boundless progress was the fact that optimism could not of itself satisfy the moral needs of a nation, nor could self-confidence and awareness yield America's necessary self-competence. As faith in humanity progressed, human sin abounded all the more. Greater and greater regulatory control was granted to the various civil estates in order to keep America's ever more progressive vice in check. With the prolific growth of the various civil establishments, particularly at the national level, the American citizenry began to look more and more to the state, eventually adopting a popular notion that the civil government itself was the author of our rights and even the repository of our daily necessities. Human aid then came in the form of material assistance, resulting in a further notion that material satisfaction could somehow replace the need for private or public virtue. Such a notion would have seemed laughable to a John Adams or the *"intelligent,"* *"learned,"* and *"sensible"* Puritans of old. The contrast between their generations and ours can best be seen by the personal hazard that they were willing to risk for the sake of their liberty and virtue, and the various forms of lavish public assistance that we so freely claim as our right.

By following John Adams's precedent, another look at America's origins might serve us well. Like Adams, it would certainly benefit our generation to undertake a more careful study of the first principles that motivated the forebearers of our forefathers and provide ourselves with a more *"learned"* understanding of our noble inheritance. Then, future generations may once again embrace the sound precepts of those *"intelligent"* and *"sensible"* people who once faithfully served the American cause.

Dan Ford, 2002

A. This is the title page of a popular pocket Bible printed during England's Commonwealth period (1653).

B. The sword of God's Word: This sketch depicts a Puritan military officer reading a typical soldier's pocket Bible.

Chapter 1: The Early Societal Reformers

The Advent of Covenantal Thought in Societal Obligations

WITH a wider scope of history we can see that there was a time in the more distant past when Western Europe began a great societal shift. About six hundred years ago, Western culture at large began to move from its system of multilayered feudalism back toward the long-forgotten idea of a more centralized and supreme potentate.

Throughout the millennium which followed the collapse of the Roman Empire, European cultures had been built around the protective structures of local castles and their localized lords. The lords protected the people, and the people obliged themselves in abject service to their masters. In the Middle Ages there was little centralized power, and though there were kings among the various lords, they typically had few additional privileges and were held in check by the courts that tended to the interests of the nobility. The Church of Rome held the most centralized and absolute sway among the vast conglomerate of multileveled medieval institutions. Then, in the later Middle Ages, prospects arose that the general temper of European culture was moving away from the ever-shifting dominions of feudalism and was gradually beginning to adopt the notion of stronger nation-states. For a number of reasons, including an ever-present threat of a Moslem invasion, the ruling Europeans began to recognize that powerful royal regimes rebuilt around a single potentate would prove to be more resilient than the often-explosive mixture of feuding courts. The parlay among those medieval courts (such as those which were themselves called parliaments) had often proven ineffective under the various combative lordships with their turbulent interests and contradictory allegiances.

The rise of centralized states evoked a necessary cultural self-awareness which would lend legitimacy to its further progress. Europe's massive cultural shift, the first since the fall of Rome, was thus accompanied by significant contemporary literature to champion its cause. With the rise of monarchical supremacy came an accompaniment of volumes of books and documents which today, as an essential part of Western history, document for us the principal ideas that lay behind the events which altered Europe's entire fabric. The French kings, for example, who most fully embraced the idea of royal supremacy, were especially fond of the philosophy of Niccolò Machiavelli. Machiavelli was a late medieval Italian author who justified the idea of an absolute monarchy. Ruling power or royal supremacy to him was not a matter of a divine moral code, but it was a matter of practical realities which required whatever means necessary to achieve a desired end.

Dan Ford, 2002

A.

B.

A. This is a sketch of the pragmatic philosopher Niccolò Machiavelli.

B. This is the title page of the 1577 pocket edition of *Le Prince*, popular with French absolutists.

According to Machiavellian philosophy, all virtue was ascribed to the intended outcome of a governmental policy, and not necessarily by following any code of morality in achieving it. A powerful and invasive state would thus be most effective and efficient in achieving its outcome-based ends.

The French court particularly liked Machiavelli's philosophy because it tended to validate the ill treatment of those who might threaten its power. It utilized Machiavelli's bold propositions to condone the widespread persecution of its most popular rival, the French Reformed Protestants (known as the Huguenots). Machiavelli's small work, translated into their language as *Le Prince*, found great favor among the courts of Henry II and Henry III in the mid-1500's. Its ideas placated those who were loyal to the king and drove them to crush any noteworthy threat. For the French Royalists, *Le Prince* spoke favorably of their pragmatic (though often harsh) treatment of those over whom they ruled:

> *... let it here be noted that men are either to be kindly treated, or utterly crushed, since they can revenge lighter injuries, but not graver. Wherefore the injury we do to a man should be of a sort to leave* [the Prince or rulers] *no fear or reprisals.*[1]

In a similar pragmatic manner, the French monarchy lavishly fancied its loyal Royalists and brutalized its opponents. Some five years after a massacre of over 20,000 French Protestants on St. Bartholomew's Day in 1572, Henry III revoked a subsequent royal 'Edict of Toleration.' He was, at the time, said to have maintained *"a copy* [of *Le Prince*] *always in his pocket, for ready reference, when he needed guidance on how to be most effectively evil."*[2] It was also at the time acknowledged that *"the chief cause of the current 'calamities and destruction' "* was due to the *" 'evil arts, vicious counsels, and false and pestiferous doctrines of Niccolò Machiavelli the Florentine.' "*[3]

In the wake of the Bartholomew's Day massacre, it soon became apparent that French society at large was being reorganized according to Machiavellian principles from the top down. But, the rise of princely absolutism did not merely mean a change in the civil government, it evoked an inquisition upon anyone opposing the absolutist ideas of personal faith, private household, orthodox church, acceptable society, or civil policy. The crown claimed a right to search out any Protestant writings, which included their French-language Bibles, and arrest the 'wayward' parent who might be found teaching its lessons to his children. Widespread persecution drove the opposition into the dark recesses of French society. From there the Huguenots valiantly fought at every hazard, clinging to

1. Niccolò Machiavelli, *The Prince*, translated by Hill Thompson (Norwalk, CT: Easton Press, 1980), pp. 34-35.
2. George Garnett, Editor's Introduction to *Vindiciae, Contra Tyrannos: or, Concerning the Legitimate Power of a Prince over the People, and of the People over a Prince*, by Stephanus Junius Brutus, edited and translated by George Garnett (Cambridge, Great Britain: Cambridge University Press, 1994), p. xxi, partially quoting from [Jean Boucher], *De Justa Henrici Tertii Abdicatione e Francorum Regno, Libri Quatuor* (Paris, 1589).
3. Ibid., p. xxi, partially quoting from the original preface of *Vindiciae, Contra Tyrannos*.

maintain the principles they knew to be true against the pragmatic French "Politiques" of the later 1500's; nevertheless, they were still able to contribute much to the societal fabric of French life.

The notion of all authority emanating from the state brought a great disturbance to all the other God-ordained spheres of human life. Family, local assemblies, societies, and communities were all brought under the absolute control of the central state mechanism. With the civil estate being supreme, it reduced the rest to abject servitude in accordance to the will of the crown. Such were the objections and charges made by several Huguenot spokesmen in opposition to the tyrannical establishment. The Huguenots' own volumes and documents which contested the assumptions of a Machiavellian vision of principalities and powers have been passed down to us. Their writings opposed an unchecked, absolutist scheme of civil governance, yet the seeds of what they proposed in return would usher in a way of understanding that set the terms for still another massive cultural turn. They set in motion quite a different societal doctrine which would determine much of European and North American culture over the subsequent centuries.

Their ideas were set forth in the early Huguenot writings such as *Vindiciae, Contra Tyrannos* (Vindication Against Tyrants), postulating a return to *"certain first principles"* in reorganizing legitimate authority and rule. From its preface (which was, incidentally, dated 1577, the year that Henry III had revoked an earlier Edict of Toleration), *Vindiciae* began with a direct affront upon the whole of Machiavellian philosophy:

> *... there could be no more certain and prompt remedy than if the rule of princes and the right of peoples (who are under them) were referred to their legitimate and certain first principles. By this means the power of both would be kept within bounds, beyond or short of which the right administration of the commonwealth clearly could not survive; nor, of course, could the teachings of Machiavelli, which are completely overturned by these principles, be accepted.*[4]

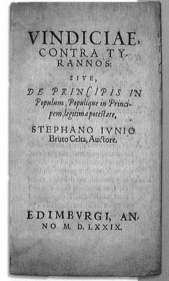

Vindiciae spelled out those *"first principles"* as the lines of obedience that God Himself had designated to run between the Almighty and all legitimate earthly rule. It called for moral means as well as moral ends in civil governance, and decried the strong arm of outcome-based pragmatism. Unlike the tyrannical Machiavellian principles at work in France, the type of prince envisioned in *Vindiciae* had his own subordinate, covenantal duty before God, to respect Him in protecting all those whom he served:

This is the title page of the Huguenot book *Vindiciae, Contra Tyrannos*, which was a biblically-based covenantal counterblast against tyranny. Not printed until 1579, it was issued in Basil with a false Edinburgh imprint to conceal the publisher's identity.

> *When the covenant is ratified between God and the king, it is done on this condition: that the people should be, and should remain forever, the people of God. Without doubt this was to demonstrate that God does not deprive Himself of His property and possession, when He hands*

---

4. *Vindiciae, Contra Tyrannos* (1994), translation of the original preface, p. 9.

over the people to kings, but that is conveyed in order to be ruled, cared for, and nurtured, just as he who chooses a shepherd for his flock nonetheless remains its owner.[5]

A. The French monarch held the nobility in his grasp, as shown in this illustration of the French king and court (1547).

Vindiciae provided a powerful frontal attack upon the idea of civil tyranny. It went on to challenge any flanking move by which a king might attempt to command his people apart from the precepts demonstrated in God's Word. "Brutus,"[6] *Vindiciae*'s pseudonymous author, laid out the biblical model for civil rule in terms of a civil covenant, or binding agreement, between rulers and people under God. Brutus stated that God had first set His own honor and standards before princes and magistrates by which to gauge the adequacy of their performance under Him. According to *Vindiciae*, they were merely His shepherds. They were always God's inferiors; thus, rulers being under Him, having been vested with authority by Him, were therefore invested with God's purpose for them. That purpose thereby bound those in any earthly authority unto God, or as *Vindiciae* put it, it bound them "with" God Himself.

Vindiciae developed its argument by pointing back to the type of rule that God had vested in ancient Israel in its *"foedere inter Deum & regem,"*[7] or "covenant between God and a king." Thus, a "federal" (foedere in Latin) civil covenant from God gave man no absolute dominion, for absolute dominion remained with God. All civil rule was a representative investment and was always accountable to Him, and, as a representative investment, it bound the ruler both to God and man. For example, even when the Israelites were allowed to have a king, he was only given kingly authority *"on this condition: that he observes the law of God."*[8] That fact alone left no room for arbitrary or absolutist power in the civil estate, and taken as a principle for all earthly rule, made any legitimate human authority covenantally bound to God.

B. The covenant which bound the Israelite people and rulers together under God was kept in the Ark of the Covenant, as depicted in this English Bible woodcut from 1549. *Vindiciae* also saw a "federal" covenant between God, the rulers, and the people as the biblical example for Europe.

Further, *Vindiciae* stated that the people were vested with their own responsibility from God, as noted in *"many passages in Scripture."*[9] For example, it noted that when Moses was dying he enumerated the terms of the covenant to the people, and the responsibilities in their own *"pacta conventa,"*[10] or contracted agreement, to keep them. The covenantal agreement of the sons of Israel, which bound both the ruler and the ruled, was kept in the *"Ark of the covenant"*[11] as a visible symbol of their constituted obligations to both God and one another.

5. Ibid., p. 18.
6. Attributed to Phillipe-Duplessis-Mornay.
7. Brutus, *Vindiciae, Contra Tyrannos*, Latin 1st ed. (Edinburgh [Basil], 1579), p. 11.
8. *Vindiciae, Contra Tyrannos* (1994), p. 23. (Also see Deuteronomy 17:18-20.)
9. *Vindiciae, Contra Tyrannos*, English edition (1994), p. 22, compared with *Vindiciae*, Latin edition (1579), p. 13.
10. *Vindiciae, Contra Tyrannos*, Latin ed. (1579), p. 13.
11. *Vindiciae, Contra Tyrannos* (1994), p. 22, compared with *Vindiciae* (1579), p. 13.

Vindiciae therefore pointed to the ancient nation of Israel as the covenantal model for Western European Christendom. As a fundamental principle of their rule, Western European kings were sub-regents of God and were, by their coronation oaths (royal oaths of office), known to be invested with their civil authority under Him: *"we see that kings are invested by God with the kingdom in almost the same way as vassals are by a superior lord with a fief* [feudal estate]."[12]

Vindiciae then looked to the specific stipulations that God had provided to all princes under His authority. In both old Israel and new Europe, all rulers were to look to God's Laws by which to both honor Him and the people that they were ordained to serve:

Just as Israel's king was bound as a bondservant to God by a covenant oath, he was also bound to the common good of the people. King Solomon's coronation was depicted in this engraved Dutch map cartouche (1672).

> *By the law of God, which we are discussing, we understand the two tables of the law handed to Moses, which, like hard and fast limits, ought to circumscribe the authority of all princes. The first comprises the worship of God, and the second duty towards neighbours: the first, I say, piety; and the second, justice united with charity, from which the preaching of the Gospel does not in the least detract, but to which, on the contrary, it lends authority.*[13]

The Huguenots were therefore not opposed to a monarchy, and even at times sought its protection against the secularist French "Politiques"; yet, the monarchy was always seen by them to be held in check by its truly constituted restraints – by its covenant with God and His people.

Such a concept of human authority was championed by a wide array of Christian reformers in other spheres of human life. The Huguenots in France and their allies in England and Scotland of the mid-to-late 1500's, clearly saw the Christian church in terms of covenantal bonds among believers. Christ's body of believers was therefore to be less structured than a massive ecclesiastical organization such as they saw emanating from Rome, and yet much more than an individual escape hatch from earth to heaven. The Reformed Christians thus saw themselves as covenantally obliged on earth with binding obligations to both God and man.

The Holy Testaments were also viewed by the reformers as covenants which mandated earthly duties to those who were heavenly-minded. Such a charge presented Christians with an obligation to maintain the true faith in covenant with others of Christ's Church in every sphere of human responsibility. For one, it imposed upon them an obligation to lend assistance to others in affliction, since avoiding such earthbound obligations would bring scorn upon Christ's heaven-bound saints:

> *Impious are all those who are Christians in name only, who want to participate in the sacred communion of the church, but who do not even sip from the cup of bitterness with their brothers; who seek*

12. *Vindiciae, Contra Tyrannos* (1994), p. 29.
13. Ibid., p. 30.

salvation in the church, but who do not care about the salvation and security of the church and its members.[14]

Though *Vindiciae*'s author was chiefly speaking of a covenantal obligation for other Christian magistrates to offer aid in the afflictions of their persecuted brethren in France, his argument stemmed from a principle of much wider obligations, as *Vindiciae* continued:

In short, they acknowledge one God the Father, and one family in the church; and they profess themselves to be one body in Christ. Yet they do not render assistance to Christ when He is afflicted in His members, or share their resources with Him when He is destitute. What do we consider shall be the punishment for this impiety?[15]

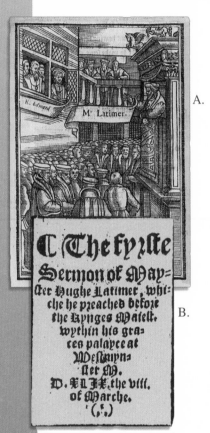

The most outspoken voice of thorough reform in England:

A. Hugh Latimer preached tirelessly (shown here before the king) to reform every sphere of English society (woodcut in Foxe's *Actes and Monumentes*, 1576 edition).

B. This is the copy block from the title page of Hugh Latimer's first published sermon (1549). He was, incidentally, martyred under Queen Mary I in 1555.

According to such comprehensive tenets of the reformers, God gave Christians multileveled covenantal obligations. They indeed had a duty to be obedient to the laws of the monarchy, but also a duty to care for those who were afflicted – for example, those persecuted by a tyrannical ruler himself. Their first obligation being to God Himself obliged all the faithful to their every earthly responsibility, whether it be in their household or local church, their occupation or local societies, as well as the commonwealth at large. Obedience to a prince or ruler as merely one sphere of Christian obligation could not exclude every other covenantal responsibility, as one duty would not annul the rest. Christians simply could not remain in covenantal obedience to God in every other obligation while absolutely obliged toward a prince in blind, passive obedience. The comprehensive nature of one's duty to God could not be commanded by a civil ruler unless one was to assume that his commands, in all things at all times, represented the very voice of God.

The rise of royal absolutism, though effective in directing Western culture away from feudalism, had brought dire consequences by presenting Europe with systems of abject tyranny. The rise of such power brought the realization that absolutism had proven no better in the state than it had in the Church under feudalism. To the Reformed Christians, the time had come to press for a restoration of the honor due God's own absolute supremacy. And, the type of comprehensive reformation that they would pursue would be one that would bind all responsibilities to God within every sphere of human existence. The tendency for the abuses and the corruptions of absolutism in both church and state had become all too apparent; and to the reformers, the time for a purer reformation had been providentially handed to them by God.

14. Ibid., p. 180.
15. Ibid.

Chapter 2: The Anglican Establishment

The Partial Reformation of England's Church and State

IN England, Henry VIII had earlier in the century begun wielding his own absolutist scepter. Throughout the Middle Ages, England, like the rest of Western Europe, had also been dominated by its feudal lords and the overarching Church of Rome. With the advent of Protestantism in Germany under Martin Luther, Henry, who had been a powerful advocate of the Roman authority in England, eventually found that the new movement provided him with a rare opportunity.

By breaking with Rome in the mid-1530's the English monarch was able to obtain a divorce from the first of his (eventual) six wives as well as gain power and wealth theretofore unseen in the British Isles. He had placed within his own grasp a venerable empire. By taking upon himself the right of personal rule over both church and state, Henry had laid claim to personal dominion over every aspect of English life. Because of the Crown's newly found wealth, it was able to dominate the new Protestant Church establishment as well as the nobility and its Parliament; and, through his royal agents, it was also free to dominate the sanctuaries of all English homes down to the meanest of tenements. Though the yoke of the feudal lords had been broken, England found herself at the whims of an untrustworthy king. Henry embraced Reformation and used Protestantism just long enough to turn against its most splendid beauties, just as he had embraced and used his new Protestant wife, Anne Boleyn, just long enough to see her head roll from the scaffold.

It was against such a ravenously royal appetite that a new vocal brand of English Protestants first put their own protests to print. The outspoken English reformer John Hooper first protested (from a safe distance) as a refugee in Zurich in the mid-1540's. He pleaded for Christ to be recognized as the true authoritative Lord and Master over England's souls, as well as its families, its church, and its commonwealth. At a time when it was thought that the peasant class had little capacity beyond blind obedience, Hooper pressed the point. When such common rabble was deemed far too ignorant to grasp the precepts of the Bible, Hooper and others strove to unveil God's own Words unto every householder, every laborer, every churchman, and every English subject. He had a heart which abounded in the Word and saw it as God's abundance for England. Hooper envisioned England's hopes through the restoration of the authority of the Bible in its homes, and accordingly wrote of the responsibility of every English father:

As the scripture teachite Christ to be the ueri trew prist ād bishope the church, prayth for the churche, satisfieth the Ire of god for the sinne of the church and only sanctifieth the churche. So doothe it proue Christ to be the Kyng Emperour and protector of the churche. And that by th of fice and property of a kyng that defendithe his subiectes, not only by his godly lawes, but also by forse and ciuile resistance. As the Ennymies of his commune wealthe shall ministre occaciō. By those too menes euery cōmune wealthe is preseruid as the scripture teachith.

A.

A. Shown here is John Hooper's historic declaration that Jesus Christ is the only true head of His Church and the only true King of His Kingdom. Christ's crown required families to honor Him to the point of civil resistance to encroachments by men (1547).

He shuld cause his familie and chyldren to rede some part of the Bible for there erudition to know god. Likwyce he shuld constrayne them to pray unto god for the promocion of his holy word and for the preservacion of the governers of the commune wealthe so that no day shuld passe withe out prayer, and augmentation of knolege in the religion of Christ.[1]

In his book, *A Declaration of Christe and of His Offyce Compylyd*, Hooper was among the first to decry any usurpation of Christ's rule in every private or public capacity. He pointed to Christ's ultimate dominion as Lord to the point of suggesting resistance to oppressive tyranny. For Hooper, Christ alone was the only absolute King in dominion, as well as the Emperor and Protector upon the thrones of church and state:

> *As the scripture teachite Christ to be the veri trew prist* [priest] *and bishope* [of] *the church, prayth for the churche, satisfieth the Ire of god for the sinne of the church... .*[2]

Henry had been given the title "Defender of the Faith" by the Roman Pontiff at a time when he was strenuously opposing Protestantism in England. Then, upon the establishment of Protestantism under his royal scepter, Henry officially declared himself "Defender of the Faith" and had his Parliament confirm the title. Hooper, though, was bold enough to declare that the title should remain with Jesus Christ:

> *So doothe it prove Christ to be the Kyng Emperour and protector of the churche. And that by th*[e] *office and property of a kyng that defendithe his subiectes, not only by his godly lawes, but also by forse and civile resistance. As the Ennymies of his commune wealthe shall ministre occacion. By those too menes every commune wealthe is preservid as the scripture teachith.*[3]

B.

B. Henry VIII saw himself not only as the "Defender of the Faith," but as the authoritative head of Christ's Church in England. He was here depicted passing the Bible into the hands of his bishops (circa 1540).

Hooper was so bold as to advocate *"civile resistance"* to royal tyranny in the cause of Christ's true Church. But, when Henry's daughter Mary I came to the throne in 1553, her own brand of royal dominion moved to eliminate any vestige of the Protestant reforms. Reformed Protestantism had been encouraged during the brief reign of her brother, Edward VI, immediately following their father's death. Under Edward, Hooper and others had been given the king's sanction to promulgate God's Word to its greatest effect. Following Edward's death, Mary turned against the reformers by again outlawing the reading of the Sacred text

1. John Hooper, *A Declaration of Christe and of His Offyce Compylyd* (Zurich, 1547), leaf Di, side 2.
2. Ibid., leaf Kii, side 2.
3. Ibid., leaves Kii-Kiii.

in English and prohibiting ownership of any Protestant writings. Households were invaded and searched. England's clergy were forbidden to marry by the forced laws which decreed that even those who had previously married must then divorce and abandon their 'illegal' spouses and children. The jurisdiction of Rome was reestablished as the official church in 1553, an act which many reformers considered as nothing less than a foreign and alien invasion of their faith. The Anglican Establishment was thus undone, Bibles were locked, condemned, or burned, and the church was structured again under the dominion of an English prelate answerable elsewhere.

Life became severe for anyone holding to the Reformed faith, as the torture conducted under Mary earned her the infamous anachronism of "Bloody" and an enduring epitaph of "Bloody Mary." Hooper was among the first to actually be put to flames, and scores of other leading voices of the reformers were silenced by her royal administrators. Hundreds of English men and women of every stature were also reduced by flames, as the nation turned toward an all-out inquisition when the Queen married another absolutist prince, Philip of Spain, in 1554. Under the united monarchy of Philip and Mary, England was obliged to the man, Philip, who above all others on earth was ardently bent upon rooting out the Reformation in faith, family, church, and state by way of the torturing arm of their inquiring agents.

A. This is the preface to an act passed under Mary I which reversed the Reformation. Among its demands, the act forced married ministers to abandon their families (1553).

B. Shown here is a woodcut depicting the public burning of confiscated Reformed Bibles and books (1550's).

It was at that point that many refugees, who had by then fled to the various Reformed sanctuaries in Germany and Switzerland, began to publish the same principles which were decades later to appear in the Huguenots' *Vindiciae*. Christopher Goodman, the pastor of the English church of refugees in Geneva, preached of obedience to God through resistance to clerical or civil tyranny. His most popular sermon was published in a 1558 treatise: *How Superior Powers Oght to be Obeyd of their subjects: and Wherin they may lawfully by Gods*

C. Shown here is a (Latin) warrant written out in the names of King Philip and Queen Mary for the civil punishment of Henry Harryson due to his excommunication by the Bishop of London. It demanded that the Warden of the Clinque *"do justice to the said Henry bodily according to the custom of England until satisfaction has been given to the holy Church both for the contempt and for the injury which have been caused her by him"* (1554).

123

by Gods Worde be disobeyed and resisted. The sermon became an early hallmark of English civil resistance, and Goodman was astute to draw the necessary link between the issues of civil tyranny with the violation of private families:

> *Wo be to you Rulers and Magistrates, from the hieste* [highest] *to the loweste: for that by your ruling without the feare of God, see your own fleshe and bloude, the very lambes of God dayly to fall by flocks, not into the diche or pit, but into the unsaciable mouthes of the wolfishe papistes: not only to be hurte and injuried, but cruelly to be devoured both bodie and goodes, and their poore wives, children, and families destroyed, and go a begginge. And yet neither the sorouful sobbes, and continual teares of the lamentable mothers, nor the pitiful cry of the spoyled infants, nor the extreme necessitie of their dispersed servants, besides the shamefull betrayinge and subversion of the whole Realme daily approachinge, can once move your harde and stonie harts with pitie to defende their cause, and delyver them from tyranny.*[4]

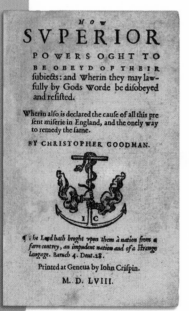

Title page of Christopher Goodman's *Superior Powers*, published by the Reformed English Church in Geneva (1558). England's Goodman (1520-1603) along with Scotland's John Knox were chosen by the refugee congregation in Geneva as its co-pastors. The English-speaking assembly at Geneva thus became the first independently covenanted congregation. Goodman, a noted first-generation Puritan scholar, also worked on the translation committee of the Geneva Bible (1560).

According to Goodman, the ancient Hebrew example showed that God's people were to be protected by their rulers. They were to be bound and covenanted together to the extent that when the people were in need, the ruler was in need, and when the nation suffered, the rulers suffered with it. The Hebrew judges, those who were chosen from among the people of Israel, were to be locked together in such a union as to be in common service to the whole, favoring neither rich nor poor in law or justice, as according to the common standard by which God had bound them all. Goodman then drew upon the inspiration of the ancient Hebrew covenant in justification of England's need to oppose Philip and Mary's regime:

> *Mattathias that worthie Captayne of the Jewes, as it is written in the First Boke of the Maccabees, coulde not so lightly excuse him self when he was commanded by the cruel officers of wicked Antiochus (which had spoyled their Tempel, rased* [raised] *their wauls* [walls]*, murthered their brethren, and set up idolatrie, in so muche as all for the most parte, applied them selves to their wicked parsuations) that he, with the residue shulde forsake the Lawes and sacrifices of their God, to worshipp strange Goddes: he made answere, to the officer of Antiochus the kinge (which would to God our Noble men had perfetly* [perfectly] *learned) That thoghe all Nations apparteyning to kinge Antiochus shulde obeye him, so the every man would declyne from the Laws of his countrie: yet I, (saieth he) my children, and brethren, wil stand in the covenant of our fathers, &c.*[5]

4. Christopher Goodman, *How Superior Powers Oght to be Obeyd of Their Subjects ...* (Geneva, 1558), pp. 91-92.
5. Ibid., p. 75.

Goodman's analogy between the ancient Hebrews and the English speaking nations was to the point. England and Scotland had like obligations which must be defended by God's faithful. In the years following Goodman's sermon, his co-pastor, John Knox, took up the cause of reformation after returning to his native Scotland. In 1564 Knox exhorted the Scottish nobility to respect its obligation to hold the crown to its covenant oath:

> *Princes are not onely bound to keep Lawes and Promises to their subjects; But, also, That in case they fail, they justly may be bridled* [by the nobility and magistrates]: *For the band betwixt the Prince and the people is reciprocall.*[6]

Even though talk of such covenantal fidelity first surfaced through the English reformers' opposition to civil and clerical tyranny, they also soon embraced the idea of such a fidelity in all their societal obligations. Any human relation that demanded virtue was seen as requiring such a godly frame. According to the covenantal model, all societies must derive their virtues from among their members, conforming themselves to the will of God. The mutual observance of God's moral code would itself provide the means of their common virtue. Those ruling from above would be in service to those under them by their submission to the moral code, and those ruled would obey them in a like dignity by observing the one and the same code. Such multitiered, mutual honor would provide their societies and larger communities with a self-governing people. Less civil regulation would be necessary from the top, yielding more God-given liberties to the governed at the local level.

To the more Reformed-minded Christians, the responsibility of self-government and godly fidelity would become defining features of their every societal duty. And, like the English refugees, many Scots viewed comprehensive covenantal reform as the cure for an entire spectrum of personal and national sins. Unified as believers into covenanted churches and united as churches covenanted together, they would find an overall strength theretofore not seen in Scotland by self-governing people. They saw that God's will would best be accomplished by a people who would, first in the societal sphere of the church assemblies, embrace His modes as their model and His precepts as their standard. In May 1559, seven Scottish congregations united themselves at Perth, Scotland to covenant themselves:

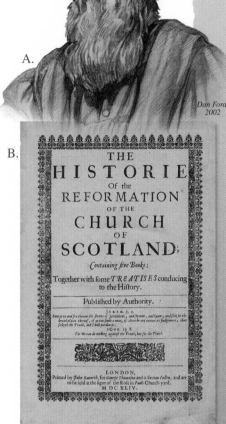

A.

Dan Ford, 2002

B.

A. The visionary giant of covenantal reform, John Knox (1514-1572), returned to Scotland from Geneva in the late 1550's and pressed his nation toward thorough Reformation.

B. This is the title page of Knox's *The Historie Of the Reformation of the Church of Scotland*, in which he chronicled the principles, debates, and events which achieved Scotland's Reformation. When the Puritans first attempted to publish Knox's *Historie* in England in the late 1500's, it was halted on the press and most of the copies were confiscated by Anglican authorities. The *Historie* was not permitted to be published in its entirety until 1644 at a time when the English Parliament was itself contesting King Charles's absolutist control over England.

---

6. John Knox to the Scottish National Assembly: John Knox, *The Historie Of the Reformation of the Church of Scotland* (London, 1644), p. 396.

[I]n the name of Jesus Christ, for setting forth his glory, understanding nothing more neccessary for the same, then to keep constant amity, unity, and fellowship together, according as they are commanded by God are confederate [covenanted] *and become bounded in the presence of God.*[7]

Dan Ford, 2002

A.

B.

A. Elizabeth I became Queen of England in 1558 and inherited its Royal Church and Commonwealth.

B. This is the text inset from the title page of the official *Articles* of the Church of England. The *Thirty-Nine Articles* prescribed by England's bishops and archbishops under Elizabeth established Reformed biblical doctrine as the recognized faith in England. However, the *Articles* also established a weighty ecclesiastical system under the crown which suppressed the possibility for a more thorough covenantal reform in practice (first complete edition of the *Thirty-Nine Articles*, begun in 1562 and not finalized until the publication of this edition in 1571).

With covenantal reform established in the hearts of the English refugees in Geneva and the first seeds of covenantal church and civil governance deposited on the soils of Scotland, the precepts of a more comprehensive Reformation had been planted on the British Isles. Following Queen Mary's passing in 1558, the English refugees returned en masse to England under the reign of her younger sister and Protestant heir, Elizabeth. They had held out hopes that a Protestant reestablishment would bring England to a thorough reformation. In her civil establishment many were initially pleased as persecution subsided and several leaders of the Reformed faith became key court counselors. In her Church settlement, Elizabeth embraced most Protestant doctrines, but much less so, the Reformed modes of church administration. Though the reading of the English Bible was reauthorized and it found a prominent place within the common English home, the church framework was structured in a system that appeared by many to be darkened with the shadows of royal absolutism. The Anglican Establishment was to the reformers a contradiction in reform: on the one hand, it was settled upon sound biblical orthodoxy, but on the other, it was structured beneath a wieldy human monarch. The Anglican Church was therefore controlled from the top down, in an elaborate hierarchy of archbishops and bishops, deans and sub-deans, down to the lowly regarded laymen. Such an inconsistency, to the reformers, meant an establishment of Christian confusion, with God's Word encouraged on the one hand, but the hierarchical system blocking Christ's administration on the other. The reformers argued that such a system ultimately bred ignorance and sin, for such an establishment could not do for England that which Christ's biblical headship was intended to do:

... surely our sins are growen ripe, our ignorance is equall with the ignorance of our leaders: we are lost they cannot find us,

7. Knox, *Historie Of the Reformation of the Church of Scotland*, p. 440.

126

we are sicke, they cannot heale us, we are hungarie, they cannot [feed] us, except they leade us by other mens lights and heale us by saying a prescript forme of service, or else feed us with homilies, that are too homely too be set in place of God's scriptures.[8]

It had become far too apparent that further reformation would not emanate from the Crown, and the time had come for the reformers' historic appeal, called *An Admonition to Parliament*. The 1572 *Admonition* was focused upon what the reformers saw as the greatest need. They pressed upon Parliament, and through it hoped to press upon the Church hierarchy for a purer reformation. Their appeal met stiff resistance from the bishops, as it had been the bishops' own prior resistance to reform which had already yielded the term "Puritan" in denoting them with satiric scorn. In their *Admonition*, though, the reformers complained of the derogatory use of the term Puritan, for it was used to cast them as simple, ignorant, and (in the royal scheme of things) as the least dignified sort of Englishmen. The preface to the *Admonition* then argued the Puritan case in return:

> *Either must we have a right ministry of God, and a right government of his church, according to the scriptures set up (both which we lacke) or else there can be no right religion, nor yet for contempt thereof can Gods plagues be from any while differed. And therfore though they link in together, & slaunderously charge poore men (whom they have made poore) with grievous faults, calling them Puritans, worse than the Donatists [heretics], exasperating & setting on, suche as be in authoritie againste them:*

8. Thomas Cartwright, et al., *An Admonition to Parliament*, excerpted from *An Answere to a certain Libel titled, An Admonition to Parliament* (London, 1572), p. 165.

A.

A. The earlier reformers such as Knox and Goodman set the precedent for the later Puritans to press for biblical reforms in England and Scotland. This woodcut depicting their earlier trumpet calls for truth appeared in a later sixteenth-century Puritan tract.

B.

> Admonition.
>
> *The Preface.*
>
> Amos. 8. 11. 12. &c. Ma. 21. 13. &c 1.Cor. 11. 30. ... any while differred. And therfore though they link in together, & slaunderously charge poore men (whom they have made poore) with grievous faults, calling them Puritans, worse thã the Donatists, exasperating & setting on, suche as be in authoritie againste them: having hytherto miserably handled them with reuilings, depriuations, imprisonements, banishmentes, & such like extremities, yet is these poore mens cause neuer the [h] worse; nor these chalegers the better; nor God his [i] hande the further of, to linke in with his against them; nor you (christian brethren) must neuer the rather without examination [k] condemne them.

C.

> Admonition.
>
> Now then, if you will restore the Churche to his ancient officers, this you must do. In stead of an Archbyshop or Lorde Byshop, you must make [z] equalitie of ministers.
>
> The sixth. Then no minister placed in any congregation, but by the consente of the people.

B. The *Admonition to Parliament* as a Reformed manifesto and an historic defense of Puritanism: Published by Reformed scholars at Cambridge University in 1572, the historic *Admonition* publicly defended the Puritans in this preface. The *Admonition* asked Parliament to intercede as England's lords and magistrates on behalf of the nation's biblical integrity.

C. The *Admonition* as a hallmark of self-government: The *Admonition to Parliament* stated that the Church was to follow the original form of choosing officers for its own government. A congregation was to be ruled under Christ by local elders and ministered unto by those chosen *"by the consente of the people."*

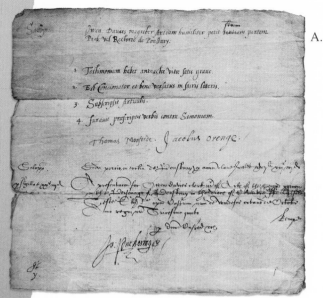

A.

A. This is a crown license to preach signed by England's Lord Keeper of the Seal, John Puckering, in 1592. In order to get such a license (here written in Latin), a prospective minister was required to subscribe to the *Articles* and acknowledge the ecclesiastical authority of the queen and bishops. Puckering also prosecuted several leading Puritans who dissented from this system of patronage.

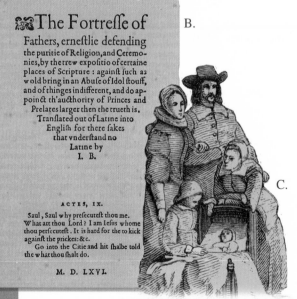

B.

C.

B. This is the title page of *The Fortresse of Fathers*, one of the great early Puritan tracts, advocating a return to original Christianity and opposing *"th' authority of Princes and Prelates larger then the trueth is"* (1566).

C. Covenantal precepts flourished in the homes of sixteenth-century Puritan families. England's later generations owed their understanding of biblical self-government to their Reformed forebearers (shown in a nineteenth-century engraving of a Puritan family).

havyng hytherto miserably handled them with revilings, deprivations, imprisonements, banishmentes, & such like extremities... .[9]

On one side of the issue, the "High Church" Anglicans argued for the dignity, stability, and security of royal control over the administration of the Church. On the other side, the "Low Church" reformers argued for an administration under localized elders and deacons. The *Admonition* brought a backlash against the reformers by the High Church Establishment, and a further published defense of the *Admonition* by the outspoken scholar Thomas Cartwright landed him in prison. Although they were forced to lay low, the Puritans did not lay idle, for they learned to quietly nurture England's future generations in their household cradles and to preach their doctrines along the royal byways, themselves ever gleaning more from the societal fount of God's Word, and then teaching its precepts to still others.

Over the following generation, the Reform movement flourished as a noteworthy subculture below the High Churchmen's watch. In spite of being handled with *"revilings, deprivations, imprisonements, banishmentes, & such like extremities,"*[10] the so-called Puritans flourished throughout England and Scotland. Similar to the ancient Hebrew captives in Egypt, they were hidden, as it were, among England's reeds and nourished as if by their Hebrew midwives below the gaze of a Pharaoh.[11] And, also similar to those Israelites of old, they then grew to become powerful people over the remaining thirty-plus years of Elizabeth's lengthy reign.

9. Preface to *An Admonition to Parliament*, excerpted from *An Answere ... Admonition to Parliament*, pp. 9-10.
10. Ibid., p. 10.
11. See Exodus 1:17-21.

Chapter 3: The Puritan Doctrine

The Proclamation of Covenantal Living in all Spheres of Life

Y the late sixteenth century the Bible had found a prominent place amid English society. It had, since the Middle Ages, already been the backbone of its laws, but by the seventeenth century it had obtained a cultural status theretofore unknown. Due to the tireless devotion of several generations of reformers, it had become the highest form of English literature and the greatest influence upon higher English thought. Not only its laws, but all public policies had to be justifiable in light of the biblical text.

Nevertheless, corruption and vice prevailed as God's Word was still too often seen in its archaic medieval light – as a high and holy book far above the peasant's comprehension, to be put aside and only handled by a few prelates and bishops. That book, though, had found its way beside the commoners' hearths due to the same tireless efforts of the reformers. As it was read by more and more of the common Englishmen, it also became all the more apparent that there was much reform left undone. Not only were the courts of the nobility and the chambers of the archbishops seen as corrupt in the Bible's inspired light, so, too, were the manners and morals of the entire nation. As commoners began to read their devotions for themselves, they likewise began to accumulate concordances and commentaries. This tended to add fuel to the fire as the moral standards of the Puritans seemed all the more consistent with a comprehensive understanding of the biblical texts. The Geneva Bibles of the later sixteenth century often came with additional tables and concordances bound in at the end which made the Scriptures still more practicable and systematic. The popular *Downame's Concordance* of the early seventeenth century which often accompanied the later Authorized (King James) translation, frequently had on its title page the timeless wisdom from the Psalmist: *"Thy Word is a lamp unto my feet and a light unto my pathes."*[1] In that century, greater and greater numbers of typical English men, women, and families would endeavor to live by those words to their fullest.

It was at the advent of the seventeenth century that the reformers began to anticipate far better prospects for a more comprehensive, covenantal culture. The idea of covenantal fidelity that had been cradled, preached, and taught by the Puritans had given rise to a popular hope for a national reformation. The Puritans had grown in great numbers, power, and wealth during the final years of the queen. With Elizabeth's passing in 1603, they anticipated more favorable encouragements from their new monarch, James I, who had himself been raised

---

1. *"Psal. 119.150."* in John Downame, *A Concordance, or Table to the Bible ...* (London, 1639), title page verse.

Dan Ford, 2002

A.

B.

THE
Kings Maiesties Speech, as
it was deliuered by him in the vpper
house of the Parliament to the Lords
Spirituall and Temporall, and to the
Knights, Citizens and Burgesses
there assembled,

On Munday the 19. day of March 1603.
being the first day of this present Parlia-
ment, and the first Parliament of
his Maiesties Raigne.

C.

At my first comming, although
I found but one Religion, and that which by my
selfe is professed, publiquely allowed, and by the
Law maintained: Yet found I another sort of Religion, besides a priuate Secte, lurking within the
bowels of this Nation. The first is the true Religion, which by me is professed and by the Law is established: The second is the falsly called Catholikes,
but truely Papistes. The third, which I call a Secte
rather then Religion, is the Puritanes & Nouelists,
who doe not so farre differ from vs in points of Religion, as in their confused forme of Policie and
Paritty, being euer discontented with the present
Gouernement, and impatient to suffer any superioritie, which maketh their Sect vnable to be suffered
in any well gouerned Common wealth.

A. This is a portrait sketch of King James I
of England (James VI of Scotland) who
severely suppressed and persecuted the
Puritans in England and the Presbyterians
in Scotland.

B. This is the title page of James's speech to
the Lords, attacking the Puritans (1603).

C. Shown here is an excerpt of the text of
James's 1603 speech in which he decried
the Puritans as *"unable to be suffered in
any well governed Common wealth."*

in Scotland on the doctrines of John Knox. But,
upon his ascension to the throne in England, the
reformers were quickly disappointed, for notions of
self-government did not sit well with James. The
church and state apparatus, as it had been under
Elizabeth, would remain in place all the more under
James.

Any semblance of local or private control
presented a threat to a crown such as his, for James
supposed himself as having a divine appointment, a
royal destiny, and a God-given right to rule
absolutely over the administration of his Church
and his State. James considered the prescriptive
duties of the crown to be established by mandates
from heaven. Yet, his claim to divine right would be
the very issue to ultimately tarnish his crown and
bring irreconcilable differences between himself
and the obnoxious "Puritanes" (as he came to call
them). The High Church Anglicans also held that
the reign of Christ was vested solely in the scepter
of James. They maintained that God's sufficiency
for England was imparted through the person of the
king, and like that of absolutist France, all authority
whether divine or human descended from there.

The Puritans, on the other hand, insisted that the
people were also vested with a mandate from God
in their own direct accountability and
responsibilities to Him. To them, James's high-
handed mechanism could neither constitutionally
nor righteously administer their own personal,
family, or local societal obligations, for those were
duties imparted by an Authority far higher than a
crown of a mere earthly king. They carefully
guarded their personal responsibilities, for it was
thought that James's absolutist Church and State
apparatus was, in effect, attempting to supplant
Christ by blocking the believers from their own
direct callings in Him. It was on that point that
many Puritans, as a sub-group known as Separatists,
concluded that the Church Establishment represented
the very kind of idolatry of which God forbade.

Most grievous to James was the fact that the
Puritans held an idea that God's moral sufficiency
was disseminated into the nation through the
subjects as well as through the king. The Crown
maintained that God's virtues descended first upon
the king and then down unto his subjects through

his crown. That civic doctrine would bring the issues of divine right and limits upon the royal prerogative to England's political table. The Puritans insisted that civil virtue was designated by God to be maintained by mutual moral obligations between the people and the prince. The Royalists countered by insisting that moral virtue was passed to the people through their subjection to the king who stood over them in God's stead. They accused the Puritans of being moral malcontents and the repositors of hatred toward any legitimate civil governance. In his first speech before Parliament in 1603, James (none too graciously) announced to the House of Lords that he had detected a political threat amid his realm. Thrown against the Puritans was his charge that they were *"ever discontented with the present Governement, and impatient to suffer any superioritie, which maketh their Sect unable to be suffered in any well governed Common wealth."*[2]

In the future light of history it would prove ironic that James's very 'unsufferables' would put forth successful models of governance in family, economy, church, and commonwealth, which would outlive his own notions by centuries. It would also become, in another sense, ironic that the Puritans' covenantal modes of self-governance would eventually lead to England's loss of the colonies instituted by James's own ordination. Yet, what would prove most ironic was the fact that the principles which would ultimately drive the offspring of those Puritan 'malcontents' to their ultimate Independence in 1776, would come from the text of Scripture that he himself had authorized to keep England pacified. James had conceded to the Puritans just one of their many demands for reformation at the Hampton Court Conference of 1604. The conference had been called due to the overwhelming "Millenary" petition brought to James by a wide faction of Reformed laymen, clergy, and magistrates. Though it was quite evident that the king would have no part in further reforms in either Scotland or England, a distinguished Oxford Puritan, Dr. Reynolds, had convinced James that an improved version of the text would serve the commonwealth. The new 1611 "Authorized" version of the Bible was at first resisted by many due to its omission of the cherished "Genevan" marginal notes. Though the Puritans at first preferred their older version, in time the "King James version" would prove its worth to both English and American Puritans. By the mid-1600's a wealth of Puritan commentaries made the Geneva Bible's notes less essential. A later generation of thirteen English colonies would find from its principles their cause to take leave of the royal ties first established under the reign of King James.[3]

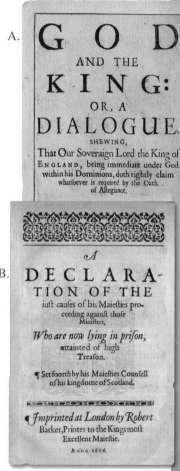

A. Allegiance to God was defined as unqualified submission to the King. This is the title page of James I's demand for an oath of absolute submission, in 1604.

B. This is the title page of James's charge of high treason against several Scottish Presbyterian ministers who attempted to meet in an unsanctioned synod (1606).

2. James I, *The Kings Majesties Speech, as it was delivered by him in the upper house of the Parliament to the Lords ...* (London, 1603), leaf B4.
3. P. Marion Simms, *The Bible in America: Versions that have Played their Part in the Making of the Republic* (New York, 1936), p. 94.

A.

A. Documenting the first era of the civil persecution of Christians:

Shown here is one of the earliest extant depictions of a Christian. It appeared on the face of a Roman oil lamp illustrating a lion devouring a believer. Christ's early faithful saw it as an abomination to bow to civil authorities as if rulers were equal to God, and they often suffered dire public consequences. Such lamps were purchased as arena souvenirs by eyewitnesses to the popular Roman sport (circa A.D. 70).

B.

C.

K I N G is a mortall God on earth, unto whom the Living G o D hath lent his own Name as a great honor, but withall told him he should die like a man, least he should be proud and flatter himself, that G o D hath with his Name imparted unto him his Nature also.

B. This is a contemporary portrait of James I's Chancellor, Francis Bacon (1561-1626).

C. Shown here is Bacon's statement on the divine authority of a monarch: "A KING is a mortall God on earth, unto whom the Living GOD hath lent his own Name as a great honor, but withall told him, he should die like a man ..." (1620).

James had simply been at a loss to understand just how much the covenantally-minded Christians revered all the institutions of government. They successfully implanted biblical governance in their homes, churches, and civil states by sounder methods than James or his son Charles I could have possibly imagined. It had been, in spite of the historic use (or misuse) of civil authorities against the Christians from day one in Rome, that the Christians revered civil institutions. It was because of the Apostles' inspired respect for God's civil institutions that Christianity kept its high regard for civil rule.

It was also despite the strong arm of the English crowns' repeated attempts to repress Reformed Christianity that Puritans never disavowed the whole idea of legitimate civil government. It would have been easy, far too easy, to develop a resentful bias against the power that God invested in the civil estate. Yet, that would ignore a legitimate investment as well as the commands of the Bible. In spite of James, the civil government itself was not viewed by the reformers as something inherently evil, as if by its earthly nature it represented a face of incarnate wickedness. The reformers fully recognized that governments were instituted divinely "for the good" of the people and the church. The Reformed-minded Christians were doctrinally armed and at the ready to drive home that point borrowed from Paul's Epistle to the Romans. What God had called good could not be deemed evil. *"Principalities and Powers,"* or the *"Higher Powers"* (as the civil authority was referenced in the Puritan Genevan and Authorized 'King James' Bibles), were all under the dominion of Christ and intended by God to render His wrath and punishments against evil.[4] It was essential therefore that the Reformed-minded know the biblical precepts all the more. It was incumbent that they know the true lines of all authority and their specific applications in civil rule. It was not an option for the Puritans to abandon such an obligation any more than it would be for them to abandon their like duty to govern their families. They were astute and went to great lengths to determine the heighth and breadth of all human authority from its reference and sanction in Scripture.

4. See Romans 13:1-5; Colossians 1:15-17; 1 Peter 2:13.

The Covenant of People and Kings

Perhaps the most thorough work concerning the Reformed ideas of human law and civil governance came from the pen of the Scottish Presbyterian Samuel Rutherford in 1644. He published his momentous treatise called *Lex, Rex* on the subject of the limits of royal prerogative (Rex) under the rule of law (Lex). As might be expected, Rutherford centered his arguments on the ascendancy of the higher Law, the biblical Law, over absolutist claims of royal prerogative. Rutherford particularly directed the readers' attention to God's own retained legal prerogative over a nation, as well as to the rule of God's moral Law over both the king and the people. To decipher the terms of such authority, he went to the Scriptures to determine the legitimate nature and extent of civil governing power:

> *The power of Government in generall must be from God: I make good, 1. Because Romans 13. -1. there is no power but of God; the powers that be, are ordained of God. 2. God commandeth obedience, and so subjection of conscience to powers, Rom. 13.5.*[5]

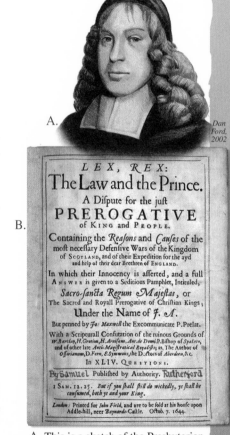

A.

Dan Ford, 2002

B.

To the covenantally-minded Rutherford, these biblical passages did not vest all human authority, much less that of the church or family, solely in the hands of a single potentate on earth. To Rutherford, such passages proved first and foremost that all governance, including civil governance, was from God, and if they were from God they were to serve a godly good:

> *Wherefore we must be subject not only for wrath (or civill punishment) but for conscience sake, I Pet. 2.13. Submit your selves to every ordinance of man for the Lords sake, whether it be to the King as Supreme, &c.*[6]

Rutherford argued that these civil commands in the Scriptures were given to all men of conscience. All men, both the rulers and the ruled alike, were obliged to submit to God. Thus the command to *"submit your selves to every ordinance of man for the Lords sake"* applied to rulers as well as the ruled, and the reformers recognized that God ruled supreme over all. And, if God had set men in a representative position to rule for Him in the civil estate, they had authority only in so far as they ruled according to God. Simply put: God's Lex ruled man's Rex (God's Law ruled man's king) and every other civil endeavor.

A. This is a sketch of the Presbyterian scholar Samuel Rutherford (1600-1661).

B. Shown here is the title page of Rutherford's key work on covenantal governance, *Lex, Rex*, in which he argued that the prerogative of God was over both that of a king and that of the people. He thus concluded that there had to be a covenantal agreement between the two parties. The work was later banned under penalty of death in both England and Scotland.

5. Samuel Rutherford, *Lex, Rex: The Law and the Prince* (London, 1644), p. 1.
6. Ibid.

133

Such a concept may seem radical to the modern mind, but it was certainly not revolutionary at the time of Rutherford. It was known that all authority emanated from God; the question that *Lex, Rex* answered was one of the basis upon which civil rule would be just and righteous as well as respected by the people. It was well accepted that civility in the people meant their due obedience to laws and ordinances; therefore *Lex, Rex* did not argue that the rulers could be disobeyed if they produced unwise or even unjust ordinances. If rulers erred in either of these ways, they would certainly be accountable to God and the people for so doing. However, if the rulers went so far as to demand anything ungodly from those they ruled, those who were ruled were to obey God's Laws first over the commands of any human king or potentate. The idea of rulers being subject to God was that which gave them the respect of the people, and in order to retain the people's submissive respect, the rulers were expected to rule accordingly. The Puritans therefore concluded that any civil establishment must (by the nature of its divine sanction) be recognized as covenantal in its nature and that all rule and submission must be tempered with respect for the highest Authority over all.

To the Puritans, then, God's purpose for civil rule was that it serve much more than its own appetite. It had indeed been vested with certain powers ordained by Him, yet they were powers that were restricted to their proper purpose and maintained within their proper sphere of His sanction. Governments would be abusive or even tyrannical when they attempted to rule beyond their authorized limits or to interfere in spheres of life not ordained to them. Consequently, more than any other people before them, the Puritans strove to delineate the nature of legitimate civil power and define the proper spheres of kings and magistrates. Once the proper lines of authority could be delineated, the nation would be better served and the king and magistrates securely obeyed.

That great struggle over the covenantal lines of civil government marked the beginning of England's historic seventeenth-century debate over the issue of constitutional governments. Rutherford explained that Scripture gave men an unqualified command to submit to the lawful authority that God had invested in the civil covenant. To him, it was evident that there was a covenant *"betwixt the King and his people"* in ancient Israel. Rutherford, then, saw England's precedent expressed in the constitutional terms of King David's coronation oath:

> *There is an oath betwixt the King and his people, laying on, by reciprocating bands, mutuall civill obligations upon the King to the people, and the people to the King, 2 Sam. 5. 3.*[7]

Rutherford and his fellow reformers therefore saw the coronation oath of their king in terms of a similar covenantal pledge before God. The king could not bear the weight of his crown without his reliance upon God, nor could he honor God without serving the people. The king was thereby covenantally obliged unto both God and man:

> *So all the Elders of Israel came to the king to Hebron, and King David made a Covenant with them in Hebron before the Lord, and they annoynted David King over Israel, I Chron. 11. 3.*[8]

7. Ibid., p. 96, quoting 2 Samuel 5:3.
8. Ibid., quoting 1 Chronicles 11:3.

The people, on their part, could not honor God without respecting the power that they had vested in their king at the time of his coronation. To honor God's authority in a civil capacity was to honor the office of their king and civil magistrates. Mutual obligations were constituted in the terms of the agreement between the rulers and the ruled as expressed in the oath. The king as well as the people were therefore faithful to God in so far as they honored the terms to which they had given their consent. As with any covenantal arrangement, there was a built-in accountability that the civil officer be loyal to God and cognizant of His mandates upon him. God would then be honored by the mutual respect between the people, the magistrates, and the crown.

Further, the Puritans saw their civil allegiance in terms of honoring the constitution of the office rather than the will of the office holder. The king or magistrate was bound by God to fulfill the duty inherent in the position he held. To attempt to wield more authority than his duty required was considered a violation of a trust. Puritans pressed the point that the lower magistrates were to be faithful to their trust rather than being duty-bound in subservience to the demands (whether right or wrong) of the king. The lower official would assist the king and the people by keeping the monarch within his own constituted bounds, and obedience was therefore considered a matter of allegiance to the overall commonwealth rather than to the potentate upon a throne.

During the period of English history known as the Commonwealth (the time when the Puritans were at their greatest civil ascendancy), the nation was vicariously ruled without the crown. During that interim (1649-1660), an officeholder's sworn allegiance to the king was replaced with sworn allegiance to the Commonwealth by way of an oath of office: *"So help you God"*:

> *You shall Swear, That you shall be true and faithful to the Commonwealth of England, as it is now Established without King or House of Lords: You shall well and truly execute the Office of Maior within the City of _____ and Liberties thereof, according to the best of your skill, knowledge and power. So help you God.*[9]

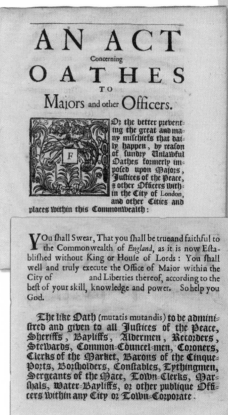

Shown here is the title page and section of text from Parliament's 1649 Act requiring mayors, magistrates, and public officers to take an oath to the Commonwealth of England. Allegiance was to be pledged under God (*"so help you [me] God"*), to the good of the nation, and to its constituted laws by way of an oath of office instead of the oath of fidelity previously required to the will, mandates, or decrees of the king.

There were constituted limits placed upon the powers delegated to any magisterial position which stood as a covenantal trust with the people. The rights

9. Parliament, *An Act Concerning Oathes* ... (London, 1649), title leaf sides a and b.

of the ruler to impose upon the people or their property were strictly limited to the powers vested by that trust; there was no constitutional right to unrighteously tread upon the people or their property. Of such constituted limits, the Puritan divine Richard Baxter wrote during England's Commonwealth period:

> *And where his* [the ruler's] *Covenants with his people limit him, he hath no power in the exempt points; e. g. if he be restrained from raising Taxes without the people's consent, if he yet command the payment of such taxes, he doth so not by Authority: For neither God nor man did ever give him Authority thereto.*[10]

A. *ICHANNES CALVINVS.*   B.

THE
Lavves and Statu-
tes of Geneua, as well concerning ecclesiasticall Discipline, as ciuill regiment, with certeine Proclamations duly executed, whereby Gods religion is most purelie mainteined, and their common wealth quietli gouerned: Translated out of Frenche into Englishe by Robert Fills.

Except the Lorde kepe the Citie, the kepet watcheth in vayne. PSAL. 127.

PRINTED AT LON-
don by Rouland Hall, dwellyng in Gutter Lane, at the fygne of the halfe Egle and the Keye.
1562.

A. Himself a French (Huguenot) refugee in Geneva, John Calvin (1509-1564) became the patron scholar of the Reformed republic. This is a later engraving of the powerful voice of reform (1637).

B. This is the title page of the first English edition of the highly influential *The Lawes and Statutes of Geneva*, modeled on the biblical example: *"whereby Gods religion is most purelie mainteined, and their common wealth quietli governed"* (1562).

The Biblical Mandate

Even by the reign of James I in the earlier 1600's, the Puritans had already developed a comprehensive understanding of covenantal governance. Like their own Puritan forefathers of the 1500's, they had modeled their lives on the texts of the Geneva Bible which was devoutly used by both generations. The Geneva version had been the product of the Reformed refugees who had escaped from England's "Bloody Mary" to Geneva, the most scholarly center of the Reformed faith at that time. Geneva drew many of Europe's most noteworthy minds during the establishment of its Reformed Academy in Switzerland (1559), which was instituted under the guidance of the foremost reformer, John Calvin.[11] The English refugees took full advantage of their scholarly sanctuary and produced their translation (1560) by a committee of their own pastors and educators. With its copious Reformed marginal notes, the Geneva Bible provided the English language with its first study Bible. Widely influential and reprinted in dozens of editions later in England, its margins overflowed with cross-references and comments on comprehensive Christian self-government. For example, the Geneva Bible's introductory *"Argument"* to the *"book of Moses, called Deuteronomie"* presented the scope of self-government intended by God for His covenant Israel:

> *... he* [God] *prescribeth here anew, all such laws and ordinances, which ... are necessary for a Common-weal: appointing unto every estate and degree, their charge and duty: as well how to rule*

10. Richard Baxter, *A Holy Commonwealth, or Political Aphorisms, Opening The True Principles of Government* ... (London 1659), chapter on: "Of Due Obedience to Rulers, and of Resistance," p. 376.

11. See *Oxford Encyclopedia of the Reformation*, vol. 1 (New York & Oxford, 1996), s.v. "John Calvin," pp. 234-240; vol. 2, s.v. "Geneva," pp. 160-163, and s.v. "Geneva Academy," pp. 163-164.

rule and live in the fear of God, as to nourish friendship toward their neighbours, and to preserve that order which God hath established among men.[12]

The fact that God had undertaken covenantal arrangements in His prior engagement with the Hebrews made them demonstrative to the Puritans. And, the fact that the Scriptures themselves confirmed their comprehensive nature was proof enough that civil responsibilities were not the only human affairs involving such bonds. For the Puritan, the covenantal character of the Scriptures was unlike any other text in the history of man. And, as it was the preeminent book of all human history, no other volume predated or superseded its authoritative character. The laudable Puritan William Perkins thus observed:

> *The Scripture contains a continued historie, from age to age, for the space of 4000 yeers before Christ, even from the beginning. Humane histories, that are of any certainty or continuance, begin onely about the time of Ezra, and Nehemiah. As for those which were written before, they are only fragments, and of no continuity.*[13]

Therefore, to the Reformed English, the whole of human history was the sweeping movement of God's providential hand upon every sphere of human governance. And, the Scriptures told of that great history of God. He created families, local faith assemblies, and civil societies in which man was bound with his fellow man. In all of these, the Scriptures provided the Puritans' model for covenantal bonds. Therefore, they sought a comprehensive moral reformation in which all aspects of human relations were brought into biblical conformity. Said Perkins of the Holy Scripture: *"it commandeth the whole man, body and soul."*[14] Their charge for such living was to fulfill God's mandate to conduct all manner of human endeavor, whether private or public, home or institutional, to the glory of God. They modeled and constructed their personal lives, household obligations, various societal relations, and their civil governance from the abundance of the biblical texts.

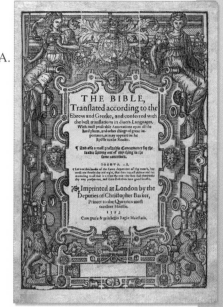

A.

A. The Geneva version of the Bible had a strong covenantal tone to its marginal notes and was favored by Reformed families over the authorized 'Bishop's' version throughout the Elizabethan era. It was also favored over the 'King James' version during the reign of James I. Shown here is the general title page of a typical Elizabethan era Geneva Bible.

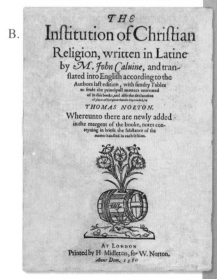

B.

B. John Calvin's greatest contribution to western thought, *The Institution of Christian Religion*, put forth terms of inward faith and outward obligations, including a chapter on civil government. It was a highly influential textbook at Cambridge University (1580 English edition).

---

12. *The* [Geneva] *Bible, Translated according to the Ebrew and Greeke ...* (London, 1594), leaf Ivi.
13. William Perkins, *The Whole Treatise of the Cases of Conscience ...* (London, 1632), p. 134.
14. Ibid., p. 133.

The English reformers looked to the Bible's great twin Testaments, from which they gleaned their own mandates, as if they were God's personal expression for every situation. These were not vague texts describing distant circumstances of ancient history. They strove not merely to delve into the facts of the biblical covenants as interesting history, but to glean from their importance in application. The Puritans desired first to understand covenants in biblical terms, but also to apply covenantal principles as if such mandates were set fresh before them by the Hand of providential timing. They were therefore presuppositional about God's Holy Word. They presupposed the Scripture's own authority and its immediacy for them on its face. They accepted its boldest statements as their own truths because God had Himself presented it to them as such in His Words. The Scripture testified of its own authority, competent and self-sufficient, so that within the text itself the reformers found all that was necessary to understand the pertinency of binding relations with God.

The reformers did not concern themselves much with the more minute nuances of the pre-Hebraic Middle-Eastern covenants. They needed no archaeological surveys or anthropological studies of the ancients to confirm their convictions. The authoritative Writ itself was enough to determine that covenants had been deposited upon the earth by the Creator before all human history in the first strokes of Genesis. Puritan scholars such as John Preston were enraptured by the mere fact that such an Almighty Being would reveal Himself, much more bind Himself, with such creatures as men:

> *If we consider it, it is a exceeding great mercy, when we thinke thus with our selves, he is in heaven, and we are on earth; he is the glorious God, we dust and ashes; he is the Creator, and we but creatures; and yet he is willing to enter into Covenant, which implies a kinde of equalitie between us; ... .*[15]

Preston was one of the most outspoken and influential Puritans of the early 1600's. To Preston and his fellow Puritans, human covenants required an overriding fidelity because a man was never in an adequate position to superintend his vows apart from his Lord. God, as Lord, would continue to superintend man's every circumstance and, as Creator, He was the Author and Definer of all existence. Any goodness that may be found in any man had been originally derived from God alone, and He would always remain the sufficiency for man's comfort, blessing, and security. Preston wrote with a typically Reformed insight on the essential connection between God's own self-sufficiency and His all-sufficiency for created man:

The six days of Creation (see Genesis 1) were pictured in these six illustrations showing God's sovereign work (represented here by His allegorical hand). Christ, as God's Word, was indeed sovereign in Creation and remains sovereign in all things in both heaven and earth: *"For by him* [Christ] *were all things created that are in heaven, and that are in earth, visible and invisible, whether they be thrones, or dominions, or principalities, or powers, all things were created by him, and for him"* (Colossians 1:16). To the reformers, the foundation of all world history rested upon the fact that He had created the earth in six literal days. These six woodcuts are excerpted portions of those used in the first printing of the complete English Bible in 1535.

15. John Preston, *The New Covenant, or the Saints Portion. A Treatise Unfolding the All-sufficiencie of God, Mans Uprightnes, and the Covenant of Grace*, 8th ed., corrected (London, 1634), p. 331.

First, consider that all that is in the creature, all the comforts, all the excellencie, all the beautie that is to bee found in them, is but borrowed and derived: God is the primitive, he is the originall, he is the first, the universal cause, the general cause of all: hence wee gather this, that there is an All-sufficiencey in him, and in him only, hee is all-sufficient, exclusively.[16]

It followed that if man derived his every semblance of goodness and sufficiency from the Creator, it was incumbent upon him to remain in league with the fount of that goodness and all-sufficiency. The Puritans saw that the way for man to maintain any form of goodness, or to do any good among his fellow man, was through his covenantal ties to God in all things. Yet, man being fallen was unable to initiate such a relation with God from a position of merit. It was necessary for God to come to man through the merit of His perfect, sinless Son. The Covenant of Grace was the means by which sinners would become Christians. The perfect and acceptable work of Christ bridged the impossible gap between the unworthy sinner and the Almighty. And, God's endowment of faith in that perfect work was the means by which the sinner was established in a justifying truce to stave off God's just wrath. Preston saw that faith also enabled the sinner to fully see Christ's all-sufficiency and to fully give himself to God in a covenantal union of sanctified righteousness:

Faith doth sanctifie & make a man righteous: and therefore Beloved (by the way) wonder not at this, that we put so much upon faith, for let a man beleeve, that God is All-sufficient, which is the Covenant, for justifying faith is but a beleeving of that part of the Covenant, and enabling a man to keepe the other part which is required; and, I say, it makes a man righteous: for when a man beleeves that God is All-sufficient, it will cause a man to give up himselfe to the Lord againe.[17]

Such comprehensive covenantal thinking brought faith and obedience together. The great gift of God's grace brought with it a covenantal obligation to man on earth, as explained by Preston:

The Puritans believed that God had ordained the societies of family, church, and civil commonwealth as the earthly settings for people to enjoy His overriding all-sufficiency:

A. The realm of the family was ordained to provide for the most intimate, private repose, as shown in this early nineteenth-century woodcut.

B. The realm of the church was ordained for local bodies of believers to gather for public worship and to be corporately discipled in His Word, as shown in this early American engraving.

C. The realm of the commonwealth was ordained to govern and protect overall society by enacting, administering, and adjudicating godly precepts, as shown in this 1641 English woodcut of a civil court.

16. Ibid., p. 27.
17. Ibid., p. 13.

139

... when he [a man] *beleeves the Lord to be all in all things to him, and it inableth him to bee in all things to the Lord againe, that is, to be holy to the Lord in all conversation. It knits his heart unto the Lord. It sanctifieth a man throughout, it makes him particular to the Lord, it makes him wholly unto him.*[18]

Grace by faith in the New Testament was just as obliging as the grace by faith to Abraham in the Old Testament. In both Testaments, faith provided the heavenly Promise of God, yet obedience provided His earthly sufficiency. Preston expanded upon that essential point in his comments on Genesis 17:1-2, in which he demonstrated both aspects of Abraham's Covenant of Grace:

I will be thy God. On the other side, 'thou shalt be mine'. ... So God expresseth himself to Abraham. And this is the Covenant on Gods part. Now that which is required on Abraham's part, is that he be the Lords, as the Lord is his, for so you see in the words following. The question only is, in what manner Abraham shall be the Lords; how that shall be declared? Sayth he, It is not an empty relation, but thou must shew that thou art mine by walking before me.[19]

Like Abraham, the English reformers viewed their covenant with God as commending them to the heavenly Redeemer as well as mandating their earthly fidelity. To them, there was little difference between high or holy obligations and those, so called, 'low' or 'profane' simply because they were performed on earth. There was no setting aside their faith as a heavenly relic, if in their covenantal obedience all things were pledged to God's honor. Such covenantal thinking brought all earthly obligations into heavenly duty, and their private and public lives were all built upon the same principles as their spiritual callings.

To the Reformed, the heavenly and the mundane were drawn from the same well of God's abundance. John Flavel, a Presbyterian divine of the mid-seventeenth century, applied such common duties as husbandry (the tending of domestic agriculture, gardens, and the like) *"to the most excellent improvements of their common employments."*[20] His popular volume, *Husbandry Spiritualized; or, the Heavenly Use of Earthly Things*, expounded on the principle of spiritual and moral lessons that God had for families in the course of everyday life. In a poetic analogy with the hard work of the most mundane of family chores, he showed the nature of every task at hand: *"In the laborious husbandman you see what all true Christians are, or ought to be."*[21] Thus, each day's labor provided a model for the spiritual life, and spiritual work was performed in the tasks of each and every day.

Dan Ford, 2002

Puritan John Flavel (1630-1691) was the author of numerous practical works, including the widely read *Husbandry Spiritualized* (1669), in which common men and women could see their spiritual service in the course of daily living. Flavel's preaching was regularly suppressed by the Anglican Establishment and he was often forced to minister in house churches.

18. Ibid.
19. Ibid., pp. 3-4.
20. John Flavel, *Husbandry Spiritualized; or, the Heavenly Use of Earthly Things* (American reprint ed., Elizabethtown, [New Jersey], 1794), subtitle of volume taken from the title page.
21. Ibid., p. 37.

Flavel explained the double obligation of the faithful, devout family member, explaining first one's everyday duty to God:

> *You find in the word, a world of work cut out for Christians; there is hearing work, praying work, reading, meditating, and self-examining work; it puts him also upon a constant watch over all the corruptions of his heart. Oh! what a world of work hath a Christian about him!*[22]

He then expanded upon the practical application of one's devotions as providing a backdrop for common family duties and the wider circles of acquaintances. Devotional living kept the heart of God in all obligations:

> *And when all this is done, what a multitude of work do his several relations exact from him? He hath a world of business incumbent on him, as a parent, child, husband, wife, master, servant, or friend; yea, not only to friends, but enemies.*[23]

To the Puritan, true faith was both domestically satisfying and earth-shattering. Even preaching and prayer without discipleship and stewardship was fruitless. There was as much holiness in a mission of godly homekeeping as there was in the mission of godly preaching; for at the cross of Christ, everyone had the same first duty to God and the like duty to their fellow man, even though they were called to differing stations. Thus, the hand at the cradle would be no more profane than the one at the pulpit if both were seen in the dignity of their like callings of God.

The Law's Great Mandate

From cradle to commonwealth, the Puritans benefited from growing to maturity with a covenantal understanding of God's Word. Weaned in youth on the *Shorter Catechisme*, the Puritan families created apt men and women fit for self-government. As they grew into maturing students and heads of families, the *Westminster Confession of Faith* provided them with the most thorough understanding of biblical

22. Ibid., p. 38.
23. Ibid., p. 39.

A. This is the title page of an early New Jersey printing of John Flavel's popular *Husbandry Spiritualized*, wherein, like Puritans of old, the citizens of the new American Republics could read of *"The Heavenly Use of Earthly Things"* (1794).

B. Reformed Christians saw a double obligation to God in the devoted life. First, they were directly obliged to God through the practice of private, daily devotions; and second, they were obliged to honor Him in devotional service to their families, churches, and wider commonwealths. Whether one was a tradesman, a shop-owner, or a farmer, whether he or she lived in a city, a town, or on a farm, such a high work standard became an enduring legacy well into the nineteenth century, when godly devotion in all things was still considered the hallmark of the nation's private and public greatness. This is an English print showing a typical example of family husbandry (1859).

141

This sketch shows the historic Westminster Assembly of Divines that met between 1643 and 1648 and established three preeminent Reformed statements of doctrine: *The Westminster Confession of Faith*, *The Larger Catechisme*, and *The Shorter Catechisme*.

doctrine and duty. Its companion, *The Larger Catechisme*, presented a more detailed summation of the composite principles of the covenantal life, beginning with its familiar first question: *"What is the chief and highest end of man?"* The answer gave the key to man's duty and unlocked the true meaning of human prosperity: *"Mans chief and highest end is, to glorifie God, and fully to enjoy him for ever."*[24] It went on to give answers to a host of doctrinal questions, accented with its copious *"proofs thereof out of the Scriptures."*[25]

Foremost in prominence was *The Larger Catechisme*'s exposé on the Ten Commandments, which was included to show God's standard for moral purity, *"as to require the utmost perfection of every duty, and to forbid the least degree of every sin."*[26] Even so, the Commandments were not specified as merely a list of personal rules for individuals' lives, they also represented covenantal obligations for all governing relations among public societies of men. They were therefore comprehensive governing statutes: *"what is forbidden or commanded to our selves, we are bound, according to our places, to endeavour that it may be avoided or performed by others, according to the duty of their places."*[27]

To the Puritan, the Commandments served several ends. They were the summation of the moral Laws that placed an individual's unshielded transgressions in the light of God's unyielding throne of judgment: *"That we might escape the wrath and curse of God due to us by reason of the transgression of the Law ... ."*[28] Thereby, the *Catechisme* laid before the reader the need of *"repentance toward God, and faith toward our Lord Jesus Christ."*[29] To ancient Israel they had also been God's great historic statutes that embodied the terms of their covenantal obedience to their Lord. Consequently, to the Puritans, they were much more than bygone statutes; they were Israel's statutes 'writ large' to the world as the moral sanctions by which God continues to rule over His dominion. *The Larger Catechisme* described the Preface of the Ten Commandments: *"wherein God manifesteth his soveraignty, as being Jehovah, the eternall, immutable, and almighty God, having his Being in and of himself, and giving being to all his words and works; and that he is a God in Covenant, as with Israel of old, so with all his people."*[30]

24. Westminster Assembly of Divines, *The Humble Advice of the Assembly of Divines... Concerning A Larger Catechisme...* (London, 1648), p. 3.
25. Ibid., title page.
26. Ibid., p. 25.
27. Ibid., p. 26.
28. Ibid., p. 45.
29. Ibid.
30. Ibid.

The Commandments, as they spoke of Israel's moral duty to their *"God in Covenant,"* thus equally spoke to the Puritans; for themselves, their families, and their culture were, no doubt, included in its phrase *"so with all his people."* The Commandments as a whole were God's consummate self-governing document and set the terms of His utmost covenantal obligations and the terms of blessings or cursings as long as mankind remained on the earth. For individuals, they represented the moral sanctions by which to govern their lives. For families, they represented the moral sanctions by which to govern the household. For the church, they represented the moral sanctions by which to govern their members. For the commonwealth, they represented the moral sanctions by which to govern the land. Thus, for the Puritans, the Commandments represented the purest ornaments of every earthly stewardship. And, being doctrinally astute, such governing stewardship was not confused with justifying their souls before God by way of Christian perfectionism. That heresy God would surely forbid! For it was well understood that the obligations of the Commandments would recommend no one for heavenly salvation, nor did God's grace eradicate sin from the earth:

> *No man is able, either of himself, or by any grace received in this life, perfectly to keep the Commandements of God, but doth daily break them in thought, word, and deed.*[31]

As to the priorities of such stewardship, the first four Commandments spoke of the moral duties owed directly to their covenant Lord. They spelled out the transcendent honor and worship owed to Him alone, directing them *"to love the Lord our God with all our heart, with all our soule, and with all our strength, and with all our mind."*[32] The last six Commandments spoke of the moral terms of the overall societal covenant between fellow men. These six were summarized in *The Larger Catechisme* as *"our duty to man."*[33] Put briefly, *"to love our neighbour as our selves, and to do to others what we would have them do to us."*[34]

The Fifth Commandment, as the first of the moral obligations among neighbors, stated: *"Honour thy Father and Mother that thy daies may be long upon the Land which the Lord thy God giveth thee."*[35] To the Puritans it represented the universal command to be subject to all legitimate authority, and lent God's own honor to all legitimate human engagements. It was indeed a moral rule with great promise, for its clause, *"that thy daies may be long upon the Land,"* carried with it far wider implications than those merely of a child and his parents:

Monuments of covenantal reform:

The historic fruits of the Westminster Assembly were its *Confession of Faith* and its two *Catechismes*, published here together in their second editions (1658). The Assembly's *Confession* heavily influenced every Reformed Christian confession thereafter, and later editions of the *Catechismes* were staples in many American families and churches well into the nineteenth century.

31. Ibid., p. 44.
32. Ibid., on *"the summe of the four Commandements,"* p. 27.
33. Ibid., p. 34.
34. Ibid. (Also see Matthew 22:37-39; 7:12.)
35. Ibid.

143

By Father and Mother, in the fifth Commandement, are meant not only naturall Parents, but all superiors in age, and gifts, and especially such as by GODS Ordinance are over us in place of authority, whether in Family, Church, or Common-wealth.[36]

The widest rules for godly governance were drawn from the moral sanctions of each of the Commandments. Though everyone was equal before God in the sense that each had an equal accounting to Him according to his or her individual calling, the Puritans believed that certain stations in life called some to greater human responsibilities than others. The higher earthly positions bringing more responsibility likewise called for a relatively higher amount of earthly respect, or *"honour."* Parents, for example, were sanctioned in the Fifth Commandment to greater honor as superiors to their children. Likewise, in the wider human societies, *"superiours"* were obliged to receive honor according to their higher responsibility. When the question was asked, *"What is the generall scope of the fifth Commandement?"*, the *Catechisme* was equally as expansive on the issue as it had been before:

The generall scope of the fifth Commandement, is the performance of those duties which we mutually owe in our severall relations, as Inferiors, Superiors, Equals.[37]

Dan Ford, 2002

William Perkins (1555-1602) was a powerful Reformed author and preacher as well as an influential lecturer at Cambridge University. English historian Thomas Fuller wrote that it was Perkins *"who first humbled the towering speculations of philosophers into practice and morality."*[*a] Perkins propagated covenantal living and was renowned for his practical approach to the great doctrines of Christian theology, or as he himself put it: *"the science of living blessedly for ever."*[*b]
*a & *b: *Compact Edition of the Dictionary of National Biography*, vol. 2 (Cambridge, 1975), p. 1642.

The renowned Puritan scholar William Perkins had previously divided the obligations of the Fifth Commandment between the categories of *"honouring of superiors,"* *"the honour unto our equals,"* and the honor *"to be yielded to inferiors."*[38] Above all of those designations was the highest reverence which was owed to God alone, as stipulated in the First Commandment. Perkins wrote: *"God is goodness itself; his goodness and his sence are one and the same: therefore Honour is due him in the first place."*[39] Perkins then ascribed the honor due to human superiors into four sub-classes of *"speciall reverence,"* *"subjection,"* *"obedience,"* and *"thanksgiving in praising God for their paines, authority and gifts ... ."*[40] Of the honor due to one's equals, he wrote: *"Equals must esteem better of others then of themselves."*[41] And finally, of the honor yielded to inferiors, Perkins wrote that it should be paid under God, *"without all contempt, in meekness of spirit, to respect them as brethren."*[42]

36. *Westminster Larger Catechisme*, Answer to *"Q. Who are meant by Father and Mother, in the fifth Commandement?"*, p. 35.
37. Ibid., Answer to *"Q. What is the generall scope of the fifth Commandement?"*, p. 35.
38. Perkins, *The Whole Cases of Conscience*, book 3, pp. 367-369.
39. Ibid.
40. Ibid.
41. Ibid.
42. Ibid.

The body of the Commandments set the covenantal demeanor as well as obligations in every venue of Puritan life. In that light, they embodied God's practical directives in accord with His revealed will. Individuals were answerable to Him according to the conditions of their singular stations, first within a family and then among the wider societies. They were inherently endowed with an obligation to be internally self-governed as well as to be externally governed (according to the *"severall relations"* of their societal stations) by the moral code of the Commandments – and all under God's watchful care.

The practical doctrine of the Puritans did not embrace such comprehensive responsibilities as if they had wide-eyed visions of a human utopia, nor were they infatuated with a classical spirit as if attempting to create monuments of rigid social stability. No, their associations were vivid, lively, and as interactive as those they saw modeled in God's Word. Their relations were indeed based on the Bible and were as interpersonally involved and (often at times) just as problematic as those that they read about in that text. They saw the covenantal role of the parents to be administered through the everyday interaction, instruction, and discipline of their children in a way that could not possibly be filled by authorities outside of the realm of their homes.[43] The parents were themselves called by God to *"train up"* (Proverbs 22:6) their offspring as those whom He had specifically appointed to the task. They saw the covenantal role of their churches as distinct, but with a like purpose of binding its members with their own obligations toward regular sustenance and mutual care for others – all in an interactive method of societal welfare that could not possibly be filled by any outside civil governance. They saw the wider civil governments as distinctly providing a general reverence of, and enforcing the overall protection for, their covenant families and churches. All societal responsibilities were therefore seen in terms of the three, distinct, covenantal spheres which were mandated and modeled in God's written Word. His commands were accepted as the standard of each, and overall cultural responsibility was motivated by a heart-driven respect for God's own all-sufficiency, under His providential care. To the Puritans, a widespread and ingrained honor for their covenantal families, churches, and civil commonwealths was therefore seen as the ultimate means for England, and then later for its colonies in America, to achieve their historic cultural successes.

43. See Deuteronomy 6:5-9.

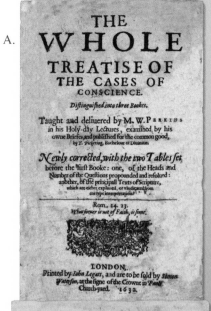

A.

B.

Spelling out the duties of godliness:

A. This is the title page of William Perkins's *The Whole Treatise of the Cases of Conscience*, a volume in which he laid out the various duties incumbent upon the faithful life (1632 edition).

B. This is the closing paragraph of the final page of Perkins's *Cases of Conscience*, in which he concluded the wider societal duties incumbent upon the faithful:

... Now to honour God, is to honour him according to his will and word, in the duties of good Conscience and good life. On the contrary, they that dishonour God, God will dishonour them befor all the World. And this must teach us, even to dedicate our selves to God and his providence, in the whole course of our callings, whether in the Church or Common-wealth.
&c. &c. &c. &c. &c. &c. &c ...

145

Chapter 4: The Covenantal Applications

The Distinction between Covenantal Integrity in England and America

THE typical Puritan pulpit sermon was divided into two major divisions: first, the doctrine, and second, the application. The preacher or "teacher" would begin with an opening passage of Scripture which could either be simply a portion of a single verse or a significant part of a chapter. Scripture would thus be the first words spoken in his oration, often merely as a brief introduction, yet always beginning with God Almighty as 'first things first' in any oratory of His Holy Word.

The oration itself would first draw out the doctrine of the passage, often one word at a time, with the meaning of each carefully outlined as though they were pieces of a meticulously assembled puzzle which would reveal the whole picture only with each piece carefully positioned with the others. Then the passage was expanded, propounded, and then expanded again, driven into its fullest meaning with side references to dozens of others like it, until the resonant principles of the doctrine would shine to full splendor from one single page of God's great text.

The second part of the sermon, which was devoted to the application, could be as equally expansive as the first part, and often comprised the majority of the entire composition. From the same text, refreshed and endowed with an abundance of doctrine, the application would be drawn, often point by point, into the clear meaning to pressing issues at hand. Whether it be concerning a care of the body, soul or spirit, household or family, church or congregation, township or freeman, or commonwealth or subject, the doctrines at hand were apt for the issue. To such ends, the Scriptures remained relevant, lively, and essential to their lives and societies, and God's Word and Spirit did their sanctifying work on the minds and hearts of the hearers. Thus it was that the Puritan covenantal doctrines (those just briefly covered in the previous chapter) indeed found their way into the lives and fabric of the wider English and American societies, and formed the cultural precedents that were carried into future generations. By reading, hearing, and studying the Scriptures, the Puritans acquired their doctrine. By prayer, repentance, fasting, intercession, thanksgiving, and especially acting in accord with their callings, they gave their doctrine its lively application.

A Solemn Covenant Sworn and Broken

The Puritan message found its way into the great pressing issues of the day. In every venue of life, God's mandates were rendered into human responsibilities by way of the sermon. *"Is not he thy Father, that hath bought thee? hath he not made thee, and established thee?"*[1] asked Puritan Minister John Ward in his sermon preached before the Long Parliament in 1645: *"... almost every where in the Books of Moses; we may hear the Prophet preaching it very plainly, both the Duty upon this very ground, and the aggravation of the sin in the case of perversnesse, and the recompence of the errour."*[2]

Ward was not giving Parliament a lesson in history or directing their attention to God's Law simply for the sake of contemplating the wisdom of an 'archaic' text. He was admonishing Parliament according to their high station before God of their own constituted duty to embrace His statutes as their own and apply His doctrine to the issues at hand:

> *... and then in your sphear, and according to your power, do honourably for God, who hath done gloriously for us all. My Lords, The matters of God are before you, as well as the affairs of the Common-wealth ... .*[3]

The thorough application of God's moral code would restore unto God the honor that He deserved, as well as relieve the terrible plague of corruption that had recently become so oppressive in England.

Especially during the wrenching Civil Wars of the 1640's, there was considerable attention to public preaching in England. There were many forceful expressions of covenantal ideas such as those of the Puritan divine Francis Taylor. As a pastor in Kent and member of the Assembly of Divines, Taylor preached before the House of Commons and addressed the issue of the king's prerogative over England:

> *Have not our princes, guided by Coutiers, and Church Parasites, countenanced Monopolies and Innovations? Have not our Parliaments stood up for our lawfull liberties? Why should wee not then stand to them to the utmost of our Estates and Lives, according to our Covenant. If it bee granted that a power abused, may not bee resisted, who doubts but a power never granted by God nor man may?*[4]

A.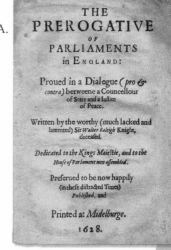

A. Sir Walter Raleigh (1552-1618), who was granted a patent to colonize America under Queen Elizabeth (but was executed under James I), supported the duty of Parliament to defend the liberties of Englishmen. Shown here is the title page of his work, *The Prerogative of Parliaments in England Proved ...* , written while imprisoned in the Tower of London (c. 1610), but first printed (1628) by Puritan allies in Holland many years following Raleigh's death.

B.

B. A powerful voice for the Commonwealth:

Unlike the idea of an absolute civil authority in the king and his lords, English civil governance required the voice of the commoners. Shown here is an engraving of the Puritan packed *House of Commons* (1642) that resisted absolute royal authority and pressed for national reforms by way of Parliament's body of local representatives. Shown in the center was a *"Speaker of the House,"* who spoke with no voice or authority other than that which the Commons had delegated to him.

1. John Ward, *The Good-Will of Him that Dwelt in the Bush: Or, The Extraordinary Happinesse of Living under an Extraordinary Providence ... a Sermon preached before the Right Honourable, the House of Lords, in the Abbey Church at Westminster, on Tuesday, July 22. 1645* (London, 1645), p. 27.
2. Ibid.
3. Ibid., p. 31.
4. Francis Taylor, *God's Covenant the Churches Plea: or a Sermon Preached before the House of Commons ...* (London, 1645), p. 19.

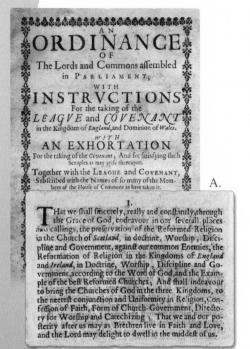

A.

B.

Two contrasting versions of *The League and Covenant*:

A comparison of the *Covenant* (A) that was sworn by Parliament in February of 1643 differs in its first clause from that to be actually sworn by the peoples of England and Scotland (B) in September. Parliament's *Covenant* uniformly bound its members, while *"All"* the people were not uniformly bound according to an *"Explication"* for cases of conscience. The *Covenant* was thereby self-limited.

Taylor was also addressing the recent treaty between England and Scotland known as *The League and Covenant*, and his sermon was a testimonial to the obliging nature of their international treaty. As the representatives of two distinct nations, it was incumbent that the two Parliaments enter their own league, as it were, with their eyes wide open. Yet, interestingly, the covenant oath prescribed *"To be taken by All Persons within the two Kingdoms of England and Scotland"*[5] (August 1643) added a clause in its first article that varied from that taken by Parliament[6] (February 1643), for it added: *"As far as we do, or shall in our consciences conceive to be according to the Word of God."*[7] Unlike the Covenant of ancient Israel which was uniformly binding on the consciences of all its leaders and people, that in England and Scotland was limited in cases of conscience.

Yet, just as a marriage covenant once entered was bound with God superintending the covenant,[8] He would likewise bind all who entered into a sworn covenant (even an international covenant) that was entered by vow or oath. It was incumbent upon oath-takers to derive covenantal virtue from the One who superintends their very existence. And, with England and Scotland's *League and Covenant* (as with marriages), it would take considerable effort to keep it from being broken. Without faithful devotion to their oath, and without ongoing submission to God, earthly covenants are too often broken, ultimately failing when put into mere human practice. The events surrounding the English and Scottish governments' abandonment of the terms of their *League and Covenant* illustrates the often tangled web of such covenant breaking.

To illustrate the ultimate failure of England and Scotland's *Covenant*, we will briefly consider its history. The reformers of both kingdoms had suffered long under King James I (r. England 1603-1625), and constitutional warfare over the royal claim of "divine right" ultimately broke out under his son Charles I (r. 1625-1649) due to the vigorous enforcement of his

5. Compare *An Ordinance of The Lords and Commons assembled ... Together with the League and Covenant, Subscribed with the Names of so many of the Members of the House of Commons as have taken it...* (London, 5 Feb. 1643), pp. 10-11; with *The New Oath or Covenant, To be taken by All Persons within the two Kingdoms of England and Scotland ...* (London, September 4, 1643), p. 4.

6. Ibid.

7. Ibid.

8. See Matthew 19:6; Mark 10:9.

absolute rule. Charles had administered a more arbitrary and ruthless suppression of Puritans and Presbyterians than his father, provoking opposition in the arenas of both politics and religion. In the late 1620's, many powerful voices in Parliament began to challenge the king's early attempts to usurp England's historic system of a shared prerogative between Parliament and the Crown. Parliament's popular civil and religious appeals forced Charles to accept its *Petition of Right* in 1628. That document was designed to prevent the king's arbitrary power to tax England without the consent of its representatives and to secure guarantees of certain historic English rights such as that of *habeas corpus* and the right to a trial by due process of law. It also prevented forced loans, excessive fines, cruel and unusual punishment, and quartering (forceful residence) of troops in private homes. The *Petition* was strengthened by the Puritans' demands in Parliament that biblically, subjects held certain fundamental rights which their rulers were required by God to vigorously respect, protect, and defend.

Following his reluctant acceptance of the *Petition*, Charles conveniently dissolved his Parliament, and for eleven ensuing years (1629-1640), he established 'personal rule' over England. Charles persecuted any who opposed his authority and worked vigorously to suppress all religious dissent. Charles also invented creative schemes to tax his subjects without their consent, such as forced 'loans' from the nobility to the crown which were never intended to be repaid, and he enforced an arbitrary system of justice through the notorious Star Chamber and Courts of Commission. His overawing inventiveness reached critical mass when he attempted to hoist Anglican forms of worship upon Presbyterian Scotland in 1637. The Scottish Presbyterians engaged themselves in a *Solemn League and Covenant* in 1638, and two brief military contests followed by which Charles was forced to call for an English Parliament to raise necessary funds to prosecute an all-out war against the Scots. Parliament, however, used the opportunity to place its own lengthy list of grievances before the king, and following Charles's unconstitutional attempt to arrest five Puritan leaders of Parliament in January 1642, civil war erupted in England. When the king raised his standard against Parliament in August, the civil doctrine of resistance to tyranny finally surfaced – the parliamentary sword of state came to blows with the Royalists' claim to a divine dominion.

A.

A. Charles I (r. 1625-1649) sought to rule England without the consent of the Lords or Commons throughout the 1630's. This portrait was included in Charles's 1639 declaration against Scotland in which he claimed that his royal authority called him to suppress its *"Religion and Liberties."*

B.

C.

England's Great Constitutional Crisis:

B. Charles demanded the arrest of the five leading Puritan members of the Commons for treason (Jan. 4, 1642).

C. The Commons answered in this *Declaration* that the king's attempt was itself rebellion *"against the Libertie of the Subject, and a Breach of Privilege of Parliament"* (Jan. 17).

149

AN
ORDINANCE
Of The
LORDS and COMMONS
Aſſembled in PARLIAMENT,

Exhorting all his Majeſties good
ſubjects in the Kingdome of England, and
Dominion of Wales, to the duty of Repentance,
(as the onely remedy for their preſent Calamities)
with an earneſt Confeſſion, and deepe Humiliation for all
particular and Nationall Sins, that ſo at length we may
obtaine a firme and happy Peace both with
G O D and Man.

To be uſed privately in Families, but eſpecially
publikely in Congregations.

A.

B.

*Dan Ford,
2002*

THE
CHARGE
OF THE
COMMONS
OF
ENGLAND.
Againſt Charls Stuart,
King of *England*,

Of High Treaſon, and other High Crimes,
exhibited to the High Court of Juſtice,
By *John Cook* Eſquire, Solicitor General;
appointed by the ſaid Court, ſet,
and on the behalf of the
People of *England*.
As it was read to Him by the Clerk in the ſaid
Court, as ſoon as Mr. Solicitor General for the Kingdom
had Impeached Him, in the name of the Commons
of *England*, at His firſt Araignment,
Saturday, Ian. 20. 1648.

Examined by the Original Copy. *Imprimatur,* Gilbert Mabbot.

London, Printed for *Kapha Harford*, at the Gilt Bible in Queens-Head-Alley
in Pater-noſter-Row. 1 6 4 9.

C.

A. Upon entering its contest with
the king, the Puritan-dominated
Parliament called for national
repentance to be observed both
"privately in Families" and
"publikely in Congregations"
(title page of the 1642 *Ordinance*).

B. Parliament triumphed over the
Crown due to the military heroics
of Oliver Cromwell, portrayed here.

C. Charles I (*"Charls Stuart"*)
was ultimately charged with
treason for waging an illegal war
upon his nation (title page of the
1649 charges against the king).

The Scots allied themselves with Parliament the following year, and after mutually engaging together in the *League and Covenant* (1643), the armies of the English Parliament and the Scottish Assembly began to triumph together over the Royalist forces. But, their crafty opponent, Charles I, after being captured in 1646, parlayed individually and separately with the Scottish and the English allies, driving a calculated wedge between the two. He played each against the other, offering impossible favors to each, and all at the other's expense. Charles, finally seizing upon his best moment, pledged himself to the Scots under pretense that he would enter the *Covenant* with them at Parliament's expense. But, Parliament's army, under the command of Thomas Fairfax (the commander in chief) and Oliver Cromwell, moved on London to expel all Scottish allies from the English Parliament in 1648, and Charles I was subsequently charged with treason for his brutal warfare as a breach of his avowed coronation oath.

Scotland raised various armies to invade England, one of which was led by Charles I's own son (1651). The younger prince Charles had also deceitfully engaged in the *League* with the Presbyterian Scots in order to obtain their backing, though by that time any semblance of a covenant was in shambles and disavowed among their more independent-minded English neighbors. Scotland tried to force the alliance and enforce the claims of the *League*, but upon its army crossing into England, the English declared Charles and the invaders both to be traitors. In a sweeping counter move, Cromwell's army then drove them back into Scotland, and God's Providence confirmed that the *League* had indeed been shattered.

Prince Charles nonetheless escaped, surviving to see better days for himself following Cromwell's death in 1658. He was subsequently restored to the English throne as Charles II in 1660, yet as a king he never honored his pretended *League* with the Scots and severely prosecuted the English who had executed his father. Incidentally, Cromwell's body was exhumed and his head was mounted on a pike as a vivid testimonial to his role in the defeat of the elder Charles. Charles II proved to be every bit as unfaithful a husband as he was a king, and overall as a man in whom little trust could faithfully be vested. Thus came the severe price that both England and Scotland paid for the failure of their oaths. Both Puritan and Presbyterian ministers suffered severely under the new regime, which illustrates the disparaging ills that can result from mismanaging or breaking sworn covenantal alliances.

Any notion of covenantal living was severely suppressed following the restoration of the English crown to Charles II. The institution of Divine Right returned with a new Oath of Allegiance that pledged English subjects to God by way of the will of their king. Accountability to God was thereby officially ascribed to the royal crown, and Charles reigned as the supreme Lord over his sovereign realm. The term "covenant" went the way of the Puritan and Presbyterian preachers, banished to private dwellings or the occasional secret meetings of covenanted congregations. The term was not employed by the new Anglican Establishment that was reaffirmed under the king's sovereignty, and it was seldom used among England's higher social strata due to its strong association with the painful political memories of the Civil War. The general idea of societal covenants certainly no longer appealed to the new, passive policies of the Royalist Parliament nor amid the politically correct literature of the day. Henceforth, any public talk of covenanting represented a spirit of rebellion and defiance amid the well-worn, though recovering, nation. There remained many powerful Puritan voices who wrote analogous poems, essays, and books, which later generations have come to revere as among the highest monuments of English literature, though at the time, public treatment for such truly noble men was often harsh, with lives and liberties severely repressed, and stories of their pitiful testimonies far too numerous.

The New England Commonwealths

Following the restoration in England, the underlying idea of covenantal bonds continued to thrive in New England, which remained as the sole nurserybed of the Puritan culture. Charles II even promoted the continuation of religious liberty in several of the American colonies in order to remove as many of the 'disreputable non-conformists' as possible away from England's immediate concern. Many ministers, deprived of their posts in the motherland, transplanted their Reformed faith to the colonies, adding new covenantal vigor to America's societal fabric.

New England's townships and churches had been built from the start around localized communities controlled by their own members. From their first plantings, they had been established more in the mode

A.

B.

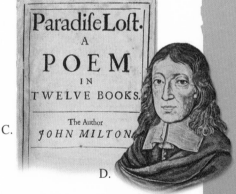

C.

D.

A. When the crown was restored to Charles II in 1660, God was seen to have placed it upon a *"Sovereign"* head, as shown by this illustration in England's *Oath of Allegiance* (1662).

B. Subjects were inviolably bound to the king's will *"as their supreme Lord"* according to these *"Grounds"* of the *Oath of Allegiance* (1662).

C. By way of contrast, Puritan John Milton (1608-1674), who was among the literary giants of the Restoration era, crafted *Paradise Lost* as an analogy of the nation's sad return to royal dominion (title page of the 1678 enlarged edition).

D. John Milton's portrait from the frontis of the third edition (1678).

151

Dan Ford, 2002

A.

B.

Dan Ford, 2001

A. Likely drafted by Separatist elder William Brewster (1567-1644), the *Mayflower Compact* joined all Plymouth Plantation's members into America's first independent, civil covenant.

B. Pledging union under God, their *"civill body politick"* combined both the Pilgrims and *"Strangers"* (resident non-Puritans) under a like obligation to conduct all public affairs according to godly precepts, and it secured the biblical foundation upon which to frame future *"lawes, ordinances, acts, constitutions, & offices."*

of Hebrew judges than that of Royalist oppressors who were ruling at home in mother England. The earliest New England immigrants had fled during the original repressive reigns of James I and that of his son Charles I, and had previously transferred the idea of covenantal fidelity to America. From the planting of the first settlement at Plymouth, the character of New England had been instilled with a miraculous sense of Providence. The Pilgrims arrived in America amid the foreboding and chilling winds of Cape Cod, deep in the Autumn of 1620. They found themselves in the precarious circumstance of being outside the recognized limits of their official English patent, and therefore engaged themselves in the first (of what would be many) of New England's civil covenants. They undertook that first solemn pact, beginning *"In ye name of God, Amen,"*[9] as to carefully place themselves steadfast under the highest possible authority. They bound themselves into a single civil body under God, as William Bradford (their second governor) later wrote: *"shuch an acte … might be as firme as any patent, and in some respects more sure."*[10] Thereby, the precedent for all subsequent civil engagements was established under God in North America by way of those first Plymouth covenanters vowing:

> … *haveing undertaken, for ye glorie of God, and advancemente of ye Christian faith, and honour of our king & countrie, a voyage to plant ye first colonie in ye Northerne parts of Virginia, doe by these presents solemnly & mutualy in ye presence of God, and one of another, covenant & combine our selves together into a civill body politick, … .*[11]

With further reflection upon New England's first successful settlement, Governor Bradford later wrote to inform their future descendants of the initial precarious circumstances. In his manuscript, *History of Plymouth Plantation*, he observed that they would have definitely perished if not for God's miraculous intervention, and he therefore admonished all those who would follow in their steps to give thanks that their forefathers had arrived in America as Englishmen, and had come with a firm reliance upon the goodness of the Lord:

> *May not & ought not the children of these fathers rightly say:* "Our faithers were Englishmen which came over this great ocean, and were ready to perish in this willdernes; but they cried unto ye Lord, and he heard their voyce, and looked on their adversitie, &c. Let them therfore praise ye Lord, because he is good, & his mercies endure for ever."[12]

9. William Bradford, *History of Plymouth Plantation* (Boston: Little, Brown, and Co., 1856), p. 89.
10. Ibid.
11. Ibid., pp. 89-90.
12. Ibid., pp. 79-80.

God's mercies endured indeed for those who followed the original American Pilgrims. Aboard the ship *Arabella* in 1629, nearly a decade after the Separatists' bold 1620 adventure, the future Massachusetts governor John Winthrop, ready to depart with his companions on their own flight to America, gave a speech which expressed the mandate of their undertaking:

> *Thus stands the cause between God and us. We are entered into covenant with Him for this work. We have taken out a commission. The Lord hath given us leave to draw our own articles. We have professed to enterprise these and those accounts, upon these and those ends. We have hereupon besought Him of favor and blessing. Now if the Lord shall please to hear us, and bring us in peace to the place we desire, then hath He ratified this covenant and sealed our commission, ...*[13]

Winthrop's farewell sermon has been memorialized through the ages as *A Model Of Christian Charity*. Upon the upper deck of the *Arabella*, while taking leave of its moorings from England, Winthrop revealed the prior model for such a grave adventure, and the conditions necessary for either its success or its utter disaster:

> *Now the only way to avoid shipwreck, and to provide for our posterity, is to follow the counsel of Micah, to do justly, to love mercy, to walk humbly with our God. For this end, we must be knit together, in this work, as one man. We must entertain each other in brotherly affection. We must be willing to abridge ourselves of our superfluities, for the supply of others' necessities.*[14]

Like the Pilgrims and Puritans who had settled before him, Winthrop knew the terms. America was, in fact, quite a foreboding wilderness, but to the covenant-minded it was not an unyielding wilderness. New England provided a clean slate upon which Puritans could covenant anew, and they came in great numbers throughout the 1630's settling themselves, one with the next, as a covenanted people bound by their honor to God and charity for each other:

> *... we are commanded this day to love the Lord our God, and to love one another, to walk in his ways and to keep his Commandments and his ordinance and his laws, and the articles of our Covenant with Him, that we may live and be multiplied, and that the Lord our God may bless us in the land whither we go to possess it.*[15]

From the advent of Puritanism's rise in England, New England's forefathers had pressed for such a reformation that would reflect scriptural lines of governance. From the time of their *1572 Admonition to Parliament* (over seventy

John Winthrop (1588-1649) was the signatory of a document drafted in Cambridge, England in 1629, pledging himself to set sail for America, *"provided that the whole government, together with the patent for the plantation, be first by order of court legally transferred and established, to remain with us and others which shall inhabit upon the same plantation."** Winthrop obtained that grant and brought covenantal self-government to the new colony of Massachusetts in 1630.
*Compact Dictionary of National Biography, vol. 2 (1975), p. 699.

---

13. John Winthrop, *Christian Charity, a Model Thereof*, from an excerpt that was included in Samuel Eliot, *Builders of the Bay Colony* (Boston, 1930), pp. 73-75.
14. Ibid.
15. Ibid.

years before Winthrop), they had pleaded that England release the Church from the reins of the royal apparatus of bishops and archbishops, to be built upon Christ-honoring modes of governance with local elders and deacons. It was known from that early date that such a restoration of Christ's rule deposited with the people would lend itself to the greater honor and glory of the civil commonwealth:

> *Not that wee meane to take awaye the authoritie of the civille magistrate and cheife governour, to whome we wishe all blessedness & for the increase of whose godlinesse, we daily pray: but that Christe being restored unto his kingdome, to rule in the same by the scepter of his worde and severe discipline: the prince may be better obeyed, the realme more flourishe in godlinesse, and the Lorde him selfe more purely according to his revealed will, served than heretofore he hath ben, or yet at present is.*[16]

Thus, it was in colonial New England that the old *Admonition* of the Puritans found its first comprehensive fruition. The original cause for which they had petitioned Parliament in 1572 was ultimately won by those who took flight from the hierarchy of bishops and prelates and settled along the northern regions of the North American coasts. With congregations established on a covenanted basis, their civil magistracy was also founded on the like model of a more localized self-governance, as both their churches and commonwealths were in cooperation amid their more intimate spheres of charity and authority. The family found its place in fulfilling its covenantal role, and the local societies and communities each served a necessary purpose, so that the commonwealth at large would thrive and not merely survive. So, more than ever before in old England, the Puritan reforms were effected and ingrained in the North American fabric, and the *Admonition*'s prayer: *"the Lorde him selfe* [served] *more purely according to his revealed will,"*[17] was foremost realized in the covenantal establishment of New England.

Providentially, in the very year that the Puritan Parliament was at the height of its pitched battle with King Charles I over the brutal enforcement of his claim to divine right, New England's most prominent teacher, John Cotton, could write from Boston in 1645 to defend the "New England Way":

> *... there is no other way given whereby a people free from naturall and compulsory engagements, can be united or combined together into one visible body, to stand by mutuall Relation, fellow-members of the same body, but onely by mutuall Covenant; as appeareth between husband and wife in the family, Magistrates and subjects in the Common-wealth, fellow citizens in the same City ... .*[18]

Dan Ford, 2002

John Cotton (1584-1652), under a threat of prosecution by church authorities at old Boston in England, fled to New England in 1633 to become the first preacher of Boston, Massachusetts. That new town took its name "Boston" in honor of Cotton's immigration.

16. *Admonition to Parliament*, excerpted from *Answere to a certain Libel...* , p. 136.
17. Ibid., p. 136.
18. John Cotton, *The Way of the Churches of Christ in New-England ...* (London, 1645), p. 4.

THE COVENANTAL APPLICATIONS

Thus, the "New England Way" appropriated covenantal engagements in all spheres of life. The earliest plantations were organized around covenanted congregations to be self-governed according to the precepts of God's Word. It was also a uniform practice for each new municipality to enter a civil engagement whereby they would be self-governed under Him. For example, the year before the Connecticut plantations of Windsor, Hartford, and Wethersfield established the first formally confederated (covenanted) constitution in 1639, the settlers of New Haven had covenanted their plantation:

> *Whereas there was a covenant solemnly made by the whole assembly of free planters of this plantation, the first day of an extraordinary humiliation, which we had after coming together, that as in matters that concern the gathering and ordering of a church, so likewise in all public offices which concern civil order, as majestrates and officers, making and repealing laws, dividing allotments of inheritance, and all other doings of like nature, we would all of us be ordered by those rules which the scripture holds forth to us; this covenant was called a plantation covenant, to distinguish it from a church covenant, ...[19]*

The New England civil magistrate acted in cooperation with the church establishment, and each within its respective sphere was bound in the service of God and the people at large. New England's governors were elected on a provincial basis with terms of one year, always to be held in strict account to those they served. Laws were legislated in a like manner with councils and representatives serving in accountable (appointive or elective) positions. Much of the day-to-day governance, as that most immediate, remained at the community or local township levels. Throughout the seventeenth century, their civil laws resonated with the virtues derived from the Scripture, though talk of "covenanted" civil government began to wane due to its association with the Scottish brand of international Covenanters, who were not admired much in Congregationalist New England. Nevertheless, the Puritan commonwealths in America viewed their engagements as covenantal, and their contracted royal charters remained in effect their national covenants. They remained pledged to God and one another, and virtue reigned over New England in sharp contrast with the vice that dominated old England's affairs of state under a potentate severely lacking in personal fidelity.

19. Benjamin Trumble, *A Complete History of Connecticut, Civil and Ecclesiastical, from the First Planters from England ...* (Hartford, 1797), excerpted from Appendix 4: "Fundamental Articles," p. 535.

A.

Dan Ford, 2003

A. Staunch Puritan Thomas Hooker (1586-1647) had helped settle an offshoot of Massachusetts at Hartford in 1636. In 1638 he preached a sermon on the covenantal nature of both the church and the commonwealth, which inspired the establishment of a biblical frame for the colony's overall civil government. Connecticut's *Fundamental Orders* (1639) became the first written constitution in North America. This sketch is based upon a sculpture of Thomas Hooker in Hartford.

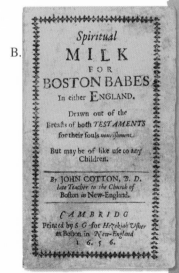

B.

B. Cradle to Commonwealth:

To assist in equipping New England's future generations, Boston's preacher John Cotton published the first children's book in America: *Spiritual Milk for Boston Babes* (1646). Shown is the title page of the 1656 edition of one of colonial America's most endearing and enduring works.

Charles R.

HARLES the Second by the Grace of God, King of *England, Scotland, France,* and *Ireland,* Defender of the Faith, &c. To all to whom these Presents shall come, or may in any wise concern, Greeting. Although We have thought fit to Issue Our Writ of *Quo Warranto* against the Charter and Priviledges Claimed by the Governour and Company of the *Massachusetts Bay* in *New England,* by reason of some Crimes and Misdemenours by them Committed;

B.

Dan Ford,
2002

A. Charles II was portrayed here later in life on the frontis of Robert Filmer's work, *Patriarcha*, a book which justified the king's absolute power (1680).

B. In 1683, Charles II announced these proceedings to prosecute against the Massachusetts Charter and put a fatal end to the Puritan commonwealths of New England.

C. After Charles II died in 1685, his brother James II appointed Sir Edmund Andros (pictured here) as the new royal governor of his "Dominion of New England" (1686).

The Dominion of New England

After decades of sacrifice and toil on the part of the Puritans to develop American resources along the New England coasts, by the 1680's their rich assets had become highly valued by the motherland. It was determined that far too many commodities had been wasted on the colonials, and bolstering their value even more was the fact that the Puritan settlements had become prized on the European stage and the objects of specific greed by France. It was therefore determined by the Crown that self-government in the covenanted commonwealths had gone too far to be tolerated, and late in Charles II's reign and throughout the reign of his younger brother, James II, each of the Puritan charters were gradually seized and replaced with the uniform English "Dominion" stamp. The colonies of New England became one under the rule of a jealous Crown, and the long-cherished liberties had come to an end.

The new "Dominion of New England" lacked the original features of covenantal self-rule, accountable taxation, or any semblance of local accountability to either God or man. The citizens of Boston protested in 1688 that, *"It was now plainly affirmed, both by some in open Council and by the same in private converse, that the people of New England were slaves, ..."*[20] The grand appetite of the Royalist administration under Edmund Andros and his secretary, Edward Randolph, brought new measures which the colonists called *"Absolute and Arbitrary."*[21] Lands were abruptly seized, township rights violated, and the independency of the Puritan churches suppressed – all in the name of conformity. The colonials petitioned – and petitioned hard foremost to their Lord. New England repented, fasted, and prayed in a *"cry to our God."*[22] Modeling the ancient Hebrews in days of old, *"... they caused the cry of the poore to come unto him, and he hears the cry of the afflicted."*[23] Massachusetts also smuggled out its most prominent ambassador of good will, the Puritan Minister Increase Mather, *"purely out of respect and the Good of his Afflicted Country."*[24]

Despite the efforts of the new administration to restrain Mather in New England, he escaped to act as its

20. Nathanael Byfield, *An Account of the Late Revolution in New-England. Together with the Declaration of the Gentlemen, Merchants, and Inhabitants of Boston and the Country adjacent* (London, 1689), p. 11.
21. Ibid., p. 9.
22. Ibid., pp. 17-18.
23. Ibid.
24. Ibid., p. 16.

political agent before the king. Through Mather, New England petitioned James II to honor the provincial principles that had theretofore been respected by the former crowns. Through Mather, they argued the Moral Laws and the English Laws, their covenantal obligations and their chartered obligations, as well as their Christian rights and their English rights, all in an effort to reestablish the way of their forefathers in America.

Their prayers and petitions were miraculously answered by the surprising events that unfolded in 1689. Along with the happy news of the overthrow of the absolutist King James II in England came a moral charge to a like conformity by the people of New England. James's royal agents, Governor Andros and Randolph, were both arrested having been overthrown by the *"gentlemen, merchants and inhabitants"*[25] of Boston. And, as would be expected, the act of reclaiming New England's historic liberties was conducted in a covenantal tone:

> *In the mean time firmly believing, we have endeavoured nothing but what meer duty to God and our Country calls for at our Hands: We commit our Enterprize unto the Blessing of Him, who hears the cry of the Oppressed, and advise all our neighbours, for whom we have thus ventured our selves, to joyn with us in Prayers and all just Actions, for the Defence of our Land.*[26]

That great event was later known in New England as the "Revolution." At the time, it brought outpourings of joy and thanksgiving for the Lord's providential intervention. Like Israel of old, God had redeemed the oppressed from bondage and set the captives free, and following the Revolution, their charters were (for the most part) restored by the new co-regents of England. Though Mather could not secure the original charters for Massachusetts, it was combined with Plymouth and Martha's Vineyard under their new grant as Massachusetts-Bay Colony. Though it had a royal governor appointed by the crown, its covenantal bonds were retained with locally elected representatives and continued enactment of definitive biblical standards. Though the king's administrator was now among them, they maintained the ascendance of God's Law as the highest civil support. And, under the terms of New England's various charters and the new Navigation Acts of Parliament, mother England ruled the waves, but the Americans continued to rule their roosts. Though the royal governors were appointed to superintend the interests of mother England, New England maintained their heavenly Father's Law in superintending all local legislation.

25. Ibid., p. 7.
26. Ibid., p. 19.

Dan Ford, 2002

A.

B.

AN
ACCOUNT
OF THE
Late Revolution
IN
NEW-ENGLAND.
Together with the
DECLARATION
OF THE
Gentlemen, Merchants, and Inhabitants of *BOSTON,*
and the Country adjacent. *April* 18. 1689.

Written by Mr. *NATHANAEL BYFIELD,*
a Merchant of *Briſtol* in *New-England,* to his Friends
in *London.*

LICENSED, *June* 27. 1689. *J. Fraſer.*

LONDON:
Printed for *Ric. Chiſwell,* at the *Roſe* and *Crown* in
St. Paul's Church-Yard. MDCLXXXIX.

A. Increase Mather (1639-1723) was the son of Richard Mather and son-in-law of John Cotton, two of the leading patriarchs of New England. A 1656 graduate of Harvard and devout preacher in Boston, Mather led the opposition to the revocation of New England's covenanted governments. He fled Andros's henchmen and petitioned on behalf of American liberties before the king in England.

B. Upon the expulsion of the Crown government from Boston in 1689, New England justified its actions through a series of tracts published under the direction of Increase Mather, its colonial agent in London. In sympathy with England's own "Glorious Revolution" against James II (1688-89), the principles for godly government were put forth as in this tract: *An Account of the Late Revolution in New-England ...* (1689).

A.

B.

C.

D.

A. The New England colonies valued their duty to govern themselves according to biblical precepts. Shown here is the title page of the *"ACTS and LAWS"* of Massachusetts, containing all statutes in effect since the grant of its provincial charter in 1692 (1759 edition).

B. Colonial legislators had an obligation to protect and defend God's institution of the family, as in Massachusetts' 1694 *"Act against Adultery and Polygamie."* Each was considered a *"Violation of the Marriage Covenant."*

C. *"Buggery,"* or sexual perversion, was considered a dangerous moral *"Sin... contrary to the very Light of Nature"* (the Creation Covenant) and was outlawed as a felony in 1696.

D. The Puritans viewed the gift of a woman's virtue as her sacred property. So, unlike any laws in Europe, in New England, the forced ravishment of a woman was a capital felony. (Shown is the Massachusetts Act of 1696).

The New England Provinces

While the new executive administrations looked quite different, New England's overall societal attitudes remained covenantal in nature. No civil legislation could be considered legitimate that violated God's overarching standards, for He would neither condone nor protect a province that adopted societal norms repugnant to His will. His Moral Law had superintended the behavior of ancient Israel, and Israel was blessed or cursed accordingly. New Englanders therefore guarded their own duty to legislate according to those precepts. And, in their members having sworn to an oath of office, colonial legislatures had a solemn obligation to preserve their right of self-government. It would then seem presumptuous for Americans to ask that God of Israel to bless their own private or public estates if they passively yielded away such covenantal obligations.

Knowing also that no societal covenants could be considered legitimate that lacked God's sanction, marriage laws, for example, were stipulated strictly by God's Word. The covenant of marriage was conducted according to His Laws, and then respected and protected accordingly by the civil laws passed to implement those Precepts. Within God's Commandments lay both the qualifying terms of all bonds and conditions for all marital conduct thereafter. The societal obligation of a marriage therefore required self-restraint, self-control, and self-governance by all. That duty put every member of society in a position of a moral trust and put the civil governments all the more in the position to honor that trust. It was not an option for the civil magistrate to avoid his charge to protect other covenantal institutions. The civil officer himself was thus doubly obliged to both God and the moral good of man. Immorality therefore found no tolerance in civil legislation, being that marriage itself was another godly societal ordinance. Adultery was thus forbidden in law as a violation of the covenant family as well as its destruction to the fabric of the commonwealth. Adultery following marriage was a breach of both a private and public covenantal trust and therefore was also a breach of the civil laws protecting that trust. The reason that Massachusetts gave for prohibiting adultery was because it violated an obligation both to God and to His foremost covenant institution: *"As the Violation of the Marriage Covenant is highly provoking to God and destructive to Families ... ,"*[27] and colonial legislation was ordained to protect the sanctity of the family institution as well as the overall moral fabric of the community. Upon conviction, the crimes of sexual perversion and ravishment resulted in death; the guilty parties of adultery were to be publicly humiliated before the community, *"upon the Gallows by the space of an Hour, with a Rope about their Neck"*[28] (among other punitive punishments) before being sent home for private repentance, restitution, and reconciliation.

Public as well as private disobedience to God had been a common problem with the ancient Hebrew people. In breaking their national obligations to God, they had repeatedly abandoned His providential protection; in the doctrinal portion of a 1733 sermon by New England preacher Samuel Wigglesworth, he pointed to old Israel's need for covenant fidelity to God: *"Their very being as a people depends on their Fidelity to God, and steadfastness in keeping his Covenant: and if they finally revolt they must expect to be rooted out, and come to nothing."*[29]

The implications of his reference was not lost on his fellow New Englanders nor on the magistrates in Wigglesworth's native colony of Massachusetts, for he was not preaching before a congregation of worshippers but an assembly of civil representatives. The application of Wigglesworth's sermon strictly admonished them as godly representatives to sharpen their judgments in legislating terror against societal ungodliness: *"And if this Great and General Assembly could indeed find its means of sharp'ning the edge of the magistrates sword, thereby rendering him a great Terror of those Evil Works."*[30] It was against such moral vices as public *"Drunkedness, Uncleanness, Prophanation*

A.

B.

A TABLE of Kindred and Affinity, wherein whosoever are related are forbidden in scripture, and by our laws, to marry together.

A man may not marry his	A woman may not marry her
1 GRANDMOTHER.	1 GRANDFATHER.
2 Grandfather's Wife.	2 Grandmother's Husband.
3 Wife's Grandmother.	3 Husband's Grandfather.
4 Father's Sister.	4 Father's Brother.
5 Mother's Sister.	5 Mother's Brother.
6 Father's Brother's Wife.	6 Father's Sister's Husband.
7 Mother's Brother's Wife.	7 Mother's Sister's Husband.
8 Wife's Father's Sister.	8 Husband's Father's Brother.
9 Wife's Mother's Sister.	9 Husband's Mother's Brother.
10 Mother.	10 Father.
11 Step-Mother.	11 Step Father.
12 Wife's Mother.	12 Husband's Father.
13 Daughter.	13 Son.
14 Wife's Daughter.	14 Husband's Son.
15 Son's Wife.	15 Daughter's Husband.
16 Sister.	16 Brother.
17 Wife's Sister.	17 Husband's Brother.
18 Brother's Wife.	18 Sister's Husband.
19 Son's Daughter.	19 Son's Son
20 Daughter's Daughter.	20 Daughter's Son.
21 Son's Son's Wife.	21 Son's Daughter's Husband.
22 Daughter's Son's Wife.	22 Daughter's Daughter's Husband
23 Wife's Son's Daughter.	23 Husband's Son's Son.
24 Wife's Daughter's Daughter.	24 Husband's Daughter's Son.
25 Brother's Daughter.	25 Brother's Son.
26 Sister's Daughter.	26 Sister's Son.
27 Brother's Son's Wife.	27 Brother's Daughter's Husband.
28 Sister's Son's Wife	28 Sister's Daughter's Husband.
29 Wife's Brother's Daughter.	29 Husband's Brother's Son.
30 Wife's Sister's Daughter.	30 Husband's Sister's Son.

A. To the Puritans, the union of husband and wife under God was the foundation of the covenant family, and the family was the underpinning of the wider societies of church and commonwealth. Protecting the biblical purity of the civil union of husband and wife was the job of the civil magistrate. Shown is a later, memorial engraving of a Puritan husband and wife, illustrated in 1863.

B. American laws that protected the family were drawn from the Bible's moral directives. The civil laws of *"Kindred and Affinity,"* which listed who could and who could not marry, were taken directly from God's mandates to the Hebrew nation. Many early American laws were enactments of God's biblical Law, as explained in this *Table of Kindred and Affinity* appendixed to a typical, early federal period New Testament (1801).

27. *Acts and Laws, Of His Majesty's Province of the Massachusetts-Bay in New England. Begun and held at Boston, the eighth of June 1692 ...* (Boston, 1759), p. 51.
28. Ibid.
29. Samuel Wigglesworth, *An Essay for Reviving Religion. A Sermon Delivered at Boston, Before the Great and General Assembly Of the Province of the Massachusetts-Bay ...* (Boston, 1733), p. 12.
30. Ibid., p. 29.

159

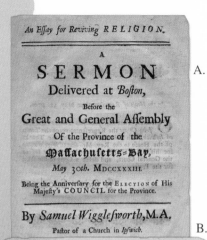

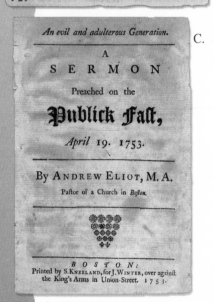

A. This is the title page of Samuel Wigglesworth's 1733 sermon, *Reviving Religion*, preached before the Assembly and Court of Massachusetts.

B. Shown here is an excerpt from Wigglesworth's sermon, in which he warned that New England's *"very Being as a People"* depended on continuing covenant fidelity to the God of its forefathers.

C. Title page of Andrew Eliot's 1753 Fast-Day Sermon, *An Evil and Adulterous Generation.*

of God's Name"[31] that dutiful magistrates were called to judge. Yet, in their judgments they were to remain tender toward the one Source of New England's virtue: *"And how can we justify our Conduct if we cast him off for ever? Surely eternal shame and Confusion will cover our Ingratitude, if we do thus requite our own and our father's God?"*[32] Simply put, Wigglesworth urged New England magistrates to rule harshly against human vice, and tenderly toward godly virtue. Thus came a typically Puritan conclusion that if the province would *"break off our Sins by Repentance"*[33] and keep New England's own covenantal obligations to God, the most glorious prospects would be in store for future generations: *"... the mercy of the Lord to everlasting to everlasting, be upon them that fear him, and his Righteousness unto Children's Children: To such as keep his Covenant, and to those that remember his Commandments to do them, Psal.103.17,18."*[34]

Likewise, two decades later at a public fast called by Massachusetts provincial magistrates in 1753, Andrew Eliot based the doctrine of his sermon on the obligation of ancient Israel to uphold God's Law. He warned that it was a failure of leadership and judicial laxity as well as an overall weak moral condition that caused Israel's demise:

> *The Heads of the people, their Rulers & Teachers taught them to err; they taught them by their Example; and there were many direct Breaches of the Law of God, which they, by their corrupt Glosses and perverse Interpretations, made the people to believe were no evil at all.*[35]

Entitling his oration *An Evil and Adulterous Generation*, Eliot's application was clear. If New England failed in its own duty to live by the covenant of their forefathers, that generation would be held responsible for the outcome. Eliot saw little difference in the moral obligation of Hebrew Israel and that of English America. In detaching themselves from the ways of their fathers, New England was also detaching its godly cords and unraveling its societal fabric.

> *Oh New-England! how art thou fallen! We are not the genuine Offspring of the first Settlers of this Land!; we are a spurious Race, risen up*

31. Ibid.
32. Ibid.
33. Ibid., p. 31.
34. Ibid., p. 36.
35. Andrew Eliot, *An Evil and Adulterous Generation. A Sermon Preached on the Publick Fast, April 19. 1753* (Boston, 1753), p. 8.

in stead of them, but very unlike them. We are guilty of great Apostasy; we have broken the Covenant, which, as we are a professing People, subsists between God and us.[36]

Such a comprehensive mantle on provincial New England invested its people with an indelible duty toward personal and private fidelity. The role of the godly family was central to New England society, as the family planted the seeds for a future commonwealth and succored another generation for the kingdom of heaven. Many of Eliot's contemporaries preached that the New England family provided its basic commonwealth, and that the home was its most basic house of worship. No less than the powerful and worthy mind of Jonathan Edwards warned of the consequence of a failure in the family's foremost duty:

> *Every Christian family ought to be as it were a little church, consecrated to Christ, and wholly influenced and governed by his rules. And family education and order are some of the chief means of grace. If these fail, all other means are likely to prove ineffectual. If these are duly maintained, all the means of grace will be likely to prosper and be successful.*[37]

Edwards carried the banner of prior American Puritans who had made the same appeal. Yet, even their call was simply a reflection of the more distant martyr John Hooper two centuries before Edwards, and that of England's Assembly of Divines following him. All Reformed Christians saw an unimpeachable duty for their families to govern themselves under God, and Edwards drew the same, familial conclusion:

> *Remembering that, as you would not have all your instructions and counsels ineffectual, there must be government as well as instructions, which must be maintained with an even hand, and steady resolution, as a guard to the religion and morals of your family, and the support of its good order.*[38]

The influence of such biblical self-governance was profound, enduring, and steeped in New England's inheritance. The doctrines that repeatedly heralded the eighteenth-century pulpits indeed echoed their Puritan forefathers and set the stage for America's future. Manifold public sermons such as Election Sermons, Thanksgiving Sermons, Fast-Day Sermons, Commemorative Sermons, Memorial Sermons, Artillery Sermons, as well as the weekly Sabbath Sermons, provided a regular diet of doctrine for every pertinent need. Perhaps more than any time before in Christendom's history, pulpits resounded amid every town with the vivid doctrine of biblical fidelity and its application of robust cultural stewardship.

Dan Ford, 2002

A.

B.

FAREWELL SERMON;

BY JONATHAN EDWARDS, A. M.

Delivered at NORTHAMPTON, June 22d, 1750.

AFTER THE PEOPLE'S PUBLIC REJECTION OF HIM AS THEIR MINISTER, AND RENOUNCING THEIR RELATION TO HIM AS PASTOR OF THE CHURCH.

PRINTED AT NORTHAMPTON, BY DANIEL WRIGHT & Co. For SIMEON BUTLER.

A. Jonathan Edwards (1703-1758) was one of the great Reformed theologians of New England's provincial era.

B. This is the title page of Edwards's *Farewell Sermon*, urging his congregation to continue in family duty (1750).

36. Ibid.
37. Jonathan Edwards, *A Farewell Sermon* (Northampton, Massachusetts, n.d.), p. 136.
38. Ibid.

Chapter 5: The Commonwealths Realized

The Covenantal Principles of the American Cause and Self-Governance

T was likely that Jonathan Edwards's pulpit had the greatest impact in preaching the saving power of Jesus Christ in the northern colonies. For him it soon became apparent that a marvelous Providence was at hand, and it was God Himself to be thanked. It was Edwards's sermons, though, that contributed much to the "awakening" of so many of New England's souls, as God's use of his preaching of grace and repentance first drove the movement. Edwards wrote in his 1736 work, *The Surprising Work of God*:

> *... there has been a great and marvelous work of conversion and sanctification among the people here; and they have paid all due respect to those who have been blest of God to be the instruments of it. Both old and young have shown a forwardness to hearken not only to my counsels, but even to my reproofs, from the pulpit.*[1]

The "Great Awakening," as it was later known, extended from the mid-1730's through the 1740's and had a powerful effect upon all of colonial America. People's hearts, souls, and minds were reoriented toward God as it was recognized that a mighty Providence was underway. The most traveled orator of America's Awakening, George Whitefield, saw Providence already at work in his first travels from Britain to the southern end of the Anglo-American shores:

> *But as certainly as Jesus Christ, that Angel of the Covenant, in the Days of his Flesh, walked upon the Water, and said to his sinking Disciples, Be not afraid it is I, ... so surely, I say, has he spoken, and at His command the Winds have blown us where we are now arrived. For his Providence ruleth all Things.*[2]

Whitefield indeed saw God's hand at work during his remaining six trips to America in which he traveled repeatedly from Georgia into the middle colonies, well into New England and back. Others, such as the powerhouse preacher Gilbert Tennent, were significantly used by God in the middle colonies, as the Presbyterian missionary David Brainerd was used among the Indians in many of the same colonies. Edwards, Whitefield, Tennent, and Brainerd were among those best remembered, but hundreds of others left unrecorded in the annals of man were also used by God to awaken thousands upon thousands of American souls.

1. Jonathan Edwards, *A Faithful Narrative of the Surprising Work of God in the Conversion of Many Hundred Souls ... in the Province of the Massachusetts-Bay in New England* (Boston edition, 1738), p. 77.
2. George Whitefield, *Thankfulness for Mercies received a necessary Duty. A Farewel Sermon Preached ... near Savannah in Georgia, on Sunday May the 17th, 1738* (London, 1738), pp. 8-9.

The Great Awakening united the colonies in a way that had not been seen before. Britain's colonial policy had always been to keep the individual colonies divided from one another. It treated each province as separate and intended to keep the interests of each independent from one another by making them compete individually for its trade. Britain severely restricted trade between the American colonies so that provincial concerns would be focused on mother Britain instead of with each other. She would reap the financial benefit of the trade and keep her colonies weakly disassembled. The New England colonies, which in the prior century had been largely united around their common faith and covenantal civil governance, had since the Revolution (1689) become considerably divided due to the British trade and mercantile regimes.

Providentially, though, the Great Awakening brought many unanticipated effects to America. What was most apparent at the time was the large number of souls that were saved, bringing a healthy dose of virtue and godliness back to America. What went largely unnoticed, or at least largely unappreciated at the time, were the Awakening's unifying influences and the greater sense of independence that it effected upon the average American mind. A Christian brother in northern New England now had unity with his continental brethren in the South. Though there remained great differences among the provinces which British colonial policy did little to help, the Awakening had a considerable consolidating effect that went far beyond the sheer number of converts. The much-improved character of the American culture grew in direct contrast with the moral decline of its much more sophisticated motherland. While Britain remained largely "High Church" with lower morals, the American assemblies remained mostly "Low Church" with high morals. Many Presbyterians, Reformed Baptists, Dutch and German Reformed, along with the occasional *"Calvinist Methodist"*[3] such as George Whitefield, joined with Congregationalists and Reformed Anglicans of an American stripe in a more doctrinally-sound fidelity than was possible under the British regime across the Atlantic. Thus, many traditional denominational barriers were softened in America. In a sustained cultural sweep, the Awakening drew the colonists' attention to Christ as their common Lord, to the Scriptures as their common doctrine, to Americans as their common brethren, and upon America as their common homeland and prime interest. In a generation soon to come, that would prove to be an explosive combination.

3. See *Encyclopedia of Colonial America* (New York, 1996), s.v. "Whitefield," p. 450.

A.

B. *Dan Ford, 2002*

C.

A. This is the title page of Jonathan Edward's *Faithful Narrative*, describing the advent of the Great Awakening in New England in 1736 (1738 edition).

B. George Whitefield (1714-1770), a powerful Reformed preacher, saw God's Awakening Providence at work in America.

C. This is the title page of his sermon, *Thankfulness ... a necessary Duty*, marking the advent of the Awakening in the southern colonies (1738).

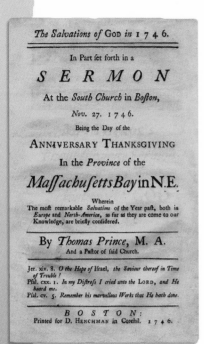

The Salvations of GOD *in* 1 7 4 6.

In Part set forth in a

S E R M O N

At the *South Church* in *Boston*,

Nov. 27. 1 7 4 6.

Being the Day of the

ANNIVERSARY THANKSGIVING

In the *Province* of the

Maſſachuſetts Bay in N.E.

Wherein
The moſt remarkable *Salvations* of the Year paſt, both in
Europe and *North-America*, as far as they are come to our
Knowledge, are briefly conſidered.

By *Thomas Prince*, M. A.

And a Paſtor of ſaid Church.

Jer. xiv. 8. O *the Hope of* Iſrael, *the Saviour thereof in Time
of Trouble !*
Pſal. cxx. 1. *In my Diſtreſs I cried unto the* LORD, *and He
heard me.*
Pſal. cv. 5. *Remember his marvellous Works that He hath done.*

B O S T O N:
Printed for D. HENCHMAN in Cornhil. 1 7 4 6.

Massachusetts had a tradition of holding an annual provincial Thanksgiving. It was called by the magistrates each year, but not merely as an historic memorial to the first Pilgrim forefathers. In fact, their annual civil ordinance specifically set aside a new day in which to gather as families and congregations to continue the necessary, ongoing practice of thankfulness, and to unitedly consider the God of their bountiful mercies. Shown here is the title page of Thomas Prince's sermon, *Salvations of God in 1746*, which extolled God's recent, miraculous deliverance against the impossible odds of a French invasion.

By the end of the Awakening, the American pulpits had grown in numbers and overall quality. While they remained (in the main) doctrinally sound, they took on the old Puritan mantle of cultural stewardship and rallied to the patriot cause in the various contests of the French and Indian Wars. American pulpits resounded with Anglo-American patriotism, and New England's pulpits cried out with the old Puritan fervor, giving thanks to God for His many intercessions. New England was once again redeemed, but not from its old spiritual foe as in the Awakening; rather, it was delivered from the manifestation of another powerful adversary. God's hand was manifested to them, time after time, throughout the French and Indian Wars. Just as it had been in the spiritual realm where the Lord had delivered thousands of souls by means of effectual salvation, in the physical realm He also delivered millions by His providential manifestation. And, God be thanked for both! For example, deliverance came in 1746 when a massive French fleet had assembled to invade the coasts of the northern colonies that had grown into maturity along the shores of New England:

> *They* [the French] *had forty thousand Arms, with proportionable Ammunition and Blankets for the Indians; ... That there were seven thousand North American Indians to join them: That upon their taking Annapolis, they expected eighteen French Ships of the Line & twenty two Spanish Men of War wou'd be sent early in the Spring to join the Fleet on these Coasts; which were a Matter generally believ'd & depended upon among them: that they were resolved to destroy the Frontier Settlements of the English Colonies, and had a Great Dependence on getting strong Footing on this Part of the North American Continent.*[4]

New England yet again appealed to their Lord in distress (2 Samuel 22:5-7).[5] And, in a surprising and immediate turn of Providence on behalf of an otherwise hapless people, an overwhelming storm overtook and scattered the invaders, turning New England's pending ruin into the ruin of the French. The massive fleet, on the verge of its landing in America, had miraculously been destroyed without the necessity of a single volley of resistance being fired by the colonists. With the enemy staved off and destroyed, the Almighty Hand of salvation had again been manifested in America:

4. Thomas Prince, *The Salvations of God in 1746. In Part set forth in a Sermon At the South Church in Boston, Nov. 27. 1746. Being the Day of the Anniversary Thanksgiving In the Province of the Massachusetts Bay in N.E.* (Boston, 1746), pp. 33-34.
5. A common Scripture passage repeated in colonial sermons that identified Americans with devotion amid trial.

Prayer throughout the Churches in this Province, on this great Emergency. And that very Night ensuing, the glorious God entirely baffled all their Purposes, and put a total End to their Mischievous enterprize. He, the mighty arose, and wrought a full Salvation for us. He sent a more serious Storm of Wind and Rain and Hail, that ever – which held to the next Day Noon – which they cou'd not stand before – which dispersed and broke them, they cou'd never get together again.[6]

In the typically Puritan fashion, Thomas Prince's sermon was quick to show that God's salvation, whether eternal (as in His Awakening) or temporal (as in His intervention to save the provinces), came by way of the same sovereign Hand of Providence. There was consequently an undeniable duty for them to give thanks in all things, in both realms of salvation:

Salvation is sometimes in Scripture used in the largest sense: As comprehending both Preservation and Deliverance from all Kinds of Evil, both of Sin, Disorder and Trouble, Both felt and threatening, in the Present State, and Preservation from every Evil in the Future; together with the Bestowment of all Kinds of Good contrary to those Evils; and all This forever. But the Salvation in the Text[7] is meant of Preservation from the threatening Host of humane, powerful and destroying enemies.

And as the sovereign GOD, in Times of His people's Danger from them, is to be eyed as having all the Parts and Powers of Nature in his Hands, both angelical, humane and elementary, and using each according to his perfect Wisdom and sovereign Pleasure; ... .[8]

Pulpits and Primers: two means of continuing cultural virtue:

A. New England's churches remained the centerpieces of provincial town culture, with their pulpits resounding in all essential biblical virtues (early nineteenth-century woodcut).

B. The popular *New England Primer* taught children biblical truths in basic learning (ABC's from eighteenth-century Primer).

From New England's pulpits there was an essential link that was understood between the Covenant of Grace and its earthly accord. The public sermon therefore echoed the common remedy of God's intervening grace for both the eternal and temporal prosperity of their souls, as was heard in Andrew Eliot's sermon a few years later:

If we be at once, by the influence of the Spirit of Grace, brought to a sincere and thoro' Repentance; God, even our God, will delight to dwell among us, and bless us. Things will go well with us. If the Spirit be poured from on high, the Wilderness shall be a fruitful field; Then judgment shall dwell in the Wilderness, and Righteousness remain in the fruitful field.[9]

6. Prince, *The Salvations of God in 1746*, p. 31.
7. Referencing Isaiah 28:29; Psalm 74:12; Jonah 2:9; Psalm 3:8; Jeremiah 3:23; and *"diverse other places."*
8. Prince, *The Salvations of God in 1746*, p. 8.
9. Andrew Eliot, *An Evil and Adulterous Generation. A Sermon Preached on the Publick Fast*, p. 26.

The Covenantal Cause

Two decades later an even greater threat would reawaken America's pulpits. The provincials had for years been resisting the intrusion of new British "innovations" in North America. In the 1760's, the British Admiralty began an invasion of the provinces which would extend well beyond their coasts, docks, and wharfs. At the same time that Parliament was encroaching upon their chartered right of self-taxation, came the alarming proposal to impose British bishops upon America as well. Again picking up the mantle of their Puritan forefathers, New England's pulpits rose to the cause by sounding the cry that those in the motherland (who should have remained their closest benefactors) were now quickly becoming their foes.

In recalling the examples of the first New England immigrants, it soon became apparent that God's deliverance would also require them to resolve upon another great sacrifice. And, similar to New England's most recent victories in the French and Indian Wars, the cause would likewise require its pulpits to call upon the people to seek divine mercies if they were once again to be unitedly delivered. *"It is hoped that this People will unitedly exert themselves ... ,"* pleaded Charles Turner before the governor and the provincial magistrates in his election sermon of 1773:

> *It is hoped that this People will unitedly exert themselves, in the methods justifiable in the sight of God, for their deliverance; and so with humblest confidence, commit their cause to the God of all grace, and mercy, and wisdom; putting up fervent prayers, in the name of Christ, to that Being who is able to save; and, in the mean time, practically considering the indispensable importance of joining repentance unfeigned with supplications, as they would rationally expect audience with Him, who loveth righteousness, and hateth iniquity: And that all persons in any places of public trust will exert themselves, according to the requirements of their several stations, to put a stop to the growing infidelity and immorality, whereby we provoke the Holy One of Israel to anger. And may the God of our fathers make bare his holy arm, for our salvation![10]*

The time had again come to preach and petition, but also to act. Massachusetts responded to Britain's forced closure of its Boston port and her dissolution of its chartered right to self-representation.[11] The colonies mourned in unison on June 1,

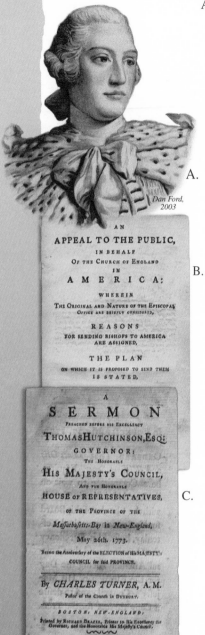

A.

Dan Ford, 2003

B.

C.

A. In the 1760's, George III began to tighten trade laws and also encroach upon America's civil and religious liberties.

B. One action that caused the American clergy their greatest consternation was this 1767 proposal to place authoritative Anglican Bishops in America.

C. By the early 1770's, it was apparent that Americans must bind their resolve under God (title page of Charles Turner's 1773 Election Sermon).

---

10. Charles Turner, *A Sermon Preached before ... His Majesty's Council, and the Honorable House of Representatives, of the Province of the Massachusetts-Bay in New-England* (Boston, 1773), pp. 43-44.
11. See Don Cook, *The Long Fuse* (New York, 1995), pp. 192-193.

1774, the day that the Boston Port Bill went into effect. Virginia observed a Day of Fasting and Prayer as a gesture in league with its Puritan colleagues to the north; shops were closed throughout the provinces and church bells were rung in solemnity. The Massachusetts Committees of Correspondence proposed a *"Solemn Covenant,"* intending to pledge the people of Massachusetts to unitedly counter the aggressive new British policies: *"being fully sensible of our indispensable duty to lay hold on every means in our power to preserve and recover the much injured constitution of our country."*[12] The covenant would mutually bind its inhabitants:

A.

Dan Ford, 2003

> *... in the presence of God, solemnly and in good faith, covenant and engage with each other, 1st, That from henceforth we will suspend all commercial intercourse with the said island of Great Britain, until the said act for blocking up the said harbour be repealed, and a full restoration of our charter rights be obtained.*[13]

The crown's newly appointed military governor for Massachusetts, General Thomas Gage, denounced the Covenant and threatened to arrest anyone involved in its signing or distribution. Gage formally dissolved the provincial council on June 17, the very day that Boston had convened a town meeting to consider adopting the Covenant. To counter that move, the Boston meeting issued its famous proposal that all the provinces convene a general (Continental) Congress. And, bolstered by an outpouring of support from other colonials (but not waiting for Congress to convene), Boston ratified the Covenant on June 27th. Over the following weeks, other provinces agreed to unite their efforts against the British "Intolerable Acts" by likewise adopting the Covenant and/or agreeing to meet in a congress.

B.

WE the Subscribers, inhabitants of the town of having taken into our serious consideration the precarious state of the liberties of North-America; and more especially the present distressed condition of this insulted province, embarrassed as it is by several acts of the British parliament, tending to the entire subversion of our natural and charter rights; among which is the act for blocking up the harbour of Boston : and being fully sensible of our indispensable duty to lay hold on every means in our power to preserve and recover the much injured constitution of our country; and conscious at the same time of no alternative between the horrors of slavery, or the carnage and desolation of a civil war, but a suspension of all commercial intercourse with the island of Great Britain, Do, in the presence of God, solemnly and in good faith, covenant and engage with each other, 1st, That from henceforth we will suspend all commercial intercourse with the said island of Great Britain, until the said act for blocking up the said harbour be repealed, and a full restoration of our charter rights be obtained. And,

2ly, That there may be the less temptation to others to continue in the said, now dangerous commerce, we do in like manner solemnly covenant that we will not buy, purchase or consume, or suffer any person, by, for or under us to purchase or consume, in any manner whatever, any goods, wares or merchandize which shall arrive in America from Great Britain aforesaid, from and after the last day of August next ensuing. And in order as much as in us lies to prevent our being interrupted and defeated in this only peaceable measure, entered into for the recovery and preservation of our rights, we agree to break off all trade, commerce and dealings whatever with all persons, who, preferring their own private interest to the salvation of their now perishing country, shall still continue to import goods from Great Britain, or shall purchase of those who do import, and never to renew any commerce or trade with them.

And, Whereas the promoting of industry, œconomy, arts and manufactures among ourselves is of the last importance to the civil and religious welfare of a community ; we engage,

3ly, That from and after the first day of October next ensuing, we will, not by ourselves, or any for, by, or under us, purchase or use any goods, wares, manufactures or merchandize, whensoever or howsoever imported from Great Britain, until the harbour of Boston shall be opened, and our charter rights restored. And,

Lastly, As a refusal to come into any agreement which promises the deliverance of our country from the calamities it now feels, and which, like a torrent are rushing upon it with increasing violence, must evidence a disposition enimical to, or criminally negligent of, the common safety : We agree, that after this covenant has been offered to any person, and they refuse to sign it, we will consider them in the same light as contumacious importers, and withdraw all commercial connexions with them forever, and publish their names to the world. Witness our hands,
June,   1774.

A. Massachusetts magistrate Samuel Adams (1722-1803) saw it as part of a sworn oath of office, and as a duty to God, to unitedly preserve America's liberties. That principle was behind his idea for a Committees of Correspondence (1772), the *Solemn Covenant* (1774), and his proposal at Boston's June 17th (1774) meeting for a general American Congress.

B. The *Solemn Covenant* was issued in the form of this broadside to be signed by towns committing under God to preserve *"the liberties of North-America"* (June, 1774).

12. Massachusetts *Covenant* Broadside (June, 1774).
13. Ibid.

The king's response to the American reaction was to engage in further Machiavellian tactics to ensure that the provincials would back down. Knowing that a new election of the British House of Commons was pending in early 1775, and that a possible majority of the British subjects might sympathize with their brethren in America, George III directed the Prime minister, Lord North, to call a special election of the House. He advised North to fix the date of the election, but not to notify the nation or any candidates who might oppose him until one week before the vote was to ensue. While the nation was still in the dark about the upcoming election, the king feathered his scheme with liberal public spending on behalf of candidates who would be of a Royalist bent. The ignorant British electorate would then be primed to back the king's allies once the election was announced, and his American policies would carry a majority in the Commons.

Secret rule or open government:

As a reaction to colonial resistance, George III enlisted the Secretary over the American colonies, the Earl of Dartmouth, to become his personal agent. Lord Dartmouth was used to privately secure the execution of the king's will in Parliament, to transmit personal orders to General Gage in Boston, and to discreetly enlist American Indians against the provincials. Among his other services, in April of 1775, Dartmouth sent General Gage the king's secret order to march on Concord, Massachusetts, beginning open hostilities in America. The British ministry had become unaccountable to public scrutiny, and Samuel Adams soon protested to the American Congress that the Earl could no longer be trusted. Shown here is an excerpt of the manuscript pay order, signed by Prime Minister North and other ministers, designating £3000 to Dartmouth for *"his Majesty's Secret Service without Account."* Payments were made for his services rendered between mid-1774 and mid-1775.

The scheme was a calculated success, and in November, Lord North could report to the king that the surprise election had indeed secured a firm majority for the crown in the Commons, and for several ensuing years his policies toward America would face no serious parliamentarian opposition. The crown also paid the Earl of Dartmouth, the British Secretary of State over the colonies, a generous stipend to secure his loyalty. Dartmouth had previously represented the colonial interests before the king, and Dartmouth College had recently been named in honor of that support. Yet, in early 1774, the Earl was secured into *"his Majesty's Secret Service without Account."* He was now the king's own agent, and no longer could American appeals gain a favorable hearing before the crown. With continuing news of America's resolve coming to the king, George III could declare back to Prime Minister North: *"The die is now cast, the colonies must either submit or triumph."*[14]

At the First Continental Congress which met at Philadelphia in September, twelve colonies came together to consider their mutual grievances and to adopt what measures were necessary to resist Britain's encroachments. Representing all of the colonies except Georgia to the far south and Canada to the far north, the American assembly appealed to Britain in a Bill of Rights which stated their various resolves, *"as that their religion, laws, and liberties may not be*

14. Cook, *The Long Fuse*, pp. 196-197.

subverted."[15] The Congress also published a circular letter to all the inhabitants of the American colonies which appealed to them to reform their lives, to pray, and to maintain an utmost godly demeanor:

> *Above all things we earnestly intreat you, with devotion of spirit, penitence of heart, and amendment of life, to humble yourselves, and implore the favour of Almighty God: and we fervently beseech his divine goodness, to take you in his gracious protection.*[16]

Though the First Continental Congress was not a governing body, it did adopt the first intercolonial legislative document among the provinces soon to become Independent States. *The Association* was a formally drafted document reflective of Massachusetts' *Covenant*, uniting the colonies in a formal pledge to act in a common purpose against Britain's oppressive policies. Among those policies were the *"several late, cruel, and oppressive Acts as have been passed respecting the town of Boston and the Massachusetts' Bay."*[17] Like the *Covenant*, *The Association* bound its assigned colonies to form governing committees *"in every county, city, or town, by those who are qualified to vote for Representatives in their legislature,"*[18] to superintend the non-importation of British goods and the non-exportation of American goods to Britain. Its pledge concluded (in part):

> *And we do solemnly bind ourselves and our constituents, under the ties aforesaid, to adhere to this association until such parts of the several Acts of Parliament passed since the close of the last war* [the last French and Indian War[19]], *... are repealed.*[20]

The Association appealed to the Puritan virtues through its resolve to *"encourage frugality, economy and industry,"*[21] and through its avowed pledge to *"discourage every species of extravagance and dissipation, especially all horse racing, all kinds of gaming, cock-fighting, ... and other expensive diversions and entertainments."*[22] By

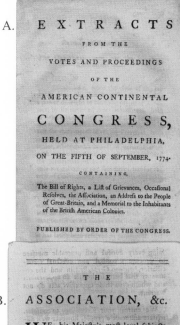

A.

B.

America's first Continental Congress brought the colonies together in 1774 to openly express their sentiments:

A. The *Extracts from the Votes and Proceedings* was its first publication and included a *Bill of Rights*, various resolves, *The Association*, and several addresses of appeal (title page of the 1774 *Extracts*).

B. *The Association* was the first official governing act with force, passed by a unified American body of delegates.

---

15. *Extracts from the Votes and Proceedings of the AMERICAN CONTINENTAL CONGRESS, held at Philadelphia, on the Fifth of September, 1774. Containing, The Bill of Rights, a List of Grievances, Occasional Resolves, the Association, an Address to the People of Great-Britain, and a Memorial to the Inhabitants of the British American Colonies* (Philadelphia; reprint ed., London, 1774), p. 3.
16. Ibid., p. 65.
17. Ibid., p. 5.
18. Ibid., p. 22.
19. Also known as the Seven Years War, 1754-1762.
20. *Extracts from the ... CONTINENTAL CONGRESS*, p. 22.
21. Ibid., pp. 18-19.
22. See Robert Middlekauff, *The Glorious Cause* (Oxford Press, 1982), p. 249.

Hannah
Zes,
2003

A.

B.

Massachusetts' declaration of its dependence:

A. Like his Puritan forefathers, John Hancock
(1737-1793), the President of Massachusetts'
1775 Provincial Congress, saw America's cause
in terms of a humble duty to submit to God.

B. It was historically consistent for the colonial
legislatures to call upon the Lord, who holds all
rulers under His sovereign authority. This public
fast was providentially called to be observed in
March 1775, a month before British troops
marched on Lexington and Concord and set in
motion the events that would determine the
ultimate judgment of Divine Providence upon
the British and the American causes.

adding standards of morality to the resolves of _The
Association_, the Continental Congress reminded America
that its virtues underpinned its civil freedom.[23]

That first legislative action of a covenantal America
would remain in place until the United Colonies ultimately
became United States in July 1776. At that time, thirteen
States (now including Georgia) pledged themselves in a
mutual _Declaration of Independence_. But, that _Independence_
was also a declaration of dependence on God by concluding:

> _And for the support of this declaration,
> with firm reliance on the protection of
> Divine Providence, we mutually pledge
> to each other our lives, our fortunes,
> and our sacred honour._[24]

Following the enactments of New England's
earlier _Covenant_ and America's _Association_ in
1774, the situation quickly worsened. It soon
became apparent that events were fast coming to
blows, and the bayonets of the motherland were
set to be plunged into the hearts of her
provincial subjects. Britain strategically chose
her target. She would strike at the center of
America's fortitude, casting her blow directly
into the heart of the covenanted resistance. The
Ministry calculated that making an example of
Massachusetts would force the remaining
colonies into compliance with its new
regulatory policies; yet before that event, the
Massachusetts Provincial Congress reaffirmed
an appeal to its Sovereign in no uncertain terms:

> _... it is highly and peculiarly proper,
> and a Duty incumbent upon this
> People; more especially at a Time of
> such general Distress, that a Day of
> publick FASTING and PRAYER should
> be observed and kept throughout this
> Colony, not only on Account of the
> present Calamity, but also in
> Conformity to the laudable Custom of
> our Ancestors._[25]

23. Ibid.
24. Continental Congress, _The Constitutions of the Several
Independent States of America ..._ (Philadelphia, [1782]; reprint
ed., London, 1783), pp. 1-4 for _"In Congress, July 4, 1776, A
Declaration of the Representatives of the United States of
America, in Congress Assembled."_
25. Massachusetts Provincial Congress, _In Provincial Congress,
... ,_ Broadside (Cambridge, [Mass.], February 16, 1775).

The leaders of that Massachusetts emergency assembly were amiss to do much by themselves against such an opponent – the most formidable military power in history – which by that time was already in possession of its capital at Boston. The first means for them to rally and confront their great oppressor was, as it had always been, to repent and rely upon God. They relied foremost upon that One who had delivered them, both bodies and souls, so many times before, and secondly, they relied on the strength of the covenantal bonds among their townsmen as those who had been weaned on the milk of *The New England Primers* and grown to manhood on the meat of their pulpits' sermons. Their duty bound them in a common cause with their Puritan ancestors who themselves had been willing to face every threat, to sacrifice all, and to risk every hazard in the name of God. Their Puritan forefathers had simply laid the charge at their feet, which was now theirs to honor and then pass along to their children. The February 1775 Provincial Fast Proclamation therefore concluded:

> *... and that we may again rejoice in the free and undisturbed Exercise of all those Rights and Privileges, for the Enjoyment of which our pious and virtuous Ancestors braved every Danger, and transmitted the fair Possession down to their Children, to be by them handed down intire to the latest Posterity. Signed by Order of the Provincial Congress, JOHN HANCOCK, President.*[26]

As long as the Second Continental Congress (which met in May of 1775) remained united, and the Continental Army remained in the field, there were many marvelous deliverances rendered on behalf of America. And, like their Puritan ancestors, it was incumbent upon them to

26. Ibid.

A.

B.

The Second Continental Congress was obliged to be thankful for God's remarkable sustenance.

A. This 1778 manuscript, *Proclamation*, asked each of the original thirteen states to declare *"a day of public thanksgiving and praise"* for God's mercies.

B. It also requested *" ... a penitent confession of our sins, and humble supplication for pardon through the merits of our Saviour."* America's cause was clearly seen as in the providential hands of an omnipotent Sovereign.

171

ascribe thanks to the Lord who went before them in battle. Upon receiving news of the first momentous American victory at Saratoga and the subsequent alliance with France, the Congress issued a proclamation for a public Thanksgiving: *"it being the indispensible duty of all men gratefully to acknowledge their obligations to him for benefits received."*[27] Their thanksgiving was accompanied by a plea for God's continuing mercies upon their precarious situation. America's 1778 Thanksgiving was not intended as a simple recollection of the Pilgrim's past gratuities in the 1620's. Theirs was meant by the Congress to be immediate, wrenching, and inspired, and like those ancestors who had gone before them, these United States saw themselves prostrated before the throne of God's sovereign mercy. There was no question as to who was in charge of the nation's fate, and its Thanksgiving brought an urgent plea for public and private repentance:

> *And it is further recommended, that together with devout thanksgivings may be joined a penitent confession of our sins, and humble supplication for pardon through the merits of our Saviour, so that under the smiles of heaven, our public councils may be directed; our arms by land & sea prospered; our liberty & independence secured; ... .*[28]

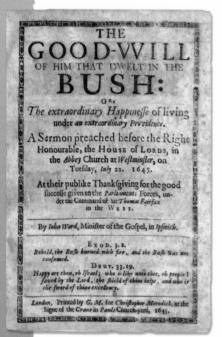

Puritan John Ward preached before Parliament after its army had won a remarkable victory over Charles I's troops at Bristol in July 1645. The Royalist forces then went into retreat and never again mustered another serious threat. The first English Civil War had been strategically won by Parliament, and Ward's *Thanksgiving* sermon therefore spoke to *"The extraordinary Happinesse of living under an extraordinary Providence"* (title page of Ward's 1645 sermon).

To honor God in each victory was to honor Him from whom continued assistance was needed. Independence from Britain did not mean independence from the Lord who had given them the protection in the field, and who was thereby providentially affirming their mutual pledge in their *Declaration of Independence*. Deep humility, thanksgiving, and praise were the proper reactions for the fledgling nation that had struggled against such outrageous odds. From the womb of its infancy America had cried out to God,[29] and even in thanksgiving for His deliverance its people would call upon Him for protection.

In the former century, the English Puritans had expressed many similar sentiments during the English Civil Wars of the 1640's. For instance, in Parliament's victory over King Charles I that foiled his efforts to establish royal absolutism, the Puritan Minister John Ward admonished England to return its thanks to God with humble praises, ascribing Parliament's success to Him: *"Not unto us, not unto us but to thy name be the praise. And to speak plainly for God; there is none other cause; for what is, or hath bin praise worthy, besides the success; and who knowes not, who sees not, that the event is of God?"*[30]

27. Continental Congress, two page manuscript *Proclamation* issued to the thirteen states (Philadelphia, 17 November, 1778), p. 1.
28. Ibid., p. 2.
29. See Psalm 22:8-11.
30. John Ward, *The Good-Will of Him that Dwelt in the Bush: ... A Sermon preached before the Right Honourable, the House of Lords, ... At their publike Thanksgiving for the good successe given to the Parliaments Forces ...* , p. 25.

It might not be surprising that following America's victory over a similar tyrannical king, the States would display similar gratitude. And, in the 1783 Thanksgiving sermon preached at Philadelphia on behalf of the Continental Congress, the Presbyterian chaplain George Duffield spoke with exacting sentiments and familiar verse as that of John Ward:

> And to him be rendered the thanks, and the praise – not to us; – not to us – but to thy name, O Lord, be the Glory. For thine is the power, and the victory, and the greatness. Both success and safety come of thee. And thou reignest over all: And shall wrought all our works, in us, and for us. PRAISE THEREFORE THY GOD, O AMERICA, — PRAISE THE LORD, YE, HIS HIGHLY FAVORED UNITED STATES.[31]

The English Puritan and the American patriot had each seen the same Lord of Israel in their deliverance, both in chapter and in verse.[32] And, as America's success was "marvelous" in his eyes, Duffield closed his 1783 Thanksgiving oration with a call for biblically grounded governance in the newly born nation of United States:

> It is that we love the Lord our God, to walk in his ways, and keep his commandments, to observe his statutes and his judgments. That a sacred regard be maintained to righteousness and truth. That we do justice, love mercy, and walk humbly with our God.[33] Then shall God delight to dwell amongst us, And these United states shall long remain, a great, a glorious, and happy people. Which may God, of his infinite mercy grant. Amen.[34]

In contrast to the earlier *League and Covenant* of England and Scotland in the 1640's, which was broken through corrupting capitulations with a disingenuous king, the three American covenants: The *Solemn Covenant* of the Committees of Correspondence (June 1774), *The Association* of the United Colonies (September 1774), and the ultimate *Declaration of Independence* (July 1776) were all solemnly pledged before God, but not broken. It was widely understood at the time that God's Providence had

A. *Dan Ford, 2003*

B.

C.

A. This is the title page of George Duffield's 1783 Thanksgiving sermon. As chaplain, Duffield discipled members of Congress in the biblical virtues of civil government and urged them to continue submitting America's independence to God.

B. Congress was composed of men such as John Witherspoon (1723-1794), President of New Jersey College (and descendant of John Knox), who understood biblical civil governance.

C. This is the title page of John Witherspoon's influential sermon: *The Dominion of Providence over the Passions of Men* (1776).

---

31. George Duffield, *A Sermon Preached ... On Thursday December 11, 1783. The Day appointed by the United States in Congress assembled, to be observed as a Day of Thanksgiving, for the restoration of Peace, and establishment of our Independence, in the Enjoyment of our Rights and Privileges* (Philadelphia, 1783), p. 25.
32. See Psalm 115:1-3.
33. Referencing Deuteronomy 30:16; Amos 5:24; Micah 6:8.
34. Duffield, *A Sermon Preached ... ,* p. 26.

Dan Ford, 2002

A.

THE
CONSTITUTIONS
OF THE SEVERAL
INDEPENDENT STATES
OF
A M E R I C A;
THE
Declaration of Independence;
THE
ARTICLES OF CONFEDERATION
BETWEEN THE SAID STATES;

B.

MASSACHUSETTS.

A
CONSTITUTION, or FRAME of GOVERNMENT, agreed upon by the Delegates of the People of the State of Massachusetts-Bay, in CONVENTION, begun and held at Cambridge, on the First of September, 1779, and continued by Adjournments to the Second of March, 1780.

PREAMBLE.

THE end of the institution, maintenance, and administration of government, is to secure the existence of the body-politic, to protect it, and to furnish the individuals who compose it, with the power of enjoying, in safety and tranquility, their natural right, and the blessings of life: And whenever these great objects are not attained, the people have a right to alter the government, and to take measures necessary for their safety, prosperity, and happiness.

The body politic is formed by a voluntary association of individuals; it is a social compact, by which the whole people covenants with each citizen, and each citizen with the whole people, that all shall be governed by certain laws for the common good. It is the duty of the people, therefore, in framing a constitution of government, to provide for an equitable mode of making laws, as well as for an impartial interpretation, and a faithful execution of them; that every man may, at all times, find his security in them.

We, therefore, the people of Massachusetts, acknowledging, with grateful hearts, the goodness of the Great Legislator of the Universe, in affording us, in the course of his providence, an opportunity, deliberately and peaceably, without fraud, violence, or surprize, of entering into an original, explicit, and solemn compact with each other; and of forming a new constitution of civil government, for ourselves and posterity; and devoutly imploring his direction in so interesting a design, DO agree upon, ordain, and establish, the following Declaration of Rights, and Frame of Government, as the CONSTITUTION of the COMMON-WEALTH of MASSACHUSETTS.

C.

A. John Adams (1735-1826) was the chief author of the *Constitution of the Commonwealth of Massachusetts.*

B. As noted on the title page of *The Constitutions of the Several Independent States* (ordered by the Congress in 1782), the text included all of the original, fundamental, constitutive documents of the nation.

C. The Massachusetts Constitution was based upon the public's foremost devotion to God. It offered *"grateful hearts"* to the *"Great Legislator of the Universe"* in its Preamble; and as a covenant, it acknowledged *"his direction in so interesting a design."*

confirmed their resolves through the heat of battle; they were not forced by Providence to concede their cause to George III; and, they stayed on the field of battle until their vows had been fulfilled with the ultimate stamp of Providence confirming their success. America never capitulated to their oppressive king nor to England's Royalist Parliament; rather, the king and Parliament capitulated in the ultimate recognition of America's rights (and to the withdrawal of British troops) through their peace treaty with America in 1783. Only then was trade restored with Britain on much more brotherly terms.

America's covenantal sentiments were expressed in many such documents of the founding period. They appeared not only in manifold public sermons, declarations, and orations of thanks of the time, but they were also inscribed on many of the civil documents which would frame the civil governments of the states. For example, the 1780 *Constitution of the Commonwealth of Massachusetts*, which John Adams contributed the majority hand, contained similar acknowledgments in its Preamble:

> *We, therefore, the people of Massachusetts, acknowledging, with grateful hearts, the goodness of the Great Legislator of the Universe, in affording us, in the course of his providence, an opportunity, deliberately and peaceably, without fraud, violence, or surprize, of entering into an original, explicit, and solemn compact with each other; and of forming a new constitution of civil government, for ourselves and posterity; ... .*[35]

That Constitution was seen by its framers to be a charter itself, as a "social compact," but not like the European Enlightenment's form of such a compact as that expressed by Jean-Jacques Rousseau. That popular European model yielded up the people's rights into the palm of the state. The Massachusetts Commonwealth's compact, however, remained a solemn covenant in a form distinctive to America in that it retained and preserved God-given (inalienable) rights with the people, saying:

> *... it is a social compact, by which the whole people covenants with each citizen, and each citizen with the whole people, that all shall be governed by certain laws for the common good.*[36]

35. Continental Congress, *The Constitutions of the Several Independent States of America*, p. 18 for "Massachusetts."
36. Ibid., Preamble of the Massachusetts Constitution, p. 18.

God reigned supreme amid the American states, and that reign was publicly acknowledged. God reigned over the rights of the people, but not through the innovative idea of humanly-derived 'rights' expressed by Rousseau's social theory. His model of state-sponsored rights would lead to the French Revolution's great horrors of the 1790's. In Massachusetts, the civil covenant recognized that the people of its civil society were vested with bonds of genuine liberty at the feet of the One who created them, who owned them, who brought them from bondage, and who required their continuing public devotion. It was therefore expressly written in the *Bill of Rights* of Massachusetts' Constitution: *"It is the right as well as the duty of all men in society, publicly, and at stated seasons to worship the supreme Being, the Creator and Preserver of the Universe ... ."*[37]

Effected in that first generation of thirteen American republics, those original principles were then passed on to the next generation. It was John Adams's son (well into the federal period) who could still savor the fruits yielded by men such as his father and the Puritan forefathers. In 1831, then ex-President John Quincy Adams spoke to a Quincy, Massachusetts audience at a memorial honoring the fifty-fifth anniversary of the Declaration of Independence. He recalled that the United States was formed as a covenanted union, and he also spoke of their nation's founding *Declaration* as if it had been penned in William Brewster's, William Bradford's, or Increase Mather's New England:

> *Each was pledged to all, and all were pledged to each by a concert of souls, without limitation of time, in the presence of Almighty God, and proclaimed to all mankind. The Colonies were not delegated sovereign states. The term sovereign is not even found in the Declaration; and far, very far was it from the contemplation of those who composed, or of those who adopted it, to constitute either the aggregate community, or any one of its members with absolute, uncontrollable or despotic power. They were united, free and independent States. Each of these properties is essential to their existence. Without union the covenant contains no pledge of freedom or independence; without freedom, none of the independence or union; without independence, none of the union or freedom.*[38]

A. Jean-Jacques Rousseau (1712-1788) was the French author of:

B. *Du Contract Social*, which proposed that citizens derived their rights from the state (1762).

C. John Quincy Adams (1767-1848) acknowledged that all liberties were derived from God.

D. This is the title page of John Quincy Adams's July 1831 *Oration*, which reminded his generation that the nation of United States was founded as a covenant under God.

Dan Ford, 2003

Dan Ford, 2002

CONTRACT·SOCIAL;
OU
PRINCIPES
DU
DROIT POLITIQUE.
PAR J. J. ROUSSEAU,
CITOYEN DE GENEVE.

AN
ORATION
ADDRESSED TO THE
CITIZENS OF THE TOWN OF QUINCY,
ON THE
FOURTH OF JULY, 1831,
THE
FIFTY-FIFTH ANNIVERSARY
OF THE
INDEPENDENCE
OF THE
UNITED STATES OF AMERICA.
BY JOHN QUINCY ADAMS.

37. Ibid., *A Declaration of Rights*, p. 19.
38. John Quincy Adams, *An Oration Addressed to the Citizens of the Town of Quincy, On the Fourth of July, 1831, The Fifty-Fifth Anniversary of the Independence of the United States of America* (Boston, 1831), p. 18.

Dan Ford, 2002

The constitution had provided that all the public functionaries of the Union, not only of the general but of all the state governments, should be under oath or affirmation for its support. The homage of religious faith was thus superadded to all the obligations of temporal law, to give it strength; and this confirmation of an appeal to the responsibilities of a future omnipotent judge, was in exact conformity with the whole tenor of the Declaration of Independence.

Covenantal continuity from Martyrs to Magistrates:

A. Many early Bible reformers paid the ultimate price, as shown in this woodcut of a public burning at Windsor Castle during the reign of Henry VIII.

B. An undying love for covenantal living drove several generations of Reformed families to New England in the 1600's. This is a later depiction of the first Sabbath service held at New Haven in 1637.

C. The United States were founded on independence from despotism and dependence on God, as shown in this illustration of President Washington's 1789 oath of office pledging his fidelity: " ... so help me God."

D. According to nineteenth-century President John Quincy Adams, the intention behind oaths of office was that they *"superadded"* godly strength *"to all the obligations of temporal law"* (excerpt of his printed speech on the *Jubilee of the Constitution* in 1839).

The roots of what our founders eventually achieved stemmed back to the original admonitions of John Hooper and the early Puritan reformers of the 1500's. Thousands were persecuted and hundreds more martyred for the cause of thorough Christian Reformation during the reigns of a long line of kings and queens in England. It was the courageous and sacrificial early Christians, as well as those who followed as refugees to America in the 1600's, who most thoroughly applied covenantal principles in their families, their churches, and their civil societies. Recent generations have unknowingly inherited a remarkable legacy from those braver souls who faithfully drew such astonishing strength by their devoted convictions to God and in their binding commitments with one another.

Nothing served early America more than when its Christians actually lived up to their name and honored their Lord's commands in every venue of life. With Reformed doctrines preached in manifold public sermons, they trumpeted a resounding call of continued covenantal faithfulness. And, in their comprehensive applications of those sermons, they triumphed in the virgin fields and forests of America. Providence Himself inspired, adorned, and endowed a new covenant nation with the bountiful fruits of liberty that those who have followed so richly enjoyed.

Yet, it is only through a broad sweep of history that Americans can appreciate the grand scope of their covenantal inheritance. With a deeper appreciation of the cause that drove our forefathers, as well as their forefathers, toward genuine freedom, today's citizens might not be as apt to forget that Creator who originally *"endowed"* us with *"unalienable rights,"*[39] nor would we be as likely to assume that we can long continue to pave a successful path on our own.

39. Continental Congress, *The Constitutions of the Several Independent States*, p. 1 for *"A Declaration* [of Independence] *of the Representatives of the United States of America, in Congress Assembled."*

Conclusion of Book II

N the early years of New England's colonial period, the covenantal principles of the Puritans found their most complete expression. The kind of civil *"foedere,"* or *"federal,"* governance that was originally sought in the Huguenots' *Vindiciae, Contra Tyrannos*, found its foremost fruition at that place and time in America. And, the kind of churches originally sought in the Puritans' *Admonition*, framed upon local elders with Christ-governed members, there assembled in doctrinal repose. They were a people who held God's Word as a common public as well as private standard, and who sought to emulate the model of moral fidelity that God put forth for the ancient Hebrew nation. With a covenantal self-awareness, the early cultural dynamic was not seen as a matter of church versus state, as if one sphere of society was pitted against the other in the public arena. The entire culture rested upon a common fidelity within its every realm of government. The father and mother, child and grandparent, planter and shopkeeper, preacher and elder, citizen and senator, each had abundant and welcomed places. Their plantations were shaped in the Puritans' sense of commonwealth, not as the church threatening the state, but as distinct yet cooperative realms; and, along with the family, each used biblical modes as its model and God's Precepts as its first principles.

The first colonial planters left following generations with a grand inheritance – one which was for each generation to secure for its own posterity. The young John Adams could indeed reflect upon his grand covenantal inheritance, replete with principles that he would emulate in helping shape a new commonwealth. The following book will therefore further examine the various bonds of those people that he saw as his example, and as those whom our founders highly revered as the *"intelligent," "learned,"* and *"sensible"* Puritans.

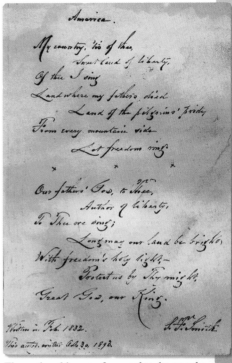

The national hymn of a people who openly professed *"Great God"* as their King:

Samuel Francis Smith (1808-1895) first published a poem in 1832 extolling the virtues of America. Its stanzas immediately became popular, and *America* was soon adopted as the national hymn of the United States. That status was not obtained by a political act, but achieved by the force of the nation's popular sentiment. Children over the next hundred years learned its verse by heart, in words that were among the most widely recognized in the English language. *America* concluded with a submissive prayer that publicly acknowledged God as both the Author of liberty and as the nation's Sovereign:

> *Our father's God, to Thee,*
> *Author of liberty,*
> *To Thee we sing;*
> *Long may our land be bright,*
> *With freedom's holy light, –*
> *Protect us by Thy might,*
> *Great God, our King.*

(Autograph manuscript dated Oct. 30, 1893.)

In the name of God, Amen.

Book III
Historic Covenantal Living

Book III Historic Covenantal Living

Introduction: The Idea of Covenantal Living

Personal and Societal Obligations under Grace and Biblical Law

GOD *hath made man a sociable creature,*"[1] wrote the Pilgrim preacher John Robinson early in the seventeenth century. The Pilgrim Separatists, as well as the larger class of Reformed English known as Puritans, were people who fashioned themselves according to a Book that defined the very essence of their lives. And to them, earthly lives could produce significant meaning only when composed from its lines.

The Bible, as the Lord's own words to man, showed God to be relational in His Being, and He created man for the purpose of engaging with Him as well as with one another. Accordingly, John Robinson derived a comprehensive understanding of God's societal mandates, and expounded upon the biblical precepts which alone would secure for man his fullest blessed benefits. Human societies were created for that very purpose, as noted by Robinson: "[God] *hath not only ordained severall societies, in which persons are to unite themselves for their mutuall welfare; but withall to dispense with his blessings, ...*"[2]

Long before the Christian Pilgrims pledged themselves to cross the Atlantic, King Solomon of Israel had expressed the same societal principle in the opening lines of a biblical proverb: *"Two are better then* [than] *one; because they have a good reward for their labour"* (Ecclesiastes 4:9). Solomon was referring to the simple, practical purpose that God intended for united lives, and it was through inspired authors like Solomon that God reconfirmed His original charge made to man at Creation that *"it is not good that the man should be alone"* (Genesis 2:18). From the beginning, then, men had been created to enjoy the goodness of friendships in societal families, as fellow creatures endowed with a necessary capacity to find genuine satisfaction only by living in a cooperative purpose.

Man's inner contentment therefore required an outward connectedness. Yet, as an outward, or societal, life involved companionship, the committed life required added, inner strength. Societal commitments were thus designed to draw upon a source of strength that was manifest in inner soundness and surety to give them the necessary resilience and endurance. Solomon likewise concluded his proverb by adding the cord of heavenly strength: *"... and a threefold cord is not quickly broken"* (Ecclesiastes 4:12). The Reformed-minded English considered Solomon's third cord as the ties of godly accountability needed in all human engagements,[3] and John Robinson and other Puritans therefore strove to bind the covenantal cord of heaven's strength around each and every society they engaged.

---

1. John Robinson, *Essayes. Or, Observations Divine and Morall ...* , 2d ed. (London, 1638), p. 345.
2. Ibid.
3. See Matthew Henry, *An Exposition of the Old & New Testaments*, vol. 3 (London, [c. 1841]), commentary on Ecclesiastes 4:12, p. 438.

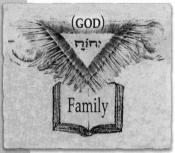

The Puritan Character

The English Puritans, who ordered their lives, line upon line, from such godly precepts, saw God as reshaping the world, line upon line, from the same biblical text. To them, God was ever reconfirming the dominion of His Kingdom on earth.[4] To the Puritan, the Lord's Prayer itself spoke of seeking procurement of that foremost Kingdom *"in earth as it is in heaven"* (Matthew 6:10). Therefore, even at the basic level of an individual prayer and its responsibilities, each petitioner was accountable for a place in establishing God's Kingdom on earth.

Such was the character of the Puritan that each individual saw it as his duty to consider the whole community, and every member was personally responsible before God for its overall good. It was well understood within each society that others would expect their fellow members to be reliable. Individual character could only be fully expressed in the context of one's overall commitment, so those bound by mutual covenant under God were, in a real sense, their *"brothers keeper"* (Genesis 4:9).

Looking to God's great Oracles, William Perkins, a key Reformed theologian of the late 1500's, wrote of a *"two-fold relation"* by which people were engaged.[5] Perkins said that a person's prime relation was indeed his single obligation to God. He argued that mankind, as the highest order of Creation, was endowed from the beginning as the unique class of beings *"whose duty is to know and to worship God according to his will revealed in his word."*[6] An individual drew that first line of duty to his Creator with a unique accountability *"touching man as he stands in relation to God."*[7] Perkins then pointed to the second line of duty necessary for every man: to be societally bound with his fellow men: *"As he stands in relation to man, he is part of a body and a member of some society."*[8] Such statements framed a basic societal tenet of Puritan life: that individuals existed foremost as covenantally accountable creatures under God, and then existed as bonded members within His various, ordained societies.

Both covenantal obligations came together in the Reformed life. And, though the Personal Covenant addressed the primary issues pertaining to one's individual character, the societal covenants addressed the issues pertaining to three larger, yet distinct, spheres of obligation. In addressing those three societies, Perkins concluded: *"some Questions concerne man as a member of a Family: some as he is a member of a Church; some as he is a member of the Common-wealth."*[9]

To the Puritans, the triune God was seen as the Author of the individual, the family, the church, and the commonwealth. Each type of human government, whether individual, family, church, or commonwealth, remained bound to Him within its respective sphere. Each therefore remained covenantal in its essence and each continued to derive its own sufficiency by way of God's eternal, all-sufficiency.

4. See Matthew 16:19.
5. William Perkins, *The Whole Treatise of the Cases of Conscience*, book 1 (London, 1632), p. 29.
6. Ibid.
7. Ibid.
8. Ibid.
9. Ibid.

The Puritans' Idea of "Relative" Living

To the Puritans, true abundance was found in contentment, and contentment was found in all people and things working together in their places. God, having initiated human societies, intended them to work according to His created order. All societies of men thus began with the union of a husband and wife as a household. Individual households fit together into the larger societal spheres, and each distinct sphere, whether it was a church or commonwealth, would be composed of families that God had placed within. So, as individuals composed families, the church was made up of individuals representing families, each within a proper place of service in the larger sphere. The civil commonwealth was likewise composed of a coordination of families, each with a place in its societal sphere.

Puritans thus organized their several societies around that logically coordinated order. They adopted the idea of "relative" (pronounced RELATE–ive) duties from their understanding of God's ordering of the earth. God had put structure in His Creation in which (despite man's fall) all things were to work together under His design and purpose. Societally, people would find their places within the logical working of the whole, adding transcendent meaning to their lives and greater purpose to their everyday functions.

For the Puritans, God set the example of *"relates"* or *"relatives"*[10] in the same way the Godhead Himself was composed of three Persons "relative" to each other. The *"Divine Essence"*[11] of the Godhead was completely one in purpose while being composed of three distinct Persons. Ipswich, New England Minister John Norton thus spoke of each distinct yet "relative" Person of the Godhead: *"The Subsistencies in the Divine Nature, are relative, and individuating: that is, they are relative properties."*[12] Norton was referring to the nature of God as He exists in the distinction of three "relative" Persons while at the same time being in exact unity of purpose. According to Reformed thinking, the three Persons of God *"are Relative, as appears in their names, viz. Father, Son, and Holy Ghost."*[13] That "relative" distinction among them spoke to the individual attributes of the Persons of the Father, the Son, and the Spirit; the unity[14] in them spoke to the Godhead's oneness of His essence: *"That all the attributes, in that they flow from the Essence, are true of every Person: because every Person has the same attributes."*[15] Thus the *"relative"*[16] functions of the

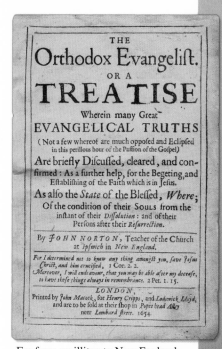

Far from an illiterate New England:

Typical of the Puritans' brand of high scholarship was this theological work by John Norton (1606-1663) of Ipswich, Massachusetts. His book, *The Orthodox Evangelist*, presented a complex array of Reformed thinking, including a fine representation of the Puritan idea of "relatives" (title page of the first edition published in 1654).

10. John Norton, *The Orthodox Evangelist* (London, 1645), p. 22.
11. Ibid.
12. Ibid.
13. Ibid.
14. Ibid., see p. 32: *"Essence of three Persons."*
15. Ibid.
16. Ibid.

three Persons of the Godhead were of one God united in His own exacting essence and purpose. And, although the *"Subsistence"*[17] of the Father, Son, and Spirit were "relative" as three distinct Persons, the Godhead's eternal existence and infinite authority were also in complete unity with His single essence and purpose.[18]

To the Reformed, then, God's "relative" oneness was both the key to understanding the nature of His *"Trinity"* (His essence) as well as understanding His comprehensive work in man's redemption (His purpose).[19] In considering the Puritans' understanding of the three "relative" Persons of God in one unified essence of one Godhead, we can begin to grasp their understanding of societal "relates" at large. To them, God's redemption of man did not merely pertain to an individual's spiritual salvation, but applied to every aspect of human existence. Redemption also brought a comprehensive reformation and a restoration of the logical, biblical order in all things, for all things related to Him. The Puritan idea of "relates" or "relatives" gave them a logical understanding of how all things, being distinct in their individual essences, still worked together under the unified overall purpose with a single, superintending Sovereign. Norton wrote that *"Every created person hath a distinct essence from another. ... though they have the same general Essence."*[20] Norton understood that although individuals were essentially distinct in their function as individual beings, their general essence and purpose remained much greater than themselves. In the Puritan sense, one's individual and distinct essence was "relative" to a general essence and purpose of all others. Everyone had an individual as well as a general accountability to his or her Maker; so, according to the Puritan worldview, each individual was unique in his or her specific calling and purpose, though grouped by God according to His overarching purpose. That logic provided a comprehensive understanding of one's individual purpose "relative" to others, while establishing the security and accountability of a unified purpose among Reformed societies of men. But, that was the logic of the entire created universe; and similar to the three Persons of the Godhead, who each functioned individually yet in unity of purpose in man's redemption, each created being also had a "relative" distinction in his or her person, yet was designed to work in coordinated purpose under God.

To the Puritans, God's societal callings were therefore both specific and general. God created specific individuals for His distinct purposes for them, but, moreover, He categorized all people according to the classification of the general nature He gave them. According to the most general nature of people, men and women were classed distinctly. As "relates," each man related to all others among his various societies according to God's ordained purpose for men, and all women related according to His purpose for women. A man was therefore called to fill a man's vocation, and a woman called to fill that of a woman's. And yet, though God created all men for distinctly male roles and all women for those befitting them in "relative" distinction, both sexes had the equal sanction of God's honor under His single, universal purpose for man. Puritan life was thereby far from drab or slavish under the dignity that God gave to both men and women.

17. Ibid., p. 22.
18. Ibid., pp. 32-33.
19. Ibid.
20. Ibid., pp. 22-23.

It was understood that men, both according to their created nature and the light of Scripture, were equipped by God for the leadership positions among their various societal relations. Therefore, a man always filled the role of leadership in both the family as well the larger societal spheres of church and commonwealth. As a member of a family, he provided the role of leadership. Therefore, outside the home, a man also "relatively" filled the roles of leadership. As an elder, preacher, or teacher of an assembly, a man would always fill the leadership positions in a church. As a magistrate, judge, or administrator, a man would always fill the leadership positions in the commonwealth. Yet, within his membership role among those wider societies, he represented his family as its delegate. Outside the home he was always "relative" to the society of his family because he represented its function in all wider societies, and his wife and children were thus carried with his voice. So, the Puritans' biblical worldview did not allow for their societies to become the modern notion of a "man's world," for a man's "relative" obligation was strictly to regard the interests of family in his every public endeavor. A heavy responsibility was thereby placed upon the head of each family to tend to its needs, whether he was at home or away. If he had a voice as a member in a public society, he spoke with the representative voice of his family; when he cast a vote, that vote was not his alone, but represented that of his loved ones.

"Relative" Authority and Welfare in the Home

Because a man was responsible to carry the voice of his family, he was also held as the responsible agent for its overall care. He was responsible to provide its home and its resources. Consequently, the general welfare of the family members was a function of the husband and father. Yet, as two parental "co-relatives," both father and mother held domestic authority as superiors to their subordinate children. The relation of father as superior, and then that of the father and mother together as co-superiors, provided for orderly lines of authority in the home. Whether regarding a more distant family relative or an invited guest, whether regarding servants or strangers, the father and mother together were the superiors to all in the home. For instance, when the husband/father was away, his wife's voice held supreme authority "relative" to the family and all subordinate guests in her home. Her voice therefore also held sway over all subordinate males as well as females within the realm of her

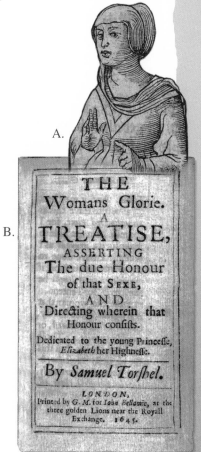

At a time when common women were seen to have little capacity for moral or intellectual learning, Samuel Torshel (1604-1650) recommended biblical education for all English daughters. As a Puritan minister, Torshel proposed that regular *"Scripture study and meditation"* would provide their finest adornment, but also warned that many were already becoming *"farre more acquainted with their Romances, than with their Sacred Historie."*

A. The frontis leaf of his book, *The Womans Glorie* (from which the above quotes were taken), included this portrait of the proverbial virtuous woman.

B. Torshel's title page extolled the *"due Honour of that Sexe."* And, published during the height of the English Civil War in 1645, it was also dedicated to nine-year-old, *"young Princesse Elizabeth,"* whom Torshel had been assigned to tutor during Charles I's royal distractions.

185

home, for her voice represented that of her husband. When her husband was home, her voice remained superior over all but that of her husband.

Puritans attempted to conform all lines of domestic authority to the Creator's logical design as well as to His expressed moral standards, in order to secure His blessing among family members. The family's government therefore worked toward the specific welfare of each of its members by all working together toward the general welfare of the whole. Each family member interacted accordingly with his or her domestic relatives, as united in both purpose and practice under the noble design of their covenant Lord.

"Relative" Charity and Public Welfare

Prominent among the Puritans were also charitable duties "relative" to the wider societies. The biblical model for public welfare was likewise served by respecting God's expressed lines for the maintenance of overall societal virtue. For example, Puritans recognized that societal responsibility of "almsgiving" (relief or welfare) came from the two societies of family and church. Those who were without a family's protection and could not meet their basic necessities required such outside assistance. According to William Perkins, God required families to give "relative" to their own *"ability that God has blessed them,"*[21] though the responsibility was limited to one's providential means to give so as *"not that others be eased, and wee ourselves grieved."*[22] The public society of the local church congregation was also called to unitedly give together from the *"almes of the [w]hole body"*[23] in order to *"maintaine the poore with things necessary, fit, and convenient: as meate, drinke and clothing."*[24] According to Perkins, the church had the higher obligation toward those that were in the most considerable need of maintenance: *"Here widowes that are desolate, without friends and goods, are commended to the liberality of the Church."*[25] However, no assistance was to be given to encourage those who rebelled against their own family or church responsibilities. Charity toward those who were fit to work but expected to reap a bounty from others' labor was a curse to the idea of "relative" public virtue. To the Puritan Perkins, alms were not to be given to those who were covenantally irresponsible or disconnected, such as *"Vagabonds, Rogues, and staggering persons, which have no calling; nor are of any Corporation, Church, or Common-wealth."*[26] Pilgrim Pastor John Robinson concurred in saying:

> *And for such persons in societies, as, in effect make account that they are onely for other mens property, and that others are for their helps, are the very moths of family, Church and Common-wealth.*[27]

Shown in these two woodcuts included on the 1639 title page of Presbyterian Thomas Young's book on Sabbath practices were:

A. A family attending the needy.
B. A pastor ministering to the sick.

21. William Perkins, *The Whole Treatise of the Cases of Conscience*, pp. 353-355.
22. Ibid.
23. Ibid.
24. Ibid.
25. Ibid.
26. Ibid.
27. John Robinson, *Essayes. Or, Observations Divine and Morall*, p. 360.

There was little place for specific monetary alms from the civil authority because it had been ordained to service the civil community with equal justice and general welfare. As the Puritans' legacy carried into later generations, America also demonstrated its concurring repugnance to that sin of inequity by the the civil estate. For instance, in an election sermon in the late eighteenth century, Puritan Pastor Zabdiel Adams cautioned his magistrates that God required their impartiality in the administration of the Massachusetts government: *"He will not allow one administration for the poor man and another for the rich."*[28] He vehemently warned that such a *"respect of persons"* was dishonoring to God: *"They should not take bribes from the rich; so on the other, an idle compassion should not lead them to befriend the poor, and indulge them in measures iniquitous."*[29]

Almsgiving by the civil estate therefore represented corruption on its face. How could the commonwealth claim to administer equal justice on the one hand while fisting out selective shillings and preferential pence with the other? The occasional public almshouse was therefore a place for the distressed to work for explicit emergency relief, and not for his general sustenance. True alms were left to those who would be most intimate, immediate, and familiar with the particular food, clothing, health, or sustenance requirements of the needy. So, if a magistrate desired to give assistance to an individual or family in need, he would do so out of his own family's purse or initiate the assistance through the deacons of his local church. To William Perkins (and those of a Puritan mind), it was indeed God's moral requirement that civil officials restrain public freeloading: *"Yea, it doth proclaim to the world, in the eares of all men, the shame of the Magistrate, who restrains it not."*[30]

A. Family charity in early America included the distribution of Bibles, as shown in this nineteenth-century American Tract Society engraving.

B. This is the title page of the Massachusetts preacher Zabdiel Adams's 1782 election sermon, in which he cautioned Governor Hancock, the Senate, and House of Representatives not to engage in public *"measures iniquitous."*

With comprehensive public compassion administered by families and churches, there was little call for hapless begging in early America because no genuine need fell through the cracks. With continued public charity appropriated by the two most local societies and equal justice administered by the overall commonwealth, there would be no legitimate cracks. Simple beggars were required to work, and any real necessities were met in coordinated order by societies most familiar with the need. In contrast, Puritan William Perkins had previously protested the disorder of his day that was caused by ignoring such godly societal models:

> It is also a great disorder in Common-wealths: For the boldest and most clamorous beggars carries away all the almes from the rest; and so relief is distributed unwisely and unequally; howsoever the good Law of our Land, [is] agreeable to the Law of God, that none should begge that are able to labor.[31]

28. Zabdiel Adams, [Election] *Sermon* ([Boston], 1782), pp. 29-30.
29. Ibid.
30. Perkins, *The Whole Treatise of the Cases of Conscience*, pp. 353-355.
31. Ibid., p. 355.

With the Puritan idea of covenantal living, overall society's needs were met by God providing an abundance to some families so that through their charity they would model His regard for those in need. Thereby, compassionate family and church charities were important components of the virtue of overall society. Civil governments were simply not seen as having been "relatively" charged with such an omnipotent compassion as to supplant God's own means of providing His care. If the civil estate, for instance, looked upon the nation's general resources to provide for the needs of its individuals, it would both usurp its ordained limits and violate the realm of the family which was charged with the care of its members. That civil government would "relatively" simply burden itself with the various demands of the hoards of its newly adopted children. On the other hand, for a man to fail in his own "relative" obligations in the home was for him to indeed invite an outside intrusion, because he would ultimately be wreaking havoc upon the outside, public societies. Individual welfare was therefore to be the obligation of the family, beginning with the husband and father; welfare outside the home was to be "relatively" left to other families and the caring congregations closest to home.

Dan Ford, 2003

Reformed women were devoted students of God's Book, as shown in this sketch based upon a Plymouth, Massachusetts statue honoring America's Pilgrim women. On the back of its pedestal was inscribed *"They brought up their families in sturdy virtue and living faith in God, without which nations perish."*

The "Relative" Satisfied Life

The Puritan man or woman could be satisfied with no other life than that which the Sacred History had directed. Though there was always an abundant variety of individual talents and personal interests to be expressed in various creative ways, overall contentment was a matter of finding one's satisfaction only where it was sanctioned by God. The Puritan man could not be satisfied with the vocation of a woman, nor a woman with that of a man. A Puritan mother could not be satisfied as an elder or a magistrate, nor with her children ruling at home in her stead. True individual satisfaction was limited to that which was modeled in the Bible, according to one's specific calling. John Preston added: *"What can a man desire more than to be satisfied?"*[32] He saw that genuine satisfaction would only be found "relative" to one's proper place of godly calling.[33] Far from wasting time trying to find contentment in chasing personal illusions or societal innovations, a man's or woman's earthly satisfaction would be found within the order which God sanctioned. God would not call an individual to a post that denied his or her created nature, that denied his or her "relative" duties, or that denied his or her family's station or circumstance, for within every societal sphere God called each to the best sufficiency in honest toil, honest gain, and honest charity:

> *Consider thy selfe, that the varieties of the sufficiencies that God gives to men, every man in his place, he may have it within his spheare, so that there shall be no want of at all.*[34]

32. John Preston, *The New Covenant, or The Saints Portion* ... (London, 1634), p. 133. (Also see James 4:2.)
33. Ibid.
34. Ibid., p. 132.

God graciously provided covenantal interconnectedness by which human societies could remain strong and resilient. He structured covenant families and communities with a framework of mutual accountability as the means to rein in personal failures and curb rampant individualism. He delegated representatives over families, churches, and commonwealths. Because God initiated families and other societies of men, their various governments themselves provided His protections from men at large – that was, only if those institutions maintained God's Precepts in their own governance. The covenantal stability of the whole protected it from the rebel, as the institutional framework itself was equipped with the temper to prevent its collapse. For example, God's covenantal structure of the family would keep the rebellious two-year-old from either becoming too detached from, or too dominating over, the whole. God ordered a "relative" structure in the home that both constrained the toddler as well as cultivated his healthy upbringing. The home was structured to raise him up as well as rein him in. The covenantal life was thereby intended as an orderly life, and because it was ordered by God, it would also be a secure and caring life for all so engaged.

THE PILGRIM MEETING-HOUSE.

This mid-nineteenth-century engraving of the first Pilgrim *"meeting-house"* depicts the unity among New England's first permanent settlers. The idea of the one **meeting-house** came out of their immediate need for general fellowship and protection in the early 1620's, but its image as a general **house** endured as a powerful symbol of the overall unity of all three societal spheres of their lives. First, individual family **household** societies are shown here assembling at the general meeting-house in union with the other family societies. Second, the church society also used the meeting-house as a sanctuary for its **household** of faith. Third, the civil magistrates used the meeting-house as their local **house** for representatives, and civil judges used it as their **courthouse**. The general **house** also served as a literal fortress of protection for all three Pilgrim societies, shown here by the men with their firearms always at the ready.

The idea of covenantal living wed the idea of a "relative" societal order with its virtuous overall societal character. God gave human societies their framework by instituting them as families, congregations, and other civil societies, and gave them His Laws to infuse His moral character within the governance of each. The Puritans believed both godly morality and a godly frame to be the necessary elements of each society. With societies of men endowed with such a character, the covenantal life offered individuals in union together God's healthy abundance on earth.

The Widest Good

The covenantal life also carried a responsibility of both spiritual fidelity and godly stewardship in the widest venues of living. There were to be no human arenas exempt from a first duty to God, as the early Christians had embraced the responsibility of consistent neighborly charity in all things. The Apostle Paul had admonished the infant church at Corinth to *"Let all your things be done with charity"* (1 Corinthians 16:14).

As the Puritans formed their own societal communities, they coordinated themselves to the greater honor of God. Honoring God was their foremost duty, as no society could remain virtuous while disconnected from the source of its virtue. The societies that emerged in England, Scotland, and America all had significant distinctions, but all held a uniform belief that covenantal societies were accountable to God. The Puritans firmly believed that man in general could not come to a genuine civility apart from the precepts of the Creator. Though not all of the earth would come under His sovereign Covenant of Grace, nevertheless, His more general mercies over the earth would be significantly maintained by the saltiness of those saints that were indeed within that gracious Covenant.[35] The remarkable Cambridge, New England preacher Thomas Shepard considered the perilous circumstances of colonial America's early settlements, and he rhetorically pondered what might happen to their beloved plantations if the Christian graces were removed from among them:

> *If God should take away this generation of Magistracy and Ministry, what would this despised Country do? then no schools for them, when no Gospel left among them, then every mans sword shall be against his brother, and God spreading the place with darkness, which through his presence is made light; what little hope of a happy generation after us, when many among us scarce know how to teach their children manners?*[36]

A.

B.

A. The duty to pray for those in authority and for those in authority to pray was central to the early American view of civil society. Shown here is a stained-glass depiction of the First Continental Congress asking God's assistance before conducting its inter-colonial affairs in 1774 (*Liberty Window* in Christ's Church, Philadelphia).

B. And, from the mouths of babes: The multigenerational Puritans taught their children to pray on behalf of continued godliness in their families, churches, and civil societies. Shown here is an engraving included in a tribute published in 1863 to honor the memories of America's Pilgrim forefathers.

A charge was before the Christians – a charge for both their own households and those beyond their own gates and fencerows. Neighborliness was more than friendship, and friendships were more than fellowship among peers. Each society needed a healthy dose of Christian service and prayer, and the Bible's mandates and margins defined that duty. Commenting on the Apostle Paul's admonition that *"thanks be made for all men"* (1 Timothy 2:1-2), the Geneva Bible footnoted: *"This word containeth all kinde of duty which is to be used amongst men in all their affairs."*[37] To the Puritans, then, there was a continual reformation to be conducted throughout each sphere of society. Being learned in God's Word and His standards gave them, all the more, a responsibility to be godly neighbors to all, to protect themselves, their families, and nonbelievers alike from the ravages of rampant societal godlessness and the complete famine from God's sufficiency. Here New England's Cotton Mather, typical of that societal ethic, saw a very active role for Christians

35. See Matthew 5:13-16.
36. Thomas Shepard, *The Parable of the Ten Virgins Opened & Applied: Being the Substance of divers Sermons on Matth. 25. 1,—13*, book 2 (1695 edition), p. 6.
37. *The Holy Bible* (London, 1649), Geneva marginal note on 1 Timothy 2:2, leaf Mmm3.

applying Solomon's threefold cord to its utmost effect; to him, the Covenant of Grace by which the Christian was redeemed called him back to the Moral Law of God as the rule of his whole life. That Law afforded him both the true worship of God in heaven and the rule of good works toward his neighbor on earth: *"... first you are to look upon it as a glorious truth of the gospel, that the moral law (which prescribes good works) must, by every Christian alive, be the rule of his life."*[38] God's overall Commandments were therefore viewed for the goodness of all men and all societies, which implied the care of each person and also the welfare of the whole. God's Commandments were considered good, not for the appeasement of His just wrath against sinners, but for the lively self-government of His covenantal communities. Jesus Christ paid the price for the former, and He confirmed His Laws for the latter. And, as the Two great Commandments of Christ were in perfect accord with His prior Ten,[39] they were likewise each given as gifts for the benefit of men and societies. The idea of covenant life thereby wed God's graciousness with all His Laws. Whether speaking of an individual or a society of men, God's graciousness and His Laws came together in a covenantal manner of living.

The general societal covenant pressed the wider issues of biblical reform. As one generation handed the charge to the next, each came with a debt to the former and a responsibility to the next. The earlier reformers had concluded that the true Christian, in accord with his personal covenants, was to honor God in all:

> *If we would truly honour our selves, we must honour God in all our waies. For God will honour them that Honour him.*[40]

Those earlier Puritans knew that to honor God was to live according to the Words that He gave for our lives: *"Now to honour God, is to honour him according to his will and word, in the duties of good Conscience and good life."*[41] Early on, they embraced the responsibility of Christians to oppose humanity's progressive abandonment of its covenantal obligations. They saw it as their own obligation to curb the world's drift toward godlessness, to hold it in check and bring it back to account, and then build their own communities established on covenanted

Dan Ford, 1996

The Pilgrims landed on the shores of New Plymouth, deep into the winter of 1620. They embarked from England on the *Mayflower* as a covenant church and then established themselves before coming ashore in New England as a covenant civil body, but they also landed their American adventure as covenant families. Finally coming ashore at their new home on the western edge of Cape Cod Bay in December, families soon began procuring their private dwellings. The *Mayflower* stayed anchored in Plymouth Harbor throughout the winter as a common safe haven for many and a secure place to store provisions. The date of May 5, 1621 was eventually set as the time for the *Mayflower* to sail back to England. Yet, remarkably united in their cause, and despite considerable suffering, loss, and death during the first winter season, not one family chose to leave for England with the return voyage. Illustrated here is a depiction of one such resolute couple resting *Upon the Rock* at New Plymouth and its recently vacated harbor.

38. Cotton Mather, *Essays To Do Good, Addressed to all Christians* ([1710]; Portsmouth, 1824 edition), p. 35.
39. Compare Matthew 22:37-40 with Exodus 20:1-17.
40. Perkins, *The Whole Treatise of the Cases of Conscience*, p. 373.
41. Ibid.

Dan Ford, 2003

ESSAYES.
OR,
OBSERVATIONS
DIVINE AND
MORALL.
COLLECTED OVT OF
holy Scriptures, Ancient and
Moderne Writers, both di-
vine and humane.
As alſo, out of the great volume
of mens manners: Tending to the
furtherance of knowledge
and vertue.

By IOHN ROBINSON.

A.

B.

GOD hath made man a
ſociable creature ; and
hath not onely ordained
ſeverall ſocieties , in
which perſons are to u-
nite themſelves for their mutuall
welfare; but withall ſo diſpended
his bleſſings, as that no man is ſo
barren, but hath ſomething where-
with to profit others .

C.

A. The English Separatist preacher
John Robinson (1576-1625) had
prepared the Pilgrims to be
biblically self-governed in Holland
prior to their departing from him for
New England in 1620.

B. In his work on practical living,
*Essayes. Or, Observations Divine
and Morall ...* (1625), Robinson
compiled the various precepts of
biblical living that he preached to
his congregation during their many
years under his care (title page of
the first London edition in 1638).

C. In Robinson's *Essayes*, he
acknowledged God as the Author of
the various human societies and
man's obligation to God within each.

terms. The former were the two callings that effected
godliness back in England, the latter was effected in the
New England commonwealths in colonial America. Just
as the earlier reformers had a charge from God over their
individual lives, their families, and their church
congregations, they saw the widest civil society as simply
another extension, but an essential extension, of that first
charge: *"And this must teach us, even to dedicate our
selves to God and his providence, in the whole course of
our callings, whether in the Church or Commonwealth."*[42]

Such reformers understood the societal mandate
before they saw its fruition. Before his congregation
sailed to America in 1620, John Robinson (who would
remain behind and not make the trip), the pastor of the
Pilgrim church in Holland, nevertheless passionately
spoke of God's loving call: *"From this love of God, as
from a Spring head, issueth all good both for grace and
glory."*[43] God's grace was unto their salvation, but their
earthly mission was for His earthly glory. All their
affliction and all of their toil was for the good:

> *Yea, by it (which is more) all evill by all
> Creatures intended, or done against us. By our
> afflictions worke together with our election,
> redemption, vocation, &c. for our good.*[44]

At the time that King James I was still seeking to
prosecute the overall Puritan society in England,
Robinson confidently encouraged his own congregation
that their great plight would yield its good fruits. Their
mission was yet before them as those who would land at
New Plymouth's rock. Robinson's words would come
prophetically true when he had spoken of their firm
covenant with God: *"By reason of it* [God's *"election,
redemption, and vocation"* of them], *the stones of the
field are in league with us."*[45]

Armed with a common Reformed background and a
shared understanding of covenantal living, the later New
England Puritans were afforded the opportunity of
building their covenantal societies from the ground up. As
they composed their communities, they also considered
the caution that to disconnect with the Bible's precepts in
any societal interaction was to disconnect with the source

42. Ibid.
43. Robinson, *Essayes. Or, Observations Divine and Morall*, p. 11.
44. Ibid.
45. Ibid.

of their virtue and unravel the fabric of any union of men. To the Puritans, the structure as well as the moral fabric of society were to follow the order of God's biblical design. To think that He commanded moral obligations and made no provision for moral order would seem that God had sanctioned anarchy and chaos. Administering His Precepts required the orderly application of His great Statutes. Modeling as best they could the good examples that they read in Scripture, the goal of Puritan communities was to decipher all its delineations and apply them within their covenantal lives. All of the stones of the field were indeed in league with them.

The New England Puritans enjoyed the fruit of all the reformers who before them had paved the way, having lived by biblical principles without seeing the outcome. Those early reformers had preached that even their widest endeavors should be invigorated with covenantal precepts. The later New England settlers were thereby provided an opportunity to build America's early societies on the same covenantal principles. They all gave their successors a legacy in their homes and churches, the lines of which ran in their own lines of succession and ultimately infused several new states with covenantal precepts as grand and godly commonwealths.

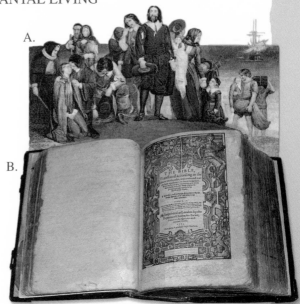

A. Plymouth's Governor William Bradford (1590-1657) was pivotal in directing the Pilgrims to adhere to godly self-government in their civil affairs. In his manuscript account of their venture, *Of Plymouth Plantation* (c. 1650), Bradford saw their small settlement as nothing less than a testimony to the entire world, describing it as *"set in the plaine field, or rather on a hill, made conspicuous to the view of all."* Their covenantal model did indeed become a model for later colonial plantations in New England and an example for biblical civil governments thereafter (nineteenth-century engraving of Bradford and the Pilgrims landing at New Plymouth).

B. A duty to effect the widest possible societal good was explicit in the Puritans' favored Geneva Bible. In its copious Reformed footnotes, they read of their obligation to put their prayers to practice *"in all their affairs"* (Geneva footnote on 1 Timothy 2:1-2). Shown here is a late sixteenth-century Geneva Bible in a like edition to that used by Plymouth Plantation's Governor Bradford.

The remaining chapters will focus further on several venues of covenantal living. They will address the nature and the character of the Personal Covenant, and the nature and order of the various societal covenants. Though addressing the same overarching covenantal topic (as well as several of the same points) as the previous two books, they will present them in a more practical manner as an organized accompaniment. Whereas the previous two books on the Christian and American inheritances focused on covenantal theology and its history, this book will focus on the many godly distinctives of covenantal living as they were "relatively" organized. It will therefore continue to draw pertinent references from the Scripture, the doctrines of the Reformed faith, and many historical references, all in the hope of providing a more authoritative understanding of covenantal living. In conjunction with the previous two books, the following few chapters will hopefully provide the reader with a basic understanding of our covenantal inheritance as it pertains to our various God-given venues in life.

Chapter 1: Personal Covenantal Living

Individual Faith and Obedience under Grace and Biblical Law

To the Reformed Christians, any society of men, whether a family, a church, or a civil body, began with its charter and its government. The charter was the original sanction that God had instituted for each type of self-governing society. For instance, when He instituted the society of the family, God set certain parameters upon it that defined its nature and its overall moral character. That nature and character was to be maintained by all people who would think of themselves as a family if they were legitimately to continue as such.

It followed, then, that there were certain inherent, godly parameters in the moral character of every societal government, for all types of societies (whether family, church, or civil) originated with the divine will of the Creator. The inherent parameters were therefore essential in defining a society's basic charter: whether it be illegitimate or legitimate, whether it be governed immorally or morally, whether it produce evil or good. Therefore, in the Reformed Anglo-American tradition, accountable, "relative" (RELATE-ive) government was always considered the hallmark of any legitimate, self-governing society. And, as all societies were composed of individuals and every soul was likewise created by God, each individual soul was likewise considered personally accountable to Him. The most basic of all the human governments, then, was an accountable personal government, and that individual self-government logically began with a "relative" accountability to the Creator who had set the moral parameters of all legitimate governments.

Maintaining that essential accountability has thus been a question for the ages, for accountability to God has always been a question of man being in some sort of relation with Him in a way that at least seemed legitimate, cordial, and appropriate. Thus, religions of men have traditionally played an essential role in the basic idea of one's self-governance on earth as well as in the matter of one's eternal repose. Being connected with God in a way that would legitimize one's acts of self-governance and procure his or her favorable eternal rest has been a most driving object of many a religionist's heart and mind. But, the idea of maintaining cordial personal relations with God might seem absurd on its face – that is, to actually maintain direct and warm relations with God on terms of human commendability to Him. First, He is infinite and we are finite. He is perfect and we are definitely imperfect. How could such a Being relate in a friendly way with such beings as ourselves?

Men have tried to endear themselves to Him through religion or prayers, pleadings, promises, pledges, praises, processions, or piles of priestly performances. But what exhaustive tokens could man throw before a Holy God to make Him ignore His greatness and our sin? What could man do to make the

Almighty crack and compromise His infinite character to wink at our self-evident corruption? Others have insisted that "God is Love" as if that was enough, and ignore the steep price He had to pay to actually appropriate it to cover our continual corruption and rebellion. Then again, we could point out to God that He made us and owes it to us to overlook our faults because we just act the way He made us. After all, we did not ask to be sinners, and maybe He is the One who owes us an explanation. But, do our few years of existence trump His everlasting glory? Does our frail stature supersede His divine wisdom, or our sense of fairness override His sovereign will?

No, the idea of even establishing good relations with God by our effort is indeed absurd on its face. If Adam and Eve could not maintain adequate self-government in Paradise, how could we expect to do so amid more turbulent lives? They were simply two individuals in a garden, while we are billions in a world; they were tempted but once, while we encounter hundreds of temptations daily; and they were originally innocent, while we are compounded in our inherited corrupted complexities. How, then, can we expect to maintain any semblance of adequate relations with God when Adam and Eve had a perfect existence and utterly failed?

The wisdom of the preacher in the book of Ecclesiastes thus opened with an exasperating salvo: *"Vanity of vanities, all is vanity. What profit hath a man of all his labour which he taketh under the sun?"* (Ecclesiastes 1:2-3). Then again, after exasperating proclamations declaring that everything under the sun was nothing but vanity, the preacher concluded with an admonition to *"Fear God, and keep his commandments: for this is the whole duty of man"* (Ecclesiastes 12:13). So there was a clue that there must be some remedy. The New Covenant's Apostle Paul also wrote several epistles touching upon the need for a consistent relation with God. In his various letters to the earliest churches he admonished his readers that a Christian's calling applied to all things, including one's entire stewardship: whether in a family, work, or church, as well as all wider obligations:

> *Therefore if any man be in Christ, he is a new creature: old things are past away, behold, all things are become new. And all things are of God, who hath reconciled us to himself by Jesus Christ* (2 Corinthians 5:17-18).

Therein lay the key to man's hope! The old man – the man of sin – was no more (or at least *"all things"* pertaining to him were reconciled with God), and all things, meaning all of his life's relations and obligations, *"become new."* In the strength of a comprehensive godly life, both secret (inward or private) sins and public (outward) wrongs were put away. Therein was the key to the Personal Covenant for finite and fallible man to engage in a cordial league with the infinite, infallible God, and in so doing, serve Him as Lord and govern one's self in every way according to His sovereign will.

The Geneva Bible's translation of 2 Corinthians 5:17: *"if any man be in Christ, let him be* a new creature. *Olde things are passed away: beholde, all things are become new,"* indicated a commandment to be self-governed in Christ, in addition to providing a statement of one's new spiritual condition before God. Puritans who read the Geneva version did indeed consider the conduct of their personal lives to be wholly accountable to the Author of the Holy Text (1594 edition).
*Emphasis added.

195

The Covenant of Grace

How could it be that man could possibly maintain a cordial relation with God, or be obedient and sufficiently self-governed if he did? Man remained imperfect and yet, God still required perfect obedience. God could still never lower His perfect standard by which to reestablish a cordial relation with man, for a perfect moral Being could not wink at sinful disobedience and remain true to Himself. Since fallen man could not present himself as blameless before God, God's requirements of perfect obedience must be satisfied by another. God could only be satisfied by the perfect obedience of a substitutional Redeemer that would fulfill the precise obligations on the part of man and thereby reconcile him with God. The renowned reformer John Preston thus spoke of a unique arrangement between God and man; one that God announced after Adam's fall. It was a kind of covenant that ran contrary to the Covenant of Works, which obliged Adam to perfect works. Preston wrote accordingly:

A.

The second is the Covenant of Grace, and that runnes in these terms, thou shalt beleeve, thou shalt take my Sonne for thy Lord, and thou shalt likewise receive the gift of righteousnesse, whiche was wrought by him, for an absolution for thy sinnes, for reconciliation with me, thereupon thou shalt grow up in love and obedience towards me, then I will be thy God and thou shalt be my people.[1]

Preston saw that God's Son would supply the work of perfect obedience necessary in the Covenant of Works. God alone would perfectly satisfy the infinite standard of a perfect moral Being. God's grace would enable men to again unite with Him, to again become His people, and to again *"grow up in love and obedience."*[2] God's grace ordered the redemption of man by the integrity of His own infallibility and His own covenantal promise of fulfillment: *"My covenant will I not break: nor alter the thing that is gone out of my lips"* (Psalm 89:34). The Geneva Bible's margins concurred that God in His divine mercy would fulfill the works on the part of fallen man: *"For God in promising hath respect to his mercy, and not to mans power in performing."*[3]

God's pledge was henceforth fixed, binding, and eternal, as was His covenantal pledge to redeem man. God alone being holy would within Himself provide the work of redemption: *"He sent redemption unto his people, he hath commanded his covenant for ever: holy and reverend is his name"* (David: Psalm 111:9).

The Law of Freedom:

A. This is the title page of John Preston's *The New Covenant*, in which he wrote that those in covenant with God own His Law in their hearts.

B. He observed that the Law does *"not onely present the outward letter of the Commandement, but there is a Law written within, ... it is a ministration of freedome, and not of bondage and enmitie"* (1634 edition).

B.

1. Preston, *The New Covenant*, pp. 317-318.
2. Ibid.
3. Geneva note on Psalm 89:34, leaf Cc7.

The work was accomplished in the actual life of Messiah so that the oppressive, inescapable disobedience that weighed impossibly heavy upon man was rendered as an absolute pardon through His gracious performance. Christ carried the whole work of redemption for the sake of hapless man, and alas! yielded up God's pure grace unto faith in the believer and thereby yielded up the imputation of righteousness.

This Covenant, though, would not be obtained by all men. To the Puritans, redemption came only to those with an "effectual calling" from God. Accordingly, man neither could nor would (even if he could) will himself into a genuinely effectual relation with God. To the Reformed, saving grace was not considered universal. As long as God remained sovereign, it would be no surprise to God that a sinner rejected Him; he rejected Him from birth and enmity toward God already encompassed the heart of every man. Individual faith was a gift from God – just as effectual calling was a gift – just as sovereign redemptive grace had been a gift. The Covenant of Grace was therefore limited to those who were sovereignly called, and thereby who truly repented and believed. Accordingly, the prominent Puritan theologian William Perkins wrote:

Jesus Christ accomplished the work of man's redemption in His complete victory over death. Shown here is a woodcut depicting God's radiant inner-love, with Christ as the Lamb of God symbolically standing triumphant (at the top) amid the dead bones of man.

God's sovereign grace was then imparted to the individual by the work of His Holy Spirit within each believer, yielding an ability to harbor the genuine love of God. The caption therefore read (in part): " ... *the lambe signifieth the quiet conscience of the faithful."* That inner love of God would then be manifest in the lives of each of Christ's true faithful. This illustration was included in Stephen Bateman's *A Crystall glasse of Christian Reformation* (1569).

> *Some think that men may be brought within the Covenant, by the doctrine of Universal grace and redemption. But this way of persuading a man that he has a title to the covenant is false and unfit. False it is, because all the promises of the Gospell, are limited within the condition of Faith and Repentance; not being universal to all, but made onely to such persons, as repent and believe.*[4]

Perkins also addressed the most common objection to the idea of God's sovereign and specific grace which was often argued in reference to 1 Timothy 2:4, *"that God would have all men to be saved."*[5] The biblically astute and societally "relative" Perkins therefore observed:

> *As for the Universality of 'all,' it must not be understood of all particulars, but of all kinds, sorts, conditions, and states of men; as may be gathered out of the former words: 'I would that prayer be made for all men;' not for every particular man ... but for all states of men, as well Princes, as subjects; poore, as rich; base, as noble; unlearned, as learned, &c.*[6]

4. Perkins, *The Whole Treatise of the Cases of Conscience*, book 1, p. 55.
5. Ibid.
6. Ibid.

Similarly, John Preston made an argument that the personal Covenant of Grace was a free gift of sonship from God and not a reward for a man's natural or innate goodness:

> *No, saith the Lord, this is an inheritance, and you are my sonnes, and you shall have it given to you freely, and given to you as it becomes a Father to give it, so you shall take it; Therefore that it might be free grace, and not of a debt, ...*[7]

The appropriation of God's sovereign redemption to those who were chosen for sonship would be demonstrated by God's specific granting of faith, so Preston saw faith as the means by which the believer entered a gracious, Personal Covenant with God, saying, *"because we beleeve the promises, and the Covenant of Grace, therefore the Lord accepts us, and accounts us as righteous."*[8] Thus, according to "relative" thinking, the same faith that God had worked in Abraham's prior Covenant was one and the same faith that He worked in the covenant Christian, as Preston also wrote:

> *Surely look how Abraham was made partaker of the Covenant, so every one of us must be: Abraham was made partaker of it by faith, and no otherwise.*[9]

The reformers saw that it was only by way of grace being sovereignly and assertively granted by God that the sinner could have faith. And, just as faith had yielded the imputed righteousness which enabled Abraham to enter a cordial covenant with God, so it was with the Christian. Responsive faith and reciprocal love was the mark of the genuine believer, so only by engaging with God in faith could one genuinely live in a Personal Covenant with Him as Lord. The work of grace was His, and the gift of grace was to each believer. God alone had initiated the Covenant of Grace as the Father; He alone had performed it as the Son; and He alone granted faith and imputed righteousness to individuals by His Holy Spirit. Individuals were therefore sovereignly and graciously redeemed from sin unto lives of faithful service that would oblige them in every way.

Internal Covenantal Living under Grace

The Apostles had urged first-century believers to present themselves wholly to their Sovereign's service. The Apostle Paul admonished the infant Church at Rome: *"I beseech you therefore, brethren, by the mercies of God, that ye present your bodies a living sacrifice, holy, acceptable unto God, which is your reasonable service"* (Romans 12:1). Though God's grace was apportioned to each man and woman as a gift without any prior meritorious service on their part,[10] once entered, the Personal Covenant was therefore completely obliging.

Puritans most aggressively preached that same obliging calling with God's grace. The prodigious, mid-seventeenth-century scholar Richard Baxter wrote that God had a useful purpose for man in His working of grace: *"The Work,"* Baxter

---

7. Preston, *The New Covenant*, pp. 365-366.
8. Ibid.
9. Ibid., p. 366.
10. See Ephesians 2:8-9.

said of man's redemption, *"was to bring sinners to God."*[11] Man was brought to God by God. God appropriated grace to man, but in conjunction with reciprocal faith, the man was to be responsively yielded back to God. By that "co-relative" engagement, the Covenant of Grace apportioned the effective work of Christ into the inner life of the believer, and the believer entered into a consensual and living covenant with his Lord, as Baxter explained:

> *With this Covenant concurs a mutual delivery: Christ delivereth himself in all comfortable Relations to the sinner, and the sinner delivered up himself to be saved and ruled by Christ.*[12]

Only by yielding to Christ in an internal subordinate relation, as in the taking of the *"Sonne for thy Lord,"*[13] added Preston, could the fallible sinner truly enjoy an amiable and cordial relation with God. And, with an active self-consciousness of being redeemed by Christ, the believer would be "relatively" all the more obliged to Him as a living, personal Lord. The Personal Covenant was therefore not merely forgiving, it was personally obliging upon the conscience of the party who was consensually obliged, as Baxter further explained: *"It is not only to acknowledge his* [Christ's] *sufferings, and accept pardon and glory; but to acknowledge his sovereignty, and submit to his Government."*[14]

The working of grace therefore did not stop with its first imputation. There were henceforth mutual obligations to be met on behalf of the believer as well as his Lord. God's grace continued the appropriation of its living work in the continued submission of the believer to his Lord. Jeremiah's prophecy of a *"New Covenant,"* in which God promised that *"I will put my law in their inward parts"* (Jeremiah 31:33), spoke to the reformers of the ongoing "sanctification" work that God would perform within. Preston concurred:

> *This Spirit being infused, written the Law in his inward parts, that is it breedes in him a holy disposition, that enables him in some measure to keep the Law, it prints in him all those graces that give him strength to observe the Commandments that God hath given him.*[15]

Dan Ford, 2002

A. A monument of Reformed scholarship, Richard Baxter (1615-1691) was both a theological and societal activist. He preached personal fidelity to his congregation in Kidderminster and preached national fidelity to the Parliament at Westminster (1660). Following the restoration of Charles II, he was prohibited from both.

B. Baxter's much admired work, *The Saints Everlasting Rest* (1650), has proven to be among the most enduring volumes in the history of English literature. In it, Baxter eloquently explained the intricate elements of a soul's covenant with God, and he wrote of one's duty to press in upon Him through patient, daily prayer: *"In a word, What will not be done in one day, do in the next, till thou has pleaded thy heart from Earth to heaven, from conversing below, to walking with God; and till thou canst lay thy heart to rest, as in the bosom of Christ, in this meditation of thy full and Everlasting Rest"* (part 4, conclusion of chapter 13).

11. Richard Baxter, *The Saints Everlasting Rest, or, a Treatise Of the Blessed State of the Saints in their Enjoyment of God in Glory*, 6th ed., part 3 (London, 1656), pp. 178-179.
12. Ibid.
13. Preston, *The New Covenant*, pp. 317-318.
14. Baxter, *The Saints Everlasting Rest*, p. 178.
15. Preston, *The New Covenant*, p. 345.

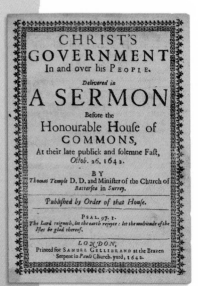

CHRIST'S
GOVERNMENT
In and over his PEOPLE.

Delivered in

A SERMON

Before the
Honourable House of
COMMONS,

At their late publick and solemne Faſt,
Octob. 26, 1642.

BY
Thomas Temple D. D. and Miniſter of the Church of
Batterſea in *Surrey.*

Publiſhed by Order of that Houſe.

PSAL. 97. 1.
*The Lord reignesh, let the earth rejoyce : let the multitude of the
Iſles be glad thereof.*

LONDON,
Printed for SAMUEL GELLIBRAND at the Brazen
Serpent in Pauls Church-yard, 1642.

The powerful Puritan scholar Dr. Thomas Temple (1601-1661) wrote that those in covenant with God had a high internal calling to govern themselves with greater inward virtue. Shown here is the title page of Temple's 1642 sermon, *Christ's Government In and over his People.*

The Personal Covenant therefore included that perfecting work that God performed on the believer *"to give us new hearts, and new spirits to sanctifie us, to make us new creatures, to crucifie the flesh, to weaken the dominion of sinne."*[16] It was imparted by Christ by way of the saint yielding to Him, *"and therefore Christ is made sanctification, that is, you derive it from Him."*[17] Preston noted that a man did not live righteously on his own strength, but asked for God's strength, and the Lord provided that which was needed. God's sanctifying work on behalf of those in covenant with Him allowed them to draw from His strength in resisting evil in themselves as well as procuring the greater good toward others. The saint's perseverance was, in that sense, an active gift concurrent with the sovereign gift of grace, providing the very fount of the saint's continuing virtue. Preston warned: *"Therefore let no man goe about his business in his owne strength."*[18] The later Puritan divine Thomas Temple reduced the principle of sanctification to its most practical terms in saying, *"The new man under the new covenant hath new strengths."*[19] The sanctified life was therefore achieved by an ongoing, willful, and active working of covenantal submission on the part of the believer, and the Lord's ongoing, willful, and active imputation of His strength on behalf of the covenant faithful.

To the reformers, such as Perkins, Preston, Baxter, Temple, and the host of Reformed-minded English of the sixteenth and seventeenth centuries, such a covenantal understanding not only represented the difference between eternal life or death, but between worldly bondage or earthly freedom in the lives of faithful Christians. The reformers desired a good life in free conscience and healthy repose, and internal freedom from the bonds of sin made their lives rich indeed as souls living in covenantal union with a glorious Lord. Baxter radiantly concluded:

> Now doth the soul resolvedly conclude, I have been blindly led by the flesh and lust of the world, and the devil too long already almost to my utter destruction: I will now be wholly at the dispose of my Lord, who hath bought me with his blood, and will bring me to his glory. And thus the complete work of saving Faith consisteth in this Covenanting, or Mystical marriage of the sinner to Christ.[20]

To the reformers, the Personal Covenant required the believer to look to God for every earthly sufficiency. This included God's *"giftings"*[21] as well as His abundance. God's giftings were particular talents and abilities useful to the believer in accord with God's providential purpose "relative" to his calling.

16. Ibid.
17. Ibid.
18. Ibid.
19. Thomas Temple, *Christ's Government In and over his People. Delivered in A Sermon...* (London, 1642), p. 11.
20. Baxter, *The Saints Everlasting Rest*, p. 179.
21. Preston, *The New Covenant*, p. 133.

Giftings therefore varied in type and degree among individuals, not according to the believer's desired purposes, but according to God's purpose in him. Speaking of the nature of that gifting, Preston noted: *"they are not his own but they are bestowed upon him."*[22] God gave giftings to be used *"otherwise,"*[23] as for the good of others in Christ's wider body on earth. Among Puritans, giftings were thereby considered "relative" to the work that God intended from the individual and were measured out accordingly: *"He that hath the lesser measure of gifts hath the lower part given to him to act."*[24] Nevertheless, the fullest earthly *"sufficiency"*[25] would always be provided for all believers by way of both God's giftings and His work of sanctification within. Thus, God's giftings and sanctification were both imparted to the covenanted man, and His earthly sufficiency would be enjoyed in its fullest abundance by appropriating man's gifts in continued submission and service to his Lord.

External Living with Internal Self-Government

The man of faith entered into a broadly based covenant with God. He obtained his heavenly, cordial relation with his Lord, and in that sense it was a private, or personal, covenant of singular redemption. As the New England author John Norton put it: *"The form of this union is the actual conjoining of the person of the form of Christ, and the person of the Beleever."*[26] That was the inward essence of the Personal Covenant by which a man was united with Christ, but as Norton continued his narrative, he explained that the union of the believer with Christ yielded a *"Tertium* [third] *being,"* which was the man's outward covenantal life.[27] Norton's so-called "third being" was to be powerfully reforming and was to be lived out both through the believer's communion among his brethren and in wider obligations among the world.

22. Ibid.
23. Ibid.
24. Ibid.
25. Ibid.
26. Norton, *The Orthodox Evangelist*, p. 287.
27. Ibid.

Though vast numbers of volumes were written by the great Reformed authors, giving us an adequate record of the covenantal life, the personal testimonies of a greater volume of typical Puritan lives have been largely lost to history. Occasionally though, incidental evidence can be found written into the margins of an odd Puritan volume of otherwise wider importance. Such anonymous records often provide glimpses into the hearts and minds of those forgotten lives.

Pictured here is a bit of anonymous poetic evidence written into the margins of a sixteenth-century Geneva Bible. And, it provides a hearty glimpse into the abundant devotion within a typical Puritan life:

Great God with Wonder and with praise
on all thy workest look
But still thy wisdom power & Grace
shine Briter in thy book

The stars th[a]t in their Courses roll
Have much Instruction Given
But thy Good Word Informs my Soul
How I may climb to Heaven

The feilds provide me food & shew
the Goodness of the Lord
But fruits of life & Glory Grow
in thy Most Holy Word

Here are my Choicest Treasures hid
Here my best comforts lies
Here my desieres are satisfyed
& hence my Hopes arise

Lord make me understand thy Law
Shew what my faults have bin
& from thy Gosple let me draw
pardon for all my Sin

That new being was indeed inwardly reflective, but was also to be outwardly productive. So, the Personal Covenant was intended to have legs on earth.[28] It represented a comprehensive self-governance within the covenant man which caused his faithfulness to be the means by which God accomplished His wider earthly reformation. And on that point, the man's Personal Covenant put him in league with God's whole earthly purpose amid every sphere of human engagement.

That certainly did not mean that a man could actually accomplish the outward work on his own any more than he could that of the inward work. A man was simply a chosen vessel[29] to accomplish God's governance on earth. The believer represented Christ's body on earth and Christ remained his Head, just like Jesus Christ had been to His disciples before. As Christ's own dominion reigned over His earthly body, the Personal Covenant did not require the believer to act on his own will, but upon God's directives on earth. Thus, the covenanted man was the vehicle by which his Sovereign Lord chose to work out His own body's activity on earth. In line with his Puritan association of godly *"relates,"*[30] John Norton presented the *"efficacy of the relation"*[31] between Christ and the believer:

> *The body is conformable to its Head; the union is mystical; the Communion (whilst in this life, and imperfect) is heaven out of heaven.*[32]

The image of father and son was a powerful "relative" in the individual Puritan mind. Taken from the concept of Fatherliness and Sonship modeled in the Bible, a father's role denoted God's love, security, guidance, instruction, and authoritative discipline for each individual under his care. Shown here is a nineteenth-century engraving of one form of that "relative" input.

The relational purpose for Christ having believers on earth was thus to effect *"heaven out of heaven."*[33] It was to effect God's governance on earth. As the nation of Israel had been of old, God continued to have His body represented on earth in the form of His new chosen vessels. And, the newer form of covenantal saint was not removed from his or her own covenantal duty any more than the individual residents of old Israel had been from theirs; both old and new saints had been called to conform to the will of their sovereign Redeemer. Though the new model believer was now a "son" of God in the sense of having that title conferred to him by way of his inheritance-rights in Christ, in an administrative or outward sense, he continued on earth as a vassal-servant of God.[34] In other words, the believer's covenant rights inwardly and directly to the Father were as a son, but outwardly and toward others the believer remained God's vassal servant. Even as an Apostle who clearly possessed sonship rights, Paul continued to refer to himself as the Lord's vassal servant toward others. Thus, the Kingdom of God continued on earth by way of a believer's fellow-sonship inheritance "relative" to Christ and as a faithful servant "relative" to God's government over it.

28. See Psalm 119:105.
29. See 2 Corinthians 4:7.
30. Norton, *The Orthodox Evangelist*, pp. 292-293.
31. Ibid.
32. Ibid.
33. Ibid.
34. Compare 1 Corinthians 7:22 with Galatians 4:4-9; also Matthew 23:8-11.

The Personal Covenant obliged the believer in service to Christ. God's grace defined the believer's responsibility of doing good, and doing good was done by obeying God's moral standards. According to New England's Cotton Mather, truth simply brought the Law into its rightful rule over the individual covenant life: *"... first you are to look upon it as a glorious truth of the gospel, that the moral law (which prescribes good works) must, by every Christian alive, be the rule of his life."*[35] Grace, then, was that which held the covenanted believer to his duty, and his duty was that which held him to God's Law. Yet, Puritans completely separated the vanity of doing good works unto salvation from that of doing good works under the higher obligations of their covenant:

> *We are not under the law as a covenant of works: our own exactness in performing good works is not the condition for entering into life; (wo be to us if it were) but still, the covenant of grace holds us to it as our duty: and if we are in the covenant of grace, we shall make it our study to perform those good works.*[36]

For the Puritans, the Laws of God were the rules for all internal as well as external governance, and their Personal Covenant obliged them to exemplify both to the world. First, living under God's statutes was a duty of gratefulness. John Norton wrote that *"The great end of obeying under the Gospel is, thankefulnese unto God for Jesus Christ."*[37] The inner motivation of obedience was thankfulness, and the Word of God called believers to do good as well as to desire goodness, so they carried gratefulness inwardly and lived it outwardly. Others could see the standard that was carried in conformity to the Gospel and that was modeled in the covenantal life, *"Which moveth by propounding Arguments, and by persuading, 2 Cor. 5. 11. By Woing, John 3:29. By Commanding, 1 John 3:23,"*[38] as noted by Norton. The obedient life was thus a persuasive and commanding model used by the Spirit of God to demonstrate God's gracious effect to others. Like God's letters written upon the pages of Exodus's twentieth chapter, the covenant life was scripted for others to read. One who then observed the lives of the saints (by way of God's Spirit) saw faith working obedience as a *"moral Suasion"*[39] to his own awakening, inner eyes. In an obedient covenant life, God therefore displayed His Laws *"in their use as a means,"*[40] but not in the pride of a show, for He drew a sharp moral line between true submission and selfish arrogance. The difference between the two drew the believer back to the true object of his or her faith, for Christ's faithful would not wear the Law as an ornament of their own valiant show, but as an adornment of His blessed grace.[41]

From one to another:

God chose to use individuals to convey His precepts from person to person. From the beginning, Christ chose His original disciples to publicly as well as privately relate His truths to others, and He has used that means ever since. His Holy Spirit has conveyed the Gospel "relatively" from one disciple to another, and the duty to model and profess His Standard has fallen on each of His covenant faithful. Though each disciple has been called to a distinct vocation and equipped with a differing capacity, all are called to employ their every private and public liberty toward that purpose. Shown here is a nineteenth-century engraving of a disciple working in a private capacity.

35. Mather, *Essays To Do Good*, p. 35.
36. Ibid.
37. Norton, *The Orthodox Evangelist*, pp. 212-213.
38. Ibid.
39. Ibid.
40. Ibid.
41. Compare Matthew 23:4-5 with Titus 2:7-10.

203

A.

B.

Biblically-reflective lives:

A key component of the prayerful, studious Puritan life was that of personal, biblical reflection. Shown in these engravings were the images of two contemplative Puritan women at opposite poles of their adult lives.

A. The young woman was shown here in reflective anticipation of her earthly future, pondering a potential future groom as she stood before the ornament of God's Holy Word (illustrated for page 141 of the magazine *The Quiver* in 1889).

B. The older woman was shown here seated in reflective memory of the richly ornamented life that she conducted here on earth. She also rested in her own reflective anticipation of Christ, that future Groom with whom she would spend a glorious and heavenly eternity (illustrated for page 840 of *The Quiver*, 1889).

By grace being put into practice in the Christian life, covenanting with Christ was anything but dry legalism. With God's redemption effected in the believer, the covenantal life became deeply personal and personally satisfying. Therefore, in the Personal Covenant both grace and obedience came together in the inward man and the outward life. Grace was both obliging and graciously comprehensive. As Preston put it: *"Now this is the covenant that God will make with you if you will be in covenant with Him, that He will be all sufficient for you."*[42] He went on to describe God's covenantal sufficiency as: *"forgiving"* and *"sanctifying,"* as well as *"providing for,"* the covenanted man.[43] God initiated redemption in eternity and He graciously initiated its complete and full work in men. God continually directed and man governed himself accordingly. God was fully sufficient and men were fully supplicant, because in the Personal Covenant, God was given to man and man was given to God.

Once grace was imparted, it infused every aspect of the believer's life. Once his obedience was modeled in the personal life, it was obliging in every societal sphere. The Personal Covenant once entered therefore reformed the believer's demeanor and obliged and modified every engagement. It carried all concerns with his or her fellow man and was carried into the bonds and commitments that would constitute one's entire life thereafter. The covenanted man was therefore uniquely obliged before God for the wider good. His influence was to be seen and to resonate in all his engagements. It was carried into that part of God's dominion that composed his household. If he was married, it would infuse his family, or when/if he was eventually to marry, it would then become the basis of the foundational relation with his wife, and in due time, direct the rearing of his offspring in their mutual covenant bonds. It was carried into that part of the Kingdom known as his local church, to which he could have true communion with fellow members of Christ's body on earth; and it was carried into that part of God's dominion known as the commonwealth, by which godly precepts could be championed among the most general human societies. All spheres were covenantally obliging to the individual believer; all were places where God's reformation was to be carried, and all were venues of wider covenantal living.

42. Preston, *The New Covenant*, p. 107.
43. Ibid., p. 134.

Book III Historic Covenantal Living

Chapter 2: Familial Covenantal Living

Household Faith and Obedience under Grace and Biblical Law

 O the Puritans, all public societies were built upon the private society that God had originally established in the home. The family was the original society of His creative ordering of mankind, and all wider, or more public, societies grew out of that first domestic order. The society of the home thus began with a compliment of two, as Adam living in perfect Paradise could not find his perfect satisfaction alone. John Bunyan explained:

> *All the glory of this World, had not Adam had a Wife, could not have completed this man's blessedness.*[1]

It remains of historic note that by God making His Genesis statement: *"It is **not good** that man should be alone"* (Genesis 2:18, emphasis added), He was making His first negative observation upon His six days of work. God had determined that man's Paradise was simply not complete aside from the advent of woman. Even amid all the splendors of the Garden, the man was found lacking, wanton, and gravely incomplete. The man could not be wholly what God had intended, as the choicest of all His creatures, without the blessed bonds with his foremost human companion. Thus was the advent of the husband and the wife; thus was the advent of the family; and thus was the advent of all human societies.

Another Puritan, Matthew Henry, supposed Adam to have announced upon the introduction of his wife: *"Now I have what I wanted, which all the creatures could not furnish me with, a help meet!"*[2] Henry then followed with a narrative that God's foremost purpose for the marriage was for husband and wife to help one another in the mutual *"cleave"*[3] of a covenantal union. As long as man remained upon the face of the earth, that cleaving was intended to be – for God Himself had created man as an intimate, relational creature with an innate and divinely sanctioned, covenantal nature. In speaking of Eve, Matthew Henry wrote of her as thus "relative" to Adam: *"that this lovely creature, now presented to him, was a piece of himself, and was to be his companion and the wife of his covenant."*[4]

The union of a man and a woman in *"wedlock"* (meaning *"covenant"* and *"seal"*)[5] was to tie the two together in a sanctified bond. It was intended for their exclusive, mutual help in personal intimacy under the sanction of godly legitimacy. All societies of men would then be established upon the stability of

1. John Bunyan, *The Works ...* (London, 1736), *An Exposition on the First Ten Chapters of Genesis ...* , p. 13.
2. Henry, *Exposition of the Old & New Testaments*, commentary on Genesis 2:23-24.
3. Ibid.
4. Ibid.
5. Noah Webster, *An American Dictionary of the English Language* (New York: S. Converse, 1828), vol. 1 for "locke" in its Saxon derivative, and vol. 2 for "wed" in its Saxon derivative.

exclusive, binding associations based in mutual faithfulness. The marriage union would thereby confine human sensual passions within God's ordained purposes for them, and prevent the unchecked anarchy of random sensual affairs. The stability of all human associations therefore began with such a union. In a domestic sense, *"Marriage was ordained for the mutual help of husband and wife,"*[6] and in a more public sense, marriage was also ordained for *"the increase of mankind with a legitimate issue."*[7]

God was the Author of marriage and all marriages were as accountable to Him as that between Adam and Eve (engraving of the first covenantal union from John Speed's *Genealogies* in the 1611 Authorized Bible).

To the reformers, the marriage of Adam and Eve represented the first society of man. All marriages thereafter were to follow the covenant form and purpose that God had placed with the first, for when He sanctified the first marriage, He sanctified every legitimate marriage. The Pilgrim Pastor John Robinson wrote that God had ordained marriage *"for the benefit of mans naturall, and spirituall life, in an individual societie."*[8] The reformers considered marriage to be so bonding that the two people uniting became *"as one"* in a covenant that ought not be broken: *"by the ordinance of God, who saith that man and wife are as one, that is, not to be divided."*[9]

Betrothal

Since its advent with Adam and Eve, the institution of marriage was to be a union formed by two consenting parties and their consenting families. There were appropriate considerations to follow in bequeathing one's fidelity, for though *"It is lawfull for all sorts of people to marry who are able with judgement to give their consent,"*[10] discretion is an obligation with lifelong implications. The Puritans' *Westminster Confession of Faith* spoke of avoiding *"Infidels"*[11] or being *"unequally yoked, by marrying with suche as are notoriously wicked in their life, or maintain damnable Heresies."*[12] Other considerations included the prohibition of marrying those *"kindred neerer in blood."*[13] John Robinson wrote of the high moral discretion required in selecting a spouse and warned of the common snares which must be avoided to prevent greater marital mischief:

> *Some marry by their eye ... and herein follow favour, which is deceitful, and beauty which is a vain thing: others by their fingers, as minding what the woman is worth, in the worlds sense: others by the eare, as specially respecting their wives title, and high birth, and so get themselves so many Lords, and masters over them as she hath friends.*[14]

6. Westminster Assembly of Divines, *The Confession of Faith* (London, 1658), p. 83.
7. Ibid.
8. Robinson, *Essayes. Or, Observations Divine and Morall*, p. 516.
9. Geneva note on Ephesians 5:28.
10. *Westminster Confession of Faith*, pp. 83-85.
11. Ibid.
12. Ibid. (Also see 2 Corinthians 6:14.)
13. Ibid. (Also see Leviticus 20:14.)
14. Robinson, *Essayes. Or, Observations Divine and Morall*, p. 516.

Robinson therefore advised that a spousal consideration should be made on the merits of virtue and godliness, for they were the further *"handmaidens"*[15] of a marriage. The wife's and husband's virtues would provide for each other's adornment: *"The virtue of the wife is the husbands ornament, so the husbands the wifes... ."*[16] After determining that priority *"goodeness,"* their mutual qualities of *"fitness"* would suit each other *"as a paire of gloves or two oxen: two alike."*[17]

Like the marriage itself, a marital espousal was a covenanted *"engagement,"*[18] in that once the promises to marry were exchanged, it was also set in devoutly binding terms. According to Thomas Goodwin's account of the ancient Hebrew practice, espousals were consensually contracted before several witnesses by an exchange of money from the future groom to the future bride by saying, *"Loe thou art betrothed unto me."*[19] The payment represented his gift of adoration and appreciation and not a purchase. It was a reserve for the bride's financial provision in the event of abandonment, divorce, or the death of the groom. The solemnities of the Israelite betrothing were usually performed under a canopy or tent as a *"tabernacle"*[20] of the engagement conducted before the families and witnesses. The betrothal was thereby much more than a statement of mere intentions, it was a publicly avowed commitment to marry. Once his proposal was accepted, the future groom would depart his tabernacle *"chamber"* rejoicing *"as a strong man to runne a race."*[21] To violate the vow of fidelity that was pledged during the proposal would be for him to commit adultery as much as it would be to do so following the later nuptials. And similarly, *"betrothing by copulation"* was strictly forbidden, *"and who so did it, were chastised with rods; howbeit the betrothing stood in force."*[22]

The English courtship and marriage traditions also drew deeply from the Hebrew precedents. The English retained the Israelites' requirement for physical purity during the period of betrothal, and often retained the old tradition of payment (the dowry) for the vows of engagement.[23] Like the precedent of ancient Israel, each family was to register its consent for the marriage prior to granting their mutual blessing to the espoused couple as *"having the Consent of those whose immediate Care and Government they are under."*[24] The engagement was also a public event as considerable public notice was required before marriage. For example, in Puritan Massachusetts, the couple was legally required to *"first publish their*

15. Ibid., pp. 522-523.
16. Ibid.
17. Ibid.
18. Thomas Godwyn [Goodwin], *Moses & Aaron. Civil and Ecclesiastical Rites, Used by the Ancient Hebrews,* 7th ed. (London, 1655), pp. 231-232.
19. Ibid.
20. Goodwin, *Moses & Aaron,* referencing Psalm 19:4-5.
21. Ibid., pp. 231-232.
22. Ibid.
23. See Genesis 34:11-12 and Deuteronomy 22.
24. *Acts and Laws, Of His Majesty's Province of the Massachusettes-Bay in New England. Begun and held at Boston, the eighth of June 1692 ...* (Boston, 1759), p. 16.

English families of centuries past were highly influenced by the ancient Hebrew model of marital espousal. The Jewish man would formally approach the father of his desired Hebrew bride and negotiate for her hand. The formalities that followed made the "engagement" a binding, public commitment (engraving of a Hebrew espousal negotiation in a 1776 English Bible).

Banns at three several publick Meetings in both towns where such parties respectively dwell."[25] If, due to circumstances, that was not possible or practical, they could publicize their betrothal *"by posting up their Names and Intentions at some Publick Place in each of the said Towns, fairly written, there to stand by the space of fourteen days."*[26] Such notice would provide fair warning to the community at large that the two were espoused and provide ample time for anyone to approach either family with any concerns regarding prior entanglements, moral lapses, or biblical prohibitions against the two individuals mentioned. According to the Reformed tradition, both parental families retained considerable input in the affair, for as they had granted their specific consent to the matrimonial engagement, any new concerns following an espousal could cause them to alter the circumstance of the engagement or even void the pending marriage.

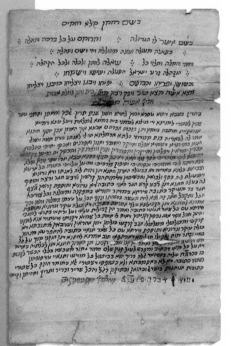

According to the long rabbinic tradition, the Hebrew marriage has always been contracted as a covenantal union. The "ketuboh," or wedding covenant, was the manuscript testimonial of a Hebrew couple's joyous union containing a written promise of the husband's continuing love, honor, and support for his wife. It was presented to the bride by the groom during their nuptials and she was charged with preserving the document throughout her lifetime. Pictured here is a typical manuscript ketuboh dating from the nineteenth century.

The Union of Two

As the Israelite espousal ceremony had been particularly central to the symbolism of the ancient Hebrew culture, Puritan historian Thomas Goodwin also observed the same "relative" meaning in their ancient ceremony of matrimony. Goodwin wrote that the Hebrew administrator, or *"the Chief of the Companions,"*[27] would lead the wedding party and their assembled guests in prayer. Taking the wedding cup and blessing God, he would speak: *"Blessed art thou, O Lord our God, the King of the World, which created the fruit of the vine."*[28] Goodwin noted that the Hebrew blessing thereby began with an acknowledgment of God as the Creator of the earth as well as the source of mankind's continued procreation. To the Hebrew newlyweds, their own hopes for future familial fruitfulness thereby began with that first acknowledgment. After administering additional, similar blessings, the chief of the nuptials continued with a further prayer that the sweetness of the bedchamber would provide God's rich adornment for their nation:

> *I beseech, thee O Lord, let there suddenly be heard in the cities of Judah, and the streets of Jerusalem, the voice of joy and gladnesse, the voice of the bridegroom and the bride: the voice of exultation in the bridechamber is sweeter then any feast, & children sweeter then the sweetnesse of a song.*[29]

25. Ibid.
26. Ibid.
27. Goodwin, *Moses & Aaron*, p. 223, quoting Genebrard.
28. Ibid.
29. Ibid.

Goodwin's observations confirmed the prophetic nature of the Hebrew wedding as it anticipated the ultimate wedding feast still to come between the Messiah, Jesus, and His faithful Bride, the Church. To covenantal Puritans such as Goodwin, the Hebrew model therefore had significant "relative" meaning for the Christians who also engaged themselves in the bonds of earthly wedlock. Beginning in the early sixteenth century, English Protestants had abandoned the Roman Catholic belief that marriage was an official church sacrament and resorted it to the original model (like that of ancient Israel) in which marriages were considered domestic and civil covenantal unions. In England, the Church still administered the wedding ceremonies, but the civil courts now legislated and administered marital laws. And, though many Puritans at the time considered the Church ceremonies far too ritualistic, the rich symbolism within the English nuptials remains a powerful testimony of the covenantal nature of all English marriages during that era.

The Protestant English Church retained many of the old Israelite ideas in solemnizing its wedding ceremonies. The bride's father was again central to the proceedings, as the English minister would ask of the assembly: *"Who giveth this woman to this man?"*[30] Only after her father's consent was acknowledged, the minister then formally received the bride's hand from him and presented it into the hand of the groom. The man then pledged his vow to his woman and the woman to her man. They individually promised themselves in such a manner that they were solemnly given unto each other *"according to God's holy ordinance."*[31] Each vow therefore ended with the covenant promise: *"I pledge thee my troth"*[32] (meaning true faith and whole fidelity). A ring was placed *"upon the book"* and handed to the minister, who in turn lifted the band and handed it to the man *"to put it upon the fourth finger of the womans left hand,"*[33] as the groom pledged:

> *With this Ring I thee Wedde, with my body I thee worship, and with my worldly goods I thee endow: In the Name of the Father, & of the Sonne, and of the Holy Ghost. Amen.*[34]

In the English tradition, the wedding ring was the seal upon the wedlock. In the manner of the official Anglican rite of the later sixteenth century, the minister of the matrimonial ceremony then offered up a prayer following the man's *"leaving the Ring upon the fourth finger of the womans left hand."*[35] Like that of ancient Israel, he blessed their union according to the vows of their covenant:

Elizabethan era weddings of the late 1500's and early 1600's tended to be very formal affairs. Though the marriage rite was no longer considered an official sacrament to be administered under the Roman Canon Law, the English ceremony adopted a high degree of Christian symbolism. Official directives for English marriage rites were included in the prayer books that were added to period English Bibles. Although some Puritans found many aspects of the ritualism to be unnecessary and even repugnant to the purity of God's marital ordinance, many others appreciated the covenantal implications of the English form of wedlock. Illustrated here is an engraving of a later Elizabethan era couple shown hand-in-hand (circa 1600).

30. *The* [Geneva] *Bible* (London, 1594), Prayer Book Prefix: *"The forme of solemnization of Matrimonie,"* leaf B7.
31. Ibid.
32. Ibid.
33. Ibid.
34. Ibid.
35. Ibid.

A. The wedding vows were spoken individually by the groom and then the bride in pledging fidelity to each other under God. Wedlock united the two vows into one charter (late sixteenth-century ordinance).

A. *O Eternal God, creator and preserver of all mankinde, giver of all spirituall grace, the author of everlasting life, send thy blessing upon these thy servants, this man and this woman, whom we bless in thy Name, that as Isaac and Rebecca lived faithfully together, so these persons may surely performe and keep vow and covenant betwixt them made (whereof this Ring given and received is a token and pledge) and may ever remaine in perfect love & peace together, and live according to the Lawes, through Jesus Christ, Amen.*[36]

At that point, their vows which had been individually spoken were fused together into the covenant charter of wedlock. Their united promises were fixed under the seal of the ring as completing each other and initiating the chartered institution of a family. And, as with the biblical examples of Adam with Eve and Isaac with Rebekah, the new couple became a new, private and public society.

B. American weddings were less formal affairs than their English counterparts. Beginning in colonial New England, the service would typically be conducted by a local civil officer. It was often a domestic affair conducted in a home among family and invited guests, followed by a reception to celebrate the blessed event. Like in old England, American wedlock was still entered by mutual vows, and in later colonial New England, services would be conducted by either a church minister or a civil officer. Either way, they were equally solemnized under God's holy ordination. Shown here is an early nineteenth-century lithograph of an American parlor wedding.

In Puritan New England, there was much less emphasis on outward formalities. The wedding would typically be administered by a magistrate rather than a minister, but the couple, all the same, entered into a holy as well as a civil union before God. Many of the formalities of the English service were abandoned for the more austere vows spoken before the families and witnesses as administered by the Justice of the Peace. The New England practice was to focus more upon the celebration of the formal engagement of the couple, and in keeping with the Hebrew manner, the families hosted a reception for the bride and groom after the nuptials as a social event. By the later seventeenth century, many New England ministers began to perform the ceremonies in the same manner as their English counterparts, though in keeping with the social practices of the engagement and reception celebrations. Whether administered by a civil Justice of the Peace or by an ordained minister, whether performed in the sanctuary of the church or that of the home, the couple was equally *"solemnized"* before God and the world. In Massachusetts, it was ordered that *"every Justice and Minister shall keep a particular Register of all Marriages solemnized before them."*[37] The family, whether residing privately at home or presenting itself publicly as members of a church, citizens of a town, or subjects of a king, was societally honored as a self-governing society by way of God's superintending Laws. The blessed union then received all the civil respect, reverence, and legal protection that was due God's ordination of wedlock.

36. Ibid.
37. *Acts and Laws, Of His Majesty's Province of Massachusettes-Bay*, p. 16.

Marriage and Civil Society

Once the husband and wife married, their unity was to be recognized outside of the home as complete. Wider societies were to view the two persons as one, for according to English law, the matrimonial husband and wife were recognized as one person. The legal existence of the woman was *"incorporated and consolidated into that of the husband."*[38] If, for instance, the wife was indebted before entering matrimony, her husband was legally bound to cover her debt: *"for he has adopted her and her circumstances together."*[39] The role of the husband was considered altogether obliging to cover his wife in her every earthly employment: *"under whose wing, protection, and cover she performs every thing."*[40] Their union was thereby legally, as well as culturally, complete. The matrimonial covenant was recognized as such a tightly bound cord that the husband and wife could not legally enter into a further contract or covenant together with each other, because to do so *"would be to suppose her separate existence."*[41]

The idea of the legal oneness of a husband and wife in English law provided the basis for the later American constitutional principle against forcing a husband or wife to testify against one another. The principle also disallowed them to testify on behalf of each other, as Sir William Blackstone noted:

> ... in trials of any sort, they are not allowed to be evidence for, or against, each other: partly because it is impossible their testimony should be indifferent; but principally because of the union of person: and therefore, if they were admitted to be witnesses for each other, they would contradict one maxim of law, no one ought to be witness in his own cause and if against each other, they would contradict another maxim, no one is bound to accuse himself.[42]

The union of wedlock was thereby definitive of all associations pertaining to the couple. With respect to the two original families of the bride and groom, the marriage had also linked them as families by way of the new couple becoming their intermediate family. So, according to the Puritan idea of family honor, even though the new family society was distinct from its former two, "relative" honor was maintained for both former households in accord with God's great family statute of the Fifth Commandment.[43] Nevertheless, the new union represented both a leaving of the old and a cleaving within the new – with all the obliging duties of a domestic household placed respectively upon the new husband and wife. Alongside

Dan Ford, 2003

COMMENTARIES

ON THE

L A W S

OF

E N G L A N D.

IN FOUR BOOKS

By Sir WILLIAM BLACKSTONE,

ONE OF HIS MAJESTY'S JUSTICES OF THE HONOUR-
ABLE COURT OF COMMON PLEAS.

A. Sir William Blackstone (1723-1780) won recognition as a brilliant legal educator and became the first professor of English law in 1758.

B. Widely popular in both England and America, Blackstone's *Commentaries on the Laws of England* (1765-1769) articulated the clear and descriptive maxims of godly law and justice (title page of a 1773 edition).

38. William Blackstone, *Commentaries on the Laws of England* (Dublin, 1773), vol. 1, chapter 15: "Of Husband and Wife," pp. 442-443.
39. Ibid.
40. Ibid.
41. Ibid.
42. Ibid., p. 443.
43. See Exodus 20:12 and Deuteronomy 5:15.

the Genesis declaration that a man was to *"leave"* his father and mother in order to *"cleave"* to his wife, the Reformed Geneva Bible footnoted: *"So marriage requires a greater duty of us toward our wives, than otherwise we are bound to show to our parents."*[44] The cleaving in marriage thus required a definitive leaving, and the couple embarked as a new covenant family, chartered under God.

Just as God sanctified the first marriage covenant in Adam and Eve, He would superintend every marriage thereafter. His active supervision over the single small society in Paradise would continue over all marriages as long as mankind remained on earth. God's right of dominion over marriage neither diminished with man's fall, nor did it suffer loss in mankind's transgression. He neither yielded His sovereignty on the day that humanity embraced rebellion, nor was He subsequently stripped of His right to reign over man or the societies of men. God would therefore continue to superintend the family centered around the nucleus of a husband and a wife, and the domestic home was to remain covenantal under Him as it had been in Paradise. In return, the domestic family secured the most intimate relations for a married husband and wife while providing them with God's representative dominion over all those under their roof.

Dan Ford, 2002

Cotton Mather (1663-1728), the son of Increase Mather, was a remarkable Boston clergyman and prodigious Puritan author. Graduating from Harvard in 1678 and ordained in 1685, he went on to write 450 works, from scholarly natural history to New England's political history, and from Puritan church polity to congregational music. Like his father, Cotton Mather resisted the royal appointment of royal governor Sir Edmund Andros, and he assisted Zabdiel Boylston in a campaign to promote small pox inoculations. Yet, in all, some of Mather's most beloved writings at the time were his numerous moral and practical essays.

As the Puritan covenantal character was built upon biblical precepts, Cotton Mather narrated the necessary nature of *"goodness"*[45] between the husband and wife. And, being as the husband's chief societal obligation was that of his *"domestic relations"*[46] with his spouse, Mather addressed the interrelative character necessary for every successful husband. A goodly man should begin by asking of himself "relative" to God's original charge to Adam: *"What shall I do that my wife may have cause for ever to bless God for having brought her to me?"*[47] Every husband was therefore obliged to act in the interest of his wife in such a way as to evoke her reciprocal thanksgiving to her heavenly Lord. If that foundational principle was indeed evoked by a husband, his wife would indeed have many sound reasons to bless God for the man that she married. And, according to Mather, a wife also had a charge "relative" to the Bible's virtuous woman portrayed in the Book of Proverbs[48] by which every wife should likewise inquire of herself: *"Wherein may I be to my husband a wife of that character – She will do him good and not evil all the days of her life!"*[49] The man would then have reason to bless God for the beauty of her character. Thus, to the Puritans, the Bible defined the gracious demeanor that God intended for each spouse, and in turn, established His gracious character in a truly covenantal union. Mather thus concluded: *"O happy marriage!"*[50]

44. Geneva note on Genesis 2:24, leaf A6.
45. Mather, *Essays To Do Good*, p. 46.
46. Ibid.
47. Ibid., "relative" to Genesis 2:22.
48. See Proverbs 31:10-31.
49. Mather, *Essays To Do Good*, p. 46, "relative" to Proverbs 31:12.
50. Ibid.

Any consideration of divorce would be exceptionally wrenching under terms that bound two parties *"unto their lives end."*[51] The *Westminster Confession of Faith* cited that once a marriage had been amiably consummated, the one deadly cause for such a radical act was *"Adultery after Marriage."*[52] To the Puritans, the act of divorcement was severe and represented the public splitting of a legal person in two. And, although an offended party could *"sue out a divorce,"*[53] the actual writ had to be granted by an outside authority and *"remedied"* according to the approval of a local *"Church or Civil Magistrate."*[54] Accordingly, John Robinson noted that God had permitted divorce with the ancient Hebrews *"only for the hardness of their hearts,"* so he concluded that it *"may justly by the Magistrate be denied to Christians."*[55] In the unusual instance of divorcement being granted, the matrimonial bond would indeed be severed, and the innocent party freed to marry again *"as if the offending party were dead."*[56] However, the offending party (as covenantally dead) was not legally permitted to remarry. In colonial Massachusetts, not only was adultery a legal *"Violation of the Marriage Covenant"* and a corporally punishable act,[57] but remarriage was a punishable felony, except in cases where a divorce had been granted due to spousal abandonment (of over seven years) or granted to a victim of adultery. Both cases legally rendered one's prior vows *"Void and of no Effect,"*[58] but there could be no consideration of escaping one's matrimonial vows by way of a no-fault petition or a plea of irreconcilable differences, for those would render divine superintendence worthless and reduce God's sovereign sanction for marriage down to base, humanistic, good intentions.[59] Matrimonial divorce was thereby exceptional among Puritan societies, by comparison with later legal systems implemented amid rampant humanism. Adultery was comparatively rare and divorce seldom granted when a violation of the marriage covenant was legally acknowledged as *"highly provoking to God and destructive of the family."*[60]

The family has survived as God's basic provision for human repose, and until recently, remained the most stable and secure institution among all human societies. The marriage, originally established by God as a covenantal union of two, has survived relatively intact as a harbinger of mutual care and support for those of each given home. That which attacks the institution of husband and wife therefore attacks God's basic provision for mankind. Yet, the household's centerpiece relation – the union of husband and wife – has remained in existence amid every culture and generation of man. As extended from the original man and woman in Paradise, each clan, tribe, and nation has, to varying degrees, recognized that central union as essential to healthy domestic life as well as to wider, public societal living.

The successful union of a Puritan husband and wife required their continued dependence upon God. By together submitting their prayers before the Lord, they further established His strength within the bonds of their matrimony. Shown here is an excerpt of a nineteenth-century memorial engraving honoring the prayerful lives of America's earliest Puritan immigrants.

51. *Geneva Bible*, Prayer Book: *"The forme of solemnization of Matrimonie,"* leaf B8.
52. *Westminster Confession of Faith*, p. 85.
53. Ibid.
54. Ibid.
55. Robinson, *Essayes. Or, Observations Divine and Morall*, p. 529.
56. *Westminster Confession of Faith*, p. 85. (Also see Matthew 19:9; Romans 7:2-3.)
57. *Acts and Laws, Of ... Province of the Massachusettes-Bay*, pp. 51-52.
58. Ibid.
59. See Matthew 19:6.
60. *Acts and Laws, Of ... Province of the Massachusettes-Bay*, pp. 51-52.

The Society of the Household

To the Reformed Christians, the most dear of all societal covenants was that of their home. The highest end of every man and woman was to honor God, and for the Puritans, the epitome of that end was to honor Him in that which was most immediate. And, as with all things covenantal, the building of a home was to be framed according to the design of God's written Word. In following His Word, the covenantal home was designed to be both hierarchical and paternal. The husband had the highest place in the family hierarchy because he bore the greatest weight of accountability to God for its care. The wife, distinct in her responsibility, held direct accountability to God as a wife, but "co-relative" responsibilities with and under her husband within the framework of the home. Though subordinate to her husband in overall governing responsibility, she had significant accountability to God in framing its practical, daily administration. The couple's marital obligations thus enforced a sense of fellow stewardship over the family's frame, and fellow stewardship reinforced a further trust in the hierarchical design of the home.

The heart of the Puritan home began with the Genesis description between a man and woman. Following His stipulation that a husband was to *"cleave unto his wife"* (Genesis 2:24), God then dignified another tier to that first family society. Through God's providential gift of childbirth to Adam and Eve, mankind was mercifully saved from extinction after the fall, and the familial covenant union of two was graciously extended into a fuller household with children. Puritan parents therefore recognized (according to biblical design) that their own offspring also belonged to God by way of that grace, and that He had (by design) entrusted those new souls to the care of their parental home.

John Robinson reminded the families of his congregation that *"God created our first parents, male and female, blessed them saying, Be fruitful and multiply and fill the earth."*[*a] Living to see many families of his Pilgrim congregation do just that by sailing to America in 1620, Robinson also saw a duty in every husband and father: *"The Lord requires in the man love and wisdom."*[*b] The family man had the prime responsibility to extend God's care for the home, providing both food and comfort for his loved ones (nineteenth-century engraving of an earlier American home). *a &*b: *Essayes. Divine and Morall*, pp. 524-530.

As the matrimonial bond was a covenant superintended by God, it followed that the society that immediately surrounded it was likewise necessarily covenantal in nature "relative" to His more expansive purpose for the home. Intimacy was closest between the husband and wife and then among those within their immediate household. The foremost consideration of the father was therefore for the care, protection, and provision of those within his household: to his wife and children first, and only then "relative" to his callings outside the home. The household served as a pivot, or the central point, for a man's outside associations, and though his outside obligations were indeed important, they were "relatively" less pressing than interests inside the home. To Puritans such as Cotton Mather, it was then perfectly proper for the family man to prioritize his "relative" responsibilities toward the home:

> ... *let every man consider the RELATION, in which God the sovereign Ruler, has placed him; and let him devise what good he may do, that may render his relatives the better for him.*[61]

61. Mather, *Essays To Do Good*, p. 46.

But, such an important familial charge conferred by God upon parents simply added to their obligation of covenantal stewardship. According to William Perkins, the children remained exclusively under their parents' *"tuition."*[62] As such, the father and mother's civil union would provide the legal covering for sons and daughters who *"are of their parents good, and neither fit to take an oath, without their consent. ...Neither are they to choose a calling, or make any contract of themselves, but onely by the one direction & advice of their parents."*[63] As the parents were responsible *"stewards"*[64] of God's gift, the children were the exclusive wards of their parents. The term *"ward"* referred to the *"villagent,"* or *"defensive,"* or *"guardian protection"*[65] that children enjoyed within a family's abode. In English law, the natural parents were the legal *"guardians"*[66] of their children. And, though the term *"infant"*[67] in common English usage pertained to children under the age of two, according to English law the term applied legally to all children remaining at home up to the age of twenty.[68] For example, an *"infant"* young man of ten years could not enter a covenant or engagement until he reached the age of twelve (and then only with the consent of his parents), because that was the legal age of an infant's *"discretion."*[69] Parental guardianship also meant that the children could not be approached by law or by any outside intrusion without that intruder going through the father – or (as in the case of a widow) the mother. There was therefore protective power given to the duty of parental guardianship as well as a duty to rightly use that power. The parents' legal obligation to their children consisted of *"three particulars; their maintenance, their protection, and their education,"*[70] for while they remained at home, the children were to be equipped for their future duties and callings. The father and mother alone had protective responsibilities to be the wardens and guardians of their children in *"warding"*[71] off all outside evils from reaching them.

Matthew Henry also warned of various *"sins of daily infirmity"*[72] that weakened the domestic fabric from within. Henry proposed not only guarding against outside infidelity, but warding off tendencies leading families away from intrinsic faithfulness. He called for household confession and repentance of all such defects and also for guarding against the kind of language and conduct that would lead in an unfaithful direction:

Parental guardianship was intended to provide a private sanctuary for all those who resided under their roof. Massachusetts magistrate James Otis defended the private sanctity of the colonial home in 1761, saying, *"Now one of the most essential branches of English liberty is the freedom of one's house. A man's house is his castle; and while he is quiet, he is as well guarded as a prince in his castle."** Shown here is an early nineteenth-century engraving of an early American family at quiet repose before their evening's hearth.
*James Otis, *Speech In Opposition to Writs of Assistance* (Boston, 1761).

62. Perkins, *The Whole Treatise of the Cases of Conscience*, book 2, p. 231.
63. Ibid.
64. Webster, *An American Dictionary of the English Language*, vol. 2 (1828), for "steward" and "ward."
65. Ibid.
66. Ibid. (Also see Blackstone, *Commentaries on the Laws of England*, book 1: *The Rights of Persons*, "Of Guardian and Ward," pp. 460-462.)
67. Ibid.
68. Ibid.
69. Ibid.
70. See Blackstone, *Commentaries*, book 1, "Of Parents and Children," p. 446.
71. See Webster, *An American Dictionary of the English Language*, vol. 2, for "ward" and "warden."
72. Matthew Henry, *A Church in the House. A Sermon Concerning Family-Religion* (London, 1704), p. 24.

> *Their vain Words, and unprofitable Converse among themselves; their manifold Defects in relative Duties, provoking one another's Lusts and Passions, instead of promoting one another to Love and to good works. These ought to be confess'd and bewail'd by the family together, that God might be glorified, and what has been amiss may be amended for the future.*[73]

Contrary to the *"vain Words"* that provoked corruption, good words – God's own Words and His Laws – were to be raised and implemented as the standard for governing the home. The Bible provided a straightforward, but thoroughly descriptive, charge to teach them in the home:

> *And ye shall teach them your children, speaking of them when thou sittest in thine house, and when thou walkest by the way, when thou liest down, and when thou risest up. And thou shalt write them upon the door posts of thine house, and upon thy gates* (Deuteronomy 11:19-20).

Paternal Honor and Duty

The Puritans put a great emphasis on the role of the head of the household. The head of the home was of chief importance to the family because he was the first in accountability to God for its earthly care. Modeling the sons of Abraham, the Puritans considered the father as the patriarch of the home and placed considerable credence in the fact that the man had the most essential role of headship. That meant an acceptance of his covenantal duty to lead his immediate family by example, and passing covenantal continuity from his generation on to the next. Good family government depended upon that line of authority; therefore, to New England minister Samuel Wigglesworth, the good father was synonomous with the godly *"governour"* of a home:

> *Family governours are as highly concerned as any to exert themselves with their Children and Servants, to impress their tender Minds with an early Sense of their great Maker, and their obligations to serve him with a perfect Heart.*[74]

The paternal father was to provide personally supervised care and discipline for his children. Consequently, he also provided adequate educational resources for their proper upbringing. Shown here is an early nineteenth-century illustration of a typical family visit to the local bookseller.

In giving the father such a fundamental responsibility, God placed the mantle of the home squarely upon his shoulders. The strength of the family therefore relied upon his manly temper and his capacity to firmly establish the home on sanctified ground. To the early reformers, the lines of family virtue were drawn upon the lines of authority originally manifested

73. Ibid.
74. Samuel Wigglesworth, *An Essay for Reviving Religion. A Sermon Delivered at Boston, ...* (Boston, 1733), p. 32.

in God's Creation and repeatedly confirmed throughout the text of Scripture. A century before Mather or Wigglesworth, the English Puritans had seen such lines of authority in the basic character of manly honor. The biblical lines of domestic leadership and subordination had been drawn for them by their Puritan forebearers. William Perkins, for example, delineated the character of paternal duty from four basic grounds of manly honor which he listed as *"virtue,"* *"representation," "paternity,"* and *"eternity."*[75] God bestowed man with those four grounds of honor at the advent of Creation and charged each man since with the concurrent role as household leader. The head of the domestic family was therefore to be honored according to the godly character of his position, and upon the following four grounds lay the domestic authority of the husband and father: *"First,"* wrote Perkins, *"man is to be honored for vertues sake, because therein principally stands the internall Image of God."*[76] The first man was created in the image of God, and woman from the man. The image of *"virtue"* was therefore delineated from the original order, first to the man and then to the woman.

Perkins went on to the second ground of manly honor involving his *"representation"*: *"because one man before another beareth the Image of Some Thing that is in God."*[77] To Perkins, the created order put man at the head of the family's order in regard to its overall duties. *"Some Thing"* referred to the responsibility inherent in the order of man's prior duties to God in Creation and his prior position of responsibility in Paradise, *"because he beareth before the woman the Image of the glory of God, yea of his Providence, Wisdome, Lordship, and Government."*[78] The man therefore carried the priority weight in conducting a faithful family government. The man's authority, derived from God, was always subject to His highest authority. Selfishness, pride, or arbitrary claims of male dominion had no place in the hierarchical order of representative, domestic leadership.

According to Perkins's third ground of manly honor, *"paternity,"* the domestic father was to mirror God's own fatherly image. Fatherhood originated with God, and each generation was charged with depositing that image with the next. The head of the family was therefore to be honored as a patriarch by the son who would carry the fatherly mantle forward. Perkins wrote: *"And so the Father is honored of the Sonne, because he beares in his person the Image of Gods Paternity, or Father-hood."*[79] Hence, the domestic father figure was given a grave and humbling charge from God. But, because no man could rise to such a measure or adequately display such an awesome image, the patriarch must indeed be steeped in the biblical beatitudes of godliness.[80]

A fatherly figure was that of a servant leader over his home. The father was to model godly authority and care within his household and set an example of representative headship by his submission to his own heavenly Superior. Above all, the patriarch was to demonstrate dependence on God by praying over all his earthly affairs, as shown in this nineteenth-century engraving of fatherly prayer over a family business.

75. Perkins, *The Whole Treatise of the Cases of Conscience*, book 3, p. 368.
76. Ibid.
77. Ibid.
78. Ibid.
79. Ibid.
80. See Matthew 7:9-12.

Perkins's fourth and final ground most vividly expressed the idea of manly leadership in its high respect for eternity. According to Perkins's ground of *"eternity,"* the aged man more immediately bore God's image as the Eternal Being. A man with age better modeled the eternal wisdom of God than did the younger, as God's eternity was modeled in the length of a godly man's days. Each generation was once more removed from God's image originally deposited with man in Paradise. The fourth ground of honor therefore recognized the family patriarch's closer proximity to both past Creation and future eternity. It acknowledged the honor due to those greater in age and of prior generations. Perkins therefore concluded: *"Fourthly, of his eternity. And hence it is that, that honour is given to the aged before the young man, because he beareth the image thereof."*[81]

To reformers such as Perkins, the idea of family governance was derived from the very "grounds" that God invested in the role of the father. All family authority was therefore to model the virtue, representation, paternity, and eternity exhibited by God in the model of biblical patriarchy. The father's duty was then to graciously model the representative dignities that God deposited within that honored position. Perkins concluded: *"Thus we see, that Divine representations doe imprint a kind of excellency in some persons, and consequently, doe bring forth honour."*[82]

The Happy Family:

Respect for the hierarchical order of the home was encouraged in the chapbooks (small story books) of the eighteenth century. Children read for moral instruction as well as for academic discipline, so the books chosen for them to read by their parents were those consistent with biblical virtues. In the popular work, *The Happy Family; or the Rewards of Virtue and Filial Duty*, children read of the duty to honor those charged with their care, and that recreation and safety were secured under parental wings, *"to preserve you from dangers"* (illustration from *The Happy Family*, 1786).

The idea of hierarchy, or the divine order of obligation and subordination, was a set fixture in the Puritan family. Accordingly, John Robinson saw that the husband and father's obligation was to lead his family by a strict rule of charity toward all those under his authority: *"Love rather descends, then* [than] *ascends; as streams of water doe."*[83] The honor of the domestic patriarch was to be warmly established by the father in the hearts of his children as a resonant principle which would then be modeled in their respect for all other elders, as Robinson also reasoned: *"so should the younger sort specially be trained up in a bashful, and modest reverence towards all."*[84] To the Puritans, the domestic family as well as larger, public societies were endowed with hierarchical roles established by God. They were not roles which could be arbitrarily juxtaposed due to the creative notions of men, women, or children. The hierarchy of the home presented children with the honorable model for the coordinated roles of women and men, and of the younger and older working together to secure the order that God originally deposited in the first human society. The younger were not created to lord over the older any more than the serpent had been created to lord over Adam and Eve. To do so would produce a similar, unsettling effect.

81. Perkins, *The Whole Treatise of the Cases of Conscience*, book 3, p. 368.
82. Ibid.
83. Robinson, *Essayes. Or, Observations Divine and Morall*, p. 537.
84. Ibid., pp. 550-551.

Family Education

To the Puritans, children belonged first to God and then were entrusted to the care of the parents. As was mentioned before, Cotton Mather observed that a father had a foremost charge to *"render his relatives the better for him."*[85] Family education was therefore a parental responsibility and an essential component of the domestic covenant.[86] A mother was next in the line of responsibility to provide for her children's education. Though second in the position of family duty, a mother was the first in line as the immediate nurturer and caretaker of her loved ones: *"... as they are most about their children, and have early and frequent opportunities to instruct them, so this is the principal service they can do to God in this world, being restrained from more publick work."*[87] Parents were counseled in the *Westminster Confession of Faith* to remove the moral weeds growing around their tender seedlings, to shed God's light upon their young fertile minds, and to keep their hearts warmed to the comforting fires of home, for they were otherwise cautioned:

> *The ground needs no other midwifery in bringing forth weeds than onely in neglect of the Husbandmans hand in plucking them up; the Ayr [air] needs no other cause of darknesse, than the absence of the Sun, nor Water of coldnesse than its distance from the Fire.*[88]

Parental neglect of home education would thus unduly expose their children to immoral weeds, godless darkness, and stifling chills of the world. It was incumbent upon parents to take charge of the child's moral, doctrinal, and academic training. The wider societal significance of that primary domestic responsibility was stated by Thomas Manton's classic charge to parents in his *Epistle to the Reader* of the *Westminster Confession*:

> *A family is the seminary of Church and State; and if children be not well principled there, all miscarrieth: a fault in the first concoction is not mended in the second; if youth be bred ill in the family, they prove ill in Church and Commonwealth.*[89]

God had specifically entrusted parents to nurture and educate their children in His ways, which John Robinson noted was a foremost family duty: *"He trusts us with the bringing them up, in his nurture, and instruction."*[90] To Robinson, it was the finest adornment of a Christian home for parents to commend their own children to godliness: *"It is an enduring fruit of God's gracious covenant when good parents by their godly care have gracious children; and that by which the faith is much confirmed."*[91]

A.

B.

Hannah Zes, 2002

C.

At home, children of each generation were properly nurtured in the manner of their reading and guarded in the subject of their text:

A. A home reading lesson pictured in Foxe's *Actes and Monumentes* (1576 edition).

B. Illustration of a typical eighteenth-century home reading lesson.

C. Woodcut of a home reading lesson from a *New England Primer* (c. 1820).

---

85. Mather, *Essays To Do Good*, p. 46.
86. See Deuteronomy 32:45-47.
87. *Westminster Confession of Faith*, Thomas Manton's *"To the Reader ... ,"* leaf C2.
88. Ibid., *"The General Epistle: To the Reader ... ,"* leaf A3.
89. Ibid., Manton's *"To the Reader,"* leaves C-C1.
90. Robinson, *Essayes. Or, Observations Divine and Morall*, p. 533.
91. Ibid.

Richard Baxter went further in lamenting that multigenerational, paternal ignorance had been the reason that common knowledge of God had for centuries been nearly *"banished from the world, and never to be recovered."*[92] Nevertheless, he went on to ask why, even though a parent's own education might be found lacking, that would free him from his current obligation to pick up educational skills as an adult: *"But if your parents did not teach you, why did you not learn when you came to age?"*[93] Thus, having lightly admonished the uneducated parent, Puritan Baxter simply went on to advise that the self-taught adult ought to teach his next generation what he has learned, even *"while you are learning your selves, teach your children what you know."*[94] And, according to Robinson, no adult had ever been adequately taught anyway (or at least never fully appreciated his or her own education) until achieving parenthood: *"Wee seldome consider the prize worthy the cares, and the paines of parents, till wee become parents our selves, and learne them by experience."*[95]

The typical New England home became the heavenly haven of family education. With Reformed colonial preachers ever beating their drums of parental duty, Cotton Mather directed the parents of his native Boston: *"Parents! How much you ought to be devising for the good of your children."*[96] For Mather, family education and virtuous character were to be the juvenile adornments given to every generation: *"carry on a desirable education for them, and an education that may make them desirable; how to render them lovely and polite, and serviceable to their generation."*[97] And, to such a studious Puritan as Cotton Mather, the disciplines of wider academics brought the issue of virtuous discretion into his children's education:

> *I would be solicitous to have my children expert, not only in reading with propriety, but also at writing a fair hand. I will then assign them such books to read, as I may judge most agreeable and profitable: obliging them to give me some account of what they read, lest they should stumble on the devil's library and poison themselves with foolish romances, novels, plays, songs or jests, "that are not convenient.*[98]*"*[99]

Similarly, as a regular aid to parents, the *New England Primer*, which had an extensive run of publication between the late seventeenth to the mid-nineteenth centuries, directed youth to their heavenly service in commonplace family study. Written for the youngest readers, the *Primer* included, along with its famously poetic ABC's, many moral lessons to be rehearsed as life's little proverbs. Teaching familial duties alongside the most basic scholarship, lessons in prayer, humility, and honorable deportment were included in the task of reading and writing:

The hand-held *hornbook* was a common teaching tool that included the alphabet, the phonetic sounds, and the Lord's Prayer (seventeenth-century hornbook).

92. Baxter, *The Saints Everlasting Rest*, part 3, pp. 361-362.
93. Ibid.
94. Ibid.
95. Robinson, *Essayes. Or, Observations Divine and Morall*, p. 536.
96. Mather, *Essays To Do Good*, p. 61.
97. Ibid.
98. Meaning: fit; suitable; proper. "Convenient" as defined in Webster, *An American Dictionary of the English Language*, vol. 1 (1828).
99. Mather, *Essays To Do Good*, p. 51.

1. Praying will make us leave sinning, or sinning will make us leave praying.

2. Our weakness and inabilities break not the bond of our duties.

3. What we are afraid to speak before men, we should be afraid to think before God.[100]

To the reformers, a thorough understanding of man's relation to God was foremost in shaping a thorough education. It was not assumed that children came into the world as blank slates, as if they were in an unfallen human condition and would undertake learning moral lessons if left to themselves:

Were it so well with the soul (as some Philosophers have vainly imagined) to come into the world as a mere blank or piece of white paper, on which neither anything written nor any blots, it would then be equally receptive of good and evil.[101]

Children, born as negatively-charged moral agents, needed a regular infusion of positively-charged biblical instruction. Through daily exercises in God's written Word, they would be shaped into fit future managers of their lives, families, churches, or business affairs. Typical of the many eighteenth- and early nineteenth-century New England miniature children's readers, *The History of the Old and New Testament*, published by the son of the famous patriot printer Isaiah Thomas, stated that the objects of its lessons were *"to mend the heart, and establish in the mind those unalterable laws of the DEITY, which lead us to the knowledge of himself, which cement us together in society."*[102] Children, as young citizens of both their home and wider commonwealth, were taught their moral, historic, and societal duties side by side – or rather, learned them as one and the same. Likewise, the *New England Primer* included the *Westminster Shorter Catechisme* to assist children in understanding the Bible's doctrinal mandates. Nearly all home-spun New England students learned of God's ascendancy, His lordship, and His rules at a tender age, and through its series of brief questions and answers, read for themselves the choicest principles that would remain at their ready in conducting their lives:

Q. What is the duty which God requireth of man?

A. The duty which God requireth of man, is obedience to his revealed will.

A.

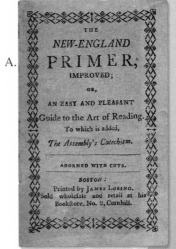

A. The direct descendant of John Cotton's *Spiritual Milk for Boston Babes* of the seventeenth century, the *New-England Primer* was a multigenerational tool employed by American families well into the nineteenth century (title page of the *"Improved"* *Primer*, circa 1800).

B.

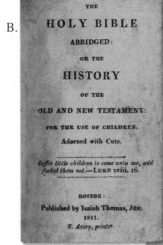

B. Although the Bible was read to children in its entirety, small abridged versions provided young students with a means to read the "history" of the text for themselves. This abridged *History of the Old and New Testament* provided children with their earliest lesson of history (1811).

100. *"Three Short Sentences,"* excerpted from *The New-England Primer* (Boston, [circa 1790's]), unpaginated leaf.
101. *Westminster Confession of Faith*, "[First] *Epistle to the Christian Reader, especially Heads of Families,"* leaf A3.
102. *The Holy Bible Abridged: Or the History of the Old and New Testament* (Boston, 1811 edition), Preface, p. 5.

Q. What did God at first reveal to man as for the rule of his obedience?

A. The rule which God at first revealed to man for his obedience, was the moral law.

Q. What is the sum of the ten Commandments?

A. The sum of the ten Commandments is, To love the Lord our God with all our heart, with all our soul, with all our strength, and all our mind; and our neighbour as our selves.[103]

Puritan parents knew that they were given the inescapable duty to follow the familial Hebrew passage to *"Train up a child in the way he should go"* (Proverbs 22:6). This included a thorough understanding of reading, writing, history, and academics, in which the student was expected to employ considerable individual effort. As the child matured, the study of moral virtue played an even greater part in his or her education. Here the parents contributed much from the example of their own character in the creative dispensing of such valuable, higher knowledge: *"consider how to enrich their minds with valuable knowledge; how to instill into their minds generous, gracious, and heavenly principles."*[104] From infancy to maturity, the covenantal parents prepared their children at home to enter the uncertain and oft unsafe world of adulthood. That task would indeed be daunting but the results would prove rewarding, as Cotton Mather concluded in his advice to parental educators: *"there is a world of good that you have to do for them."*[105]

The Family Altar

The covenantal responsibilities of Puritan families went well beyond the duties of the husband to wife, the wife to husband, the parents to children, or the children to parents. The biblical admonitions to spousal love and honor, and the proverbial charge to "train up" their children, also had significant devotional implications. To keep those commandments was for them to first honor the true object of all family devotion. To love, honor, and train those of their family meant that they first worship the Creator, the Sustainer, and the true Lord of their home.

To the Puritans, it was not assumed that children were born with inherent spiritual knowledge by which to engage with God in a meaningful relation, or that they naturally inherited a heart inclined toward His proper worship. So, like the child's moral and academic training, spiritual education and discipline also began under the watchful care of the parents. On the one hand, the household covenant required the governor of the family to see that those under his care were trained for suitable earthly employment, and on the other, it required him to disciple all those under his roof in the character and conduct of heavenly faith. To the Reformed, the whole counsel of Scripture was to be used in directing him toward that end. Matthew Henry saw the noble constitution of the ancient Hebrew

---

103. *The New-England Primer*, leaf C2.
104. Mather, *Essays To Do Good*, p. 61.
105. Ibid.

patriarchal family as the model for every family of faith, observing that *"where-ever Abraham had a Tent, God had an Altar in it, and he himself serv'd at that Altar. Herein is left us an Example."*[106] For him, the patriarchs set an example for a fatherly duty to lead corporate worship, reading, and study, and they passed the father's example to the next generation of familial faithful. With a household subject to God, each successive patriarch was the primary exemplar of God's honor in his own household of faith. Accordingly, to Henry, the Christian father would do great good to honor the Creator of his natural and spiritual offspring, holding a special reverence for the example that God had set with Old Covenant Israel:

> *Especially adore him as the God of the families of Israel, in Covenant-Relation to them, having a particular Concern for them above others, Jer. 31:1. Give Honour to the Great Redeemer as the Head of all the Churches, even those in your Houses; call upon him the Master of the Family, and the great Upholder and Benefactor of it; for he it is whom all the Families of the earth are blessed, Gen. 12:3.*[107]

According to Richard Baxter, for a father to disregard such a fundamental duty was for him to bear the very image of God's great adversary: *"if anything that walks in the flesh may be called a devil, I think it is a parent that hindereth his children from salvation."*[108] Thomas Manton also lamented the failure of fathers to provide for the appropriate devotional discipline of their loved ones: *"This covenant-breaking with God, and betraying the souls of their children to the devil, must lie heavy on them here or hereafter."*[109] The father's spiritual charge was therefore much more than moralizing or maintaining the formalities of religious activity, as a failure to regularly and carefully place one's family before the household altar represented a covenantal breach of the highest order:

> *They beget children, and keep families, merely for the world and the flesh: but little consider what a charge is committed to them, and what it is to bring up a child for God, and govern a family as a sanctified society.*[110]

The family provided the most private sanctuary before God's throne of grace. Men, women, and children could each bow their knee within their private closet or jointly together before the family hearth. Cambridge, New England's first pastor, Thomas Shepard, spoke of the woeful neglect of *"meditation"* as a *"deep*

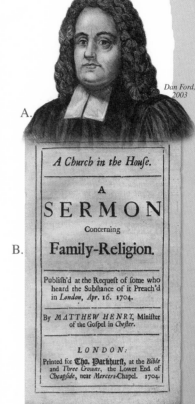

Dan Ford, 2003

A.

B. A Church in the House.

A SERMON Concerning Family-Religion.

Publish'd at the Request of some who heard the Substance of it Preach'd in *London, Apr.* 16. 1704.

By *MATTHEW HENRY*, Minister of the Gospel in *Chester*.

LONDON:

Printed for **Tho. Parkhurst**, at the *Bible* and *Three Crowns*, the Lower End of *Cheapside*, near *Mercers-Chapel*. 1704.

A. Matthew Henry (1662-1714) was a non-conforming (independent) English scholar best known for a voluminous set of Reformed commentaries: *An Exposition of the Old & New Testaments* (1708-1714).

B. A strong advocate of active family worship and prayer, Henry published *A Church in the House* in 1704. He saw private family devotions as the key to overall, national virtue: *"Family-Religion, if that prevail will put a Face of Religion upon the Land, and very much advance the Beauty and Peace of our English Jerusalem"* (title page of *A Church in the House*).

---

106. Henry, *A Church in the House*, p. 22.
107. Ibid., p. 23.
108. Baxter, *The Saints Everlasting Rest*, part 3, p. 361.
109. *Westminster Confession of Faith*, Manton's *"To the Reader,"* leaf C2.
110. Ibid.

A.

B.

The regular practice of family devotions staved off many ills in earlier American culture. When families found contentment in the God of the Bible, class jealousy was held in check, as depicted in these two nineteenth-century illustrations:

A. Engraving of a father leading a humble, poorer family in devotions.

B. Lithograph of a father leading a humble, wealthy family in devotions.

mischief plotting against New-England."[111] And, he concluded: *"Oh therefore seek the Lord still in private."*[112] As a regular covering upon the whole family, Cotton Mather also implored the Christian parent to daily lift each of his children before God's throne of grace:

> *Let me pray daily for my children with the greatest constancy and fervency; yea, let me daily mention each of them by name before the Lord. I would importunately beg for a suitable blessing to bestow upon them; that God would give them grace, and give them glory ... .*[113]

To the Puritans, regular and devotional reading of the Scripture with the entire family together would provide hearty opportunity to *"go through the Bible,"* beginning at a time *"when the olive-plants around my table are capable of being so watered."*[114] Regular cultivation begun at such a tender age would bear its fruit in the middle and later years of growth, as the steady sustenance in reading, singing, praying, and rich family fellowship would stave off the infections of cultural paganism and childish imaginations. Children were also encouraged to be self-disciplined in their personal reading, prayer, and private reflection, and then to converse with their family about the state of their souls: *"I will frequently remind them that there is a time, when they must appear before the holy Lord; and that they must now do nothing which may then be a source of grief and shame to them."*[115]

Everyday duties likewise went hand in hand with family devotions, as regular devotions prepared the household members for their daily tasks. Work was forbidden on the Sabbath, but so was idleness during the remainder of the week. Even though the Puritan household would on any given Tuesday, Wednesday, or Thursday, be days removed from its weekly Sabbath's rest, the Sabbath's devotions would never be so far removed. As the family covenant made even the mundane holy, that which was holy was also a part of every day. Even the distinct duties that each member owed privately to God, such as prayer and Bible study, went hand in hand with one's family duties and daily tasks – as well as the weekly Sabbath's rest. With regard to regular and intimate prayer, William Perkins had encouraged: *"The house or the field is as holy before God as the church."*[116] Later, the Westminster Assembly confirmed that *"God is to be Worshipped every where, in Spirit and Truth: as in private Family daily, and in secret, each one by himself."*[117] Thus, regular prayer and family devotions were heavenly duties that

111. Thomas Shepard, *The Parable of the Ten Virgins Opened & Applied* (London, 1660), p. 166.
112. Ibid.
113. Mather, *Essays To Do Good*, p. 52.
114. Ibid.
115. Ibid.
116. Perkins, *The Whole Treatise of the Cases of Conscience*, pp. 162-163.
117. *Westminster Confession of Faith*, on *"Religious Worship and the Sabbath Day,"* pp. 71-72.

went together with the family's daily purpose. Regular devotions equipped household members to keep God in their covenant and to keep their covenant close to God. Private and family prayer, as well as private and family worship, actively kept all the family before the heavenly altar of God: to give Him due worship, honor, and thanks for who He is and all that He has done, and to keep the glow of His warmth at the heart of every task.

Even with all the devotional duties incumbent upon the domestic family, the family itself could not be considered a Christian congregation unto itself. The Sabbath was the regular time for various families to corporately gather and to unitedly hear the Word and to worship their common Lord together. The church, even if it met in a home, would be open to other families. To the Reformed, the church ought to be represented within its families, but a family itself could not be the church. The later seventeenth-century Puritan author John Owen made the following observation of the churches established by the Apostles among the various first-century Christian homes:

> It cannot be proved ... that ever they confined a Church unto a Family; or taught, that Families, though all of them Believers and baptized, were Churches on the account of their being Families.[118]

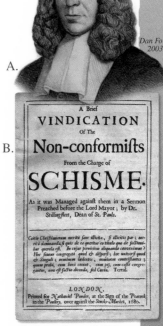

Dan Ford, 2003

A.

As a staunch *"non-conforming"*[119] independent who was very skeptical of the established Anglican Church, Owen recognized that a local body was formed *"... from the Voluntary Spiritual Consent, of those whose whereof it consists, unto Church order."*[120] However, in exampling the biblical churches described in the New Testament, he also argued: *"Neither is there any mention in Scripture of a constitution of Churches in private Families."*[121] Families were therefore recognized as having significant devotional duties, but a true communion of saints was not restricted to those of one home: *"Possibly a Church may be in a family, or consist only of members that belong to a Family. But a Family as a Family neither is nor can be a Church."*[122]

B.

Even so, the home provided the most accessible, frequent, and important place for devoted Christian lives. The *Epistle to the Reader* of the *Westminster Confession of Faith* talked of a *"double account"* for parents to first watch over their own souls and then over all those committed under their care: *"every Private Christian that hath a Soul to look after, yet upon a double account ... as having themselves and others to look after."*[123] Puritan parents were thereby obliged to keep themselves and their loved ones at the foot of the Redeemer, and those such as Thomas Manton saw little difference between a father's spiritual duty over a home and a pastor's duty over the church:

A. John Owen (1616-1683) was a defender of sound, biblical doctrine taught in the home.

B. This is the title page of Owen's *Vindication Of The Non-conformists From the Charge of Schisme* (1680), in which he argued for fidelity in the home and the church.

---

118. John Owen, *A Brief Vindication Of The Non-conformists From the Charge of Schisme* (London, 1680), p. 44.
119. Ibid., title page.
120. Ibid., pp. 44-45.
121. Ibid.
122. Ibid.
123. *Westminster Confession of Faith*, "The General Epistle: To the Reader," leaf A2.

225

Families are societies that must be sanctified to God as well as Churches; and the governors of them have as truly a charge of the souls that are therein, as pastors have of the Churches.[124]

Family prayer, confession, and worship were to begin with the mother's hymn at the cradle and the father's instruction upon his lap, as consistent devotion before the family altar placed their children at the very foot of God's throne. The crowning achievement for years of family leadership, education, devotion, and discipline would be for the parents to accomplish the task of preparing their beloved sons and daughters for their own future affairs. And, again, Cotton Mather concluded that the highest aim of the family altar was therefore in pointing their offspring toward that most essential of all future engagements:

Private devotions put each family member before God's throne (woodcut from a New England Primer, circa 1790).

If I live to see the children arrive at marriageable age, I would, before I consult with heaven or earth for their best accommodations in their married estate, aim at the espousal of their souls to their only Saviour. I would, as plainly and as fully as I can, propose to them the terms on which the glorified Redeemer will espouse them to himself, in righteousness and judgement, favour and mercies forever; and solicit their consent to his proposal and overtures: then I would proceed to do what may be expected from a tender parent for them, in their temporal circumstances.[125]

Familial Virtues versus Family Values

The first table of God's great Law (the first four Commandments) mandated that household faithfulness begin at the family altar, so familial reading, praying, singing, thanksgiving, repenting, and Sabbath resting were all necessities of the well-governed home. The individual household could not hope to be sanctified within its walls merely through an association with even the best of outside institutions. Healthy societal influences, such as godly friends and neighbors or the best churches and civil communities, could not, in themselves, equip the private domicile with its necessary virtues.

Familial virtue came directly from above and had to be secured within the family gates. Moral character was derived solely from God and was designed to flow from the home out into the wider societies. In fact, the Puritans' "relative" principle behind the idea of societal virtue was that it proceeded from the inward to the outward, from the smaller into the larger. As such, societal virtue followed a path from the domestic domicile into the wider church or household of faith, and from the private corridors of home into the public halls of state. No innovative social programming could reverse that divine, original model; no amount of societal engineering could rework that which God had designed and ordained. So, unless both morality and virtue were consistently cultivated from within, neither could be found residing at home.

124. *Westminster Confession of Faith*, Manton's *"To the Reader,"* leaf C2.
125. Mather, *Essays To Do Good*, p. 56.

FAMILIAL COVENANTAL LIVING

Bound by such "relative" (RELATE-ive) accountability, there was no place in the home for relative (REL-a-tive) social values. The Puritans surely did not write of "family values" any more than they wrote of "Christian values." They did, however, speak of the absolute strength that God Himself brought to families and the other societal spheres. They did speak of familial virtues that He secured which could not be effected at home if reduced to human commodities. Though the Scriptures did speak of both virtues and values, values described things that fluctuated in their worth. Values could vary according to one's selective desires; virtues could not. Virtues spoke of the absolute strength that families required from on High to give them a sound and steady temper – strength which was only procured by lives devoted to God and dedicated to one another.

Thanksgiving was an ongoing practice among Puritan families. Thanks to God was given for things visible such as food and shelter and for things invisible such as safety and virtue (sketch of a family's thanks over an evening meal).

Familial virtues pointed to the divine strength vowed in the wedding ceremony, whereas the 'family values' prioritized picking and choosing from an ambiguous range of changing social norms. If the solidity of godly virtues was reduced to relative values, the family's covenantal cord would be stressed to breaking by sacrificing its original, divine strength for the unstable, evolving ethos of mankind. Admittedly, neither men, women, nor children could hope to live up to God's mark of absolute virtue even in the most faithful covenant home, but His standard of perfect fidelity would always remain rock-solid before them. The Rock of all virtues, Jesus Christ, never spoke of social, family, or Christian 'values.' He affected men and women with His godly virtue. For example, a woman who was plagued with an *"issue of blood"* was not healed by Jesus' 'Christian values' – she was infused with Christ's strength by setting her resolve solely upon Him, as was noted in the Gospel that *"virtue had gone out of him"* (Mark 5:25-34). Had Christ been merely the progenitor of Christian values, the woman would have missed the mark of truly effectual faith.

The Puritan family required that sort of virtue. The covenantal family devoted to the Almighty could not hit its effective mark by lowering its sights to a world of fluctuating values. Reformed homes were therefore defined by the virtues described in God's Word, and maintained by their concurrent duties among the family's members. The stewardship mantle worn by the parents worked to prevent unhealthy societal intrusions and ensure that God's strength undergirded all the souls within. The father's obligation was to lead the home and raise his children with clear expectations of what God required of them and not leave them to grasp for their life's meaning amid the clouded shadows of changing values. Abundance was found by men and women living as husbands and wives, and then as fathers and mothers working together in the distinct roles that God had ordained. Man's strength was maintained through the coordinated work and mutual help of the whole – and not in unsatisfied illusions of individual fulfillment. With the domestic domicile established on the foundation of God's Laws, and with His Decrees inscribed upon the family gates, those inside could rest assured. Genuine satisfaction was found within the home while it provided the seedbed for the godly virtues of wider society. The remaining two chapters will therefore consider the larger societies of church and commonwealth.

Chapter 3: Church Covenantal Living

Assembly Faith and Obedience under Grace and Biblical Law

F the massive number of volumes that rolled off the Puritan presses, by far the most ink flowed over the issue of the church. The earliest battles of the Reformation were fought over the nature of true faith, the form of pure doctrine, and the right mode of godly worship. Those debates continued well after the first European settlements were planted in America, and the same issues have captivated the minds of nearly all who still endeavor to plant and cultivate new Christian assemblies.

When John Hooper published his *Declaration of Christe* in 1547, he was appealing to the English throne to allow a kind of Christian fellowship and worship that would recognize Jesus Christ as the true *"Kyng Emperour and protector of the Churche."*[1] He recognized that neither the king nor his ecclesiastical establishment were qualified to rule in the place of Jesus Christ. Those who would not *"harken unto his voyce"*[2] had no authority in His Church. According to Hooper, Christ had covenantally *"bound his churche to receive his doctrine,"*[3] and that no arbitrary structure of men could supersede the dominion which Christ Himself appropriated to His Church. According to Hooper, Christ had deposited His earthly authority first in the Apostles who served the early church and provided all to come after them with the testimony of the New Covenant Scriptures.[4] Then, by way of His Spirit, God's dominion was mutually granted to all believers, as overseen by elders and deacons with pastors and teachers, each in the service of His dominion of saints.

When *"the mother of Zebedees children"* (meaning the disciples James and John) requested that Jesus put them in the positions of highest dominion, she asked: *"Grant that these my two sons may sit, the one on thy right hand, and the other on the left, in thy kingdom"* (Matthew 20:21). Jesus told her that those positions were not His to give, but were to be granted by His Father. When His other disciples were moved with indignation over her audacious request, Jesus (with another mild rebuke) told them that they were each to be His servants and none of them were to rule with kingly dominion over His faithful:

> *Ye know that the princes of the Gentiles exercise dominion over them, and they that are great, exercise authority upon them. But it shall not be so among you: but whosoever will be great among you, let him be your minister. And whosoever will be chief among you, let him be your servant* (Matthew 20:25-27).

1. John Hooper, *A Declaration of Christe and of his Offyce Compylyd* (Zurich, 1547), leaf Kii.
2. Ibid., leaf biii.
3. Ibid.
4. Ibid.

Matthew Henry noted that *"the constitution"*[5] of Christ's Kingdom would be quite different from the lording Gentiles, in that those who ruled as His apostles and administrators were *"to teach the subjects of this kingdom, to instruct and beseech them, to council and comfort them, to take pains with them, and suffer with them"*; and thus Henry added: *"You are not to lord it over God's heritage, 1 Pet. v.3, but labour in it."*[6] Likewise, to the earlier reformers, Christ's own government superseded that of any earthly king, potentate, or humanly-devised system attempting to reign over His Church. Hooper and the earliest sixteenth-century reformers had been determined to restore the Church of Christ to the order and ordinances of the Scriptures. They knew that Christ was the dominion Head of the church, and that the church was to be ordered according to biblical mandates and not ruled by an English monarch.

Similarly, in the 1640's when Parliament had wrestled the English Church away from the crown, there was a considerable contingent of *"Erastians"*[7] who would have had the church governed directly by the Parliament. George Gillespie's resounding defense of *"The Divine Ordinance of Church-Government"*[8] which he titled *Aarons Rod Blossoming*, argued for a church establishment distinct from the civil commonwealth like that of the ancient Hebrews: *"The jewish churche was formally distinct from the Jewish State."*[9] The Presbyterian Gillespie affirmed his argument in dedicating the volume to the Westminster Assembly, saying, *"Christ hath a Kingdome and government in his Church, distinct from the kingdomes of this World."*[10] He pointed to the fact that though the role of the church was cooperative with the state, and that both were established by God, the earliest Christian assemblies had been set upon a covenantal foundation that was wholly distinct from that of the Jewish or Roman civil magistrates. And, as a staunch Presbyterian, Gillespie knew that Christ had a differing administration over His covenant saints than the one that God had implemented over the commonwealth. Christ's Church, as a body of saints, had been sealed by His personal sacrifice and must be distinguished as a realm different from the general government or civil estate, as Gillespie concluded: *"that Christ himselfe suffered to the death for it, and sealed it with his blood."*[11]

Overwhelming the counter-arguments by the Erastians in the Assembly, Gillespie's position prevailed and the government of the Church was recognized by Puritans and Presbyterians as distinct from either the crown or Parliament. The church and state were henceforth seen as two distinct callings with two distinct governing administrations, yet both under the One and the same Lord.

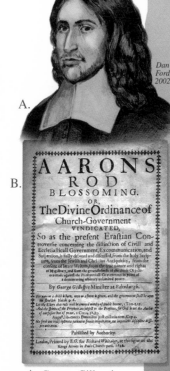

Dan Ford, 2002

A.

B.

A. George Gillespie (1613-1648) was an outspoken Scottish member of the Westminster Assembly and helped draft the first chapter of its *Confession*.

B. Shown here is the title page of *Aarons Rod Blossoming. Or, The Divine Ordinance of Church-Government*, which was a powerful statement for a spiritual jurisdiction of church government (1646).

5. Henry, *Exposition of the Old & New Testaments*, vol. 3, commentary on Matthew 20:25-27, pp. 115-116.
6. Ibid.
7. George Gillespie, *Aarons Rod Blossoming. Or, The Divine Ordinance of Church-Government Vindicated, ...* (London, 1646), *"To the Reverend and Learned Assembly of Divines Convened at Westminster,"* leaf a.
8. Ibid.
9. Ibid., p. 6.
10. Ibid., leaf a.
11. Ibid.

The Local Assembly

The stories of the earliest settlements in New England were framed around similar issues as those of Gillespie. The Puritans, during the reign of James I, had argued a similar point when confronted with the strong civil arm over his ecclesiastical administration. Several of the more determined congregations known as Separatists removed themselves from the established Anglican Church and began to meet independently. They were subsequently forced from their homes and several congregations were forced to flee to Holland, but remaining loyal Englishmen, they published a joint *Humble Supplication* to James in 1609, petitioning the Crown that they be allowed to return to their homes with *"libertie to enjoy and observe the ordinances of Christ Jesus in the administration of his Churches in lieu of humane constitutions."*[12] Their appeal was for them to be formally exempted from the formal Anglican *Constitutions* that James wielded to suppress the Presbyterian or Independent assemblies. While acknowledging the king's authority over them in the *"care of matters civill,"*[13] they presented England with a veritable manifesto for an independent congregational ordination:

A.

> ... *the favour humbly sollicited by us, is, that whereas our Lord Jesus hath given to each particular church or ordinarie congregation this right and priviledge, viz. to elect, ordeine, and deprive her owne Ministers, and to excercise all other parts of ecclesiasticall jurisdiction under him, your Ma[jesty] would be pleased to take order as well.*[14]

James rejected the congregationalist *Supplication* in scathing terms, though one of the refugee congregations providentially arrived at Cape Cod in the fall of 1620 under the flag of the king. That notable exception was due to the fact that James had been convinced that a few, small, independent congregations could still be quite beneficial to his Crown if they were allowed to settle in America, yet simply remain English possessions. The idea suited the king, and the idea was befitting the Puritans. Thus, in a move to enlarge his own dominions, James unwittingly, though providentially, enlarged the Kingdom of Christ under a banner of congregational independency.

Two decades later, after the successive immigrations of hundreds of similar Puritan refugees to North America, the pastor of the infant town of Boston, John Cotton, would write in defense of their local church bodies: *"It is part of all Christians, who look for salvation by Christ Jesus, to joyn themselves (if God give them opportunity)*

A. Several covenanted assemblies made attempts to flee James I's rigid, centralized Church policies. This nineteenth-century engraving depicted the Pilgrims' first attempted flight to Holland in 1608.

B. The English refugees in Holland published this *Supplication* in 1609, requesting James's acceptance of their churches ruled by local elders.

12. [Holland English Separatists], *To the right High and mightie Prince, JAMES by the grace of God, ... An humble Supplication for Toleration ...* ([Holland], 1609), title page.
13. Ibid., p. 6.
14. Ibid., p. 14.

to some one or other such a particular visible Church of Christ."[15] By the 1640's, New England had been well established in independency from Anglicanism and it rested squarely on the Puritan mode of orthodox administration, worship, and theology. At that time, when those first settlers were still precariously perched with their backs against a wild and untamed wilderness, John Cotton appreciated the necessity of believers to unite themselves for their mutual care and corporate strength and to wholly give themselves to God as:

> *... the fellowship and estate of church, we finde not in Scripture that God hath done it any other way then by entering all of them together, (as one man) into an holy covenant himselfe, To take the Lord (as the head of the church) for their God, and to give up themselves to him, to be his Church and people.*[16]

In New England the churches were formed as covenanted members. They became independent congregations which were administered by elders, deacons, ministers, and teachers according to God's holy ordinance. The keys of heaven were administered by the local congregation and the civil sword was administered by the colonial Governor and the magistrates:

> *The power of the keys is far distant from the power of the sword and though one of them might need the helpe of the other, when they go astray, and administered, the one of them doth not intercept, but establish the execution of the other.*[17]

As authority in the New England churches was distributed among the members and the administrative rulers of each congregation, the "New England Way" was charged by some in England as being a *"Democraticall government."*[18] Cotton dismissed the notion out-of-hand in saying, *"It is unworthy ... to prefer Athens before Jerusalem, pregnant wits before sacred hearts."*[19] Cotton's point was that although their churches were not under the English king as was the Anglican Establishment, neither were New England's churches under the people as if a democracy. To Cotton, each New England assembly modeled its congregation as a *"mixt"*[20] form of government beginning with Christ *"who is head and wise Monarch of the Church,"*[21] then by the *"elders"*[22] who had power to restrain *"where not the will of each man bearth the sway"*[23] as in a pure democracy:

> *... the government of the Church is not meerly democraticall, but (as the best governments be) of a*

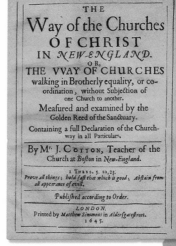

Defining the New England Way:

John Cotton, sometimes called the "Patriarch of New England," was chosen as the "teacher" of the first church of Boston. Shown here is Cotton's *The Way of the Churches of Christ in New-England. Or, the Way of Churches walking in Brotherly equality, or coordination, without Subjection of one Church to another*, which was highly influential in establishing the independency of American congregations.

15. John Cotton, *The Way of the Churches of Christ in New-England. ...* (London, 1645), p. 2.
16. Ibid., p. 2.
17. Ibid.
18. Ibid., pp. 100-101.
19. Ibid.
20. Ibid.
21. Ibid.
22. Ibid.
23. Ibid.

A.

B.

AN ACT
For the promoting and propagating the
GOSPEL
OF
JESUS CHRIST
IN
New England.

Whereas the Commons of England assembled in Parliament, have received certain intelligence, by the testimonial of divers faithful and godly Ministers, and others in New-England, That divers the heathen Natives of that Countrey, through the blessing of God upon the pious care and pains of some godly English of this Nation, who preach the Gospel to them in their own Indian Language, who not onely of [...] are become Civil, but many of [...] their accusto[...]

C.

mixt temper; in respect of Christ (whose voice must be heard, and his rule kept) it is a Monarchy; in respect of the peoples power in choosing officers, and joynt power with the officers in admitting members, in censuring offenders, it is a Democracy; in respect of the officers instruction and reproof of the people in publike ministry, and in ordering all things in the Assembly, it is an Aristocracy; what is good in any civill government, is in Church-government.[24]

With Christ as King, the administrators as servants, and the people mutually obliged for the good of the whole, the fledgling New England churches had undertaken a most thorough reformation. Likewise, many *"converted Indians"*[25] also desired to enter into covenantal congregations. Under the influence of Puritan missionaries, the Christian natives had also separated from their former tribesmen to form themselves as worshipping assemblies of saints. Martha's Vineyard missionary Thomas Mayhew wrote similarly in a letter to his parent *Society for the Propagation of the Gospel in New-England* of those who had fled the dark spiritualist modes, as: *"Indians there, who are solemnly Covenanted together."*[26] Whether American natives or English imports, the early New England Christians were formed as bonded communities of Christian individuals and families who pledged themselves to worship God together in spirit and truth. As with their English counterparts, the early Indian assemblies were composed of those who not only sought mutual protection from the formidable native hazards, but who also strictly limited their numbers to those of an orthodox faith and a sound life in Christ. According to Mayhew, they received *"none into their Fraternity or Combination, but those which give good proofs of their upright desires."*[27] He went on to describe at length the manner in which about fifty Indians *"desiring to joyne with the Worshipers of God, ... entered into Covenant"*[28] with them:

> *... all of them came confessing of their sinnes, some in speciall the naughtinesse of their hearts, others in particular, actuall sinnes they had lived in: and also they all desired to be made better, and to attend unto the Word of God, to the end looking*

A. Edward Winslow (1595-1655) was one of the founders of Plymouth Colony in 1620. He was appointed its agent to the Indians and befriended Chief Massasoit. As a devoted Puritan, Winslow was sent to England on several occasions to represent the colonial interests of Plymouth and Massachusetts Bay, and he was responsible for the first English missionary society in America (nineteenth-century engraving).

B. *The Society for the Propagation of the Gospel of Jesus Christ in New England* was established in 1649 (at the request of Winslow) as an independent missionary endeavor. This 1649 Act ensured that the Puritan mission projects would be completely self-governed and funded by free-will contributions from England.

C. The Puritan missions established self-governed congregations among the Christian Indians (nineteenth-century engraving of a Puritan mission to a New England tribe).

24. Ibid.
25. John Eliot, William Leverich, and Thomas Mayhew, *Strength out of Weakness. Or the glorious Manifestation of the further Progresse of the Gospel amongst the Indians in New-England* (London, 1652), p. 16.
26. Ibid.
27. Ibid.
28. Ibid., pp. 30-31.

onely to Christ Jesus for salvation. I observed also that they generally came in Families, bringing their children with them, saying, I have brought my Children too, I would have my Children serve their Parents have them say something to shew their willingness to serve God: and when the Commandments were repeated, they all acknowledged them to be good, and make Jehovah to be their God, promising to walk according to his councils: And when they were received by them that were before in this generall Covenant, it was by loud voices thanking God that they were met together in the wayes of Jehovah.[29]

Members of the Reformed congregations were composed of a citizenry destined for Christ's eternal Kingdom. The English Puritan Thomas Temple explained in a 1642 sermon: *"This should be the ligament of the Christians society: their relation to Christ, as they are fellow citizens of the heavenly Jerusalem, and the Household of God, and knit together under one King."*[30] Temple was speaking of the saints' vertical *"relation to Christ,"* their true King, as the *"ligament,"* or tie, that bound them together in their earthly household of faith, just like He did the citizens of His heavenly city.

Temple continued his narrative by describing the character that such a knitting of saints implied: *"Wee should desire to keepe the same company, we shall doe in heaven: there our company should be God and the Saints; so it should be here."*[31] Those in Christ's *"company"* were accountable to take care in preserving the moral as well as the spiritual character of the whole. Cambridge, New England's Thomas Shepard similarly warned of the obligation to keep the congregation free from moral corruption: *"Take you heed of Coming to Church Fellowship with defiled hearts, and to defiling God's holy things, for do you know where you are?"*[32] The local church was composed of members who brought godly virtue with them into the assembly, who were clothed in His righteousness, and who respected others as *"God's holy things."* The assembly was considered holy only because of that distinctive dignity. The purpose of congregating was, first, to worship Him and publicly hear His Precepts, but also to model His holiness in brotherly fellowship, for the New England Puritans defined a true assembly as *"Such as not only attained the knowledge of the principles of religion, and are free from gross and open scandals ... but also walk in blameless obedience to the word."*[33]

Dan Ford, 2002

A New England Sabbath assembly represented the congregation of local families. The focal point of the service was the Lord, to whom they gathered together to worship. The psalms and songs that were sung were specifically devotional and directed toward God's honor and glory, and their teachings and sermons were focused upon His written Word for the common equipping of the body. *"All things,"* the Apostle Paul had written in the text, were to be *"done unto edifying"* (1 Corinthians 14:26).

The intellectual level of their services also followed that of the biblical text, meaning that each teaching was delivered for the understanding of the governor of the home. He would then, in turn, apply the sermon within his household and reduce the discourse (if necessary) down to the level of his particular children's understanding. This sketch is based upon a nineteenth-century engraving of an early New England Sabbath assembly.

29. Ibid.
30. Temple, *Christ's Government In and Over His People*, p. 23.
31. Ibid.
32. Shepard, *The Parable of the Ten Virgins Opened & Applied*, p. 6.
33. Synod of New England Churches, *A Platform of Church Discipline Gathered out of the Word of God, and agreed upon it the Elders, and Messengers of the Churches assembled in the Synod at Cambridge in New-England. ... Anno. 1649* (Boston, 1772), p. 22.

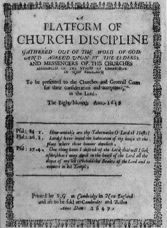

A.

B.

A. Richard Mather (1596-1669) was the patriarch of the multigenerational Mather dynasty in New England. After becoming Reformed in his pastorate at Toxteth Park in England, he was repeatedly "silenced" by Anglican officials. In 1635, Mather fled to America with his family and settled as the preacher of the congregation at Dorchester. He soon became one of New England's leading theologians, and along with John Eliot and Thomas Weld, published *The Bay Psalm Book* (1640), the first English book printed in America. Shown here is a contemporary woodcut of Richard Mather.

B. Richard Mather also helped draft the (Cambridge) *Platform* (1649), the seminal statement of faith adopted by a synod of New England churches. It was the first independent American church constitution, focusing more upon church polity than upon theological doctrine.

Admission to Covenant Assemblies

Although membership into a local assembly usually came by way of being born into a resident family in good standing, new membership was commonplace amid the growing and shifting populations of New England. Membership was nearly automatic for families coming to a new church community if they had been recommended by their former local assembly. If they had not, they could visit the new assembly as guests, although evidence of their personal confession of Christian faith would be required over time before their admittance as covenant members, with full rights of participation in the communion of saints. Generous accommodations were likewise made for Puritan families that had recently immigrated from England, or those who came to New England with recommendations by Puritans remaining on the mother soil. There were, however, more formal considerations required for those who had never partaken in a church covenant before.

The manner of becoming members by those *"that were never in church society before"* began by a *"profession of faith and repentance."*[34] The profession provided that those who would newly join a covenanted congregation had a conscious awareness of their redeemed standing before God. They must, themselves, have entered into an individual covenant relation with God in Christ by way of a personal confession that *"must be made by each at admission."*[35] According to New England's *Platform of Church Discipline* (1649), it was essential that prospective members have an adequate understanding of the nature and terms of a true conversion before being allowed to join. The new Christian (or the newly Reformed Anglican) typically came before the leadership of the congregation for an *"examination"*[36] in which he or she would openly make a profession of faith before entering into a *"full communion."*[37] Once the profession was accepted, he or she would then take the seal of the covenant through the sacrament of individual baptism, and partake of the communion of saints by regular, corporate partaking in the sacrament of the Lord's Supper with the assembly.

For those who had been born to member families and baptized while under their legal *"infancy, or minority, by virtue of the covenant of their parents,"*[38] a trial or examination of any newly confessing child or young adult was also required, *"being grown up unto years of discretion."*[39] Most Puritans (as

34. Ibid., pp. 46-47.
35. Ibid.
36. Ibid.
37. Ibid.
38. Ibid.
39. Ibid.

those of early New England) considered that children baptized under the covering of their parents were *"in full covenant with God,* [and] *have the seal thereof upon them, viz. baptism"*; but, even though that alone did not make them truly regenerated Christians, living in a Christian home afforded them recognition as living in the covenant way: *"if not regenerating grace, yet are in a more hopefull way of attaining regenerating grace, and all the spiritual blessings both of the covenant and seal."*[40]

On the other hand, Puritans such as John Bunyan had a different take on the nature of covenantal baptism. Though they also associated baptism with covenantal church membership, Bunyan and others saw the sacrament as pertaining only to converted, professing believers. To Bunyan, baptism represented the symbolic outward sign of the "death" of the old, sinful man and the "resurrection" of the new, redeemed man who had actually been infused with God's Spirit upon conversion:

> *All that I have ever conversed with have declared it to be Baptism with Water, by the Direction of the Spirit ... where Men by Baptism are said to be planted into the likeness of his Death; and Col. 2. 12. we are said to be buried with him in Baptism; all which, together with the consent of all Christians.*[41]

So, to Bunyan and a growing number of Puritans of the later seventeenth century, covenant baptism represented the believers' consent to covenant with the faithful, and the faithful's consent to have them join. The sacrament, then, was the rite by which newly professing Christians entered into a full covenant fellowship with a body of believers after their conversion. In either the case of 'infant' baptism or that of 'believers only' baptism, one's full communion with a covenant body (such as admission to the sacrament of the Lord's Supper) was restricted to those who had indeed made a profession of their faith and repentance. Even in the early years of New England, all members partaking of the *"full communion"*[42] were required to profess their spiritual regeneration. And, those who remained with only the seal of infant baptism were considered in the meantime *"under church-watch,"* in hopes of their full conversion, but also in their church discipline *"... for the healing and amendment, as need shall require."*[43]

To the Reformed, it was known that the earliest models for church communities were those that had existed under the Apostles as locally governed bodies of saints. It was also recognized by the Puritans that in Christianity's earliest years, the faithful had not only survived but had thrived as believers covenanted together with their brethren in "visible" community-oriented churches. Thus, to the Reformed Christians of early New England, consistency with their ancient forefathers called each of their towns to likewise worship as a public society, or *"visible church"*;[44] and that meant for them to live as multiple families in the bonded commitment of their local body, or as New England's Cambridge *Platform of Church Discipline* put it:

40. Ibid.
41. Bunyan, *The Works*, vol. 2: *An Exhortation to Peace and Unity*, p. 827.
42. *A Platform of Church Discipline*, pp. 46-47.
43. Ibid.
44. Ibid., p. 22.

... being in a specific form consisting of a company of saints by calling, united into one body by a holy covenant, for the public, and mutual edification of one another, in the fellowship of the Lord.[45]

The local church was therefore a company of believers who had entered covenant together as a quite visible, public society. The body was composed of those who had established themselves (vertically) with God in their effectual callings, and had knit themselves together (horizontally) as a public community under Him. Therefore, all believers were called to be part of His visible congregation on earth. And, according to Bunyan, all believers entering by covenant into such societies *"are"* to visibly act as a *"body, building, house, hands, eyes, feet, and* [with] *other members must be united, or else (remaining separate) are not a body."*[46] To him, entering a church covenant was the only way for the faithful to truly become *"knit"*[47] together by consent into a genuine Christian society: *"This form is a visible covenant, agreement or consent, whereby they give themselves unto the Lord, to observe the ordinances of the Christ together in the same society."*[48] That kind of league with God recognized each new member as having a significant (inward) spiritual status, higher than any other earthly calling, but his or her new league with others also required a significant (outward) demeanor of warmth, charity, and self-sacrifice equal to the most humbling duty in bonded service to Christ.

Dan Ford, 1996

Among the "extraordinary" callings within the church was that of the evangelist. John Wycliffe (1324-1382) not only translated the entire Bible into English and was responsible for hundreds of manuscript copies published before the invention of printing, but he sent dozens of well-discipled evangelists out across England to teach biblical precepts to a largely ignorant nation. The office of evangelist was thus called to serve a wider community beyond that of a local congregation. Shown here is a sketch of Wycliffe's extraordinary mission, based upon a painting by W. F. Yeames, called *The Dawn of Reformation*.

The Offices of the Church

In its largest or "universal" sense, the church was composed of the entire Kingdom of Christ under His sovereign reign. England's Westminster Assembly prioritized that highest office, saying, *"There is no other Head of the Church, but Lord Jesus Christ."*[49] In agreement, New England's *Platform of Church Discipline* proclaimed the *"supreme"* head of the church *"(by way of gifting from the Father) is the Lord Jesus Christ."*[50] In its widest context, then, Christ's Church consists of a congregation encompassing all the faithful, both Old and New Testament, that have ever been (or ever would be) on earth as an august assembly to be gathered together as His corporal body in eternity. That magnificent assembly, known as the *"catholic"*[51] or *"universal"*[52] church, is composed of a community far too extensive to be of one denomination, or of one nation, or of any one people, one

45. Ibid.
46. Ibid., p. 25.
47. Ibid.
48. Ibid.
49. *Westminster Confession of Faith*, p. 89.
50. *A Platform of Church Discipline*, p. 86.
51. Ibid., p. 21.
52. Ibid.

place, or one time on earth. Nevertheless, as the *"King and head of His Church,"*[53] Christ authorized representative church officers and ministers to serve under Him. His universal church officers, whom the reformers described as *"extraordinary,"*[54] were the *"apostles, prophets and evangelists."*[55] Each of those offices were ordained by God's Word to disciple people in a multitude of locations or to serve among many local congregations. Those extraordinary ministries often covered several communities and provinces, and at times even crossed international borders in service to the wider body of Christ. So, according to New England's Platform, such men were called directly by God, and the local congregation was *"given no direction about the choice or course of the apostles, prophets or evangelists."*[56]

On the other hand, the offices of the local congregation were, in a *"ministerial"*[57] sense, *"ordinary"*[58] positions of service. Unlike the wider, or *"extraordinary"* service of the evangelists, the local assemblies required regular administration and oversight in which to ensure both purity and order in their worship, doctrine, and moral frame. The New England churches therefore had a long list of obligations to be internally managed in obedience to their Lord:

> *That the Church which Christ in his Gospel hath instituted, and to which he hath committed the keys of his kingdom, the power of binding and loosing, the tables and seales of the Covenant, the Officers and censures of his Church, the Administration of all his publick Worship and Ordinances, is, Coetus fidelium, a Communion of Saints, a Combination of faithfull godly men, meet for that end, by common and joynt consent.*[59]

The Scriptures had commanded that they *"set in order the things that are wanting* [lacking]*, and ordain elders in every city"* (Titus 1:5), and the Puritan immigrants to New England saw their elders as men called by *"Christ, out of his tender compassion,"*[60] to govern and maintain the congregation's *"well-being."*[61] Those charged with the regular care of the local assembly began with the highest office of administration as *"ruling elders."*[62] To the Puritan churches of New England, eldership represented a position of a great honor proportionate to the greater service that was to be rendered by such men in every well-governed assembly. Since they saw the governing role of the church as societally significant (yet distinct from that of the commonwealth), the New England churches installed their elders with an oversight befitting the adequate administration and discipline of a self-governed body.

Dan Ford, 2002

Bound by strict biblical qualifications for office,* the elders of New England assemblies were to exhibit soundness of doctrine and maturity of leadership. This sketch is based on the statue, *The Pilgrim* [Elder], in Fairmount Park, Philadelphia, sculpted by Augustus St. Gaudens (1903-04). *See Titus 1:6-9.

53. *Westminster Confession of Faith*, p. 101.
54. *A Platform of Church Discipline*, p. 28.
55. Ibid.
56. Ibid., pp. 29-30.
57. Ibid., p. 28.
58. Ibid.
59. Cotton, *The Way of the Churches of Christ in New-England*, p. 1.
60. *A Platform of Church Discipline*, p. 29.
61. Ibid.
62. Ibid., p. 30.

According to the *Cambridge Platform*, elders indeed had an extensive service to perform: *"Of which sort these be as followeth"*:

> *1. To open and shut the doors of God's house, by the admission of members approved by the church; by ordination of officers chosen by the church, and excommunication of notorious and obstinate offenders denounced by the church, and by restoring of penitents forgiven by the church. 2. To call the church together when there is occasion, and seasonally to dismiss them again. 3. To prepare matters in private, that in public they may be carried to an end with less trouble, and more speedy dispatch. 4. To moderate the carriage of all matters in the church assembled; as, to propound matters to the church, to order the season of speech and silence, and to pronounce sentence according to the mind of Christ, with the consent of the church. 5. To be guides and leaders to the church, in all matters whatsoever pertaining to church administrations and actions. 6. To see that none in the church live inordinately, out of rank and place, without a calling, or idly in their calling. 7. To prevent and heal such offenses in life or in doctrine, as might corrupt the church. 8. To feed the flock of God with a word of admonition. 9. And as they shall be sent for, to visit and pray over the sick brethren. 10. And at other times as opportunity shall serve thereunto.*[63]

The elders thus set the doctrinal direction of the congregation and guarded its fidelity to the Lord. In that regard, they ruled over the pastor, though he, too, could be chosen as an elder. The elders made provision that all who would join the assembly were of the orthodox, Reformed faith and of a moral temper suited to their calling in Christ. The elders were therefore given authority to administer censures that were *"necessary for the reclaiming & gaining the offending Brethren"*[64] among other, non-corporal brotherly disciplines, *"for purging out that Leaven which might infect the whole Lump."*[65]

The fully-equipped local church was prepared for a variety of needs within the assembly. A family in genuine need would find comfort and assistance through the church's office of "helps." A deacon was pictured in this nineteenth-century engraving attending a destitute family.

In New England, all authoritative officers were to be approved by the congregation, as *"No man may take the honor unto himself, but that he that is called of God, as was Aaron. Heb. 5. 4."*[66] They were to *"be first tried, and proved, because hands are not suddenly to be laid upon any, and both elders and deacons must be honest and of good report. I Tim. 5. 22. and 7. 10. Acts 16. 2 and 6. 3."*[67] The elders were chosen by the assembly of saints because *"A church being free, cannot become subject to any but by election."*[68] There was therefore great faith in the authoritative integrity of the whole covenanted body, though once an elder's election was confirmed, he was delegated sufficient, accountable authority, for the body was to *"most willingly submit to their* [elders'] *ministry in the Lord."*[69]

63. Ibid., pp. 31-32.
64. *Westminster Confession of Faith*, p. 102.
65. Ibid.
66. *A Platform of Church Discipline*, p. 34.
67. Ibid.
68. Ibid.
69. Ibid.

Next to the elder in the administration of the assembly was the position of deacon, also known as *"helps."*[70] The office was strictly limited to the *"care of temporal good things of the church."*[71] It was indeed an honored position and an office of highest trust, for it was in the service of the necessities of the body's physical and financial sustenance, and *"the Scripture tellest us how they should be qualified: 'Grace not double tongued, not given to much wine, not given to filthy lucre.' "*[72] Those who were specifically qualified for such a high calling then *"must first be proved, and then used,"*[73] meaning that good intentions were not enough to qualify one for the role of a deacon. As a ministry that attended to the nurturing of some and the nursing of others, the *Cambridge Platform* also recognized an historic precedent of the ancient church: *"The Lord also appointed ancient widows (where they may be had) to minister in the church in giving attendance to the sick, and to give succour unto them, and others in the like necessities."*[74] Therefore, long before there was the notion of a secular nurse or a (civil) government welfare worker in the modern sense, the local church had already provided for the *"attendance"* of the physical comforts of its sick and the financial needs of its own weakest members.

The Pastor/Preacher and the Teacher

The church offices that historically have drawn the most public attention were those of pastor and teacher. Differing from the office of elder by lesser administrative authority and by more ministerial prominence, the office of preacher was given the responsibility of regularly delivering God's Word in exhortation: *"The pastors special work is, to attend to exhortation, and therein to administer a word of wisdom."*[75] The teacher, similar to the pastor in his public prominence though with even less an authoritative charge, was to *"attend to doctrine, and therein to administer a word of knowledge."*[76] Both pastor and teacher were assigned to assist in the service of Baptism and the communion of the Lord's Table, with *"either of them to administer the seals of that covenant."*[77]

Cotton Mather wrote that the pastor and the teacher should be foremost offices in the front-line work of God, *"that they who are 'men of God' should always work for God."*[78] And then as men of God they were to be servants to the people:

> *It is necessary that you carefully consider the state of your flocks; and bring them such truths, as will best suit their present circumstances. In order to do*

The position of a preacher required a thorough, working knowledge of God's Word. Unlike Anglican sermons that were formally read from prayer books to an audience, Puritan sermons demanded biblical astuteness on the part of both the speaker and the hearers. Their sermons ranged in subject matter from the most precious grains of spiritual doctrine to the wider nuances of political polity. And, though plain in the style of their delivery, they were distinguished in simplicity, lacking any formal verbiage that would distract from a purity of message (nineteenth-century engraving of an earlier Puritan preacher at work).

70. *A Platform of Church Discipline*, p. 32.
71. Ibid.
72. Ibid.
73. Ibid.
74. Ibid., p. 33.
75. Ibid., p. 30.
76. Ibid.
77. Ibid.
78. Mather, *Essays To Do Good*, p. 72.

this, you will observe their condition, their faults, their snares, and their griefs; that you may "speak a word in season."[79]

In the seventeenth century, Richard Baxter spoke frankly to his fellow shepherds as the *"Ministers of the Gospel"*[80] of Christ's flock. The pastor's foremost duty was to preach Jesus Christ, and it was incumbent upon him to safeguard against preaching either for himself or that which the people would like to hear:

> *God forbid that you should spend a weeks study to please the people, or to seek the advancement of your own reputations. Dare you appear on the Pulpit on such a business, and speak of yourselves, when you are sent and pretend to speak for Christ?*[81]

Nearly a century later, Newberry, Massachusetts Pastor Thomas Barnard similarly preached at a pastoral ordination service of the kind of humility fitting that revered Christian office, and warned of the grave and humbling responsibility that ought to accompany the regular preaching of Christ's sovereign Words:

> *You preach not yourselves but Jesus Christ, Lord. From him you gain every Principle of the Faith you instruct your people in, every Rule of Life you advise them to, and every Foundation of hope you encourage them to rely on. – You teach Men the Way to Virtue and Happiness, not after our own Imaginations or any humane Scheme, but by the Laws and Directions of him, who shutteth and no man openeth.*[82]

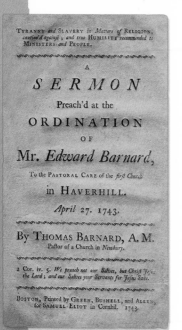

Thomas Barnard's 1743 pastoral *Ordination Sermon* (preached to Edward Barnard) recommended 2 Corinthians 4:5 on its title page: *"We preach not our Selves, but Christ Jesus the Lord; and our Selves your Servants for Jesus Sake."*

The office of pastor, minister, or shepherd was to bring, admonish, and exhort the covenant assembly in the Words and will of God. The role of the teacher in the assembly was one less of exhortation, but more of direct instruction to the disciples of Christ. Cotton Mather thus described the office of teacher: *"their employment was to explain and defend the principles of the christian religion, unto all whom they could be concerned."*[83] The teacher had the primary roll of catechizing believers in the Christian faith as well as in the duties incumbent upon all those in the church: *"here was the catechist, with reference unto whom the apostle says: Let the catechised communicate unto him in all good things."*[84] As notable tokens of their humility, many early New England pastors, such as the prolific author, preacher, missionary, and Bible translator John Eliot, preferred the title of teacher over that of a pastor or preacher. Still, other men of exceptional service and sound doctrine were also described by Mather as *"teaching elders."*[85] In that office, they would assist the pastor *"to administer the seals of that covenant, unto the dispensation whereof they are the alike called."*[86]

79. Ibid., p. 75.
80. Baxter, *The Saints Everlasting Rest*, part 3, p. 319.
81. Ibid.
82. Thomas Barnard, *Tyranny and Slavery in Matters of Religion, caution'd against; and true Humility recommended to Ministers and People. A Sermon ...* (Boston, 1743), p. 27.
83. Cotton Mather, *Magnalia Christi Americana*, vol. 1 (Hartford, 1820), p. 497.
84. Ibid., p. 498.
85. Ibid., p. 497.
86. *A Platform of Church Discipline*, p. 30.

The Church and the Family

Cotton Mather also described the labors of Thomas Shepard, who in 1635 became the pastor and teacher of an infant Massachusetts town, *"taking his station in Cambridge, with several of his good people, did on the ensuing February, ... with a declaration of what regenerating impressions the grace of God had made upon them; and then they entered into a covenant and became a church."*[87] Retold from the words of Shepard's diary, Mather noted Shepard's personal laments and his spiritual preparations for a day of fasting (circa mid-1640's):

> *May not I be the cause of the church's sorrows, which are renewed upon us? ... The people committed to me: they are not pitied so much nor prayed for, nor visited, as ought to have been; nor have I shewed so much love unto them. The family, I have not edified nor instructed, nor taken all occasions of speech with them.*[88]

Thus was the intertwined character of the local church with the local family in the colonial societies of New England. The family was to be a support of the covenant assembly as the church and pastor were to be the strongest supports of the covenant family. The family and church were designed to societally work together for their mutual support and thereby together for the greater work of God in the community at large. The local covenanted body of families was to regularly worship and fellowship together as one congregation. That involved the essential principle that those of families remained as families in the church. The assembly was not to be divided into disjointed individuals. The church was composed of many people of whom some might be single adults, but it would not split the family, neither segregate the children from parents, nor form arbitrary groupings of peoples that the ministry might find more convenient.[89] To do so would be to work for its own ultimate harm.

According to the eighteenth-century southern colonial Presbyterian Samuel Davies, churches were to respect and honor God's foremost institution, as families themselves *"are the materials of which they are composed; and as churches and kingdoms are formed out of families, they will be such as the materials of which they consist."*[90] The Sabbath was a day of family rest and a time of togetherness from the long week's labors that too often drew the family members apart. The families therefore attended divine services together and sat together, all with an obligation to listen attentively to the

Cotton Mather's *Magnalia Christi Americana: or, the Ecclesiastical History of New-England* (1702) was the most complete church history published during America's colonial era. It represented a voluminous composite of the various church plantings of New England and detailed the *"Wonderful Providences"* of God that secured and preserved them. Through *Magnalia Christi*, Americans were intended never to forget the marvelous events and noble lives that originally established covenanted churches on their continent.

---

87. Mather, *Magnalia Christi Americana*, vol. 1, p. 348.
88. Ibid., p. 356.
89. Such arbitrary groupings could include segregation by: age, marital status, life-situation, spiritual maturity, etc.
90. Samuel Davies, *Sermons on Important Subjects*, vol. 2 (Philadelphia, 1794), p. 61.

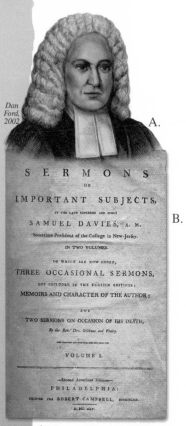

A.

B.

Dan Ford, 2002

A. Samuel Davies (1723-1761) was a Presbyterian minister who won acclaim as a Reformed orator in the southern colonies.

B. His collected *Sermons on Important Subjects* ranged from private piety to public patriotism (title page of the 1794 edition).

C.

C. Puritan sermons were delivered before entire families, and attentively listened to by the fathers who would then teach them to his loved ones (woodcut from the title page of Thomas Young's book on Sabbath practices, 1639).

expounded Words of God. All would hear the same message that could, should, and often would be later discussed around the table at home. Davies likewise reminded the heads of families: *"You find David returning home from the solemnities of public worship to bless his house 2 Sam. v. 20."*[91] In line with the precedent of the ancient Hebrew home, Davies also admonished the heads of Christian families to explain the nature of such public worship to their loved ones:

> *And must not parents now be under superior obligations, to inform their children of the more glorious doctrines and ordinances of the gospel?*[92]

By worshipping together as families in the assembly, the whole family would together hear God's Oracles preached from the pulpit. And, according to God's charge to the husband and father, he had a "relative" obligation to interpret and apply the sermon to the domestic needs of the home. The father would expound again upon the message with his family to domestically render that which they all had publicly heard. Davies thus reminded fathers of the principle behind their duty: *"Their souls, Sirs, their immortal souls are entrusted to your care."*[93]

A man was therefore obliged to be very attentive to the delicate art of hearing a sermon. Over a century before Davies, William Perkins had warned the man to *"Take heede how ye heare,"* for according to him, true hearing was to have both *"a Right disposition in hearing, and duties to be practiced afterward."*[94] To the Puritans, there was sufficient self-examination and preparation required before attending the sermon. These involved laying aside *"all corruptions both of heart and life"* and lifting *"up our hearts in prayer to God, that he would give us the Hearing eare."*[95] He then explained such duties *"to be performed after hearing, are these:"*[96]

> *First, the doctrine delivered, must be treasured up in the heart, and practiced in life, Psa. 119. 11 ... . Secondly, a man must meditate on the Word which he hath heard, with lifting up his heart unto God. Lev. 11. ... Thirdly, he must have experience of the Word of God in himselfe, Psal. 34.8. ... Fourthly, he is to examine himselfe after he hath heard the Word. ... Psal. 119. 5. ... Fifthly, he must be obedient to it, and testifiie his obedience, yet not at all times, yet whensoever occasion is offered, Jam. 1.22. Be ye doers of the Word, and not hearers only ... .*[97]

91. Ibid., p. 72.
92. Ibid., p. 277.
93. Ibid., p. 69.
94. Perkins, *The Whole Treatise of the Cases of Conscience*, p. 170.
95. Ibid., p. 171.
96. Ibid.
97. Ibid., pp. 173-174.

The sermon was both grist for the mind and meat for the soul. Accordingly, all of the diligent labor of the preacher's preparation would not go for naught, nor slip through the cracks of the mind as if the sermon was merely entertainment, nor would it be quickly forgotten when rearticulated by the father down into the sweetest milk for his most tender babes. Here the church would be of great service toward its families. The sermon was given to propound God's Word, and when orated truthfully and publicly, would not fall to the ground without accomplishing the Sovereign's purpose.[98]

Another service of the church was the brotherly visits of the pastor to the various homes of its members. Cotton Mather advised *"taking one afternoon in a week for the purpose."*[99] The purpose was to *"not only do good, but also get good, by your conversation with all sorts of persons, in thus visiting them 'from house to house.' "*[100] He saw such visits as helping the families build character and godly order in the home, in encouraging parents *"to maintain family-prayer,"* in adding reminders to *"care of instructing their children and servants in the holy religion of our Savior,"*[101] and in asking the *"younger people"*[102] to read from the Scriptures and then explain what they had read. In addition, Mather suggested that the pastor might provide families with tracts or small volumes to read, explaining that an *"incredible deal of good may be done, by distributing little books of piety."*[103] As a Puritan, he saw the encouragement of familial reading as essential to good counsel and saw the pastor as a chief agent toward that end. Pastoral duty called for directing families to regularly read God's Word for themselves and also in recommending a wide variety of additional volumes which could further assist them in their particular circumstances:

The pastor was often the chief outside counsel to the families of a church. He would not only advise them corporately from a public pulpit, but come to greet them privately and discreetly in their homes. It was there that he could best get to know those whom he was to pray for and shepherd, and it was there he could offer them individual assistance or even frank advice for daily living. Shown here is a nineteenth-century engraving of a preacher talking privately, man-to-man, in a home.

> *... books for all persons and circumstance: books for the old and for the young – for persons under afflictions or desertions – for persons who are under the power of particular vices – for those who neglect domestic religion – for sea faring persons ... By good books a salt of piety is scattered about a neighborhood.*[104]

Mather especially advised a pastor that he visit the poor as well as the rich, not only to bring his own alms to the needy, but to also *"mention the condition of the poor in your conversation with the rich."*[105] In all, Mather could speak from experience that a pastoral shepherd *"will seldom leave a family without having observed many tears of devotion shed by all sorts of persons in it."*[106]

98. See Isaiah 55:11.
99. Mather, *Essays To Do Good*, p. 79.
100. Ibid., p. 80.
101. Ibid., p. 78.
102. Ibid., p. 80.
103. Ibid.
104. Ibid.
105. Ibid.
106. Ibid., p. 79.

Church Doctrine and Worship

Sound doctrine was always to remain at the heart of every good Reformed assembly. John Robinson wrote from Holland to his (soon departing) congregation who had returned to England to make preparations for their immigration to America in 1620. As their most recent pastor, he sent with them a warning to take more care regarding what they would build upon their doctrinal foundation than the care they might take in framing their homes:

> And as men are carfull not to have a new house shaken with any violence before it be well setled & ye parts firmly knite, so be you, I beseech you, brethren, much more carfull, yt [that] the house of God which you are, and are to be, be not shaken with unnecessarie novelties or other oppositions at ye first setling therof.[107]

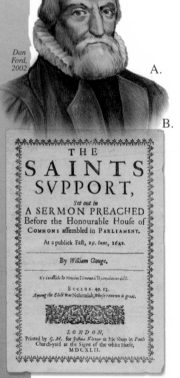

Dan Ford, 2002

A.

B.

THE
SAINTS
SVPPORT,
Set out in
A SERMON PREACHED
Before the Honourable House of
COMMONS assembled in PARLIAMENT.

At a publick Fast, 29. *June*, 1642.

By *William Gouge*.

Ει ενκάλκσ δε Νηφαλει ἐ ἐνεντα Τὸ μνμελεσσο ἀΰτ.

ECCLUS. 49. 13.
Among the Elect was Nehemiah, whose renown is great.

LONDON,
Printed by *G.M.* for *Joshua Kirton* at his Shop in *Pauls* Church-yard at the Signe of the white Horse, MDCXLII.

A. William Gouge (1578-1653) was a highly prolific Puritan author and scholar. As a leading member of the Westminster Assembly, he was a strong advocate of the Presbyterian form of church government.

B. Title page of Gouge's sermon, *The Saints Support*, in which he put forth many essential doctrines of public faith (1642).

The reformers indeed strove to build the strength of their churches on strong doctrine. There were many great and essential doctrines of the Christian faith, but central to them all were those of God's own Being. Without a right understanding of who God is, there could be no right understanding of faith, worship, or the covenant, because without knowing the proper object of faith, worship, and covenant, all other truths vanish into irrelevancy. Like all Puritans, the stalwart William Gouge saw God's central Being portrayed in the doctrine of *"The Trinity in Unity."*[108] He saw that knowledge of the covenantal relation between the Persons of the Father, the Son, and the Holy Spirit was essential to the believer's understanding of his own interactions with God: *"... we know and beleeve that the Spirit which proceedeth from the Father and Son, and helpeth our infirmities, enableth us to doe the will of God and establish us against all assaults."*[109]

To Puritan ministers, maintaining God's truth was mandatory to the shepherding of every congregation, for without a well-defined understanding of the "relative" nature of God with His people, the society of saints was ill equipped for the rigors of the covenant life. John Bunyan added that pastors should be constantly feeding upon the essential truths of biblical faith and doctrine, and then feeding them to Christ's congregation: *"Thus Paul tells Timothy, that if he put the brethren in mind of the truths of the Gospel, he himself should not only be a good Minister of Christ, but should be nourished up in the Words of Faith and of good Doctrine. I Tim, 4. 6."*[110] Christ's command to worship God in both *"spirit and truth"* (John 4:24) included an undeniable mandate that His body of believers have a thorough understanding of the biblical doctrines of their faith.[111]

107. John Robinson's letter, as quoted in William Bradford, *History of Plymouth Plantation* (Boston: Little, Brown, and Co., 1856), p. 66.
108. William Gouge, *The Saints Support, Set out in A Sermon* ... (London, 1642), p. 9.
109. Ibid.
110. John Bunyan, *The Works*, vol. 1, p. 438, on *Christian Behaviour*.
111. See Titus 2:1.

Complete worship was thus multitasked and multipurposed, but limited to God's specific directives in its practice. The *Westminster Confession of Faith* observed: *"The acceptable way of worshiping God, is instituted by Himselfe, and so limited to his revealed Will, that he may not be worshipped according to the imaginations and devices of men, or the Suggestions of the Satan ... ."*[112] To the Reformed, the way to know the difference between true worship and idolatry was not only to recognize its correct object, but also its genuine, biblical means of practice. The *Confession* thereby summarized the *"parts"* of true worship as:

> *Prayer, with Thanksgiving, ... The reading of the Scriptures with godly fear, the Profound Preaching, and conscientious hearing of the word, in obedience unto God, with understanding, faith, and reverence; singing of Psalms with grace in the heart; also the due administration, and worthy receiving of Sacraments instituted by Christ;... .*[113]

The Puritans recognized that worshipping God involved unified hearts as well as corporate minds. Bunyan noted the Bible's admonition: *"... we are exhorted, by one Spirit, with one Mind, to Strive together for the faith of the Gospel, Phil. 1.27."*[114] He also noted that the assembly's worship was much more than common corporal activity: *"the Mystical Body of Christ holds an Analogy with the natural Body of Man: As first, In the natural Body there must be a Spirit to animate it."*[115] With God Himself being a Spirit, His Church was to relate to Him on His spiritual terms. His Spirit was to be that which motivated true worship, therefore the meaningful corporate worship of God was neither to be reduced to the dry, priestly performances described in the Anglican *Constitutions*, nor to be expanded by innovative modes of human expression, as if church music was performed for the assembly as full-blown entertainment upon a stage. The reformers decried both. New England's Thomas Barnard asked concerning the dry, ritualistic Anglican modes imposed by the king: *"Can we receive Laws and Constitutions for the Worship of God, from any Man without placing him in God's Stead, and being guilty of Idolatry?"*[116] Similarly, William Perkins preached against novel, entertaining *"recreations"* being used in worship: *"Recreations may not be in the use of holy things; that is, in the use of the Word, Sacraments, prayer, or in any act of Religion."*[117] Thus, the Puritan assemblies owed their worship to a worthy Lord who was ascended much higher than the whims of men and popular modes of the day. The Puritan congregations therefore exercised their corporate hearts as directed by God's Word, and conducted their spiritual worship together in harmonious accord with its text:

> *And let the peace of God rule in your hearts, to the which also ye are called in one body: and be ye thankfull. Let the word of Christ dwell in you richly in all wisdom, teaching and admonishing one another in psalms and hymns, and spirituall songs, singing with grace in your hearts to the Lord* (Colossians 3:15-16).

---

112. *Westminster Confession of Faith*, pp. 67-68, *"Of Religious Worship, and the Sabbath Day."*
113. *Westminster Confession of Faith*, pp. 68-70.
114. John Bunyan, *The Works*, vol. 2: *An Exhortation to Peace and Unity* (London, 1737), p. 825.
115. Ibid.
116. Barnard, *Tyranny and Slavery in Matters of Religion, caution'd against*, p. 19.
117. Perkins, *The Whole Treatise of the Cases of Conscience*, p. 343.

Supports of the Commonwealth

The local Puritan churches were societies in which their members pledged themselves together to obey the Word of God, and they were designed by God to work harmoniously alongside both the family and the commonwealth. In New England, covenants were the societal underpinning of all three – each self-governed by their members, each with mutually "relative" purposes under God. Each had its own distinct spheres of delegated authority that worked with the others to restrain the intrusive power of either of the other societal spheres. The societal realm of the church was not only highly respected by, but considered essential to, the success of the family and civil governments. And, each being covenantal in nature, the church worked harmoniously with the community at large in a common purpose to effect safety, stability, and the godly virtue of overall New England society. By cooperatively appreciating such multisphered and interdependent self-governments, New England achieved an extraordinary degree of overall societal cohesion. Thus, as early as 1636, Boston's preacher John Cotton could write to his Puritan friend Lord Say and Seal back in the motherland, of the reasons for his confidence that New England would preserve its overall liberties:

> *Purity, preserved in the church, will preserve well ordered liberty in the people, and both of them establish well-ballanced authority in the magistrates. God is the author of all these three, and neyther is himselfe the God of confusion, nor are his wayes of confusion, but of peace.*[118]

Cotton had therein related the foremost principles that defined the "New England Way." The earliest churches of Connecticut were similarly described by the later eighteenth-century historian Benjamin Trumble as cooperative and cohesive with their civil governments: *"The most perfect harmony subsisted between the legislature and the clergy."*[119] The historian Trumble went on to record the deep respect that still existed between the church and the state, as Connecticut's various civil administrations had always made full use of the clergy, who were often the most educated members of their communities and their greatest pillars of support: *"In no government have the clergy had more influence, or been treated with more generosity and respect, by the civil rulers and people in general, than in Connecticut."*[120]

New England's legacy of multisphered covenantal cooperation was consequently adopted as the typical model for the societal role of American churches amid their civil communities. The churches' principles of virtue and self-government provided the learned examples for the wider civil establishments and planted the unique character of Christian liberty within the American societal fabric. That

The centerpieces of New England towns were their churches, as steeples once commonly adorned the American skyline (early nineteenth-century engraving of a typical New England skyline).

118. John Cotton, from Appendix 3 in *The History of the Colony of Massachusetts Bay. From the First Settlement Thereof in 1628, until its Incorporation with the Colony of Plimouth, Province of Main, &c.*, by Thomas Hutchinson (London, 1765), p. 500.
119. Benjamin Trumble, *A Complete History of Connecticut, Civil and Ecclesiastical, from the Emigration of its first Planters from England...* (Hartford, 1797), pp. 301-302.
120. Ibid.

which originally typified the Puritan understanding of societal virtue had become embedded in the very American idea of liberty. Over a century after Cotton, another Massachusetts preacher, Ebenezer Bridge, spoke before the Governor, Council, and House of Representatives of his continuing gratitude for the long and historic cooperation of *"patriotic ministers"* with their *"counsellors and statesmen"*:

> *How happy our nation also, in having in her some raised up by God from time to time, and by divine providence put in places of the greatest importance, who have proved true to her liberties and interests – As, patriotic ministers, noble counsellors and statesmen.*[121]

A.

The societal role of the church was defined as being patriotic in that it promoted the interests of godliness in the general commonwealth. But, the church was not to be blindly patriotic to every whim of civil inventiveness or be blindly partisan toward nationalistic pride at the expense of God's specific virtues. There were far too many calls for repentance, fasting, and prayer within American churches in the colonial and early federal period to countenance the ill-defined theme of "God *Bless* America" to national patriotism.[122] The Puritan-influenced churches tended rather toward propagating the more urgent and humble "God *Save* America" theme. The colonial and early state governments overwhelmingly agreed. For example, in early 1776, Massachusetts heartily thanked its churches for the service they provided to the overall stability of its colonial government at a time when it was under suppression from Britain:

B.

> *And, as the ministers of the Gospel, within this Colony have during the late Relaxation of the Powers of Civil Government, exerted themselves for our Safety, it is hereby recommended to them, still to continue their virtuous labours for the Good of the People, inculcating by their public Ministry, and private Example, the Necessity of Religion, Morality, and Good Order.*
>
> *In Council January 19. 1776. ...*
>
> *GOD Save the PEOPLE.*[123]

A. The typical, late eighteenth-century proclamation for public fasting and prayer urged local churches to pray for the good of their state and the entire nation. This 1799 state proclamation concluded: *"God Save the Commonwealth of Massachusetts!"*

B. This broadside, issued just before America's independence, appealed for churches to help maintain civil order. In contrast to royal proclamations which ended *"God save the King,"* this was the first use of an appeal, *"GOD Save the PEOPLE"* (January 1776).

121. Ebenezer Bridge, *A Sermon Preached before His Excellency Francis Bernard, Esq.; Governor, His Honor Thomas Hutchinson, Esq. Lieutenant Governor, The Honorable His Majesty's Council, and the Honorable House of Representatives, of the Province of Massachusetts-Bay in New England ...* (Boston, 1767), p. 40.
122. See 1799 Commonwealth of Massachusetts, Broadside for *Fasting, Humiliation & Prayer* (Boston, 1799), for *"God Save the Commonwealth of Massachusetts!"*
123. The Great and General Court of the Colony of Massachusetts-Bay, *A Proclamation*, Broadside ([n.p.], January 1776).

Josiah Whitney likewise preached of necessary multisphered cooperation before the Connecticut Governor, Council, and House of Representatives at the time that the various states were debating the adoption of their Federal Constitution in 1788: " ... *when the clergy, and that religion that they faithfully preach, have been most honoured, and respected by a nation, then things went best among them, and they were most honoured, and respected by nations around them.*"[124] Whitney also warned his statesmen: "*The best preaching will ordinarily be but to little purpose, if rulers in general by their practice say the fear of the Lord is not before our eyes.*"[125] The church could only lend genuine support to the commonwealth when it remained as God's true standard-bearer. Whitney thus went on to preach of the endemic godly character of their state, its governance, and the resulting blessings when godly truth was recognized: "*The joys of HEAVEN, consist not in epicurean indolence, nor in stoic apathy, nor in enthusiastic raptures, nor in the sensual gratification of the Koran – But in conformity to the image of God – doing his will, and enjoying him.*"[126] The supportive role of the Connecticut churches toward the civil establishments (as they had existed from the first days of their settlements) remained infused in the state long after the federal period ensued among the United States.

Just as it had as an infant English colony, Connecticut had always relied on the essential support of its clergy and churches. It would not be surprising, then, that in 1792, the state government appointed a committee of ministers, including Dr. Jonathan Edwards, Jr., to send missionaries into its northwestern regions to establish towns to assist in civilizing the native Indians. After initiating several remarkable missions, the committee reported back to the state the following year:

> *What a glorious service must it be, to plant regular churches and ministers, to promote christian morals and diffuse the blessings of literature, civilization, regular society and undefiled religion, in the initial settlements throughout such extensive countries. ... We are taught without ceasing "Thy kingdom come." but who, with any sincerity or consistency, can make that prayer, while he neglects the means and opportunities of advancing that kingdom.*[127]

Dr. Edwards understood the inseparable and reciprocal link between the role of the church and that of the civil governments in order to secure the general blessings of both liberty and prosperity. In an Election Sermon the following year (1794) before the Governor, Council, and Representatives of the state, Edwards spoke on behalf of the Connecticut "*Pastors of churches*" in saying, "*We are deeply interested in the prosperity*

A
NARRATIVE
OF THE
MISSIONS
TO THE
NEW SETTLEMENTS
ACCORDING TO THE APPOINTMENT
OF THE
GENERAL ASSOCIATION
OF THE
STATE OF CONNECTICUT:
TOGETHER WITH
AN ACCOUNT
OF THE
RECEIPTS AND EXPENDITURES
OF
THE MONEY CONTRIBUTED BY THE
PEOPLE OF CONNECTICUT,
IN MAY, 1793,
FOR THE SUPPORT OF THE MISSIONARIES,
ACCORDING TO AN ACT OF THE GENERAL ASSEMBLY OF THE STATE.

NEW-HAVEN—PRINTED BY T. & S. GREEN. 1794.

The civil government of Connecticut encouraged churches to evangelize its northwestern borders. There was no surer way to bring civility to its frontiers than to promote (though not officially establish) the Christian faith, so like the earlier Puritan missions, funding was provided by freewill offerings from state residents (title page of the 1794 Connecticut report on frontier missions).

124. Josiah Whitney, *The Essential requisites to form the good Ruler's Character, illustrated and urged* (Hartford, 1788), p. 32.
125. Ibid., p. 31.
126. Ibid., p. 39.
127. General Assembly of the State of Connecticut, *A Narrative of the Missions to the New Settlements According to the Appointment of the General Association of the State of Connecticut ...* (New Haven, [Connecticut], 1794), p. 16.

of the state, ... It is our business to study and teach christianity, and thus to promote the political good of the state as well as the spiritual good of the souls of our hearers."[128] He therefore concluded with a "co-relative" covenantal mandate of the church and state to his magistrates: *"But if you and the good people of the state in general will unite to practice virtue and christianity, and promote the wisest and best men among us, we shall doubtless be that happy people described in the text* [quoting Psalm 144:15]. *"*[129]

There was wide continuity throughout the earlier, virtuous years of America's colonial and early federal periods. God's basic societal institutions were not only respected but relied upon by the civil societies in order to maintain overall virtue and thereby preserve the people's God-given liberties. As God's standard bearer, the societal role of the church was thus ordained for the good of the state, and the civic role of Christianity (as embodied in the local church) was, at the time, undeniable. The earlier Puritans saw that the church was ordained not to compete with either the role of the family nor of the commonwealth, but to interact with them both for the mutual benefit of each, as the local churches were instituted for both the salvation of souls and effecting Christ-like service and support to the general community.

THE CHURCH ESSENTIAL TO THE REPUBLIC.

A

SERMON

IN BEHALF OF THE

AMERICAN HOME MISSIONARY SOCIETY.

PREACHED IN THE CITIES OF NEW-YORK AND BROOKLYN,

MAY, 1848.

BY

EDWARD NORRIS KIRK,

PASTOR OF THE MT. VERNON CHURCH, BOSTON,

NEW-YORK:

PRINTED FOR THE AMERICAN HOME MISSIONARY SOCIETY,

BY LEAVITT, TROW & CO., 49 ANN-ST.

1848.

Among numerous nineteenth-century sermons encouraging a very active cultural role for the church was Edward Kirk's *The Church Essential to the Republic*, which he preached before the American Home Missionary Society in 1848.

To the Reformed English and Americans, the covenant of the church was unlike any other, for though it represented Christ's citizenry at the gates of an eternal, heavenly Kingdom, its earthbound members were described as a body, a family, a society, and a kingdom. Covenanted saints were therefore considered as His hands, His sons, His members, and His subjects as long as they remained below. They were to uplift, encourage, and help one another as well as represent God, as living standard bearers to the world. Thus, they were not to be disjointed or detached from one another, but were called into common service to proclaim the inward message of God's grace and the outward moral consequence of His Laws.

Such multifaceted obligations necessitated a more intimate fellowship of saints with whom local believers were to be committed with one another on a regular and ongoing basis. In covenant assemblies there were to be ministers and administers such as preachers and teachers, and elders and deacons to faithfully conduct their worship of God and their fellow service among the community of saints. Activity within the assembly included preaching, praying, singing, and administering the sacraments. God's written Word was revered and employed to exhort, to edify, and to provoke the saints to faithful Christian action. So, outside the assembly, the members (thus exhorted, edified, and active) were to tend to the spiritual and physical needs among one another as well as to procure His standard within their every venue of life, whether at home or in service to the wider commonwealth. Thus, the final chapter of this book will consider the reformers' understanding of that wider obligation regarded as the Civil Covenant.

128. Jonathan Edwards [Jr.], Pastor of the Church in New-Haven, *The Necessity of the Belief in Christianity by the Citizens of the State, in order to our political Prosperity* (Hartford, [Connecticut], 1794), p. 44.
129. Ibid., pp. 46-47.

Book III   Historic Covenantal Living

Chapter 4: Civil Covenantal Living

Commonwealth Faith and Obedience under Grace and Biblical Law

HEN the men aboard the *Mayflower* put their names to their *"civill body politick,"*[1] they bound themselves together as an independent governing body. They were no longer merely a refugee Separatist church set adrift from the powerfully authoritative Anglican Establishment; they had set foot in America as a people – as a whole and united people – a commonwealth, covenanted together under God. Accordingly, just prior to their departure from England to America, their pastor, John Robinson, wrote them an appropriate letter with encouragement and advice:

> *... wheras you are become a body politik, using amongst your selves civill govermente, and are not furnished with any persons of spetiall eminencie above ye* [the] *rest, to be chosen by you into office of goverment, let your wisdome & godlines appeare... .*[2]

Robinson was aware that among those first inhabitants of a new Anglo-American colony, there would be no men of nobility or of worldly eminence. That would have been a disadvantage under the old English system, but prove most advantageous in America where there was no established system of royal supremacy. Robinson's advice was for them to resort back to the first principles of civil government, proposing a biblical foundation for their civil affairs. They had been born and raised under the English system of monarchs and lords, and they had lived for years under the more republican modes of government in Holland. Yet Robinson, in preparing his beloved with a few carefully chosen words, went back to the first principles of civil society – back to basic biblical covenantalism. He was able to point them to the fundamental precepts of the best governance, with a representative administration of delegated rule strictly covenantal in its character as accountable to both God and the people:

> *... let your wisdome & godlines appeare, not only in chusing shuch persons as doe entirely love and will promote ye commone good, but also in yeelding unto them all due honour & obedience in their lawfull administrations; not behoulding in them ye ordinarinesse of their persons, but Gods ordinance for your good, not being like ye foolish multitud who more honour ye gay coate, then either ye vertuous minde of ye man, or glorious ordinance of ye Lord. But you know better things, & that ye image of ye Lords power & authoritie which ye magistrate beareth, is honourable, in how meane persons soever.*[3]

1. William Bradford, *History of Plymouth Plantation* (Boston, 1856), p. 90.
2. John Robinson's letter, as quoted in Bradford, *History of Plymouth Plantation*, p. 66.
3. Ibid., pp. 66-67.

Knowing the continuing mandate that rested on those who were departing for America, Robinson had prepared his beloved congregation to live in both a church and a civil estate. And, being Reformed, the terms of their civil covenant would follow similar lines of delegated authority as that of the church congregation. The Pilgrims knew that in both spheres, authority emanated from God to the people, through the people to their chosen rulers, and then from their entrusted rulers back to the general good of the entire body of people. That was the form of the ecclesiastical polity, or church government, that they saw modeled in the Bible, and that would be the form of civil polity, or general commonwealth, to be modeled on the same text.

A. John Robinson prayed over his beloved brethren as they bid him farewell at Delftshaven, Holland. The scene was movingly portrayed in this nineteenth-century memorial engraving.

The Pilgrims had been primed before their departure for America in the nature of their undertaking. They were well aware of the purview of God over their entire adventure; they were well aware of the godly responsibility of their New Plymouth magistrates; and they were well aware of the only sure source for their civil laws. Being English, they had lived for years as refugee families in a covenanted congregation in Holland, and landing in America they bound themselves under a wider, civil oath for the mutual good of a new English commonwealth. They (and all who would join them) were no longer limited to the Christian obligations of their church orientation, but were thereafter also obliged in their Christian obligations of their wider estate. Their civic, or "commonwealth," affairs were therefore covenanted under a more general, but nonetheless, equally binding commitment to each other, beginning with the historic words *"In ye name of God, Amen."*[4]

... Haveing undertaken, for ye glorie of God, and advancemente of ye Christian faith, and honour of our king & countrie, a voyage to plant ye first colonie in ye Northerne parts of Virginia, doe by these presents solemnly & mutualy in ye presence of God, and one of another, covenant & combine our selves togeather into a civill body politick, for our better ordering & preservation & furtherance of ye ends aforesaid; and by vertue hearof to enacte, constitute, and frame such just & equall lawes, ordinances, acts, constitutions, & offices, from time to time, as shall be thought most meete & convenient for ye generall good of ye Colonie, ...[5]

B. The *Mayflower Compact* was the first covenanted agreement for civil self-government in America. It was signed by the 41 male adults on the *Mayflower* in November 1620, just prior to a scouting party disembarking to locate the first permanent English settlement in New England. This manuscript of the covenant (minus signatures) was redrawn from the copy in Governor Bradford's account of Plymouth's founding.

4. Bradford, *Plymouth Plantation*, p. 89.
5. Ibid., pp. 89-90.

That covenantal model would become the established civil mode for them as well as for droves of later Puritan settlers over the following decades. The model would thus become a fixture of the typical American way of thinking about civil affairs. The following decade, when Boston preacher John Cotton wrote back to Lord Say and Seal in England in 1636 to commend the "New England Way," he not only spoke of the essential role of godly virtues in individuals and church congregations, but also the indispensable necessity of godly virtues in their overall commonwealth. In describing the godly ways of his infant town of Boston to a Puritan brother back in England, Cotton left no doubt as to the single source of all civil virtue:

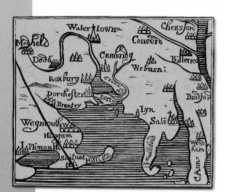

The seats of America's first two 'Bible Commonwealths' were Plymouth and Massachusetts Bay. This 1667 map shows a significant number of local settlements which, by then, composed those two original Puritan colonies. (North was oriented to the right.)

It is very suitable to God's all-sufficient wisdom, and to the fulnes and perfection of Holy Scriptures, not only to prescribe perfect rules for the right ordering of a private man's soule to every blessednes with himselfe, but also for the right ordering of a mans family, yea, of commonwealth too.[6]

With the Scriptures acknowledged as the highest source of their laws, and the covenantal model as the frame of their governments, New England found itself – or rather, was intentionally founded – upon the most noble foundation that they could establish. New England was not a utopian dream, but a living reality. They had the Sourcebook of all virtuous Law and a multitude of Reformed commentaries, as well as a solid civil frame for a remarkable kind of liberty suited for a devoutly covenantal people.

The Covenantal Civil Body Politic

As with any covenantal society, the civil society was seen as a body of members. But, unlike the more specifically-defined societies of the family or the church, the civil society pertained to all men in a common community, as in Plymouth's *"civill body politick."* Thus, all things civil pertained to the general or common population of a given region or realm, and terms such as *"civil rulers"* or *"civil liberties"* pertained to all sorts of freemen as fellow *"citizens"* of a given community or commonwealth.[7]

A covenantal civil government would be one in which that community or commonwealth recognized and was committed to live obediently under the one true Sovereign who reigns over all civil affairs. Thus the English Puritan Richard Baxter described a *"Commonwealth properly"* as a *"society of God's Subjects ordered into Relations of Sovereign and Subjects for their common good, and*

6. John Cotton, from Appendix 3 in *The History of the Colony of Massachusetts Bay* by Thomas Hutchinson, p. 497.
7. Webster, *American Dictionary of the English Language*, vol. 1 (1828), for "civil," definition 2 as an adjective.

pleasing to God as their Absolute Sovereign."[8] As to the *"form"* of a commonwealth, the Reformed Baxter also called it a *"civil body politic,"* and the two principals or "relatives" within the body were the rulers and the ruled, or as Baxter put it: *"The subject matter* [commonwealth] *is a civil body, or Community of God's subjects: The relate and the Correlate are the Sovereign* [the rulers] *and the Subjects* [those ruled].*"*[9] He concluded that for any legitimate civil body to exist, there had to be representative authority and subjection to that authority. In order for there to be civil order, there had to be delegated sovereignty in the voice of the ruler and consensual subjection by the ruled: *"Where there is no Subject there is no Sovereign ... the Relate cannot be without its Correlate."*[10] The rulers were therefore vested only with authority accountable to the people and granted only with a limited sovereignty over them. So, to the Puritans, a pure democracy would be a *"falsehood,"*[11] because if all the people ruled among one another equally, the government would be without a "co-relative" order and lack the necessary distinction between the rulers and those who were ruled.

God provided rulers with His Sacred Word, *"Biblia Sacra,"* for the reformation of civil government, as was depicted in this seventeenth-century woodcut, *"Senatus,"* of a Puritan-packed English Parliament (1642).

With the principle of hierarchical rule within a civil body being established, the Puritans saw that all such rule was necessarily covenantal in nature, meaning that every representative governor was obliged to both God and those he served. Baxter again noted: *"No King* [or ruler] *hath any power, but what is for God and the common good."*[12] Being vested with authority originating from God, the rulers were obliged to rule for the good of the whole civil body and work to protect and defend all the people in common. In every true commonwealth then, the rulers (as subjects of God) were bound within their stations for the good of the whole, and the people (as subjects of God) were bound within their stations for the good of the whole. Baxter concluded: *"Every subject is by nature and Relation, bound to preserve the Commonwealth in his place, as well as the King* [or ruler]*; and no one can be instruments against it."*[13]

The Reformed English therefore considered all *"rights"*[14] as specific liberties and obligations that distinguished the various parties in the commonwealth. God alone retained the only absolute right over the civil body politic. He alone could intervene, according to His sovereign purpose at any level of authority or any place or time, to prosper or punish, to enact or judicate His highest executive will. The rulers were then given certain rights (as specific liberties and obligations) by which they were distinctly accountable to Him according to their "relative" charge to the people. And, the people had other distinct rights (as specific liberties and obligations) according to their "relative" submission to God and the ordinances of their rulers. Thus, a covenantal agreement between the two

8. Richard Baxter, *A Holy Commonwealth, or Political Aphorisms, ...* (London, 1659), p. 59.
9. Ibid., p. 61.
10. Ibid., p. 64.
11. Ibid., p. 63.
12. Ibid., p. 419.
13. Ibid.
14. Ibid., p. 429.

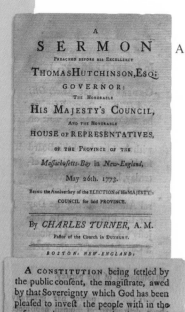

A.

B.

A. Colonial election sermons addressed essential principles of biblical civil government to magistrates (title page, 1773).

B. Preached to the colonial government of Massachusetts just prior to its hostilities with Britain, Charles Turner's 1773 sermon included the covenantal principle of a constitutional government by consent under God's sovereignty.

C.

C. Turner's election sermon was based upon the familiar passage of Romans 13:4, which he said indicated that a colonial magistrate was a civil *"Minister of God."* The magistrates were therefore obliged to defend the God-given rights of the people (opening page of sermon).

earthly parties (the rulers and the ruled) was necessary to spell out the full extent of the various rights between them. That agreement, in either the form of a written document and/or a verbal agreement, became the covenant of the civil body under God. Such agreements as *"fundamental Constitutions,"*[15] had as their chief object the protection and defense of the rights granted by God's revealed Word, as well as all those 'rightfully' contracted between them. The fundamental end (or purpose) of the civil government was thus to secure and defend those rights. The body of people also had a like charge to be diligent and hold their public officials accountable. Therefore Baxter wrote:

> If in the fundamental Constitutions, any rights by contract be received to the people, and the King obliged to maintain them, the people may lawfully defend those Rights, (proportional to their worth) against the king that violateth them.[16]

The Civil Ministers Unto Thee for Good

The Reformed concept of the covenantal civil society can be traced back well before the time of the Presbyterian Baxter or of the bold, independent-minded adventures of Robinson and Cotton in New England. To the earlier English and Scottish reformers, one of the most definitive biblical passages that spoke to the godly temper of civil governance was the Apostle Paul's admonishment in his Epistle to the Romans. It was known by way of numerous accounts of his public ministry and preaching of the Gospel, that Paul, as a Roman citizen, had been very astute of both the Roman legal system and the overall godly purpose of civil government.[17] Incorporating the citizens' and the subjects' duty to be obedient to the (civil) *"higher powers"* (Romans 13:1) with the obligation of the rulers to govern for the *"good"* of the people, Paul had concluded that the civil rulers were *"ministers of God to thee for good"* (Romans 13:4).

To a Christian of Paul's era, such words linking that fundamental principle of civil rule with that of the servant minister of God, would have had definitive covenantal implications. Paul's words certainly did – to the sixteenth-through eighteenth-century reformers! Paul, as a first-century Roman citizen, had certainly used his citizen rights to champion

15. Ibid.
16. Ibid.
17. See Paul's civil appeal before Felix: Acts 24:10-21; Paul's defense against being whipped: Acts 22:25; and Paul's civil appeal to Caesar: Acts 25:8-11.

the cause of Christ. The Christians of the sixteenth century who were being robbed of their chartered English rights by a brutally illegal regime saw that the roles of both the minister and the civil magistrate were definitively answerable to one and the same God. The Christians of the kingdoms of Scotland and England could then expect their earthly sovereigns to conform to the will of their avowed heavenly Lord. They indeed recognized a sharp distinction in the roles of the family, church, and civil estates under God, but there was always (and would always be) One and the same ultimate Sovereign at the helm of the family and church, as well as the great ship of state.

To those earliest reformers, all civil power was to be exercised for the good of the commonwealth. Alongside Paul's instructional passage of Romans 13:1: *"Let every soul be subject unto the higher powers. For there is no power but of God: the powers that be, are ordained of God,"* the reformers' beloved Geneva Bible commented in its margins:

> *Now he sheweth severally, what subjects owe to their magistrates, to wit, obedience: from which he sheweth that no man is free: and in such sort, that it is not only due to the highest magistrate himself, but also even to the basest, which hath any office under him.*[18]

To the reformers, government was binding upon all people of a commonwealth. The Geneva Bible's notation that *"no man is free"* meant that no man was free from the constraints of the various civil estates that God had placed over him. And, by Paul using the term *"higher powers"* (as Paul would have understood them to be in the Roman regime), it also pointed to multiple powers as the multilayered constitutional system of any well-ordered government. And further, as each ruler was called to be His minister for the good of the people, the reformers interpreted that fact as the means by which differing magistrates were charged by God to keep each other in check from becoming tyrannical. In his 1558 book, *The Appellation*, the Presbyterian reformer John Knox interpreted the *"higher powers"* as including the magistrates under the king: *"That all powers be God's Ministers, ordained for the weal, profit, and salvation of their subjects and not for their destruction."*[19]

Governments therefore consisted of both higher as well as lower orders of magisterial responsibilities: of local as well as more general offices, and of township and county magistrates, along with the more general civil councils. Both the subject and the citizen were therefore required to understand the jurisdiction of the various levels of office by which they could know their rightful obligations to the proper spheres of obedience on any particular matter. The local magistrate could not legislate the payment of a national tribute any

Like the Parliament which legislatively held the Crown's power in check, the lower, or local, magistrates also had their own "jurisdictions," or spheres, of authority upon which the national government was not to encroach. Provincial, county, or township governments not only conducted local affairs, but their very existence limited the encroaching ability of the higher authorities. Shown in this seventeenth-century engraving are English magistrates voting on local issues.

18. Geneva note on Romans 13:1, leaf Iii.
19. John Knox, *The Appellation of John Knox, From the cruell and most unjust Sentence pronounced against him, by the false Bishops and Clergie of Scotland: With his Supplication and Exhortation to the Nobility, States, and Communalty of the same Realme* (London, 1644), p. 11.

more than the crown could dictate the minute affairs of a lawfully incorporated township. To be obliged to the king in a case where obedience to the local magistrate was constitutionally ordained would be a breach of the citizen's biblical duty to *"Submit your selves to every ordinance of man"* (1 Peter 2:13). Local government had its constituted place, which no superior power but God Himself ought wrest from the local community, as Reformed Scottish Presbyterian Samuel Rutherford in the mid-seventeenth century noted in his work, *Lex, Rex*, that *"the resisting of the inferior Magistrate in his lawful Commandment, is the resisting of God's Ordinance, and a breach of the fifth Commandment, as is disobedience to parents."*[20] With each level of the various civil administrations called by God to be mutually duty-bound with the people, all rulers were constituted according to the same godly purpose to be *"ministers of God to thee for good."* Each magistrate existed with the same overriding purpose to ensure justice within his constituted sphere of authority, but each and every one had a civil, or common, ministerial purpose under God toward men.

The Power of the Sword

Beside the civil charge to promote the common good, the reformers saw that all rulers and magistrates had a charge to guard against the moral cancers that might infect and weaken the body of the commonwealth. According to John Knox, God gave civil government its purpose:

> *God the Supreme Lord and King of all the world, hath ordained civil magistrates to be under him over the people, for his own glory and the public good; and, to this end, hath armed them with the power of the sword, for the defense and encouragement of them that are good and for the punishment of evildoers.*[21]

To Knox, the civil covenant bound all inhabitants to submit to civil rule, but also required all civil rulers to submit to the charge to execute godly laws and justice. In speaking of the magistrates, he therefore wrote that *"... lawfull powers is given the Sword, for the punishment of malefactors, for the maintenance of innocents, and the profit and utility of the subjects."*[22] Rutherford, again, later pointed to the same Scriptures for the proper mandate: *"HE is but a minister of God, a revenger to execute wrath upon him that doeth evill."*[23] Rutherford described the purpose of the sharp edge of the civil sword. On the one

John Knox's *The Appellation ... to the Nobility ... of Scotland* (1559) was an appeal for God's civil rulers to take up the *"power of the sword"* in defending the nation against evildoers. He argued the point *"from the plain Word of God."** Shown here is the opening page of the 1644 edition. *Page 3.

20. Samuel Rutherford, *Lex, Rex: The Law and the Prince* (London, 1644), p. 162.
21. Knox, *The Appellation*, p. 11.
22. Ibid., p. 12.
23. Rutherford, *Lex, Rex*, p. 195.

hand, rulers had an unimpeachable duty to protect the civil society by executing judgment upon offenders, *"therefore the Law saith: He cannot pardon, and free the guilty, of the punishment due to him."*[24] For a ruler to condone moral offenses by ignoring moral repugnance was, itself, tyrannical – indicating his lack of respect for both God and the people he served. On the contrary, each and every ruler owed civil society his utmost moral protection, taking care not to *"draw the sword against the innocent."*[25] For a ruler to prosecute the innocent or persecute the godly was equally tyrannical – indicating his utter contempt for God and the people he was "relatively" charged to serve. Men were therefore not given power to oppress, punish, or prosecute the legally innocent, but as God's stewards they were strictly charged to punish the morally guilty. Magistrates and judges owed their civil power to both God and the people they were "relatively" charged to protect. Thus, to Rutherford, God's Will alone was supreme: *"and God only is essentially King. Ps. 97. 1. Ps. 99. 1. and all men in Relation to him, are meere ministers, servants, legates, deputies."*[26]

God therefore had "relatively" given civil governments the power to execute His judgment upon evildoers. But in giving that power, God granted it only for a purpose "relative" to His own judgments of good and evil. Magistrates were obliged to define civic good and evil accordingly. Richard Baxter (Rutherford's contemporary) also wrote that civil governors were obliged to rule by their *"duties of relation and society."*[27] Governments among men were therefore given a godly doctrine by which to ascribe societal laws that were in line with the will of their Maker, as Baxter put it: *"man is a creature and must be instructed by Doctrine and ruled by the use of Laws."*[28] To the Puritans, sound government was a matter of enacting, executing, and judicating godly morality, and good law was the passing and enforcing of God's standard for civil societies. As sound rule required higher judgment, so too, good law required higher Laws – and Baxter concluded with simple reason: *"if God have Laws, he will have judgment according to his Laws."*[29]

Knox had similarly proposed that the proper way for kings and magistrates to demonstrate their respect for the heavenly Sovereign was for them to enact and enforce His Laws. Knox asked his generation, *"How do Kings serve the Lord but in feare, but in punishing, and by a godly severity forbidding those things which are done against the Commandments of the Lord?"*[30] The

A. England's legal educators once defined good law as that which conformed to God's written Will. Shown here is the title page of the earliest English-language treatise on equity law, called *The dialoges in English, betwene Doctour of Divinitye, and a Student in the lawes of England* (1569 edition).

B. English Law itself began with the revealed *"lawe of God"* for *"the politicall rule of the people, the whiche bee called Judicials."*

C. The *"second ground"* of English Law was *"for punishement of them that offended against the lawe of God."*

24. Ibid.
25. Ibid.
26. Ibid.
27. Baxter, *A Holy Commonwealth*, pp. 14-15.
28. Ibid.
29. Ibid.
30. Knox, *The Appellation*, p. 11.

Westminster Assembly also acknowledged God's Laws as England's supreme standard, and that He "armed" England's magistrates (including Parliament) *"with the power of the sword, for the defense and encouragement of them that are good and for the punishment of evildoers."*[31] Consequently, with the Reformed understanding of the moral character of law, the offenses that were to be prohibited by New England's magistrates were, among others, *"idolatry and blasphemy"* as well as *"venting corrupt and pernicious opinions, that destroy the foundation* [of civil society].*"*[32]

Quiet and Peaceable Lives

Once the commonwealth was established with godly laws suited to a godly people, the people were not at liberty to live licentiously. Civil societies required the structure of constituted laws and an orderly commonwealth required uniform obedience to those laws. Only with godly laws and uniform submission to those laws, would the people enjoy their God-given liberty and freedom from any punitive or oppressive civil restraints. Only under such an establishment could people realize the necessary freedom to enjoy truly peaceable lives, as Paul had exhorted Timothy to pray:

> *I exhort therefore, first of all, supplications, prayers, intercessions, and giving of thanks, be made for all men; For kings, and for all that are in authority; that we may lead a quiet and peaceable life in all godliness and honesty* (1 Timothy 2:1-2).

England's courts were to be seats of authority where godly laws reigned supreme. Petitions could be brought before an appropriate court in order to obtain a remedy at law. Actions could be brought against individuals such as private persons and public officials, or brought against corporations such as companies or civil governments. According to biblical mandates, justices were to be impartial and nonprejudicial in all judgments. Shown in this sixteenth-century woodcut are plaintiffs (those bringing an action) and defendants (those accused), each arguing their case before the bench (seat of judgment) in an English court.

In Paul's exhortation to his fellow saints, he predicated the demeanor required for godly civility. Individuals were to live *"quiet and peaceable"* lives, praying for higher and lower magistrates as well as for governors, legislators, and judges, being *"all that are in authority."* Private individuals, then, ought not complain of the oppressions of their magistrates if they had not undertaken the duty to pray for them. And, under good civil governance, godly law reigned above all those in power, meaning that anyone genuinely grieved could petition through the courts to find their remedy at law according to equitable justice. Any legitimate offense between the government and the people could thereby find its cure in an appropriate court. On one hand, rulers were to take suspected lawbreakers to court to determine guilt before executing justice; on the other, private individuals could also sue the government for any legitimate grievance, or even sue against unjust laws, as Baxter noted:

31. *Westminster Confession of Faith*, p. 79.
32. *A Platform of Church Discipline*, p. 64.

If the Law be above the King [or rulers], *then may we do what the law alloweth, though against his will. If it allows us to sue the king in his courts of Justice, we may do it: If it allows us to sue his Agents, as subjects that have broken the Law, though be by his command, we may do it.*[33]

Consistent with Paul's statements on the nature of good government in both Romans 13 and 1 Timothy 2, and according to the Reformed understanding of the nature of godly laws such as those expressed by Richard Baxter, magistrates had a clear obligation before God to see that the people could indeed live quiet and peaceable lives. That placed a solemn charge at each and every magistrate's feet to respect and protect godly and obedient subjects or citizens. The magistrates themselves would be answerable to God if they did otherwise, because rulers of every rank had the same high charge to promote godliness and prevent harm from coming to the peaceable subjects, either from themselves or from one another.

The goal of Christian civility was to enable peaceable people to enjoy their God-given liberties; and with godliness reigning supreme, they could partake of life's quiet repose. Shown in this eighteenth-century engraving was a typical, quiet scene of peaceful civility.

Rulers were further charged to secure a level playing field for all people to safely procure peaceable lives in both private livelihoods and public commerce. There was no equitable place for a governor to meddle with private commerce other than to safely secure the equal status of all men and their companies under the law. To play favorites toward one individual, company, or corporation against any others would be a severe breach of justice and raise a standard of abject wickedness amid the privileged seats of civil authority. If rulers demonstrated such an abject disrespect for their own honored positions, they would have failed in their primary charge before God and lost the necessary respect of the people they were charged to serve. Though corruption might put wealth into the pockets of a few disreputable public ministers, it represented the ruin of the whole civil community; magisterial corruption, besides provoking God's judgment upon the entire civil body, exposed the private citizen to unrestricted injustice. Corruption in high places therefore ultimately rendered Paul's desire for *"quiet and peaceable"* lives into disorder and havoc, for corrupt rulers undermined the very heart of all civility regardless of any noble framework of government, as Baxter also noted: *"It is no meer frame of government, whether Monarchy, Aristocracy, Democracy, or mixt ... that will make happy a Common-wealth in the hands of imprudent, impious men, so much as one of the other forms, supposed worse, will do in the hands of men of prudence, and the fear of God."*[34] Thus, any form of covenantal or *"mixt"* civil government certainly required integrity, fidelity, and virtue among the people and magistrates alike, and according to that great Apostle to the Gentiles, all civil affairs required the faithful support of abundant Christian prayer.

33. Baxter, *A Holy Commonwealth*, p. 430.
34. Ibid., p. 224.

The common good was to be the object for civil government, for the only reasons power had been granted by God to the magistrate were that they ensue uniform justice and suppress public evil. Good civil order obliged the individuals to obey the laws and ordinances of the magistrates, as individuals under civil authority had no power aside from the courts to annul any laws, ordinances, or civil powers. For a private person to disobey constituted laws and ordinances at his discretion would be as destructive to the commonwealth as it would be for a child to disregard household rules. Such a personal, uncivil action would be considered rebellion according to the Bible's Fifth Commandment, which obliged due obedience to all legitimate superior powers, as Rutherford noted in *Lex, Rex*: "*By what reason a family hath a Power of Government, and of punishing malefactors, that same power must be in societies of men.*"[35]

The general community would suffer if its members became a law unto themselves, nevertheless, such circumstances did present themselves. If, for instance, in the home, a father were to order his children to violate their primary obligation to God's Law, he would simply breach his authority in the matter. For the father, who was "relatively" charged by God to defend righteousness in the home, to demand evil of his loved ones would undermine the charge of his authority and his lawless demand must be righteously disobeyed. Likewise, in a commonwealth, such a circumstance would present itself if the rulers placed demands upon the people outside of the rulers' authority or required them to disobey God's higher Laws. Individuals would likewise be obligated in such a peculiar circumstance to disobey a civil ordinance, as according to Baxter:

> If a Lawfull King be Limited, if he Command the subjects beyond his Limits, in matters exempted from his power, or else in matters that the nature of his office extendeth not unto, that command is not an act of power; and therefore it is not a resistance of Power to disobey it.[36]

When people suffered under the king's oppression during the English Civil War, they petitioned for relief. A poor Devonshire widow was shown in this 1643 woodcut praying for pity from her countrymen.

Nevertheless, with even the most unjust ruler still holding the lawful sword of authority, there would certainly be a price to pay, as Baxter also cautioned: "*It is the subjects Duty to submit to suffering, and not resist the Power of their Rulers, in cases where they may not lawfully obey.*"[37] He was referring to the necessary Christian's willingness to suffer the unjust consequence of even unrighteous civil retribution. The private individual, though acting righteously in refusing to violate God's Law in accord with a tyrant's demand, was not to resist the civil prosecution which would result, as he was then obliged to faithfully bear the backhand of injustice. Nevertheless, the lower magistrates – and only the magistrates – were charged by God to come to the rescue of such victims of unrighteous decrees. The people had no authority within themselves to overrule any civil action apart from those whom they had vested with authority, yet they could counter the most highly placed tyranny through intervention of duly elected lower magistrates.

35. Rutherford, *Lex, Rex*, p. 4.
36. Baxter, *A Holy Commonwealth*, p. 375.
37. Ibid., p. 372.

Those lower magistrates, who were themselves fully answerable to God for their part in good government, were to secure justice by interposing themselves on behalf of the people. John Knox had exhorted them to defend the realm even if the crown itself refused. If the crown failed in its obligation, it was the lower magistrates' duty to act as surrogate princes: *"God hath appointed you Princes in the People, and by very reason thereof, requireth of your defense of the Innocents troubled in your dominion."*[38] So, it was indeed the people's obligation to pray to God, but also to plead and petition every level of magistracy to perform their full civil duty. And, when the lower magistrates rose to the cause, it was then the duty of godly people to support them.

That explained the genius of the covenant-minded Samuel Adams when the British oppression of the American colonies became severe. When Massachusetts Governor Thomas Hutchinson refused to allow its constituted General Court to convene an assembly to lawfully address its grievances, Adams called for a network of local town assemblies to take up the cause. At a 1772 Boston town meeting, he proposed a Committee of Correspondence *"to state the Rights of Colonists, and of this Province in particular, as Men, as Christians, and as subjects; to Communicate and Publish the same to this Province, and to the World."*[39] The lower governments thereby intervened to exercise the legitimate authority that had been vested in them. So, in spite of mother Britain's use of raw force, the people had a vehicle of constitutionally sanctioned civil government to exert godly opposition to repugnant, anti-charter and anti-covenantal tyranny. Then, on the eve of America's Independence in 1776, John Witherspoon, the great Presbyterian educator, congressman, and direct descendant of John Knox, spoke of the people's reciprocal civic duty to commend themselves unto heaven's protection:

> *It is therefore your duty in this important and critical season, to exert yourselves every one in his proper sphere to stem the tide of prevailing vice, and promote the knowledge of God, the reverence of his name and worship, and obedience to his Laws.*[40]

THE
VOTES and PROCEEDINGS
OF THE
FREEHOLDERS and other INHABITANTS
OF THE
Town of BOSTON,
In Town Meeting assembled,
ACCORDING TO LAW.

[*Published by Order of the Town.*]

To which is prefixed,
As Introductory, an attested Copy of a Vote of the Town at a preceeding Meeting.

BOSTON:
PRINTED BY EDES AND GILL, IN QUEEN-STREET,
AND T. AND J. FLEET, IN CORNHILL.

The 1772 Boston town meeting called Americans to act with Christian civility in their cause. This pamphlet published their legal case against Britain, proposed a "Committee of Correspondence" with other towns, and suppressed personal, civil rebellion.

Witherspoon had drawn parallel callings between one's sincere, private regard for God and one's patriotic, public regard for the civil estate, saying, *"Whosoever is an avowed enemy of God, I scruple not to call him an enemy to his country."*[41]

In drawing the lines of civility between the magistrates' vows to assertively act for the common good and the people's charge to assertively pray for the commonwealth, Puritans had set forth the biblical model for a civil covenant. Later, Christians such as Adams and Witherspoon simply followed the principles of those preceding them in restoring America's own quiet and peaceable lives.

38. Knox, *The Appellation*, p. 2.
39. [Town of Boston], *The Votes and Proceedings of the Freeholders and other Inhabitants of the Town of Boston, In Town Meeting assembled, According to Law* (Boston, 1772), p. iii.
40. John Witherspoon, *The Dominion of Providence over the Passions of Men ...* (Philadelphia, 1776), p. 52.
41. Ibid., p. 51.

England's Attempts at Commonwealth Living

The historic influence of covenantal civil thought in both England and America was profoundly significant. As early as the brutal reign of England's Mary I in the 1550's, exiles such as John Knox and Christopher Goodman had postulated covenantal arguments against any notion of civil tyranny. Upon Mary's death in 1558, most of the exiles returned home and integrated themselves into the English societal fabric. Then, throughout the formative years of the youthful Elizabeth I's reign came a significant influx of covenant-minded Huguenots due to a series of massacres of the Protestants in France. Both the returned English exiles and the new French refugees brought with them profound ideas of the nature of civil government which soon worked their way to the ear of the queen.

Elizabeth did not consider it a virtue to have a woman sitting upon the English throne, once telling her House of Lords: *"We are not ignorant of the imbecility and unableness of Our sex to governe such a powerfull and mighty Kingdom."*[42] She therefore positioned a variety of counselors close at hand, among whom were several prominent Reformed ministers of state. In marked contrast to her father, Henry VIII, and her elder sister, Mary I, Elizabeth enumerated the principles of a covenantal commonwealth in a speech before the Lords in 1572:

> *We find that Princes have as neere a relation; and as strict an obligation to their Subjects, as Subjects have to them; secundum morem principis, after the manner which a Prince can be ingaged or obliged, that is, by the bond sealed to the people at the Coronation; every Prince covenants with the people, to defend them from all injuries, domesticke and forraigne, to institute and ordaine good and wholesome lawes for their security, from opressions one from another, and from the Prince himselfe.*[43]

Thus, in remarkably fine biblical form, Elizabeth had drawn her English precedent from the distinct precepts of ancient Israel: *"A Prince should therefore be toward the people, as that great Prophet Samuel was toward the Israelites."*[44] She carried the analogy home in her application to the body of English nobility:

> *This my Lords, we in Our consideration and resolution, set downe as Our president in the government of this Our English Israel, whom with God's mercies have nourished his particular people, and this we shall ever accomplish, the due administration of Justice.*[45]

A. A youthful Queen Elizabeth was shown in this 1576 woodcut, seated beside three of her closest advisors. She considered her female crown as an unpleasant necessity in order to block an untenable royal succession.

B. In her 1572 *Speech* before the Lords, Elizabeth acknowledged the covenantal obligation of her royal coronation (first edition, 1643).

C. England's civil covenant was to secure the people *"from all injuries, domesticke and forraigne."*

42. Elizabeth I, *Speech, Delivered by that Mirrour and Miracle of Princes, Queen Elizabeth ...* (London, 1643), p. 1.
43. Ibid., p. 4.
44. Ibid.
45. Ibid., p. 5.

Such a direct acknowledgment of God and her godly obligation was fully appreciated by Elizabeth's contemporary, Reformed-minded advisors, but, under her two immediate successors, James I and his son Charles I, opposition to covenantal Puritanism became harsh. Parliament, as the House of Lords and the House of Commons, interposed itself on behalf of the nation to resist Charles's tyrannical regime. The process of defeating Charles brought a revival of covenantal principles, but parliamentarian factioning resulted in the dissolution of both the monarchy and the House of Lords. In 1649, the Commons ordained itself a democratic Commonwealth with a *Declaration "That the people are under God the Originall of all just power,"*[46] to which it annexed a copy of the king's *"Covenant"*[47] (coronation oath) that he had broken by waging an unjust war against his subjects. Charles was found guilty of high treason in a judicial court called by the Commons. The "Rump" Parliament then mistakenly attempted to rule England without a chief executive or a constitution, leading to disjointed political power.

When the military commander, Oliver Cromwell, was eventually appointed as the "Lord Protector" of England in 1654, Parliament attempted to establish its national government under a system of shared powers between a chief executive and a legislative body. Cromwell therefore spoke of a constitutional union to the Commons: *"The government by a single Person* [a chief executive] *and a Parliament* [a legislative body] *is a Fundamentall: it is the Esse. It is Constitutive."*[48] Cromwell realized that the *"Esse"* (essence) of good government was the mutual accountability of both branches to each other, and that their representative duties to the people should be framed, or spelled out, in a fundamental or *"Constitutive"* document. He therefore further explained to England's body of representatives: *"In every Government there must be somewhat like a Magna Charta, that should be standing, and unalterable."*[49]

Through its exhaustive struggle to establish a godly government, England was shown that a truly civil commonwealth required more than the brute power of a single king, more than the disjointed power of a legislative body, and more than the disordered will of the people. The heart of a well constituted civil commonwealth was therefore the union of a chief executive officer and a legislative body of magistrates. Both were to be held accountable to the people, and all were to be held under the rule of God's Laws. That covenantal principle was what the Puritan Cromwell had come to know as a basic *"Fundamentall."*

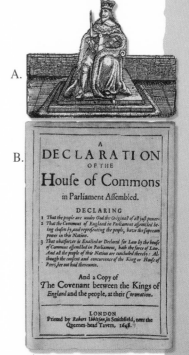

A.

B.

A. Charles I attempted to govern by "personal rule." "His Majesty" was shown in this contemporary woodcut.

B. In this 1649 *Declaration*, the Commons proclaimed its democratical rule and attempted to govern England without an executive office.

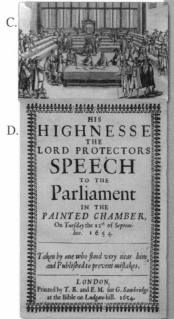

C.

D.

C. The Commonwealth era Parliament was shown in this contemporary engraving.

D. Cromwell urged England in this 1654 speech to frame a fundamental constitution.

46. House of Commons, *A Declaration of the House of Commons in Parliament Assembled. Declaring That the people are under God the Originall of all just power...* (London, [January, 1649]), p. 3.
47. Ibid., pp. 3-4.
48. Oliver Cromwell, *His Highness The Lord Protectors Speech to the Parliament in the Painted Chamber ...* (London, 1654), pp. 30-31.
49. Ibid.

New England's Idea of Commonwealth Living

Cromwell, who himself had earlier attempted to immigrate to New England, also decried the plight of so many worthy English families who, under his royal predecessors, had been forced to flee to America. And, he well knew the reason they had sacrificed so much to escape there: *".... where they have for Liberty sake stripped themselves of all their Comfort, and the Enjoyment they had, embracing losse of Friends, and want, then [than] be so ensnared, and in Bondage."*[50] Decades prior to Parliament's short-lived attempt to establish itself as a Commonwealth, the plantations of New England had begun to take advantage of their *"wildernesse"*[51] situation to form themselves as covenanted communities. Each of New England's earliest towns had been framed as a covenanted commonwealth with signed documents and sworn oaths binding each in mutual accountability under God. Even the earliest Christianized Indians established such a civil estate which, according to the first English missionary, John Eliot, had been framed on the precepts of the Book of Exodus:

> *... with Prayer to God I read and Expounded to them the 18th of Exodus, which I had done several times before, and finally they first chose a Ruler of a Hundred, then they chose two Rulers of Fifties, ... and lastly for that days work every man chose who be Ruler of ten, the Rulers standing in order and every man going to the man he chose.*[52]

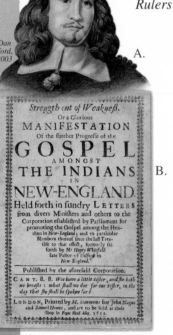

Dan Ford, 2003

A.

B.

Just as the Israelites of old had done before, the first of many "praying" Indian villages had *"entered into a Covenant with God and each other, to be the Lord's people, and to be governed by the Word of the Lord in all things."*[53] The staunch Puritan Eliot recorded that their 1651 covenant formed *"the first public Record among the Indians."*[54] And, as the fundamental governing charter of native-born Americans directly under God, it was quite notably void of all royal impositions (as translated by Eliot):

> *The words of which Covenant are these in English: We give ourselves and our children unto God to be his people, he shall rule us in all our affairs, not only in our Religion and affairs of Church (these we desire as soon as we can) but also in our works and affairs in this world, God shall rule over us. Isa. 33:22. The Lord is our Judge, the Lord is our Law giver, the Lord is our King. He will save us; the Wisdom which God has taught us in his Book, that shall guide us and direct our way. Oh, Jehovah, teach us wisdom to find out the Wisdom of thy Scriptures, let the grace of Christ help us, because Christ is the Wisdom of God, send thy Spirit into our Hearts, and let it teach us; Lord take us to be thy people, and let us take thee to be our God.*[55]

A. John Eliot (1604-1690) was an amazingly prolific Puritan missionary. He published the first Indian-language Bible in 1663, an Indian Primer in 1669, and founded several self-governed Indian towns.

B. Eliot's letters included in *Strength out of Weakness* gave the first account of civilly covenanted Indians.

50. Ibid., p. 32.
51. Ibid.
52. John Eliot, excerpted from *Strength out of Weakness. Or a Glorious Manifestation Of the further Progresse of the Gospel Amongst the Indians in New-England* (London, 1652), pp. 10-11.
53. Ibid., p. 11.
54. Ibid.
55. Ibid.

Not surprisingly, the first formally adopted constitution to establish a civil government was also drafted in Puritan New England. At the very time when their English counterparts were still suffering without the benefit of Parliament under the personal rule of Charles I, a small group of settlers (who had recently fled his regime) were able to establish a framework for consensual government by way of a formally written vehicle for self-rule. The Puritan Minister Thomas Hooker inspired a union of three Connecticut townships that would not only ensure the choice of their own officers, but allow the people themselves to define and establish constitutional bounds and limits of their own civil authorities.

Connecticut's historic *Fundamental Orders* occasioned the desire for a confederation of the local inhabitants of Windsor, Hartford, and Wethersfield. And, with all three settlements being of Reformed civic stock, they knew that *"where a people are gathered together the Word of God requireth that, to maintain the peace and union of such a people, there should be an orderly and decent government established according to God."*[56] The Connecticut frame was as much the model of good government as had ever been adopted by man because it was the handiwork of people who were both thoroughly knowledgeable in the Scriptures and uniquely free to form themselves as a new confederation. As Puritans, their constitution had the features of a covenantal, or mixed, form of civil government with representatives elected to form a *"Court of Electors."*[57] Then, their general court and chief executive governor were chosen by those elected. Both the governor and the general court were likewise answerable to their charge: *"which being chosen and sworn according to an oath recorded for that purpose, shall have power to administer justice according to the laws herein established, and for want thereof according to the Word of God."*[58] In return, every citizen "freeman" was to take an "oath of fidelity" in order to freely inhabit within the

A.

B. *THE original conftitution of Connecticut, formed by voluntary compact,* 1639.

FORASMUCH as it hath pleafed the Almighty GOD, by the wife difpofition of his Divine Providence, fo to order and difpofe of things, that we the inhabitants and refidents of Windfor, Hartford, and Wethersfield, are now cohabiting and dwelling in and upon the river of Connecticut and the lands thereunto adjoining, and well knowing where a people are gathered together the word of GOD requireth that, to maintain the peace and union of fuch a people, there fhould be an orderly and decent government eftablifhed according to GOD, to order and difpofe of the affairs of the people at all feafons, as occafion fhould require: do therefore affociate and conjoin ourfelves to be as one public STATE or COMMONWEALTH; and do, for ourfelves and our fucceffors, and fuch as fhall be adjoined to us at any time hereafter, enter into combination and confederation together, to maintain and preferve the liberty and purity of the gofpel of our LORD JESUS, which we now profefs, as alfo the difcipline of the churches, which, according to the truth of faid gofpel, is now practifed amongft us; as alfo in our civil affairs to be guided and governed according to fuch laws, rules, orders, and decrees, as fhall be made, ordered, and decreed, as followeth.

A. The first settlers of Hartford were people who immigrated from New Town (later Cambridge), Massachusetts in 1636. Thomas Hooker, the leader of the Puritan contingent, believed that Christian civic responsibility followed Christian liberty. As a strong proponent of self-government, Hooker preached that *"the choice of magestrates belongs to the people by God's allowance,"* and he added the covenantal principle that *"they who have the power to appoint officers and magestrates, it is in their power, also, to set the bounds and limitations of the power."*[*] Shown here is a nineteenth-century engraving of Hooker preaching to Hartford's first immigrants.
Encyclopedia Britannica, Eleventh Edition, vol. 13 (New York, 1910), p. 674.

B. Connecticut's *Fundamental Orders* framed the first written civil constitution adopted by a free people. The Preamble stated that its purpose was *"to maintain the peace and union."* It united the towns of Windsor, Hartford, and Wethersfield into a *"confederation"* (civil covenant) of local governments, to *"preserve the liberty and purity of the gospel of our Lord Jesus, ..."* Shown here is the Preamble, first published in Benjamin Trumble's *History of Connecticut, Civil and Ecclesiastical* (1797).

56. Benjamin Trumble, *A Complete History of Connecticut, Civil and Ecclesiastical, from the Emigration of its first Planters from England*, p. 528.
57. Ibid., p. 529.
58. Ibid.

265

confines of the union. With its strictly limited terms of office and its multitiered layers of magistracy, the constitution ensured a sound administration of government on the level closest to where the people lived, and established a uniformly accountable leadership higher up. There was no vestige of royal prerogative or lordly privilege in the American brand of covenantal commonwealth, for rule was established strictly for its biblically defined purpose: as for the uniform good of the whole body directly under God.

The towns were to send deputies to a general colonial court as each town was to *"give notice distinctly to the inhabitants of the same, in some public assembly or by going or sending from house to house"*[59] to elect its representatives. Thus, Connecticut families enjoyed a mixed, or limited, form of government with legislative as well as executive and local as well as overall colonial rule, securing liberty and providing ample guardianship for the inhabitants of the commonwealth. Its structure of mutual accountability provided an exceptional model for other covenantal constitutions to follow, as there was little room for tyranny or corruption on the part of the rulers, or for disunion or licentious living on the part of the people. All were pledged in accord to the civil glory of God, of His Laws, and toward the common good of the whole.

Dan Ford,
2003

A.

B.

A. John Davenport (1597-1670), who fled to Massachusetts in 1637, retained a wide reputation as a Reformed scholar. He graciously declined a seat on the Westminster Assembly in 1642, and the local Quinnipiac Tribe knew him as *"the big-study man."* (*Compact Edition of the Dictionary of National Biography*, vol. 1, 1974, p. 561.)

B. Davenport played a leading role in drafting the New Haven Constitution. It was a carefully considered document that ensured local rule as well as submission to the moral character and structural framework modeled in Scripture. (Excerpted Preamble from Trumble's *History*, 1797.)

In the meantime, another immigration to the Connecticut region had begun in 1638. The new colonists that settled along the southern coast immediately drew up the New Haven "plantation covenant," which also recognized the Scriptures as the supreme guide to their civil affairs. The following year they met in an assembly to frame a more comprehensive civil frame that they called *"The fundamental articles,"* which served as the *"constitution of the colony of New Haven."*[60] John Davenport led the proceedings of ratification, *"praying them to consider seriously in the presence and fear of Almighty GOD, the weight of the business they met about."*[61] The first query to be considered for the consent was:

> *Whether the Scriptures do hold forth a perfect rule for the direction and government of all men in all duties which they are to perform to GOD and men, as well as families, and commonwealth, as in the matters of the church?*[62]

The query unanimously carried, *"assented by all, no man descenting, as was expressed by holding up hands."*[63] The next query considered the nature of the public magistrates and officers

59. Ibid., p. 531.
60. Ibid., p. 533.
61. Ibid.
62. Ibid., p. 534.
63. Ibid.

"*making and repealing laws.*"[64] As with the first, the second query "*was assented unto by all, and no man gain-sayed* [against] *it.*"[65] The constitution was ratified by a succession of six such queries all going to the heart of godly covenantal government, and with each of its tenets being "*formed by voluntary compact.*"[66]

The character of New England's mixed and multitiered civil governments, with the local townships respected and relied upon by the wider colonial government, became an important feature of civil life in colonial America. Each tier of colonial government performed duties that were best suited to its respective position and locality. So, unlike England, there was a greater sense of power emanating from the local governments to the general confederations. Local families formed local communities, therefore the town representatives dealt with issues involving the interests of their resident families. The wider colonies were composed of those townships, and therefore the towns and the people in general were represented in the larger colonial governments. Civil power tended to flow upward from families to townships and then to colonies; accountability tended to flow down from the province to the towns and then back to families. In Connecticut, for example, representatives from the various households within each town were to "*assemble themselves together, to elect and choose certain deputies to be at general court then following, to agitate the affairs of the commonwealth.*"[67] Families and towns thus sent representatives 'up' to the colony-wide governments who were accountable back 'down' below in their good service. Connecticut's residents and families thereby enjoyed a system of multitiered, shared political authority within an internally, self-limiting structure of civil power. And, with each tier of authority having a legislative as well as an executive branch, each 'mixed' government provided ample public guardianship for the personal liberties and private property of the commonwealth.

The security of the Bible's moral Laws provided for the kind of character requisite in a sound public administration. With biblical morality respected in every ordinance, statute, or act of state, there was little room for civil disunion or licentious living on the part of the people. And, with multiple checks built within the framework of all public civility, there was little room for tyranny or corruption on the part of the rulers. Remarkably, colonial laws were also passed that acknowledged the inalienable liberties of the colonial inhabitants, securing them against all unconstitutional impositions. The various plantations were therefore vigorous in their moral, structural, and administrative integrity, and to a large extent, even equipped to withstand outside interference. For example, when greater Britain tried to impose an outside tax on colonial documents and local publications in the 1760's, the Assembly of Rhode Island passed an Act intended to further bolster the constituted liberties of its inhabitants:

A LAW,

Made and paſſed by the General Aſſembly, at their Seſſion in Newport, on the Firſt Day of *March*, A. D. 1663.

An A C T, declaring the Rights and Privileges of His Majeſty's Subjects within this Colony.

BE it Enacted by the General Aſſembly, and by the Authority thereof it is Enacted, That no Freeman ſhall be taken or impriſoned, or be deprived of his Freehold, or Liberty, or free Cuſtoms, or be out-lawed, or exiled, or otherways deſtroyed, nor ſhall be paſſed upon, judged or condemned, but by the lawful Judgment of his Peers, or by the Law of this Colony : And that no Aid, Tax, Tallage, or Cuſtom, Loan, Benevolence, Gift, Excife, Duty, or Impoſition whatſoever, ſhall be laid, aſſeſſed, impoſed, levied or required of or on any of His Majeſty's Subjects within this Colony, or upon their Eſtates, upon any Manner of Pretence or Colour whatſoever, but by the Act and Aſſent of the General Aſſembly of this Colony.

The General Assembly of Rhode Island had previously passed this Law in 1663. By legally acknowledging the rights of *"Freehold, or Liberty"* and guaranteeing juries composed only of one's *"Peers,"* the law effectively served as a statutory "Bill of Rights." The law also guaranteed the colony's exclusive right of overall taxation, safeguarding both its own self-rule and the property of its inhabitants from outside impositions. (Excerpted from *Acts and Laws ... of Rhode-Island*, Newport, 1767 edition.)

64. Ibid., p. 535.
65. Ibid.
66. Ibid.
67. Ibid. ("Agitate" meaning: to debate all sides of the issues.)

A.

B.

A. Rhode Island's *Acts and Laws* asserted the authority of the General Assembly and required several officers in each town to retain printed copies for local use (title page of the 1767 edition).

B. This excerpt of a 1765 Act confirmed the colony's exclusive constituted right *"to lay Taxes and Imposts"* on its residents.

C.

D.

C. In this correspondence, the Selectmen and Town Clerk of Cambridge required Constable Dana to announce a public meeting to address America's emergency measures against British encroachments. It then requested local citizens who are *"Qualified to Vote for Representatives"* to assemble at the county courthouse.

D. The conclusion requested the resident freemen to act in obedience to the resolves of the Provincial and Continental Congresses to secure their liberties.

... the General Assembly of this Colony have, in their representative Capacity, the only exclusive Right to lay Taxes and Imposts upon the Inhabitants of this Colony: And that every Attempt to vest such Power in any Person or Persons whomsoever, other than the General Assembly aforesaid, is unconstitutional, and hath a manifest Tendency to destroy the Liberties of the People of this Colony.[68]

In the mid-1770's, when an alarmed Massachusetts government attempted to defend itself against continued encroachments by Britain, it was required to ask each township for jurisdictional support. For example, in December 1774, the Provincial Congress sent a request to the town of Cambridge to determine whether it would back the colony's defensive measures. The local magistrates, in turn, requested *"In His Majesty's Name"*[69] (meaning in a clearly chartered manner) that its Constable, Benjamin Dana, announce a public meeting of the local inhabitants: *"To know the Minds of the Town whether they will* [be] *agreeable to the recommendation of the Provincial Congress ... ."*[70] The voice of the resident freemen was therefore the voice of the town, and an emergency town meeting was required to direct the colony in its pertinent business from the bottom up, according to its truly constituted authority "in the people's name." The townsmen were therefore asked in conclusion:

To take under their Consideration such of the important Resolves, either of the Continental, or Provincial Congress as to them shall seem meet; and to act upon the beforementioned Clauses as they shall think expedient; also to act and do any thing that they shall think proper for the recovering, and securing, our Just Rights and Liberties.[71]

68. Rhode Island Colonial Assembly, *Acts and Laws of The English Colony of Rhode-Island and Providence-Plantations, in New England, in America* (Newport, Rhode Island, 1767), p. 227.
69. Cambridge Selectmen and Town Clerk, bifold manuscript notification to *"Warn the Freeholders & other Inhabitants ... ; Qualified to Vote for Representatives that they Assemble at the Court House in Cambridge ... on Monday the Second Day of January next at One of the Clock, in the afternoon on said Day"* (December 26, 1774), p. 1.
70. Ibid.
71. Ibid., pp. 1-2.

Another important feature of the covenanted civil arm was that of the citizen soldier. Companies of private militiamen had been instrumental in the early success of the Puritan resistance to Charles I in the 1640's, and they would prove even more so in the success of American efforts in the 1770's. Though colonial militias were not regarded as soldiers of a professional army, each of the New England colonies required all able-bodied men to own firearms and regularly assemble to be trained for any extraordinary defense of their fellow citizenry. Actual mustered enlistments were therefore typically short and the companies disbanded at the conclusion of a given crisis.

Nevertheless, the local militias offered the colonial governments their most formidable and ready arm of civil defense. They were regulated by the wider colonial laws, but because they were composed of men living for the most part in private capacities, they were mustered at the local level. Militias had been key to the survival of the northern colonies during their conflicts with marauding Indians in the later seventeenth century, and the British colonies owed their very existence to the militias that served throughout the French and Indian Wars. Yet, in all, they were most notably remembered for their essential contributions during the period of armed conflict over America's liberty which ultimately led to Independence in 1776.

The province of Massachusetts began calling for an immediate, ready citizenry in 1774 when Britain stationed its "Regulars" in the colony as a means of intimidation. And, the colony once again was placed in the position of relying upon local consent not only for assistance, but for its survival. The counties assembled and the local citizenry rose to the cause. The existence of their militias, featuring private soldiers affording their very corporal lives in the defense of the wider civil community, offered one of the most sublime images of multi-covenantal living. Militias of private men in the sacrificial service of their fellow countrymen linked the covenant of family with commonwealth. The colonies could not – and would not – have succeeded in the cause of liberty, had it not been for such Christian patriots serving as citizen soldiers.

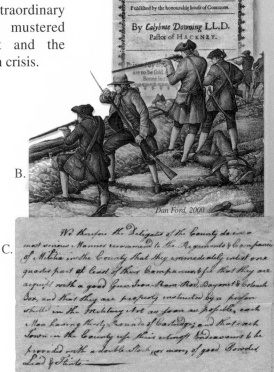

A.
B.
Dan Ford, 2000
C.

A. The Puritan Artillery Sermons that were preached during the early years of the English Civil War awoke soldiers to the cause for which they were offering their lives. Calybute Downing's 1640 sermon preached before the London militia was the first such sermon, teaching that war itself is *"an appeale to heaven"* if in a *"just defense."*

B. The colonial militias were used to mark a powerful line between the people's liberties and arbitrary tyranny. This inked sketch portrays the line of defense by the Massachusetts militias on Bunker Hill in June 1775. The motto on many New England flags read: *"An Appeal to Heaven."*

C. Like many other Massachusetts jurisdictions, Bristol County answered the call of the Provincial Congress by enlisting its militias in the colonial cause. This manuscript excerpt from Bristol's *"Convention"* at Taunton on January 4-5, 1775, recommended *"in a most serious Manner"* to *"the Regiments & Companies of Militia in the County that they immediately inlist one quarter part at least of their Companies, & see that they are acquipt* [equipped] *with a good Gun Iron... ."*

269

The Nursing Fathers of the Church

Being a power ordained by God, the rule of the commonwealth was to provide ample support for all its resident societies. It was to work in a conjunctive role with its covenant families to provide them with civil protection and offer them a safe place to labor for their own provision. It was likewise to offer the covenant church assemblies a secure setting to thrive in, according to their biblical mandate.

According to the historic Reformed understanding of the "co-relative" role of the commonwealth with the church, they were to function distinctly yet in coordination with each other under God. On one hand, all local churches and church members were bound as subjects or citizens in their various civil communities. All Christians were thereby subject to all civil laws, as Richard Baxter observed: *"All persons, even Pastors of the Church, are bound to this subjection to Magistrates."*[72] On the other hand, he also observed that there was a reciprocal obligation of civil officers toward the church and its members: *"Magistrates are the guardians of the Church, and must see to the execution of Gods Laws, by all their subjects in their places."*[73] According to their historic, "co-relative" purposes, the church has provided the civil communities with self-restrained, self-supporting, and law-abiding subjects, citizens, and families of a commonwealth. The commonwealth has provided the church with protection and support for its own biblically-mandated ministry, administration, and mission upon the earth.

In looking to the Scriptures for such a protective and supportive role that the commonwealth was to provide for the church, the most endearing image came from a prophetic passage in the Book of Isaiah wherein God foretold the place of Gentile (earthly) kings and queens in His Kingdom:

Shown here is an excerpt of Isaiah 49:22-23 from the *Authorized*, or 'King James,' version of the Bible, printed with its Geneva Bible sidenotes (1649).

Thus saith the Lord GOD, Behold, I will lift up mine hand to the Gentiles, and set up my standard to the people: and they shall bring thy sons in their arms, and thy daughters shall be carried upon their shoulders. And kings shall be thy nursing-fathers, and their queens thy nursing-mothers: ... (Isaiah 49:22-23).

The Reformed Geneva Bible noted that Isaiah had prophesied that Gentile kings shall *"bestow their power and authority for the preservation of the church."*[74] Thus it followed in the reformers expectations, that in spite of the historic opposition and persecutions of Christians, God had nonetheless ordained the civil estate to work in such a way that preserved Christ's Kingdom.

The Reformed axiom of *"nursing-fathers"* meant that civil communities and nations were intended to nurture the church, but not for them to suppress that which Christ had ordained, or for them to dominate His own establishment. They were, however, obliged to succor Christ's establishment and offer it a fruitful repose, as Boston's original preacher, John Cotton, observed of New England, where its magistrates ruled in the place of *"kings"* and *"queens"*:

72. Baxter, *A Holy Commonwealth*, p. 355.
73. Ibid., p. 301.
74. Geneva note on Isaiah 49:22-23, leaf Hh6.

... our Christian Magistrates are nursing Fathers to the Church, and the Churches now established, are carried not only with a pious desire to enlarge the kingdom of Christ, but also with brotherly love to such as intend so good a work.[75]

New England's *Cambridge Platform* of 1648 also noted that rulers of commonwealths were to support the church through the civil administration of *"both tables"* of God's Law, meaning to honorably serve both God and their fellow citizenry: *"The magistrates are nursing fathers, and nursing mothers, and stand charged with the custody of both tables ... ."*[76]

New England's attitude concerning the healthy, cooperative roles of the civil establishment and the church prospered both covenants over its ensuing centuries. Ebenezer Bridge's election sermon of 1767 recognized such cooperation as central to the historic success of the colony. He extolled the temper of the most recent monarchs that had followed England's *Glorious Revolution* in 1689, establishing the crown under an explicitly constitutional system of rule. Bridge preached that since that time, England's kings and queens *"... have proved nursing fathers, and nursing mothers, having made the laws of the realm the rule of their conduct."*[77]

Later, after the United States were established in their independency, the same cooperative demeanor was carried into the various state republics. David Parsons's election sermon delivered at the advent of America's federal period extolled Massachusetts Governor Hancock and the magistrates to their obligation to support the cause of Christ in their civil positions:

> *It is by no means beneath the dignity of the greatest magistrate or monarch on earth, to yield the most profound subjection to God, and pay homage to the Redeemer of men; nor to consecrate themselves, their power and authority, to his service. God requires that they co-operate with him in his designs to effect the best interest of his people, ... that they should be patrons, and nursing Fathers of the church of Christ; and use their utmost endeavours to advance his kingdom.*[78]

The covenantal nature of the civil establishment as well as the family and the church found true expression in early America more than at any other place or time on earth since that of Abraham, Moses, David, and the prophets. Early on, John Cotton had proclaimed the uniquely covenantal way of

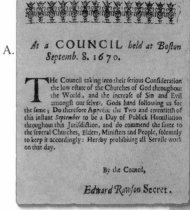

A. New England's governments were aware of the need to back their churches in suppressing evil. Shown here is an early civil call for *"Publick Humiliation"* to thwart *"Sin and Evil"* (1670).

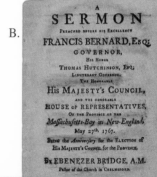

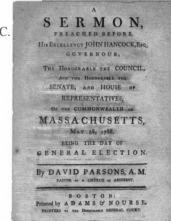

B. Ebenezer Bridge's 1767 election sermon acknowledged the English King as a nursing father in as far as the crown respected America's liberties.

C. David Parsons's 1788 election sermon urged all magistrates to *"consecrate"* their power by being *"nursing Fathers."*

75. John Cotton, *The Way of the Churches of Christ in New-England*, Proposal 5, p. 7.
76. *A Platform of Church Discipline*, p. 43.
77. Ebenezer Bridge, [Election] *Sermon*, p. 39.
78. David Parsons, *A Sermon Preached before His Excellency John Hancock, Esq. Governour ...* (Boston, 1788), p. 12.

life amid the newly-settled American plantations: *"whereby a people free from naturall and compulsory engagements, can be united or combined together into one visible body, to stand in mutuall Relation, ... by mutuall Covenant."*[79]

Whereas America remains composed of various civil governments still recognizing their union as being "One nation under God," the covenantal lives of Robinson, Winthrop, Cotton, Eliot, Davenport, Mather, and on and on through Hancock and the Adamses of the early federal period, point to a definitive distinction between their effectiveness and modern rhetoric. Today, Americans function relatively: first, to the 'possibilities' within each individual, and then, to the vague social rubbish of 'human potentiality.' Earlier Americans functioned "relative": first, to God, and then, toward the common good – and only then, to the concurrent societal blessing unto each individual. That distinction made all the difference. Earlier Americans sought their societal engagements to the honor of God within their families, churches, and commonwealths. They were infected with a greater sense of accountability by devoutly relying on Precepts that required faithfulness and obedience to God and to one another. Their various societal institutions obtained a formidable accountability that infused their lives with biblical virtues instead of human values, and effected genuine honor, commitment, and mutual strength, that most today can only distantly imagine.

All aspects of their Reformed societies were designed to work together to the common and greater good. The civil commonwealth served the family, and the family vested godliness in the common estate. The local body of Christ functioned to the good of the commonwealth, and the commonwealth served as the civil support of the church. Each institution rested within its proper place, but all stood together in an overall league with the others under God. Ironically, from within the confines of his Bedford prison, John Bunyan could recognize such societal cohesion as the adorned beauty of faithful Christian lives:

The seventeenth-century author John Bunyan was shown in this illustration being visited in prison by his beloved daughter. Bunyan, that self-sacrificial champion of the English tongue, was well-qualified to write of the essential "relative" role of families and churches amid the wider commonwealth (mid-nineteenth-century engraving).

> ... *it is amiable and pleasant to God, when Christians keep their Ranks, Relations and Stations doing all as becoming their Calling. When Christians stand every one in their Places, and doe the Work of their Relations, then they are like the flowers in the garden that stand and Grow where Gardener hath planted them, and they shall both honour the garden in which they are planted, and the Gardener that hath so disposed them.*[80]

In living covenantal lives, the Puritans strengthened the fiber of their entire existence; and with God as their centerpiece, He secured them in every earthly engagement. As it was well-known to them, they were each far from perfect or from establishing any system of perfect societal relations on earth. Nevertheless, their union was pledged to the Lord of both heaven and earth, and their confidence rested assuredly upon the only One who provided them a secure foundation and added His genuine strength to all those devoted to biblical, covenantal living.

79. John Cotton, *The Way of the Churches of Christ in New-England*, p. 4.
80. John Bunyan, *Christian Behaviour* from *The Works*, vol. 1 (London, 1736), p. 418.

In the Name of God, Amen.
Conclusion

THERE was a time when average Americans revered the lives of the men and women who built their nation. Books, magazines, and pamphlets were full of scenes and stories of the lives who, like us, lived with their feet on the ground, but unlike us, had hearts and minds fixed upon heaven. The story of American liberty was told and retold in the abundant prose and pictures from the past, which we hope these three books have documented for more current readers.

Earlier Americans knew that the historic reformers of the sixteenth through the eighteenth centuries left an important legacy of liberty and self-government. America's ancestors understood the character of biblical covenants, which afforded them a comprehensive means to be knit together with meaningful and significant lives. They were pledged under God as private families, local churches, and public commonwealths, allowing them to live in considerable abundance despite the most trying circumstances, and in so doing, they deposited rich examples of prosperous lives in the annals of English and American history.

Western cultures have lost their appreciation for such noble lives, as we have steadily fallen for the great illusion of humanity's autonomy from God. Humanity has instead become enamored with its own mirrored reflection, as if mankind itself were somehow capable of the wonders manifest by God's ascendant glory. Consequently, over the past two centuries marked by rampant self-infatuation, western civilization has undergone severe changes and suffered much as a result. Several societal movements, each marked by demands to remove the God of ancient Israel from the public arena, have already reaped severe consequences. The extinct French Republic of the eighteenth century and the extinct Soviet Socialist Republic of the last are but two notable examples among many radical social efforts of transient mankind. But, each has shown that humanity devastates itself when set adrift from its necessary corporate bonds with God. Nonetheless, mankind keeps trying to improve itself, by itself, and for itself, ever drifting further from the fount of its original strength and sustenance. And, as the past two centuries have demonstrated, mankind is determined to set itself adrift from any sincere and credible public accountability to God as it ever seeks satisfaction and abundance amid the dying vineyards of material and sensual gratification.

God's two Testaments, though, have presented man with quite a different model, for they both proclaim the deep riches of God's explicit truths. As a case in point, after Jesus Himself had fasted for forty days in the wilderness, He was offered a series of the most delectable human and material gratifications. Yet, He vanquished His tempter by way of citing a passage from the Old Testament, and rebuked the evil one by reminding him that *"man shall not live by bread alone, but by every word of God"* (Luke 4:4). Those historic Words were not spoken merely for the benefit of Christ's adversary, for that opponent was not a man who could have taken advantage of the advice. Neither were they spoken for Christ's own benefit, because, though He was fully a man, He was also fully God and was at the time speaking the very Words by which His sovereign divinity was being manifest. Christ's Words that *"man shall not live by bread alone, but by every word of God"* were therefore being spoken by God to all mankind as a universal standard, just as they had been previously spoken to the ancient nation of Israel[1] – as a sweeping rebuke to all godless *"power"* and all human *"glory"* (Luke 4:6).

Christ's additional reminder that *"Thou shalt worship the Lord thy God, and him onely shalt thou serve"* (Luke 4:8) was likewise a repudiation of Western Civilization's current infatuation with similar temptations of human power and glory. Also drawn from the pages of the Old Covenant,[2] Christ's declaration that *"him onely shalt thou serve"* was hence reconfirmed in the New Covenant, showing that men must still look to heaven in order to see the nature of legitimate human engagements, and then must govern themselves according to God's divine design in order to truly enjoy the fruition of their earthbound blessings.

Any fruitful understanding of the obligations of godly living starts with a basic knowledge of the historic relations between God and man. The opening chapter of the Bible therefore described the beginning of all things, including the beginning of man's existence when God unveiled the first glimpse of the essential relations between the Creator and His Creation. The Genesis narrative explained that God spoke upon each of the first six days of history, and all of universal Creation ensued at His Commands. And, what great marvel occurred at His beckoned call? What massive power must have been demonstrated at His sole authoritative voice? Yet, the Holy Text calmly tells us that all time, all space, all energy, and all matter came into existence upon His few, simple commands, each beginning with the sublimely understated words: *"God said..."* (Genesis 1).

Likewise, from the beginning, God created a rich fount of relations between Himself and man. On God's sixth and final day of creative work,[3] He ordered the creation of man: *"God created he him; male and female created he them"* (Genesis 1:27). In such concise Words, God initiated all individuals and all human societies to be forever bound to Him. Mankind was not created simply to exist as a mass of unattached individuals nor under the common yoke of human despotism, because each and all have come into the world with inescapable obligations to God and one another. Both vertically and horizontally *"created he them"* in their specific (vertical) obligations to God and in their manifold (horizontal) duties to each other. The Reformed commentator Matthew Henry thereby described the Bible's second chapter of Genesis as *"that part of the history which relates immediately to man."*[4] Adam and Eve's Genesis Paradise marked the beginning of man's covenantal relations with each other under God, as Henry also noted: *"under the obligations of a law and covenant."*[5] God, then, had chosen to relate with man through covenants. The universal nature of individuals within the fabric of their societies was, from the beginning, created to exist in such obligating commitments.

---

1. Compare Luke 4:4 with Deuteronomy 8:3.
2. See Deuteronomy 6:13.
3. See Genesis 1:26-2:2.
4. Matthew Henry, *An Exposition of the Old & New Testaments*, book 1 (London, [c. 1841]), commentary on Genesis, introduction to chapter 2, p. 6.
5. Ibid.

CONCLUSION

In His continuing mercy toward mankind, God then put His moral will into more concise and understandable terms. He reduced the sum of His unfathomable moral perfection into Ten distinct Commandments which contained all the wisdom of the ages.[6] Then, in God's gracious incarnation as a man, Christ Jesus reconfirmed the Ten as Two unified Commandments with such sublime clarity that they have ever since been easily committed to memory. His first was simply: *"Thou shalt love the Lord thy God with all thy heart, and with all thy soul, and with all thy minde"* (Matthew 22:37). Thus, Christ's first great command spoke of a universal obligation to have the Creator God as the first object of all human concerns. Christ then followed with His second command: *"Thou shalt love thy neighbour as thy self"* (Matthew 22:39). Thus, He spoke an additional mandate to consider others equally as well.[7] In the Christian sense, that meant preferring the good of others over one's own; for instance, in the love of a man for his wife, the wife was to be the man's foremost concern next to God. Each of Christ's commands dispelled the notion of individual rights for the sake of human appetite or self-gratification. The husband was granted his spousal and fatherly rights in order to responsibly protect and defend his earthly beloved in obedience to his heavenly Lord. Christ Himself had modeled that principle of manly leadership by preferring His own beloved earthly Church and sacrificing His life for her.[8] With the Two Commandments knit together, Christ infused the infinite richness of God's love with universally obliging truth, yet He presented them in such a marvelously simple way as to be clearly understandable by all.

Christ then concluded that *"On these two commandments hang all the law and the prophets"* (Matthew 22:40). In Messiah God directing His disciples to look back to ancient Israel, it would be evident to them that God had hung all His covenantal statutes (*"all the law"*) and all His covenant promises (*"the prophets"*) upon those two overarching covenantal principles. Christ thereby pointed his followers back to their own covenantal inheritance as a means for them to understand Him as their true Covenant Lord. Both the Covenant Law and the Prophets had pointed the way to Him, as the covenantal Law and covenantal promises came together in the eternal reign of Jesus as (Messiah) Christ. The Commandments that had formerly been essential in defining the covenant nation of Israel were reconfirmed as the moral statutes of Christ's continuing dominion as the King of Kings. They were essential in obliging a nation then, and remain obliging in all legitimate forms of government thereafter. The permeating moral character of Christ's commands thereby obligated all the covenantal faithful to maintain them in the conduct of their lives on earth.

The Puritans were merely people who embraced such a comprehensive understanding of the biblical relations between God and man. They saw that under the same God as that of Adam, Noah, Abraham, and ancient Israel, all legitimate engagements remained covenantal in their nature, for all earthly engagements remained under God's authority and were accountable to Him. Whether regarding their families, their churches, or their communities at large, the Puritans were bound in each sphere of living to God's honor as well as toward the mutual good of their fellow members.

6. See Exodus 20 and Deuteronomy 5.
7. Compare Deuteronomy 6:5 and Leviticus 19:18.
8. See Ephesians 5:25.

As Reformed Christians, the Puritans saw Providence guiding their steps in a multigenerational Reformation, first in England and Scotland, and most notably in colonial America. But, their families did not triumph in all covenantal virtues from the beginning of the Reformation; their churches were not at once returned to the precepts of genuine covenantal communion; and their commonwealths were not immediately established in covenantal fidelity. Their families, churches, and commonwealths were reformed by years of Christian service and generations of patient improvement. At the time, true societal Reformation was not seen in the rise of noteworthy Puritan authors or in the advent of Reformed preachers and magistrates, as much as it was in the marvelous, gracious timing of the sustaining hand of God. They faithfully looked to God, and comprehensive redemption was realized only through years of patient toil. The English Reformation was engaged by relatively few in its first generation, but by greater numbers in the next, and by multitudes of faithful in the latter. It was first envisioned as theological reformation in one generation, embraced as a worldview by the next, and comprehensively effected by that which followed.

Those old covenantal Puritans, then, still have much to say to more current generations of Christians, just like the prophets of old had much to say to them. The renowned Puritan William Gouge certainly spoke with apt words fit for the faithful of his day from the timeless verse of Israel's prophet Amos:

> *Woe, saith the Prophet, woe to them that are at ease, &c. that stretch themselves upon their couches, and eate the Lambs out of the flock: that chant to the sound of violl: that drink wine in bowles, and anoint themselves with the chiefe ointments: but they are not grieved ... . What good can be expected from these dispositions?*[9]

Like Gouge, we might ask why we are not grieved as was Amos for his generation! And, then we might ask why we are not grieved as was William Gouge for his nation! What good ought we to expect from our hopes of reform if we do not plead as did they, to *"let judgment run down as waters, and righteousness as a mighty stream"* (Amos 5:24)? And, what good ought we to expect if we do not learn to live in appreciation of such an historic Christian inheritance? Living as we do in the shadow of the *"intelligent," "learned,"* and *"sensible"* Puritans,[10] we might look back to our covenantal inheritance so that our sons and daughters, and those who follow them, might live healthy, hearty, and genuinely "relative" lives – with families, churches, and commonwealths each pledged once again in the Name of God, Amen.

---

9. William Gouge, *The Saints Support* (London, 1642), p. 15, referring to *"Amos. 6.3 &c."*
10. John Adams, *A Dissertation on the Canon and the Feudal Law*, printed as part of *The True Sentiments of America...* , published by John Almon (London, 1768), p. 117.

"Virtutem Doctrina Parit" was portrayed in this 1643
woodcut of England's scepter and sword
resting upon an opened Bible.

APPENDICES

APPENDIX A

On the Reformed Christians and the Reformed Movement

The term "Reformed" applies to Christians who, beginning in the mid-1500's, pressed for thorough biblical reforms throughout Western Europe. They were part of the larger Protestant ("those who protest") movement which itself emerged decades earlier. Protestantism, in general, arose due to a broad-based protest of the corrupted superstitions and practices which had become entrenched in Western Christendom. The key earlier movement known as the "Protestant Reformation" began in 1517 when Martin Luther, an Augustinian monk, nailed his famous *Ninety-Five Theses* on his local church door at Wittenberg. Luther's *Theses* was simply a list of grievances that addressed the reforms needed in the Roman Church, but the sharp magisterial reaction to Luther's proposals by the 'official' Church led to a wider eruption of Protestantism throughout northern Europe.

Originally led by men such as Martin Luther, Huldrych Zwingli, and many others in Germany, Switzerland, and France, the Protestants did not just complain of corruption in Church doctrine and polity, but advocated the cure. They proposed that the Church return to the authority of the Bible for its doctrine, and that it institute much less pompous modes of worship than those which dominated Europe throughout the Middle Ages. The Reformation's leaders rejected the Church's cultic veneration of saints, its pilgrimages, and its use of indulgences (paid contracts for pardon of sin). They greatly reduced the number of sacraments and agreed that worship services should be conducted in the language of the common people. They therefore undertook translating the Scriptures in the tongue of the laity (non-clergy) so that they could read for themselves the great doctrines of the Bible and understand for themselves the original nature of the true Christian church.

Although many early Protestants questioned Rome's claim to authority over all of Europe, the movement took a significant shift away from Rome when Luther was excommunicated in 1520. Prior to that time, excommunication had signified damnation, but with the case of Luther, it represented the liberation of Protestantism. No longer would Protestants try to reform the Roman Church from within, but they were henceforth free to establish themselves upon the original foundations that they read in their Holy Text. That moment signified the official establishment of "Protestant" affiliated churches. Thereafter, all of Western Christendom was no longer tied to the authority of Rome or bound under a single (human) potentate.

The Protestant regions of northern Europe, though, did not obtain the Holy Roman Emperor's sanction until 1555 by the *Peace of Augsburg*. In that treaty, which (on paper) ended Roman efforts to destroy the Protestant churches by open force, the legitimacy of individual Catholic and Protestant principalities was officially recognized by each other. The treaty served to place great religious authority in the hands of the Protestant princes and magistrates of northern Europe.

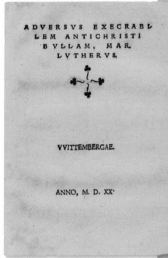

ADVERSVS EXECRABL LEM ANTICHRISTI BVLLAM, MAR. LVTHERVS,

VVITTEMBERGAE.

ANNO, M. D. XX.

Shown here is the title page of Luther's historic response to the threat of excommunication in 1520. He wrote that God's Word, which teaches freedom, ought not itself be restrained or abridged of its freedom.

279

Beginning in the later 1530's, small communities of Protestants in Switzerland and France began to emerge using a more specific title of *"Reformed."*[1] These churches saw the Reformation as an ongoing movement that had not yet hit the mark of being thoroughly reformed. The Roman Church gave its back-handed recognition to the new group by calling them a *"religion that claims to be reformed."*[2] These reformers, though, found significant support in the protective confines of Zurich under Heinrich Bullinger and of Geneva under John Calvin. Around these two municipalities, more than any others, the most comprehensive understanding of covenantal theology was developed.[3]

While a refugee in Geneva during the 1550's, the renowned Protestant John Knox fully embraced the Reformed movement. His book, *The Historie of the Reformation of the Church of Scotland,*[4] the first history of the Reformed faith in Scotland, was an uncompromising tome on the Reformed position and its covenantal responsibilities. He began the work with an indictment of Scotland's corrupt Church establishment, writing that *"Impietie, Ignorance, and Wickedness came to such a height among the Church-men of all ranks, degrees and professions ... ."*[5] Knox then reflected upon God's merciful hand in sending the Reformed faith to expel the corrupt *"Church-men"* from Scotland:

> *... God being, after so long patient, in a manner vexed with them, did stirre up the people to chase them from the service of his House, and to put others in their places, as you will see in the following Historie, whereunto I referre you.*[6]

In England, a Reformed-based petition called *An Admonition to Parliament* (1572), was placed before an already semi-Reformed Protestant establishment. Though written in a much milder tone than Knox's work, it also called for purer reforms in the worship and administration in the Anglican Church. The *Admonition* employed the term "Reformation" to describe a need for a continuing and comprehensive push toward purity in the Anglican doctrine and polity. Its key concern was that England's Church be established as *"God's church"* according to the recovery of His *"true religion, ..."*:

> *Seeing that nothing in this mortall life is more diligently to be sought for, and carefully to be looked unto than the restitution of true religion & reformation of God's church.*[7]

With that historic appeal, the growing Reformed movement found its legs in England. Even so, it was not until the early seventeenth century that reforms were pressed with sufficient force to effect their desired aim. For example, Dr. Layton's work, *An Appeal to Parliament,* called for the complete

Shown here is the title page of Dr. Layton's 1628 *Appeal to Parliament* for Reformation.

1. *Oxford Encyclopedia of the Reformation*, vol. 3 (Oxford, England, 1996), p. 395.
2. Ibid.
3. Ibid., vol. 1, pp. 228, 229, 241.
4. Knox's manuscript was written between 1559 and 1576.
5. John Knox, *The Historie of the Reformation of the Church of Scotland* (London, 1644), *The Preface*, leaf h2.
6. Ibid.
7. Thomas Cartwright, et al., *An Admonition to Parliament*, excerpted from *An Answere to a certain Libel titled, An Admonition to Parliament* (London, 1572), p. 19.

overthrow of English Prelacy and an entire revamping of the Anglican Church.[8] Dr. Layton was summarily fined, pilloried, branded, tortured, and then imprisoned.

Throughout the ensuing decade, the reformers of England and Scotland were met with further severe measures by their King, Charles I. In England, he ruled without a Parliament between 1629 and 1640, often evoking severe punishment on the Puritans who resisted his bishops' innovative and elaborate Episcopalian formalities of worship. In Scotland, Charles's agents attempted to enforce conformity to the Anglican Prayer Book, setting any reformation in reverse and causing severe tumults between the two nations.

In the early 1640's the Reformed cause was finally addressed by the English Parliament. The Scots soon petitioned against the king and his agents, and the Parliament's 1642 *Declaration to the Subjects of Scotland*[9] called for a covenantal alliance between the two British nations for the sake of reforming the Anglican Establishment. With an alliance secured in 1643, Parliament then immediately pressed hard for Reformation with its *Ordinance*[10] to establish the prestigious Westminster Assembly of Divines. The face of true reform had again returned to Britain, and though the Assembly acted in the capacity of an advisory body, it produced the most remarkable documents of church and doctrinal reform that had yet been seen. The Assembly's renowned legacy of pure reform has survived in the hundreds of Reformed churches and associations that have thrived over the ensuing centuries.

8. Dr. Layton, *An Appeal to the Parliament; or Sions Plea against the Prelacie* (1628), frontis and title page.
9. English Parliament, *The Declaration of the Lords and Commons assembled in the Parliament of England, to the Subjects of Scotland, &c.* (Oxford, 1642).
10. English Parliament, *An Ordinance of The Lords and Commons Assembled in Parliament. For the Calling of an Assembly of Learned and Godly Divines, ...* (London, 1643).

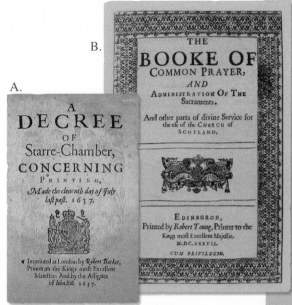

A. The infamous *"Starre-Chamber"* was one of the courts employed by Charles I through which he could rule the English Church at will. This *Decree ... Concerning Printing* banned the publication of any strongly Reformed texts and sanctioned searches of private dwellings for banned books or pamphlets (1637).

B. Great tumult ensued throughout Scotland when English Prelates unveiled this 1637 Anglican *Booke of Common Prayer*, published in Edinburgh. It was intended to force Scotland to abandon its Presbyterian form of church government.

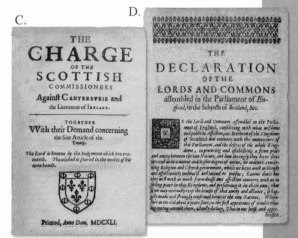

C. Scotland repeatedly protested in opposition to the Anglican suppression of its churches. It issued this *Charge ... Against Canterburie* (the Archbishop) in 1641, a time when the Puritan Parliament was also meeting to address its own grievances with the king.

D. The English Lords and Commons issued this *Declaration* to the Scots, stating their desired alliance to oppose the innovative and provocative tyranny of the royal Church Establishment (1642).

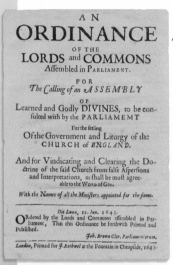

A. In England, Reformation was undertaken again in the 1640's when the English Parliament appointed an Assembly of Reformed ministers and scholars who met over several ensuing years to define the true doctrines of Scripture and the genuine nature of church government. Shown here is one of several early editions of Parliament's *Ordinance* that established the Westminster Assembly of Divines in 1643.

B. In America, Reformation was undertaken beginning in the 1620's by Reformed churches made up of refugees who had fled from England, meeting according to biblical directives. This nineteenth-century engraving depicted the *"First Sabbath"* service that was held on New England soil in 1620. It was conducted by a Pilgrim scouting party that was exploring Clark's Island just prior to their discovery of the perfect location for their new settlement within the (new) Plymouth Harbor.

New England's colonies had been established from their beginning beyond the reach of the royal establishment. Then, following the return of the harsh Episcopalian system in England and Scotland in the later seventeenth century, the colonies gained in population due to waves of persecuted immigrant "non-conforming" Puritans and Presbyterians. The Reformed tradition therefore thrived in New England, where it had merely survived back home. New England became known as the bastion of Puritanism, while Presbyterians settled throughout the lower British colonies over the century that followed.

By the 1770's, America would find itself well equipped to resist Great Britain's new, innovative encroachments on its chartered civil and religious liberties. Because of their similar, Reformed inheritance, New England's (northern) brand of Puritan descendants and America's (southern) brand of Presbyterians then led the fight together with many Reformed American Episcopalians to preserve their historic freedoms. That struggle, which ultimately resulted in a revolutionary new nation, was to a large measure engaged to preserve the same kind of liberties that the British Puritans and the Scottish Presbyterians had previously sought.

Though the term "Reformation" is remembered primarily as an historic period of great theological and political tumult in the 1500's, to those who continued to press for biblical integrity in all venues of English society it was always considered a matter of continuing biblical reform. Throughout the 1600's, Reformation was considered much more than a mere ecclesiastical struggle or a political cause. Church government and state polity were but two important venues for which it was fought. True Reformation represented a comprehensive, active way of living in accord with the precepts of the comprehensive, active, and living God. Reformation was not considered an event or a period of history, it was an aggressive, lively process with an ongoing aim of improving individuals, families, and churches, as well as the wider civil community.

To the reformers, a lack of continuing Reformation meant falling back into the stench of pagan human depravity – no matter how dignified that paganism might appear on its surface. Reformation was therefore to always be pressed onward to carry the timeless, orthodox standard of God's truth in the earth. The byword was always to look forward to *"further and more perfect Reformation,"*[11] because without constantly pressing for biblical reforms, the old corruptions were sure to return in whatever their newness of form.

11. Ibid., leaf A2.

APPENDIX B

The Bible Edition Quoted in this Volume

Because of its contemporary association with the other source material used in this volume, biblical quotes in all three books are taken from the 'King James' version of the Bible. Easily recognizable on its face is the fact that the "Authorized Version," or 'King James' version, is just that. It is merely one "version" of the English text translated from the original tongues as best could be accomplished at the time. The Authorized 'King James' itself followed several competent earlier renderings of the original languages. The translators of the 'King James' version, in fact, relied heavily upon the previous translations in rendering its textual form and style. Since its original publication in 1611, the 'King James' version has also undergone several linguistic improvements which have somewhat altered several passages; we therefore quote from a single, early "period" edition for the sake of overall continuity.

Biblical references are specially taken from the 1649 "Commonwealth" edition for several reasons. By 1649, the Authorized version's high lingual integrity had been well assimilated into the common English tongue. And by 1649, the Authorized version had also become widely accepted by the majority of the Puritan churches in England, Scotland, and America. The feature most appealing in this particular edition is the insertion of the older "Geneva" version's marginal notes. Those notes had been previously banned from inclusion in all prior editions of the Authorized Bible due to James I's and Charles I's strong objections to their Reformed tone. The Geneva Bible (1560+) had provided English readers with often exhaustive notes and references besides the biblical text, which were widely popular with earlier reformers. This edition also included *"brief exhortations of Theo. Beza upon the hard places,"*[1] giving it an even more decidedly Reformed flavor. Theodore Beza had been prominent in the development of covenant theology in Geneva during the later sixteenth century, and his commentary was held dear by many Englishmen. Following the removal of James's son, Charles, from the throne in 1649, the Geneva's notes were authorized to be included, though by the mid-1650's, other readily available Reformed commentaries and concordances overtook the need to continue the Genevan notes with the biblical text.

Shown here is the general title page of a 1649 edition of the English Bible. At first glance, it appears to be the same as all previous quarto size editions of the 'King James' version, however, it adds: *"Which* [Genevan] *notes have never before been set forth with this new Translation: But are now placed in due order with great care and industrie."*

Referencing this edition affords us an opportunity to both quote from the 'King James' version with its superior textual form and tone, and also quote from concurrent Genevan marginal notes in context from a single volume. This edition both respects the heritage of the 'King James' version, which had a considerable effect on later generations, as well as honors the Reformed doctrines of those who had paved their way.

1. *The Holy Bible* (London: The Company of Stationers, 1649), New Testament title page, leaf Aaa1.

INDEX

commonwealth (continued) 159, 161, 177, 182, 183, 185, 187, 189, 193, 204, 221, 227, 229, 246, 247, 248, 249, 250, 251, 252, 253, 255, 256, 258, 260, 261, 263, 264, 266, 267, 269, 270, 272, 273, 276

Commonwealth, English 114, 135, 136, 263, 264, 283

Commonwealth, Israelite (see Israel)

communion (also see Lord's Supper) 92, 100, 101, 119, 234, 239

communion of saints 100, 102, 201, 204, 225, 234, 235, 237, 276

Confession of Faith, Westminster 90, 91, 93, 94, 102, 141, 142, 143, 206, 213, 219, 225, 226, 229, 236, 237, 238, 245, 258

Constitution, Federal (see Federal Constitution)

Constitution of Commonwealth of Massachusetts (1780) 39, 174, 175

contentment 81, 82, 181, 183, 188, 224

Continental Congress, First (1774) 168, 169, 190,

Continental Congress, Second (1775) 171, 173

Cotton, John 154, 155, 157, 221, 230, 231, 246, 247, 252, 254, 270, 271, 272

Counter-Reformation 3

Courts of Commission 149

Covenant
    Covenant of Grace 13, 26, 27, 31, 32, 33, 82, 91, 92, 96, 97, 99, 105, 106, 107, 139, 140, 165, 190, 191, 196, 197, 198, 199, 203
    Covenant of Redemption 14, 105
    Covenant of Works 23, 25, 82, 105, 196, 203
    covenant community 93, 100
Covenanters 155
covet/coveting 48, 78, 79, 80, 81, 82
Creation Covenant 23, 24, 26, 59, 60, 64, 67, 70, 73, 77, 81, 100, 158
Creation Covenant, New (also see Noahic Covenant) 26, 27, 73, 81, 195
Cromwell, Oliver 150, 263, 264

D

Dartmouth, Earl of 168
Davenport, John 266, 272
David, King 20, 58, 70, 76, 85, 86, 87, 88, 90, 97, 98, 101, 104, 105, 107, 134, 196, 242, 271

Davies, Samuel 241, 242
Decalogue (see Commandments, Ten)
Declaration of Christe and of His Offyce Compylyd, A 6, 122, 228
Declaration of Independence (1776) 170, 172, 173, 175
democracy 50, 231, 232, 253, 259
devotion
    to God 52, 53, 55, 56, 58, 59, 70, 79, 98, 99, 107, 174
    family 36, 82, 103, 223, 224, 225
    personal/private 129, 141, 201, 222, 223, 224, 226
"diatheke" 19
discontent 78
Dissertation on Canon and Feudal Law 111, 112, 276
Divine right 7, 29, 41, 67, 87, 130, 131, 148, 154
dominion (man's) 23, 25, 29, 64, 73, 107, 118, 217
Dominion of New England 156-157
Downame's Concordance 129
dowry (also see espousal price) 69, 207
Duffield, George 173
duty 24, 36, 50, 52, 61, 63, 64, 65, 66, 86, 97, 102, 107, 117, 120, 125, 132, 135, 141, 142, 143, 158, 161, 165, 167, 170, 171, 172, 175, 182, 189, 190, 193, 199, 202, 203, 212, 214, 215, 216, 217, 218, 219, 220, 221, 222, 223, 225, 240, 243, 254, 256, 257, 258, 261

E

Eden/Paradise 23, 24, 25, 26, 77, 105, 195, 205, 212, 213, 217, 218, 274
"Edict of Toleration" 116
education/training 37, 53, 62, 82, 97, 161, 185, 215, 219-222, 226
Edward VI, King (r. 1547-53) 3, 6, 7, 122
Edwards, Jonathan 161, 162
Edwards, Jr., Dr. Jonathan 248, 249
Egypt 15, 16, 28, 38, 39, 40, 41, 43, 44, 45, 46, 47, 48, 50, 51, 55, 59, 63, 66, 75, 82, 94, 101, 102, 103, 128
elect/election (as in God's elect) 12, 14, 19, 20, 45, 105, 192
election
    of authorities 39, 48, 155, 157, 168, 260, 265, 266, 267
    of elders 238
election sermons 161, 166, 187, 230, 248, 254, 271
Eliot, Andrew 160, 161, 165

Eliot, John 21, 234, 240, 264, 272
Elizabeth I, Queen (r. 1558-1603) 126, 128, 129, 130, 147, 185, 262, 263
engagement (also see betrothal) 15, 69, 207, 208, 209, 210, 226
England 3, 4, 8, 91, 102, 103, 107, 114, 119, 120, 121, 122, 123, 124, 125, 126, 127, 128, 130, 131, 133, 134, 135, 136, 145, 146, 147, 148, 149, 150, 151, 152, 153, 154, 155, 157, 161, 172, 173, 174, 176, 190, 191, 192, 209, 210, 211, 230, 231, 232, 234, 236, 244, 250, 252, 255, 257, 258, 262, 263, 267, 271, 276, 280, 281, 282, 283
Enlightenment, European 174
enmity (with God) 58, 197
espousal price (also see dowry) 69
Essayes. Or, Observations Divine and Morall 68, 181, 186, 192, 206, 213, 214, 218, 219, 220
Essays To Do Good 102, 191, 203, 212, 214, 219, 220, 222, 224, 226, 239, 243
Eve 24, 25, 50, 64, 80, 82, 105, 195, 205, 206, 210, 212, 214, 218, 274
Exposition of the Old & New Testaments, An 26, 27, 181, 205, 223, 274

F

Fairfax, Thomas 150
falsehood 57, 75, 77, 253
family altar 36, 56, 222, 226
fatherhood 36, 46, 56, 61, 62, 63, 64, 69, 82, 87, 94, 103, 104, 121, 143, 144, 185, 188, 202, 207, 209, 212, 214, 215, 216, 217, 218, 219, 223, 224, 225, 226, 227, 242, 243, 260, 275
federal 118, 177
Federal Constitution 248
federal period 48, 86, 159, 175, 247, 248, 249, 271, 272
fidelity 38, 50, 68, 69, 70, 92, 125, 129, 135, 138, 140, 152, 155, 159, 160, 161, 163, 176, 177, 189, 199, 206, 207, 209, 210, 225, 227, 238, 259, 265, 276
Flavel, John 140, 141
"foedere inter Deum & regem" 118
"foedus" (covenant) 21
Foxe, John 5, 7
Foxe's Book of Martyrs (The Actes and Monumentes of the Martyrs) 5, 6, 7, 60, 80, 87, 92, 93, 94, 120, 219
fraud 73, 74, 77, 174
French and Indian Wars 164, 166,

Index

Index

In y̌ name of god Amen: we

the loyall subiects of our dre

Ly y̌ graco of god, of great

defendor of y̌ faith, &c

Haueing vndertaken, for y̌ gl

of y̌ christian faith, and honour of

plant y̌ first colonie in y̌ No

by these presents solemnly & r

one of another, couenant, & con

Ciuill body politick; for y̌ our bettor

therance of y̌ ends aforsaid; a

constitute, and frame shuch

Acts, constitutions, & offices. fra

most meete & conuenient for y̌ g

which we promise all due subm

wher of we haue here under s

Codd y̌ .11. of nouember, in y̌ y

Lord king James of England

and of scotland y̌ fifto fou